PRAISE FOR
BUILD REAL ESTATE WEALTH

Joel did a great job in this book explaining how to make money in real estate without taking all of the risks that many investors take. He makes the case it doesn't take money or credit to buy houses and he's a living example of what one can achieve as a real estate investor. **I wish I had his book when I started.**

Ron LeGrand
Legendary real estate investor, educator, and author

Build Real Estate Wealth is the REAL DEAL of real estate investment advice. Real estate investment guru Joel Miller makes you feel 100% confident that you can "acquire the right properties in the right way to support the growth" of your portfolio. (In fact, this book is making me seriously consider wrapping up my 37-year career in public relations and pivoting to real estate.) If you truly want to play the game of real estate investing and start making winning plays, then Build Real Estate Wealth is the only coach you'll need. **Miller's well-written book is THE comprehensive, step-by-step *definitive blueprint* for constructing your own residual, cash-producing real estate portfolio.** Anyone else here on out who tries to write a book about how to invest in real estate is just wasting their time — or just echoing what Joel just wrote.

Jeff Pizzino
Chief Authentic Officer, www.AuthenticitypPR.com

Want to be a Real Estate Millionaire?! Joel Miller's book is out of the park! A gamechanger for the industry. **This book is one you'll pass down for generations.** Fire it up!"

Real Estate Steve Szumigale

Joel Miller's *Build Real Estate Wealth* **belongs on every real estate investor's desk.** After its initial read, it will serve as an excellent reference guide to turn to over and over again. It does an astonishing job of breaking down and simplifying each aspect of the real estate game, providing a blueprint for every nook and cranny. It provides specific tips and examples that will save thousands and help maximize returns. **Even the most seasoned real estate investor will learn something from this book.** It is the (investment encyclopedia) for real estate investment.

Travis Yates
Lecturer in Economics; Penn State University

Seasoned real estate expert, Joel Miller, offers an invaluable guide for aspiring investors. With meticulous detail, the book breaks down each step of the process of successfully investing in real estate. What sets this book apart is its balanced approach; the author thoughtfully outlines the advantages and disadvantages of various strategies, providing a realistic blueprint that anyone can follow. Whether you're a novice or looking to refine your existing portfolio, **this book is an essential resource that demystifies real estate investing and empowers readers to achieve their financial goals.**

Dan Lane
Rental Income Podcast, www.RentalIncomePodcast.com

Rich Dad, Poor Dad was the first book that got me to believe that investing in Real Estate could actually be a possibility. But there wasn't much practical advice. If I would've had *Build Real Estate Wealth* to read back then, it would've saved me thousands of dollars and years of trying to figure it out on my own. **Joel's experience and ability to give you step by step guidance will be the building blocks for your guaranteed success in Real Estate!**

Matt Petruso
President, Benefit Advisors Insurance Group & Petruso Properties LLC

Life is too short to make all of the mistakes on your own. Joel takes 45 years of investing experience and condenses it into an easy-to-read guide. **This is the type of book that will always be on your desk, full of notes and dog-eared pages, as you will want to come back to the content over and over again.** I skipped immediately to the chapter on taxes, then went back through the rest of the book, and I was amazed at how Joel has taken really complex topics, and simplified them for readers at all levels of experience.

Adam J. Williams, Esq.
Co-founder, Pennywise Tax Strategies, LLC.

Joel Miller is the consummate real estate investor. He has been a leader in the NW Pennsylvania real estate investing scene for decades. Joel walks the walk when it comes to building wealth with his real estate investments. Joel runs his real estate investment business to the letter of the law with ethics and a high standard for the quality of his rental properties. He continues to be a pillar of leadership in our local NW PA landlord association, serving for many years the president. **If you want to build wealth and financial freedom with real estate investing, buy Joel's book and do exactly what he says.** Joel's recipe for success in this business is repeatable and will work for any person who applies it. Joel, thank you for writing this book and sharing your vast reservoir of real estate success!

Joseph P. Herbert
CCIM, Broker

This is **the best book I've ever read to teach the beginning real estate investor** the facts of life.

Judd Kessler, Esq.
licensed in real estate for over 50 years and
over 30 years as an attorney in Rancho Santa Fe, CA

Joel Miller gives us a roadmap, along with his personal guidance, for investing in rental properties—without letting it drive you crazy!

Matt Bennett
real estate investor

Joel has done a tremendous job of creating the only book you will ever need regarding building wealth via real estate investment. This is an absolute must read for anyone looking to gain wisdom from one of the best in the business"

Jason Pero
Brick & Mortar / Pero Real Estate

I've known Joel Miller since before I knew the phrase "real estate." We became friends in the early 1960s, attending elementary school together and living around the corner from each other. In the decades since, while I followed my own circuitous path in the arts, Joel, in his pursuits, came to understand the economics of the world. While it's too late for Joel to be your friend for over sixty years, **it's not too late for you to benefit from what he's learned and brought forth in this thoughtfully crafted book.**

David Greenberger
artist

THE
BIG BOOK
ON INCOME PROPERTIES

BUILD
REAL
ESTATE
WEALTH

Enjoy the Journey
of Rental Property
Investment

JOEL MILLER

Ordering Information:
Quantity sales. Special discounts are available on quantity purchases by corporations, associations, and others. For details, contact the publisher at the address above.

Orders by U.S. trade bookstores and wholesalers. Please contact:

JOELBOOK@OUTLOOK.COM

ISBN: 979-8-9911736-0-5

First Edition

CONTENTS

Because they are my "why," this book is dedicated to my beautiful and loving wife Tiffany and my amazing son Brandon. Being with them makes it all worthwhile.

FOREWORD

It is said that wealth is not built overnight, but through dedication, perseverance, and a deep understanding of the principles of prosperity. In *Build Real Estate Wealth* (which had a working title of *Get Rich Slow* during its creation among the author's associates), my dear friend Joel Miller shares his wealth of knowledge and experience accumulated over four decades as a successful entrepreneur, landlord, and investor.

My first knowledge of Joel Miller was as "DJ Joel" when he was the regular DJ at the local high school dances I attended in the early 1990's. I thought he was cool then as the disc jockey who was always the person playing the best music and controlling the dance floor. As a scrawny and awkward teenager, little did I know that the guy behind the spinning records would become a good friend and mentor in life and business.

After high school and upon graduating college, I knew very little about money and personal finance. That changed when I stumbled upon *Rich Dad Poor Dad* by Robert Kiyosaki which is really the playbook for entrepreneurs and real estate investors. Reading that book changed my life and started my trajectory as a real estate investor in 2001. With help and tutelage from mentors in my life like Joel I was able to leave a lucrative corporate career at age thirty-five in 2012, and I have continued to live a life of dreams that I would have never dreamed imaginable. From buying single family homes to large apartment complexes, the principles are the same. The wisdom is timeless, and as I've often heard from mentors: learn the basics and stick with what works, but more importantly do the things that make you happy, and pursue that happiness.

Early in my career Joel Miller became one of those "Rich Dads" that Robert Kiyosaki writes about. I have personally seen Joel's humble and nurturing nature impact countless lives over the years, including mine. He is a man of integrity, devotion, teaching, mentoring, and has a really warm and good heart. The type of friend that we should all be so lucky to have in life. Joel and I had the pleasure and honor of serving with each other as board members and ultimately Vice President and President for each other in the Apartment Association of Northwestern Pennsylvania.

Having had the privilege of being mentored by Joel myself, I have witnessed firsthand the transformative power of his guidance and wisdom. Through his practical advice, insightful strategies, and unwavering commitment to financial, personal, and spiritual growth, Joel has not only enriched his own life but has also uplifted countless others on their journey toward financial independence and personal peace.

In a world filled with get-rich-quick schemes and fleeting opportunities, Joel's approach stands out as a beacon of sustainability and long-term success. His emphasis on patience, prudent decision-making, and the importance of laying a solid foundation for wealth creation resonates deeply with all who seek to build a secure and prosperous future. When one turns to social media or late-night television, one can often get drawn into the glamour and sizzle of the get-rich-quick schemes. With *Build Real Estate Wealth,* the sizzle and the glamour is that the principles and lessons will serve you as timeless and ageless wisdom that will help you achieve true wealth, both financial and personal.

Remember to not lose yourself in the pursuit of success. Joel's lessons and wisdom will help you there. You can build a life of financial independence while enriching your life with the things that truly matter like family, friends, charity, hobbies, and experiences.

As you delve into the pages of *Build Real Estate Wealth*, I urge you to embrace Joel's teachings with an open mind and a willingness to learn. Whether you are a seasoned investor or a novice in the world of finance, the timeless principles shared in this book will undoubtedly inspire you to take control of your financial destiny and pave the way towards lasting prosperity. May Joel's words serve as a guiding light on your path towards wealth, and may the insights contained within these pages empower you to achieve your financial goals with confidence and clarity.

All the best,
JASON PERO
Brick & Mortar / Pero Real Estate

ACKNOWLEDGEMENTS

- Although they will never see this because they've both passed, I must acknowledge my **parents Fred and Vera Miller**. My dad worked side by side with me on all my properties until he passed away in 1993. He was never an investor, but he provided me with my work ethic, my understanding of the importance of volunteering, my initial interest in bookkeeping and accounting, my example to follow as a father, and as much information about using tools and doing home repairs as I was willing to absorb. My mother helped me achieve by always challenging me to know what I was doing. Sometimes we need someone in our life who does not always agree that we can do something so that we make sure we get it right. Ultimately, she became my biggest cheerleader, and I do not know of anyone prouder of me than my mother.

- My **sister Linda Bremmer** who served as my editor and creative consultant. She has a master's degree in English and is retired from teaching writing skills at the college level, so she was a natural to ask for input. Linda is thirteen years older, and my earliest memories of her are when she changed my diaper and wiped my face. In other words, she's been helping me with my messes all my life, and that carried into my attempt to write this book. We disagree about several major stances in life, but we've always maintained friendly fights including the ones that resulted in me rewriting a good portion of this book about five times until I got a passing grade!

- **John Baldwin** as the author of *Landlord 101* which is the instruction course offered to members of the Apartment Association of Northwestern Pennsylvania (of which he was a founding member in 1978). As a frequent instructor of "Landlord 101," I have learned much from John's writings. The principal tenets of "Landlord 101" have supplied inspiration throughout this book.

- **Harold "Bud" Crandall** as my mentor in the hard money lending business. Bud preceded me as president of the Apartment Association of Northwestern Pennsylvania, and he led the board in encouraging me to succeed him...which turned out to be an extremely rewarding 6-year segment of my real estate journey. I have always had Bud to turn to for inspiring investing and lending advice.

- **Dan Lane** as the creator and host of The Rental Income Podcast www.rentalincomepodcast.com. Dan was the first to ask me to be a guest on a podcast, and we think a lot alike about rental real estate. Dan was also the first to encourage me to author this book...and continued to encourage me until its completion.

- **Steve Szumigale** as the generous contributor of an entire bonus chapter of this book. Steve and I (as well as our families) have many treasured connections, and you will read my full description of Steve, the master architect of deals, in Chapter Two.

- **Joe Herbert** as a friend, fellow real estate investor, and author who kindly allowed me to include some of his material as noted in this book. Joe's works include the book *The 6 Life Assets*, the eBooks *The Clarity Tool Kit* and *Goal Mastery*, and the study course *How To Buy A Rental Property in 90 Days or Less*. His website is SelfMadeWealth.co.

- **Jeff Potts** as a friend, fellow real estate investor, and (as a career mortgage broker) my go-to guy for input regarding borrowing money for rental property investing. You will benefit from Jeff's inside info at several points in this book.

- **Matt Bennett** as a friend, investor, entrepreneur, and avid reader of real estate investing books. Most importantly, though, as the enthusiastic promoter who came along side me as the publicist for this project. Matt was the first to read the manuscript and suggest some changes that resulted in the version you are reading. He then went on to create my website and the related promotional materials along with the plan for rolling out the book on social media.

- **Jason Pero** who graciously accepted my request to write the forward to this book. Jason was my VP when I was president of the Apartment

Association, and when he followed me as president, he requested I continue as his VP. While I've known him, Jason has truly gone from zero real estate investments to the stratosphere by operating everything from tiny residential rentals to syndicating large apartment complex offerings. His and his wife's journey puts the "real" in real estate.

- **Caerus Kourt**, who is the newest member of the team. When the time came, I was blessed to connect with Caerus to create the cover and design the interior layout of my book. She was the final strategic pit stop that propelled this project across the finish line. So, if you like the book, credit her with the look!

HOW TO GET THE MOST OUT OF THIS BOOK

You will quickly notice that this book is not laid out in the typical fashion with line after line of uniform text forming paragraph after paragraph. I wanted the text to be very readable with lots of white space. The message is presented with many sections of bullet points, so that the delineation of the subject matter can be clearly seen for easy reference. This way, it is much easier for you to highlight items and make notes in the margins.

You will also notice that many sentences are in bold type like this. And if it's _really_ important, I'll underline it! The sentences in bold type are the key statements being made. Uniquely, these sentences have been selected so that you can use different techniques for absorbing the thoughts being presented.

- If you just want to get a taste of the subject matter, **only read the words in bold type**.

  o String the bold type words or sentences together like they had been written that way without the rest of the text.

  o Use a highlighter to emphasize the ones you find important, and make notes.

  o If you like what you're reading, go back and read everything in between.

- Read the book normally, including regular and bold type text.

  o Use a highlighter, and take notes as mentioned.

○ Afterward, it will be easy to review any section just by looking at the bold type words and sentences even if you haven't done much highlighting.

In any case, as I hope you have been doing with any other publications you've been reading on the subject, **I hope you not only make notations in the margins, but also write down points that impress you in a separate notebook or computer file.** Organize your notebook or files by subject matter for easy reference. Don't just make multiple notations that would require searching to find what you need.

I hope what you are about to learn will change your life in a terrific way!

INTRODUCTION

INTENTIONS

Thanks for buying this book. I know it is a little pricey, but that is just so I know that you have some skin in the game when it comes to absorbing the information contained here. It is so I know that you will place value on the commitment to read this book all the way through. And I promise it will not be a waste of your time and money.

My purpose is to show you how you can add to your life—to whatever extent you want—the investment of income-producing rental real estate, and enjoy it. It is the single investment category that has made more people/ families/companies rich over the entire span of human existence than anything else. How? From cash flow and equity growth.

This book will change your mind if you are a skeptic, and it will give you confidence if you do not believe you can "deal with tenants." **You are about to learn about plain and simple real estate investing that will, at the very least, get you rich slowly.** This is about the simple rentals to own and operate—the single-family or two to four-unit properties or even small apartment complexes. Not the big stuff—just the smaller properties that can barely be a distraction to you while you are living your life. Of course, there are plenty of real estate "gurus" that can teach you how to take it to another level beyond this book and accelerate your journey to financial independence and wealth.

This is a book about growing your income…perhaps to the point of financial independence, which I define as the ability to do what you want (only the stuff you like to do), when you want (on your own schedule) and with whom you want. You may not want to follow the path to the type of complete financial independence which allows you to leave behind everything you do now for money, and that is OK. You may have a passion for a career or a job or a hobby or a volunteer position or anything that brings you significant fulfillment, but which leaves you hoping for more fulfilment in the bank account area. But you do not feel you want to give up fulfillment from your passion just for more money. Still, **something tells you that things would be better if you just had an extra source of income, and you are willing to dedicate at least part of your life to growing that extra income.**

Equipped with the information in this book, you can address this money issue by confidently adding rental real estate to your life. You can choose to take on just enough to make a noticeable difference in your finances while you maintain your involvement in a full-time passion. Or, you can keep adding and adding until you feel you are ready to make rental real estate your main source of income. It is your choice, and it is entirely possible. I have done both, and I have seen others do it time and time again.

Why real estate, you might ask, instead of other traditional investment vehicles? Basically, it is about control and foreknowledge. Let's lump stocks, mutual funds, commodities, bonds, and precious metals (or anything you buy in units on an "exchange") into one pile and compare them to rental real estate. **Simply put, there is literally nothing you can do to affect the value of anything in that pile during your ownership like you can do with a rental property by making improvements to the property and raising the rents for more cash flow.**

Secondly, your foreknowledge of how property values and rental rates are trending in a given community is much more accurate than any foreknowledge you would have of the likely direction and timing of any of the other types of investments in that pile.

Many occupations that are trades like plumbing, barbering or sales can be successful, but if you stop doing the work, the money stops coming in. **With rental real estate, the rent checks are obligated to keep rolling in every month whether you "get out of bed or not."** Manufacturing and retail can be lucrative, but you are always chasing trends and looking for new things to make or sell. You must go to work every day, and there is this annoying thing called inventory that you have to concern yourself with every moment. **Couple that with the fact that rental real estate is virtually the opposite of a labor-intensive business as you can literally grow a fortune in real estate and never have a single employee**. You can see that rental properties hold a clear advantage over other common forms of investment.

I did not author this book blindly with no idea what the results would be if people actually did what I was recommending. **I wrote it from experience and with some vision of the results that you could expect to achieve.** I know there are readers who believe that real estate investing is for other people and not for themselves. But I believe that through reading this book, some of them will be inspired to try it and significantly alter their lives.

I think most other books on real estate investing assume that every reader wants to get rich as quickly as possible. The writer then overwhelms the reader with how to accomplish this, often creating unmanageable timelines and unrealistic expectations. Sometimes, the reader fails to take action due to the "paralysis of analysis" or gets discouraged and gives up. So, I am going to be a little different in my approach here. **I am going to teach you how to "get rich slowly" if you want to, but also how to eventually ramp that up and reach financial independence, if that is your goal. Then, I am going to explore the differences between being rich and being wealthy. You are going to learn how to BUILD REAL ESTATE WEALTH!**

This book will define and guide you through the sure and steady "tortoise wins the race" way to wealth. **I am presenting a mindset and a toolbox that does not leave you thinking that "this works for other people but not for me."** Do I object to getting rich fast? Absolutely not! Do it if you can, and I know many of you will figure out that you can. However, I do object to people NOT investing even casually in real estate just because they think they can't, and I hope that you will finish this book believing that you CAN.

Since the vehicle I am working with in this book is real estate, I think it would be fitting if the book were laid out in a parallel to how a building is constructed. Consequently, the sections of the book will be titled after the major elements of bringing a building to the point of occupancy. Let's start with The Vacant Lot.

THE VACANT LOT

The vacant lot is where the ideas start to come to mind and the possibilities for improving the land are identified. Picture yourself looking at a vacant lot where you want to build a custom home that was designed just for you. Maybe a building lot in a subdivision or out in the country. You don't own the lot yet, but you believe that having a home there is what you want for you and your loved ones. So, you are willing to find out what you need to know and to do to make that happen. That's where your mind is right now as you contemplate this real estate journey to grow your income.

You will notice that this PREFACE section is a little larger than you might expect. In fact, I am going to spend more time here with you than for some of the actual chapters. That is because, like when constructing a sound building, a good foundation must be laid first before getting into the later phases (chapters) of the project. But this is still the PREFACE, and we are not even going to get to the FOUNDATION until Chapter 2. We're still in the VACANT LOT phase now because I believe you need to get your mind in the right state regarding the building project (your real estate investing journey) while you are still gazing at the vacant lot. **The foundation of your real estate journey will be the physical income producing properties that are in your portfolio.** You must acquire the right properties in the right way to support the growth of the portfolio. **So, I guess you could say that in this PREFACE we are going to lay the foundation for the FOUNDATION** by making sure that we are thinking straight.

I am sure you are thinking about the possibilities right now. But at some point, you must make the move from dreaming to making a plan to making a commitment. Just like building a real structure, if you start breaking ground while you are still dreaming, it will be a disaster. **A dream is just a dream until you have a plan. But you still must commit to your plan.**

In his essay on the power of commitment, Johann Wolfgang Von Goethe wrote "Until one is committed, there is hesitancy, the chance to draw back, always ineffectiveness." He goes on to say that Providence moves when one commits oneself, and things occur to help you that never otherwise would have happened.

If Goethe is right (and I believe he is because I have personally experienced the flow that follows commitment many times), isn't it exciting and comforting to think about the moves Providence is going to make on your behalf once you make a COMMITMENT to adding some rental real estate to your life? You are not going to regret it!

So, the object of commitment is success. But some people, unbelievably, actually sabotage themselves because they have a fear of success. They never make a commitment because they are afraid of the success that might come with it. I believe that could be for one of two reasons. One, they do not believe they deserve the success (good things happen to other people and not to me because I'm not worthy). Or two, they are terrified of a perceived pressure (from who knows where) to continue succeeding after obtaining an initial success, so they just avoid their first success in order to avoid the pressure of succeeding again. The people in the first group are *content* to lose, so they just live in that rut, while the people in the second group think they are capable of some success, but they are *afraid* to lose. I hope you do not see yourself in either of these camps.

Scott McGillivray on the Bigger Pockets Podcast # 435 says that the difference between successful people and unsuccessful people is that **if you do not like to lose you will never give up (success or die trying). But if you are just afraid to lose you will not even try (failure to launch).**

In this book, the vehicle I am going to present to you which will carry you on your journey toward getting rich slowly, is rental real estate. Income property is said to be an IDEAL investment because of what it offers above all other investments:

I   D   E   A   L

INCOME   DEPRECIATION   EQUITY   APPRECIATION   LEVERAGE

Here is the rental (income) real estate game in a nutshell:

1. Find a way to acquire property that other people will use.
2. Let the people who use it buy it for you with their payments which are greater than your expenses.
3. Put up with minor irritations from the people, and the maintenance issues along the way, while you enjoy the cash flow and the equity growth.
4. Repeat steps one through three to build your portfolio.

My friend Dan Lane, who originated and hosts the Rental Income Podcast, blasted this out one day to all of us who subscribe to the podcast:

"I was talking the other night with a friend that wants to start investing in rentals. He really wants to start investing, but his biggest fear is that he will lose money. The more I thought about his fear, the more I realized that **it is hard to lose money on rentals over a lengthy period.** If you follow a simple formula of building a portfolio of good properties in good neighborhoods, you screen your tenants, and either hire a good property manager or learn how to manage yourself, your odds of being successful are really rather good. Of course, it is not 100% guaranteed that you are going to make money, and there will be tough times along the way. But you should be able to raise rent a little each year, and your mortgage balance is going to get paid down a little each year. Hopefully, your property will also appreciate in value over time. Once your mortgage is paid off, you are going to own an asset that your tenants bought for you, that has appreciated in value, and is generating more income than it was when you bought it."

This is not some esoteric way to make money. I think you will agree that this is basic and simple once you hear me out by reading this book. Getting money for allowing other people to use your property probably predates manufacturing, retail, or food service. There are a lot fewer moving parts in this business than most others such as retail or wholesaling where you have thousands of different inventory items to keep in the right supply rotation. Or manufacturing, or food service, or even a trade where the money stops when the work stops. And then there are all the employees for those endeavors. Also, all those types of businesses must keep looking for their next sale. With rental property you put a little effort into making one sale (finding a tenant) which then keeps sending you money month after month without any further marketing or sales pitch! **Everyone needs a place to live, and some prefer to rent. You might as well be the one who provides the location!**

Perhaps you are turned off by the prospect of needing to make repairs to your rental property. **One of the hopes of this book is to get you past the mythical "I don't want to fix a toilet in the middle of the night" mindset that you may be harboring.** That mindset may be keeping you from buying your first rental. I believe *that* particular obstacle is one of the three main reasons why people do not believe rental real estate is for them, and I want to dispel your fears about this area. Repairs are part of the game, but they should not be a deterrent. You do not even have to do them yourself if you do not want to. Repairs always involve the trades (plumbing, electrical, carpentry, etc.), and there are plenty of tradesmen out there who are in the business of responding to your needs. We will talk about that in detail later.

The second of the three main reasons is the fear of losing money. **The over-arching theme of this book is to prepare you to confidently not lose money.** Good property selection, skillful tenant selection, and sensible property management are the keys to not losing money. We will be discussing those topics as well.

The third main reason for not investing in rental real estate is not wanting to interact with tenants. Unless you have a property manager or Realtor who does all the interfacing with tenants (and this is totally a possible thing to do), you will have to occasionally deal with the people who are willing to send you hundreds of dollars every month. Generally, they will do this with little or no personal contact with you, but there are definitely situations where interaction is necessary. Be assured, I'm also going to talk a good bit about "dealing with tenants" in this book. **Not all interaction with tenants will be unpleasant, but some may be. The real way to avoid this—and the way we will be keying in on—lies in not renting problem properties to problem people in the first place.**

Can you see that the keys to avoiding reasons one, two and three are identical... good property selection (ones without unfixable features where such features would be a financial drain and attract the wrong tenants), good tenant screening (so that you put the right people in there in the first place) and good property management (so that you don't turn over an apartment with issues to unsuspecting people while you hope they won't mind the problems)? All these practices can be learned, and I will be covering property selection, tenant selection, and apartment preparation extensively.

So, you see, I am trying already in this VACANT LOT section to get you to not focus on the negatives. If you are not willing to let go of the perceived negatives, you will not be open to the positives I am going to lay out in this book. These "perceived negatives" could very well be keeping you from taking a major step in your life toward the financial betterment you are seeking, and I want you to see that these views are easily overcome with good "how to" knowledge combined with the encouragement/incentives provided by the positives.

I would ask you to think of it like this...If you focused on divorce, you would never get married. If you focused on how kids can screw up, you would never have children. If you focused on how people let you down, you would never have friends. So, stop looking so intently on what you perceive as the negatives about rentals and embrace the mindset and toolbox to getting rich (actually, wealthy is a better word) ...even if it is slow. Not that it must be slow, though, if you really want to hit it hard.

Here is a true story about achieving the mindset I am talking about regarding minimizing the negatives. At the conclusion of the final session of an Apartment Association of Northwestern PA Landlord 101 class that I had taught, the students were beginning to file out. Some swung by the front of the classroom to thank us, ask a question, or make a comment. Their heads were full of "real estate stuff," and there was an air of confidence and excitement. One middle aged guy waited patiently for the others, and he then approached me when he could be sure he had my full attention. He told me he had written down a quote in his workbook of something I had said. He said, "The thing that you said that I will remember most from this class is when you stated that a little bit of aggravation is more than made up for by the checks that roll in every month, even if you don't get out of bed." We had a good chuckle, but I knew he meant it.

So, to sum it up, what you need is some knowledge—and you don't have to have ALL the knowledge before you start. You also must have the willingness to use the knowledge, the confidence to apply the knowledge and a belief—which should be well-founded by the time you finish reading this book—that **the same rules and principles for investing in rental real estate apply to everyone. You just need to get in the game and start making plays!**

Benjamin Zander, the English conductor, founded the Boston Philharmonic Orchestra in 1978 and the Boston Philharmonic Youth Orchestra in 2012. Also, from 1965-2012, Zander was on the faculty of the New England Conservatory of Music. The Benjamin Zander Center website says he enjoys an international career as a speaker on leadership. When he emailed me with permission to use this quote, he told me that the best-selling book, *The Art of Possibility* (Zander, R. and B. 2002. New York, NY: Penguin Random House) which he co-authored with leading psychotherapist Rosamund Zander, has now been translated into twenty-six languages (and counting). I want to share this quote from Ben and Roz Zander from *The Art of Possibility* that has been under the clear desk pad in my office for decades. It says "Goals can be energizing—when you win. **But a *vision* is more powerful than a *goal*.** A vision is enlivening, it is spirit-giving, it is the guiding force behind all great human endeavors. Vision is about shared energy, a sense of awe, a sense of possibility."

So, right now I want you to have the vision that adding rental real estate to your life would not only be a good thing, but it is possible. Do not worry now about setting any goals about it. Just believe it is a path you can be happy that you took. But, as our next step, let's stop gazing at THE VACANT LOT of possibilities. Let's move ahead from embracing the vision of the future to taking action in the present. We will go "back to the future" later, but **the present is where the action must take place**.

Mark O. Haroldsen used to publish a great magazine mostly about real estate investing called *The Financial Freedom Report.* I contributed several articles to it back in its heyday in the 1990's, and I always got a lot out of reading it. I remember Mark editorializing that **it is so easy to get caught up in forward thinking.**

He said we do that, especially when we have clearly visualized our objective, when we are always living in the future and thinking about how wonderful everything is going to be. His point was that, **once we have our vision for our future, we must bring our thinking back to living and taking action in the present**... the only place of the sensory realm. He believed that becoming totally absorbed in our mission was what would eliminate the anxiety that comes with obsessing about the vision while not having a good plan to achieve it.

Coupling what Mark said with the Zander's view on a vision being more powerful than a goal, I would add that you should draw your inspiration, energy, and belief from your vision for the future while you concentrate on the tasks at hand. I will say that **too much forward thinking can derail the present and make us anxious. Set goals if you must, but make them achievable, purposeful, and most of all adjustable. Craft your vision, but once that vision is set, you have got to start taking action in the present to achieve that vision.** I promised you I would show you how to add rental real estate to your life and not regret it, and that is what we are going to start to do next! Let's go!

1
EDUCATION (SITE CLEARING AND BREAKING GROUND)

As I mentioned in the INTRODUCTION section, I'm going to name the chapters of this book after the major elements of bringing a building to the point of occupancy. So, I'm going to name this chapter in reference to the phase of construction where the land is prepared for construction to begin. Most people think that the foundation is the beginning of anything you build. Rightfully so, they point out the foundation must be right, or the endeavor will eventually fail. But I believe there are things that must go on before the foundation is laid which are just as important. I will talk about the foundation of your rental portfolio in the next chapter, because **I consider your actual physical rental properties to be the foundation of your rental property business.** Without the rental properties, you don't have a rental business, and the properties (which are the only source of income to the business) not only provide all the cash coming in, but they are the reason any cash goes out or any time is spent. So, **everything else in this business is built on the properties being in place as a base for all activities.** Consequently, I will discuss the acquisition of property in the next chapter.

The first thing that must occur, before the foundation is laid, was covered in the INTRODUCTION where the main point was getting your mind in the right place regarding the landscape of owning rental property. I made a parallel to gazing at a vacant building lot and imagining the possibilities. Nothing has happened to the land yet...it's just there for our viewing while inspiration and confidence begin to grow in our minds.

But there's another step before the foundation can be laid. That step is when the land is cleared of unwanted vegetation and the ground is dug or leveled in preparation for the footer to be poured and the foundation blocks to be set in place. **This is equivalent to the necessity for you to get some education about rental property investing before you start acquiring the property that will be the foundation of your activities. Notice I said, "some education." You don't need to wait until you have a "master's in real estate" before you buy your first rental.** In fact, I've seen many people over the years who never really did much in real estate investing because of the "paralysis of analysis." They kept thinking they needed more and more education before they got into the game, so they did little or nothing. They just kept going to seminars, coming to networking meetings, trolling the internet, and otherwise trying to reach some sort of level of knowledge that they had given themselves as a bar to achieve before they thought they were finally ready. Consequently, instead of being content to absorb enough of the rudimentary concepts that would have allowed them to begin buying and operating some typical residential rentals, they did nothing. Kind of like the student who keeps getting degree after degree and never gets a real job. Getting started—while not yet knowing everything there is to know about rental property—with some typical basic rentals like duplexes or single-family homes would have been better than doing nothing. Although they would have made some mistakes at first, they probably would be making some money, and I have to say that **actually owning and operating rental properties is the best education (and foundation) you can get.** There's nothing like doing something when it comes to learning how to do it better and gaining more confidence to do it bigger. It kind of works like this: If I tell you about it, you will forget it. If I show it to you (like reading this book), you will understand it. But **if you DO it, you will learn it.**

So, what I'm saying is that after you've stood gazing and dreaming about the possibilities for the vacant land you've found, the next step is an action step that is made back in reality mode. That was the point of the quote from Mark Haroldsen at the close of the INTRODUCTION. **That step is to educate yourself enough to get started on the construction of your dream.** By getting some education, you are clearing your mind of unwanted vegetation (confusion about the rental property business), so you can see more of what the land (the business) has to offer. Also, when you break ground, you're digging under the surface (getting more facts) so that you're on solid footing (confidence) for laying the foundation (starting to buy property).

Even when you're building a house, for example, when the site is being cleared you don't have to know everything about the house. In other words, you need to know what the footprint of the house is supposed to be before you break ground so that the ground is dug up in the right shape, but you don't have to know exactly what all the paint colors and light fixtures are going to be just yet. Speaking allegorically, you would clear the land and break ground differently if you are going to build the foundation of your financial house with income property as opposed to with retail stores. So, your only decision right now concerns **what kind of financial house you are going to build for your life?** Will you build a career on a job choice and just trade your time for money? Will you start or buy a business where the money only comes in when a sale is made, or a service is provided? Or will you acquire income producing properties where the properties themselves produce the income, instead of your time and efforts producing the income??

OR, as I'm hoping to get across to you as a perfectly viable path, **do you want to do a combination of financial houses where you continue to pursue a job or vocation or other type of business that you have a passion for while you add rental real estate to your life as a "side hustle" that you can expand on later??** In this case you don't want to give up your "day job" for whatever reason, but you would like to make some investments in real estate that you can control (unlike things bought on an exchange as I discussed earlier) and which throw off regular and predictable income that will make a difference in your finances. Maybe you even recognize that a few well-chosen properties can be your retirement when they're paid off.

You'll notice a lot of this book is devoted to the thinking and philosophy behind creating wealth and, in particular, holding rental property. The nuts and bolts and the building blocks will be presented as well. But you must have your head straight and your mind right as well as some confidence about it. Otherwise, you won't be able to build anything out of the pile of nuts and bolts lying in front of you on the table of life. And the building blocks will just look like a pile of children's toy blocks you glance at during playtime. You are sure some other kid is going to make something out of them, so you had better not touch them. I want you to understand you have just as much right to those nuts and bolts and blocks, so to speak, as anybody else. **If you take the time to go to the knowledge store (i.e., books like this) as well as networking with likeminded people in some fashion, then you can confidently do something you are proud of.**

In the PREFACE I laid out an abbreviated "nutshell" version of what the rental reals estate business is all about. Let me expand on that a little:

1. Buy a property by putting some of your own money down (or possibly with no money down).

2. Use Other People's Money (OPM) by borrowing the rest of the purchase price and agreeing to pay it back in monthly installments of principal and interest over many years (a mortgage).

3. Let tenants "buy the property for you" by allowing them to use the property in exchange for paying you rent every month at an amount greater than the total of the payments you are making on your mortgage and your expenses (such as property taxes, insurance, and maintenance).

4. Either live off the difference between your cash in and your cash out (cash flow) OR save your profits to put down on another property.

5. Do this over and over.

6. Enjoy the reduction of taxes due to your depreciation deductions (see below).

7. Watch your equity (the difference between the property's value and the amount owed on the mortgage) grow as the property increases in value and the mortgage gets paid down.

8. Enjoy increased cash flow as rents rise yet the mortgage payment remains the same.

9. Enjoy even more cash flow after the mortgage is paid off (tenants keep on paying you even if the property is all paid for).

10. Refinance the property (get a new larger mortgage that replaces the first one) and get tax-free cash (loan proceeds are not taxable income).

11. Sell the property and pay tax on the gain at a lower rate than your ordinary income (assets held longer than one year are taxed as a long-term capital gain).

In item #6 above, I said to see below. This is because I wanted to take a little more space than what was allowed above to talk about depreciation. The use of the word "depreciation" here is not in reference to the decrease in value of something over time due to use or some other factor that makes it worth less than when it was new. For example, a car depreciates with age and mileage. That is the opposite of appreciation. **Most rental properties typically increase (appreciate) in value over time for a variety of reasons such as inflation, improvements made, increased rents, and overall market demand for residential property to name several causes.** This is true even though the property is getting older and used. Yes, any property can potentially go down in value, but that would not generate any kind of deduction on your annual tax return any more than appreciation in the property's value would be cause for income to be reported on your tax return.

Depreciation, as it relates to item #6, is a bookkeeping term which refers to the calculation of a particular expense the IRS allows in determining the amount of income (or loss) from the operation of an income property or any business that has purchased a big dollar asset for its own use. The net income, after taking into account the deduction for depreciation, is the amount of income that is taxable. However, unlike all the other expenses of the operation which arise from the expenditure of cash, **depreciation does not involve any cash. Consequently, depreciation will lower your taxable income even though you haven't paid out any cash**

to get that deduction. Sometimes the depreciation deduction is enough to make the property show a loss (which reduces your taxable income from other sources too) even though the property actually had more income than cash expenses. This is called "positive cash flow." We will cover more of the particulars of depreciation in the chapter on tax implications. **Being able to take large depreciation deductions is one of the big positives of real estate investing.**

From a financial perspective, the techniques for acquiring properties can range from the simple to the exotic. **But the eleven-point outline above is pretty much the gist of how typical rental real estate investing is done in both large and small properties**. You can move the wealth-building needle faster with certain techniques that involve accepting more risk and/or committing more personal time. But keeping in mind that the purpose of this chapter is to help you to first understand the importance of getting good education and secondly to clear your mind of negative preconceptions, I would just say at this point that there are many qualified teachers of those techniques whom you could seek out. You probably will begin to learn them when you are networking with other local investors. However, **I believe you probably do not have to do anything more than what is in this book to change your financial life significantly for the better.**

So, I hope you're starting to get the concept, but you may figure there must be more to it than that. Of course, there are some finer details, and we'll be getting in deeper in the upcoming chapters. But frankly, **this whole rental property thing is just not that complicated!**

If you can:

- Grasp some basic math
- Will yourself to interact professionally with tenants and contractors
- Exercise some discipline with handling money
- Use some basic tools (hammer, screwdriver, pliers, and a saw) for minor repairs
- Pick up the phone to call someone to do whatever you don't know how to do
- Set aside false preconceptions (both positive and negative) about the business

...then you can probably accumulate significant wealth with income property. And remember, **you can do it while you are still involved with some other vocation.**

As I have alluded, buying a rental is not like buying a lifetime sentence of fixing toilets, cleaning apartments and painting rooms. Those things happen, but they are far overshadowed by the monthly checks that come in the mail from people you talk to a couple of times a year—not to mention the appreciation in value that is silently accruing. Besides, if you do this right, it will be other people you are engaging whose business it is to fix things, clean things, and paint things. Most likely, these will be subcontractors whom you pay on an as-needed basis, and not employees.

So, as we wrap up the chapter about clearing away the weeds on the vacant lot of possibilities (and considering again that one of my main points you **don't have to do everything yourself to be successful at this**), let's touch on the positions on your team you will want to start filling as you get rolling. You will not need to have all these people lined up before you buy your first rental, but you are likely to need relationships with people who fill these roles eventually. And, again, **your need for these people will depend on what you are willing and able to do yourself.**

Here are some team members to consider:

- A good Realtor who understands investment property
- An insurance agent familiar with writing policies for rentals
- A lawyer with a specialty in real estate contracts and law
- Lenders
  - Traditional banks who have an appetite for rentals
  - Hard money lenders
  - A good mortgage broker who can connect you with traditional lenders outside of your area
- Contractors
  - Plumbers
  - Sewer and drain openers
  - Roofers
  - Electricians

- Painters
- Drywall hangers and finishers
- Heating and air conditioning (HVAC)
- Masons for brick and foundation repairs
- Carpenters / Handymen
- Siding installers
- Gutter installers
- Glaziers (for glass repairs)
- Flooring installers
- Tile installers
- Insulation installers
- Cleaners
- Carpet cleaners
- Window washers
- Locksmiths
- Kitchen designers (they probably work where you buy your kitchen cabinets)
- Décor designers (may also be your Realtor because they know what sells)
- Exterminators
- Landscapers
- Trash haulers
- Tree trimmers
- Concrete and paving installers

Notice the contractors are listed in the plural. That is because it's a good idea to have relationships with more than one in any specialty. These professionals have educated themselves to collaborate with you. They, in turn, need to know you have educated yourself in your own business of rental real estate. They want to work with you, and they are not hard to find. **You do not have to know how to do everything; you just need to know the people that do. <u>Two of the biggest skills you will develop are selecting team members and selecting tenants.</u>**

To this point, I have been focusing on the mental preparation for entering the real estate investment world. I have discussed having a proper mindset as well as the necessity for absorbing education in the field before you start investing. **If you want your journey into adding rental real estate to your life to be something you do not regret, you must have the right attitude coupled with necessary knowledge.**

In a *Financial Freedom Report* article in the 1990's, A. D. Kessler's Ten Rules for Success in Real Estate were published. They are:

- Deal with motivated people.
- Be prepared to do business. You'd be amazed at the amount of people who don't have the slightest idea what to do when a deal comes at them.
- Write offers. Don't talk them. Don't think about them.
- Don't over leverage.
- Limit your liability.
- Prospect continuously. Prospect, prospect, prospect.
- Buy and sell to get cash. Don't over create yourself without getting some cash. Make sure you buy and sell from time to time to get some cash.
- Work hard at establishing a good cash flow.
- Learn and use modern technology. Be computer literate.
- Keep accurate records.

So far, I have presented a lot of general information, and now it's time to get more specific. As we move on to Chapter Two, I will begin covering the pertinent "how to" information about various aspects of acquiring and managing rental property. I will cover everything from buying property to managing the property to eventually selling the property. I hope that in the end you feel ready to take the steps that will change your life!

2 ACQUIRING PROPERTIES (THE FOUNDATION)

To recap what I've covered so far, the main points to absorb are:

- Income property can coexist profitably in your life along with something else like a job or another commitment you prefer to keep.

- You can grow your real estate activities to the point that you leave your job if you choose.

- Property owners can control the value and cash flow from their rentals to a much greater degree than the owners of stock or similar investments can.

- Rental property income is residual income that comes in routinely because you own the property, and not because you performed a particular task as in a job.

- Work that is needed on apartments can be done by other professionals you choose.

- You need to clear your mind of preconceptions about real estate which are either too negative or too positive in order to give proper consideration to investing.

- You need to get some education before you start investing, but you don't need to know everything beforehand.

- No matter how much education you get, it takes action to see results and it takes commitment to your vision to see success.

In the INTRODUCTION you found your "vacant lot" (the landscape of real estate investing) and imagined the possibilities of what could develop. Then, in CHAPTER ONE, you began "clearing the brush and breaking ground" on that lot as you considered the importance of education. But now it is time to get into the "how to" sort of information that is necessary for successful investing in rental property.

Now, in CHAPTER TWO, the topic I'm going to tackle is property acquisition. Future chapters will cover what to do with the property after you own it, but laying the foundation is what comes next in the building process after you clear the lot. And **I consider the physical properties you own to be the foundation of your rental property activities, because without your portfolio of properties, no money comes in.** All your thoughts and efforts are built on the existence of the properties. The weight of producing profits is on the properties. **If you want to expand the footprint of rentals in your life, you do it by adding properties like building blocks to your foundation.**

I think it's fair to say that, after looking back over around a half century of investing in rentals, **I believe the hardest part is finding good deals.** It's the weakest link in the chain, so to speak, not because of the actual mechanics of purchasing property, but because you can't control the *deal flow* as we call it. Even **finding the money to buy the property is easier than finding the property itself.** You can control virtually every other aspect of this business from property improvements to tenant selection to selling your property, but you can't just go into the income property section at a big box store and grab a 2-unit off the shelf when you decide it's time for another property. You can *affect* your deal flow with your search efforts, but sometimes the availability of a good deal boils down to simply good fortune.

I'm going to take you through the phases of acquiring property which I consider to be:

- Creating the legal entity which will hold title to your property
- Searching for property that fits your criteria
- Negotiating the deal to buy the property
- Checking out the facts relating to the property (doing due diligence)
- Financing the purchase
- Preparing for the closing

Please understand that the volumes written, courses taught, seminars presented, and real estate guru's fortunes made on each of these individual phases are literally countless! Each of these topics can be broken down, dissected, and repackaged endlessly. It would be impossible for me to present an exhaustive study of any one of them in this book, let alone all of them. I want to keep it simple enough that the process does not seem intimidating. However, I assure you that enough of the basics will be supplied here that will enable you to get started. **Remember, you don't have to know everything to start taking steps toward buying rental property. Just start taking action, and things will start happening that clear up questions, give you confidence and create opportunities. The first couple of deals are the hardest, but then momentum kicks in and everything becomes easier.**

One thing you will find when you are investing in real estate is that you will get interested in certain techniques. You will discover that there are multiple techniques for searching for property, evaluating deals, getting properties under contract, financing property, rehabbing property, and vetting prospective tenants just to name several of the major areas. **There is no *one* right way to do any of these things; you must decide which methods are best for you in your location with your resources, your skills, and your comfort level.** That's one of the cool things about this type of investing. You literally can choose from a smorgasbord of action plans that are described throughout a variety of resources from authors, instructors, and other investors with whom you will network. **The key, then, is to develop expertise in a few techniques that work for you and then to use them consistently.** Always work to refine your techniques and discard them when they stop working. Don't try to learn too many ways of doing things at one time, or you will get discouraged.

PHASE ONE: CREATING THE LEGAL ENTITY IN WHICH TO HOLD TITLE

Before even starting to look for property to buy you must know how you are going to hold title to the property. The two main choices are whether you want to own the property in your personal name (either just your own name or along with other partners such as your spouse) or in the name of a legal entity which you've created. If the latter is your choice, **it's especially important to create your legal entity in advance of making offers on property because it can take a while to set up an entity**. You don't want complications to arise due to your entity not yet being legally in existence while you are waiting to close on the purchase of your property. **Ultimately, your choice of how to take title to the property will be driven by the necessity (or lack of necessity, however you view it) to protect your assets from creditors and by income tax reporting considerations.**

The purpose here is to give you an overview of the possibilities so that you can see the plusses and minuses relating to your particular situation. **You should discuss your preference with a legal advisor to arrive at your final decision.**

Many of you reading this will have already decided on the fashion in which you will hold title to your property, and you already know whether you need to form a legal business entity for that purpose. In that case, you may find the rest of this section tedious reading because it covers information you do not need to know. You have my permission, then, to skip to PHASE TWO while remembering that the following is a resource if you have occasion to consider a change in your business structure. **Let's cover the typical ways in which the title of real estate is held.**

- YOUR PERSONAL NAME. Anyone can simply take ownership of property in their actual legal personal name. Although there are arguments as to whether there are better ways to do it, this is the way most people take title to their personal residence. No extra preparation is necessary to use your own name. Your name would appear in the public records at the courthouse as the owner of the property. There would be less paperwork and hoops to jump through if you were obtaining a loan while using the property as collateral.

    The biggest disadvantage of using your own name is that your personal creditors could include the property along with all your other personal assets when they are forcing your assets to be sold to repay your debt to them. This means, for example, if you fail to pay a large balance on your personal credit card, and the credit card company gets a judgement against you in court, they could record that judgement at the courthouse. The courthouse would then automatically attach that judgement to all property you own (no matter whether it is a personal residence or a rental property) so that the property cannot be sold without the judgement being paid off. The credit card company, believe it or not, could actually foreclose against the property even if you have a mortgage from a bank already on the property. They would do this in hopes of the property selling for enough at the Sheriff Sale to cover the bank's mortgage as well as their judgement. Or, if nobody bought it at the Sheriff Sale, the credit card company would become the new owner, and they could sell the property on the open market to satisfy their claim. They would have to pay off the balance on your mortgage, but they could keep the rest even if it was more than what you owed them.

Similarly, **if a claim arose against you that originated from the ownership of rental property that you held in your own name, the ability of the creditor to satisfy their claim is not limited to the property itself.** So, for example, if a tenant successfully sued you for something your property manager did that was not covered by your liability insurance, the tenant would have a claim against your other personal assets that had nothing to do with the operation of the property. They would have the same remedies against your personal residence, your car, and your boat that the credit card company had in the previous paragraph. **Protection from personal liability is the main reason investment real estate, businesses, and a variety of types of property (all of which carry with them some inherent risk) are not held in personal names. They are typically held in some sort of separate legal entity that has its own name and which insulates the owners from personal liability.**

- PERSONAL NAMES OF YOU AND YOUR SPOUSE. Pretty much everything that was said above regarding taking title in just your own name can be repeated when it comes to taking title in your and your spouse's personal names. Assuming you hold it as "joint tenants with right of survivorship" (JTWROS), then if one spouse dies the surviving spouse automatically inherits the property and then owns it 100%. **If one spouse has a debt that is solely their responsibility and which has nothing to do with the other spouse, then that creditor cannot force the sale of jointly held property to satisfy the debt. However, a debt owed by both spouses jointly can be satisfied by a claim against property that is jointly owned by both spouses.** Keep in mind, too, that a creditor can attempt to collect 100% of a joint debt from the resources of either one of the spouses since joint debts are not actually 50-50; each debtor is 100% responsible for full repayment.

- PARTNERSHIP WITH SOMEONE OTHER THAN YOUR SPOUSE. This is similar to taking title with your spouse, but there are some significant differences. You could just take title in both of your personal names (or multiple people's names) and state that it is held JTWROS, in which case your partner(s) will automatically increase their percentage of ownership in the property upon your death. In essence they inherit your share of the property proportionately. All partners remain 100% responsible for the mortgage if any.

Holding property JTWROS when the partners are not spouses or other close relatives is rare, however, since generally each partner wants their share to be inherited by their own heirs and not just be given to their partners. Usually, property that is held jointly by unrelated parties is held "tenants in common" in which each partner owns an undivided percentage of the property. So, for example, if two partners owned it as "tenants in common," they would be presumed to be sharing equally in the benefits of the property. However, their interests are undivided in the sense that they each have access to all the property and its benefits all the time. It would not be the case that each had use of only one half of the property from a geographic standpoint or from a time standpoint. Then, when each partner died, their 50% interest would be passed on to their heirs who collectively (if there were more than one heir) would also share undivided interests in the rights to the property along with the other original owner and eventually the heirs of the other original partner. Only half of the value of the property at the time of death would be included in the assets of the estate of each of the original partners at the times of their deaths.

Holding property as "tenants in common" may work fine for property that is intended to be passed down in a family like, for example, if two brothers bought a vacation property that they intended for their respective kids to inherit and use. The property is presumably not producing any income, and all they must do is split expenses like the property taxes and mortgage interest which they perhaps claim as itemized deductions related to a second home on their tax returns. However, **if the property is income producing like a rental property, this type of arrangement is impractical from an income tax reporting standpoint.**

- TRADITIONAL GENERAL PARTNERSHIP. A more practical way for unrelated people to participate in a business or income producing property is to use a general partnership. **Each partner can have their own percentage of ownership as far as how they divide up the profits or losses, and that percentage can be arrived at however they wish.** So, in a three-way partnership, one partner could own 40%, a second partner 35% and the last partner 25%. These percentages could be derived from the relative amounts of cash that each partner put in, or they could be agreed upon by what value each partner otherwise brings to the business. Perhaps the first partner has not put in any cash, but they are bringing knowledge that the business needs to be successful. The other two partners are going to put in cash of different amounts, but they all agree that the first partner's contribution is worth 40% of the business going forward.

    In my example, the partners would split up the profits according to the percentages of ownership. However, that does not mean that they each must work in the partnership according to the same relative hours or that their work must be valued the same. To take the example further, let's say that the partner who contributed no cash is actually going to work full time in the business and use their expertise to operate the business. So, that partner is going to receive a salary that is paid directly to them which is income to them, but which is an expense to the partnership. The payment to that partner does not have to be paid through an actual payroll like would be used for other employees, although it *could* be, in which case that partner would have W-2 income and withholdings like the regular employees. If the partner is not paid as a W2 employee, the payment to that partner would be in the form of a "guaranteed payment" as the IRS calls it, and not subject to withholding taxes like with a paycheck for an employee. In this case the partner would report their guaranteed payments as self-employment income on a Schedule C (for calculating income tax) as well as on Schedule SE (for calculating self-employment tax). Self-employment tax is essentially the way self-employed people pay into the Social Security System like employers and employees are required to do for W-2 jobs.

Again, referring to my example, let's say that the partner who owns 35% of the business is not going to work in the business at all, but the partner who owns 25% is going to come in a couple of times a week and do the bookkeeping. For this, that partner is also going to receive a guaranteed payment that is valued at a different rate compared to the partner who works there full time. In each case, the amounts of the guaranteed payments are counted respectively as income by each partner, and the total amount of these payments is counted as an expense of the partnership in determining net income to be reported by the partners according to their percentages of ownership.

After making the guaranteed payments, if the partnership has a profit that it wishes to distribute, then the cash is distributed according to the percentages of ownership. It's important to note that the distribution of cash profit to the partners is not an expense of the partnership like the guaranteed payments are. They are just a release of what's left after the expenses are paid. They may reflect the profits but, in fact, even if the partnership uses the cash method of accounting (as opposed to the accrual method), the distributions of cash from a partnership rarely equal the amount of the profit reported for tax purposes. That's because there can be non-cash expenses such as depreciation expense which affects the net reported income but not the checkbook. Also, if there is a mortgage payment that includes an amount applied to principal, the checkbook is affected, but the amount paid toward principal is not a deductible expense.

Also noteworthy is the fact that the partnership is not <u>required</u> to distribute its profits. It may want to stockpile cash for business purposes. However, partners are taxed on their share of the profits whether or not those profits are actually given to them by the partnership through a distribution. Similarly, if a partnership has accumulated cash from prior years of operations, and it distributes that cash all in a future year, the partner is still only taxed on the net profit from just that year.

When it's time to file taxes, the partnership, as an entity, files a report with the IRS called a Form 1065 which reports the various items of income and expense from the past year's operations. From the information on the 1065, each partner is given a statement called a K-1 which lists their share of the profits or losses as well as the total of the guaranteed payments they received. This information is then used by the partner to translate their participation in the partnership onto their personal tax return.

Notice that the partnership tax return is just an informational return and that the partnership itself does not pay any income taxes. The required information is shared both with the partners and the IRS. The IRS then compares the information provided by the partnership with that turned in by the partners similarly to the way they check to see if the amounts reported by an employee are the same as what their employer reported.

A partnership is called a "pass-through entity" because it simply passes through the information needed for the partners to pay taxes on their income from the partnership at whatever their individual tax rates are. So, you can see that the general partnership method of holding rental property is quite convenient for paying partners, distributing profits, and reporting income for tax purposes.

But wait! **There are major drawbacks with general partnerships. First, all partners are liable 100% for the debts of the partnership.** If a creditor is not satisfied by the partnership, then it can seek payment from any or all the partners individually outside of the partnership. In that case, any asset owned individually (as opposed to jointly like with a spouse) by the partner would be vulnerable to the creditor. Secondly, **this 100% liability of each partner individually is the case no matter which partner may have created the liability for the partnership.** All the general partners are responsible for the actions of all the other general partners. So, although a general partnership is convenient, it offers no protection of your personal assets from obligations that arise from the operation of the partnership.

- LIMITED PARTNERSHIP. A limited partnership is just like a general partnership except that it does not consist of two or more general partners. Instead, it consists of at least one general partner and at least one limited partner. Everything said in the prior section about general partners in a general partnership also applies to general partners in a limited partnership. The general partners still run the business and are exposed to the same liabilities. But **the limited partners are special because their personal assets are protected from the liabilities of the limited partnership. They are given this protection in exchange for being prohibited from having any "material participation" in the operations of the partnership.** In this way they do not have any say over the actions of the partnership that could create a liability. Consequently, a limited partner's risk of loss is limited to whatever they invested in the partnership. If the limited partnership goes out of business owing creditors, limited partners do not have to come up with any money beyond what they've already invested. General partners must, on the other hand, kick in money to cover any shortfall or risk losing personal assets.

  A limited partnership is a great way to take in a partner who contributes cash in anticipation of sharing in the profits if the prospective partner is not interested in participating in the business, and the partner desires protection from liability. A limited partner is assigned a percentage of interest in the partnership based on the cash or the value of some other asset that is contributed to the partnership, and each limited partner would share in any distribution of profits from the partnership based on that percentage along with all the other general and limited partners. Note that **a limited partner could not get a guaranteed payment for their services because that would mean that they are materially participating in the operations.**

Do not assume, however, that a limited partner must only have a small percentage of ownership in the business. In fact, in many limited partnerships, the general partner, or the total of all the general partner interests, is very small compared to the total of all the limited partner interests. This could be the case if, say, one or two people are willing to organize and run a company that is going to pay them a salary, but most of the money to start the company comes from limited partners. The general partners have created a paying job for themselves, but they will have to split up the profits with the limited partners.

- C CORPORATION. The C Corporation is the typical type of entity structure that you think of when you think of a company being a corporation. It must have a board of directors, and there are formal annual record-keeping and reporting requirements. The owners of the company are called shareholders, and they hold their interest in what are called shares. The shares are presumably all equal in value, and each share represents an exact percentage of the worth of the company as a whole. So, for example, if a corporation has issued (sold) 100 shares in itself, then each share represents 1% of the company's value. If all the company owns is, theoretically, a one-hundred-dollar bank account, then each share is worth one dollar. Corporations typically own a variety of assets that have a subjective value, so the value of a share of stock in the company is always open to interpretation. This is evidenced by how the prices of stocks traded on a stock exchange change minute by minute according to the belief of the public as to what the company is worth, even though nothing actually changed at the company in the past minute.

  Although there is no limit on the number of different shareholders a corporation may have, corporations do not have to be large and have their stocks traded publicly on the stock market. The same type of document called the Articles of Incorporation can be used to form a small company where maybe just one or two people are the only ones to ever own the shares. In fact, many companies that became large and whose names we all recognize actually started out with just a couple of shareholders, and they are still operating off the same original Articles of Incorporation!

It's easy for a corporation to add or change owners just by the existing shareholders selling them some of their shares. Or the corporation can issue more stock for sale at whatever price per share someone will pay. These new shares would be added to the number of outstanding shares held by the existing investors, so the profits would be divided equally by a greater number. The profits of a corporation are paid according to how many shares someone owns. This is why the payouts are called dividends. Issuing more shares, though, is a terrific way for the company to raise capital for expansion. Typically, each share is allotted one vote when the shareholders meet to make decisions. Different types or classes of stock can be issued, however. For example, preferred stock could come with the privilege of receiving dividends before any profits are paid out to regular shareholders.

In the history of business structures, the standard corporation was probably our first attempt at creating a way for the risks and rewards of operating a business to be contained within the business itself. This sort of arrangement became necessary as the owners of sole proprietorships and the general partners of any kind of partnership realized that their assets outside of the business could become vulnerable to creditors from within the business. There had to be a better way to protect owners and allow for a business to grow by taking on more owners.

The concept of a corporation is to create a legal entity that essentially has independent standing almost like an individual person in the eyes of the law and for taxation purposes. The good news is that the liabilities of the corporation do not extend to the personal assets of the shareholders unless, of course, a shareholder personally guaranteed a loan to the corporation. The corporation can get loans, hold property, and do business all in its own name. The names of the people who are starting a corporation are public record when the Articles of Incorporation are filed with the state, and certain officers and shareholders must be listed in the annual filings of a publicly traded corporation. But otherwise, the owners of a corporation (the individual shareholders) are not known to the public. **Since the titles to assets held by the corporation are held in the name of the corporation as opposed to that of any shareholders, assets do not need to be retitled (or transfer taxes paid as is the case when real estate changes ownership) even if all the shares are sold to new owners.**

The bad news is that corporations, as stand-alone legal entities, are required to pay income tax just like people are. Granted, corporate tax rates are different from individual tax rates, but the result is that the profits of a corporation are taxed twice...once when the corporations make them, and again when they are distributed to the shareholders as dividends. The corporation pays tax on its profits (whether it pays out the profits or not) from its own funds, and each shareholder pays tax at their individual tax rate when the dividends are added to the rest of their income on their tax return.

- S CORPORATION. The so called "Subchapter S" corporation is named after the section of the Internal Revenue Service Code that outlines the rules for this type of entity. It is the same entity structure as a regular corporation, but its name refers to its elected method of taxation, not its formation. After realizing that the double taxation aspect of C Corps was a big negative to endure just for the sake of removing personal liability of company owners, a vehicle was created to provide the best of both worlds. The Sub S Corporation is essentially a regular corporation with shareholders that can buy and sell their shares and have the same standing as was discussed for a C Corp earlier including insulation from creditors. Sub S corporations are limited to 100 shareholders who must be U.S. citizens or residents. Also, owners can only get common stock which has voting rights, since no preferred stock is allowed. A board of directors is required, as is the keeping of corporate minutes like for a C Corp.

The big difference is that the Sub S Corp has made an official election with the IRS to be treated as a partnership for taxation purposes. That's right! Sub S corporations do not pay their own income tax; the profits and losses are passed through to the owners on a K-1 just like in a partnership. It's important to note, though, that the owners of Sub S Corps and partnerships must include their share of the net income or loss from the business whether those profits are distributed to the owners or not.

Furthermore, the **profits from a Sub S Corporation are not considered by the IRS to be self-employment earnings for the owners** of the corporation; they are ordinary income which is only subject to income tax. Consequently, the S Corp advantage is that **you only pay FICA payroll tax on your employment wages.** The remaining profits from your S Corp are not subject to self-employment tax or FICA payroll taxes.

Please note the implication of what was just stated about wages. While S Corp profits are not considered self-employment earnings, and profit distributions of cash are neither a deduction to the S Corp nor taxable income to the shareholder, **anyone who performs a significant service for the S Corp must be on the payroll.** Their wages would be subject to all the ordinary payroll taxes. So, the temptation for the owners of a Sub S Corp is to not pay themselves a wage so that they avoid self-employment tax on the company profits (which are then higher due to their would-be wages not being taken as a deduction by the corporation). **If the business of a Sub S Corp is to perform a service or sell a product, somebody needs to be paid a reasonable wage to make that happen.**

You cannot work in a Sub S Corp as an owner and not be on the payroll while trying to skirt the self-employment tax. To quote the IRS, "The definition of an employee for FICA (Federal Insurance Contributions Act), FUTA (Federal Unemployment Tax Act) and federal income tax withholding under the Internal Revenue Code include corporate officers. **When corporate officers perform a service for the corporation and receive or are entitled to payments, those payments are considered wages.** The fact that an officer is also a shareholder does not change this requirement. Such payments to the corporate officer are treated as wages. Courts have consistently held S corporation officers/shareholders who provide more than minor services to their corporation and receive, or are entitled to receive, compensation are subject to federal employment taxes. If an officer does not perform any services or only performs minor services and is not entitled to compensation, the officer would not be considered an employee."

I must point out, however, that **income from rental real estate is *not* considered <u>earned income</u>; it is <u>passive income</u> which is not subject to self-employment tax or payroll taxes.** So, if your Sub S Corp only owns rental real estate (and does not perform a service or sell a product), the above discussion may not be a concern. I will discuss more on taxation in Chapter Ten.

Due to the liability protection coupled with the elimination of double taxation of corporate profits, many smaller companies chose this form of organization. However, read on for even more attempts at simplifying business structure while retaining protection from liability for the owners.

- LIMITED LIABILITY COMPANY. LLC's have become exceedingly popular in recent decades for the formation of all types of businesses including ones that will invest in real estate. **They are very similar to Sub S corporations in that they also protect the owners from business liabilities or debts, and they are pass-through entities for tax purposes.** However, the owners are called members, and their ownership is divided into membership interests. Just as a corporation could conceivably have just one shareholder, "single person LLC's" can be formed where there is only one member if desired. However, if any one member leaves an LLC, then it must be terminated, and a new LLC started to reflect new members if the business is to carry on. Interestingly, **profits can be distributed however you want, even if it differs from the percentage of ownership.**

An entity can form as an LLC, but then elect to register with the IRS as a Sub S. Corp. According to the IRS, "Depending on elections made by the LLC and the number of members, the IRS will treat an LLC as either a corporation, partnership, or as part of the LLC's owner's tax return (a "disregarded entity"). Specifically, a domestic LLC with at least two members is classified as a partnership for federal income tax purposes unless it files Form 8832 and affirmatively elects to be treated as a corporation. For income tax purposes, an LLC with only one member is treated as an entity disregarded as separate from its owner, unless it files Form 8832 and elects to be treated as a corporation. However, for purposes of employment tax and certain excise taxes, an LLC with only one member is still considered a separate entity."

One of the reasons that LLCs are so popular, especially for small businesses, is that they are easier to start and maintain. They are sort of a hybrid between corporations and partnerships in that a board of directors is not required, but an annual meeting of the members may be required. Also, **although company records such as meeting minutes may be required, generally the LLC record keeping requirements are less formal than a corporation's.** Rules vary from state to state.

This all equates to more flexibility in management, but make no mistake...**formal record keeping is required to keep the LLC in good standing.** People make the mistake of forming an LLC and then forgetting about them all the while believing they are fully protected personally from liabilities. The reality is that when an entity that is supposed to shield the owners has a liability that cannot be satisfied, the creditor's lawyers will try to go outside of the entity and "pierce the corporate veil" by trying to "unwind" the entity and challenge its validity. Commonly, the specific wording of the documents from the formation of the entity will be attacked, but an easier path is to point out that the ongoing record keeping requirements are not being met. The legal theory is that, **if the entity is not meeting its record-keeping requirements, it has lost its status and so the owners are no longer protected from claims.**

- LIMITED LIABILITY PARTNERSHIP. The LLP is quite interesting. It is just a traditional general partnership that, at the time of its formation or at some point in its existence, has officially elected to be treated as a limited liability partnership with its state of formation. **All its partners are general partners, but by law they are afforded the same protection from creditors as limited partners in a limited partnership, shareholders in an S Corp or C Corp, or members in an LLC.** Otherwise, it's just like a general partnership in that it passes the income and losses through to the partners according to their pro rata shares of ownership. Most uniquely, though, compared to the other organizational forms I've mentioned that offer liability protection for the owners, **LLPs are not required to have a board of directors, officers, meetings, or any kind of ongoing formal record keeping of meeting minutes. Also, unlike a limited partnership, all partners are free to participate in the day-to-day operation of the business.** For some businesses, the LLP can be the best of all worlds when it comes to ease of operation.

There are numerous other types of entity structures that meet specific needs for the owners such as the Professional Corporation (PC), trusts of a seemingly infinite variety, and closely held corporations to name a few. Each has its own rules and requirements to maintain good legal status and for tax treatment. Also, with a few exceptions, entities can be shareholders/members of other entities or own other entities. **One popular technique, for an extra layer of protection, is to have a master LLC that owns your other LLC's as you open and close them for specific projects. Or you may form an LLP to be the general partner of all your limited partnerships so that the general partner is not an individual, just to give a couple of examples.**

It's worth noting that you can own and operate rental property inside your IRA. The law says that you can invest in virtually anything inside your IRA with only a few exceptions. Most people think that only financial assets such as stocks, bonds and mutual funds can be held in your IRA, and that is what typical brokerage houses are set up to help you do. These brokerages only offer to be the custodian of your IRA if you fill it with traditional assets that you buy through them. But **there are IRA custodians that are set up specifically to help people invest in all kinds of nontraditional assets from precious metals to real estate.** They typically charge a reasonable annual fee based on the value of your account.

Owning income producing property (or even flipping property) inside your IRA is worth considering because the profits are tax free if it is a Roth IRA or at least tax-deferred if they are in a traditional IRA. The main rule is that you can't touch the money in that all income (like rents) must go directly from its source into the IRA account, and all expenses for the property must be paid directly from the IRA. These transactions are precisely what the non-traditional IRA custodian is set up to do. Also, you can't work on the property yourself; you must hire out all the work and have the IRA custodian pay them at your direction. You are, however, allowed to make all the management decisions. It's not impossible for an IRA account to get a mortgage to buy a property, but it's not the same as getting a mortgage personally nor is it usually a good idea. **The basic technique is to move your holdings from your IRA with the big brokerage house to a new account with a custodian that specializes in nontraditional assets. This is not a taxable event.** Then, when you find a property you want, liquidate your holdings, and pay cash for the property. Any profits will just accumulate inside the IRA account. Then, if it's a Roth IRA, the profits and principal can be withdrawn tax free after you turn 59 ½.

Business entities are typically formed in the state in which they will initially exist and do business. This is done with the Department of State for that particular state using the forms, laws and procedures prescribed by the state. Sometimes there are reasons to form the entity in another state like, for example, to take advantage of favorable laws regarding liability, taxation, or privacy. Delaware and Nevada often come up in those conversations. Initial and annual fees may be different for residents vs. non-residents of the state in which you organize. Also, you may be required to pay a company to be your in-state address if you don't live or otherwise do business in your state of organization. If you do business in a state other than the one in which you organized, you will probably be required to register as a foreign entity in that state. So, if you live in Pennsylvania but form your corporation in Nevada, you still must register with the Pennsylvania Department of State and pay an annual fee.

As should be obvious from this discussion, protecting the personal assets of the owners of a business from liabilities that arise from the operation of the business is of prime consideration. There are several legal entity structures that allow for that to occur. But what about if an owner of the business has a *personal* creditor that wants to satisfy their claim by acquiring the *personal assets* of the owner? That individual's ownership in the business could be up for grabs. Could this jeopardize the business and/or the interests of the other owners who have nothing to do with the issues of the individual in question? The short answer is that **you must make sure that your formation documents contain language which says that, if an outside creditor obtains an ownership interest in the company in this fashion, the creditor cannot participate in operating the company.**

There's a lot to this topic which is too detailed for this discussion. Briefly, **the legal concept is that you want to make an ownership interest in your company appear to an outside creditor to be what is known as a "poison pill" so that the creditor will not pursue the owner's interest in the company.** Positioning the interest as a "poison pill" means that, although the creditor would acquire an ownership interest, *having* the interest would actually be less desirable than *not having* the interest. This is primarily done by pointing out that the creditor would have no say in how or when profits would be distributed, nor could they dictate the salaries of the owners who work in the business. As a result, the creditor would be forced to pay tax on income they didn't receive from a partnership, for example, because the management decided not to pay it out. Or management (presumably the other owners) could decide to boost their salaries and bonuses to make up for not distributing the profits with the end result being that there are no profits for the creditor. **Having the proper language in its formation documents can force an outside creditor to think twice about attempting to acquire an interest in someone's business to satisfy a personal debt.**

Obviously, this is not an exhaustive study of business entities. My purpose here is to give you some slightly-more-than-basic information that will spark discussions with you and any potential partners. **This discussion needs to be continued,**

then, with an attorney who can help you make your final decision as to which type of entity you will use, if any, to hold the rental property you are going to operate. This could be an attorney you know locally, but now there are numerous online law firms that specialize in helping people set up businesses. They may even provide you with forms you can use over and over to create identical entities that you file with the state on your own. Your main considerations are:

- How profits are taxed

- How profits are distributed

- On which forms profits and losses are reported to the IRS and the owners

- How owners are protected from liabilities arising from within the company

- How the company is protected from liabilities of the owners that originate from outside the company

- How the owners are to be paid if they also work in the business

- How easy it is to form the business and what the costs are

- How easy it is to run the business in terms of management decisions, reporting and record keeping requirements

- How easy it is to add or eliminate owners

- How easy it is to transfer ownership by sale or inheritance

- What state the business will be formed in

Before we move on to PHASE TWO, **I want to make it clear that you should not be forming a business entity that protects you from personal liability with the idea in the back of your mind that you are going to somehow get out of paying legitimate debts. The liability protection we are primarily talking about is from claims that arise from successful lawsuits against your company that don't end up getting covered by your business' insurance.** These could come from anywhere like the operation of company vehicles, regulatory fines, negligence, and personal injuries to tenants or employees just to name some of the more popular sources of suits.

Keep in mind that, since your entity can borrow funds from any source, you as an individual may choose to lend to your entity. Injecting cash in this fashion does not change everyone's percentage of ownership in the company. It *does* make you a creditor of the company, so make sure all the details of your loan are documented at the time of the loan.

If your company buys goods or services on credit, borrows money, or accepts money in advance of providing goods or services to a customer, you need to plan on making good on those transactions. I once owned an unprofitable corporation 50-50 with someone, and when the company was being closed, there wasn't enough money from the sale of the assets to cover all the debts. I paid all the creditors in full using my own money with no help from the other owner because my reputation was more valuable to me than the money. I would have a claim against the other owner if I wanted to pursue it, but he took the low road out and declared bankruptcy so he wouldn't have to pay me.

The reality is that, **if you form an entity for the operation of a small business, and that entity wants to borrow or get credit in its own name, then you will likely have to personally sign as an owner to guarantee the loan.** So, if you get a mortgage on a rental property that your LLC owns, the bank will make you sign personally. If your partnership wants to open a trade account at a supply company, you will have to sign as well. **The bottom line is that there are ways to protect your personal assets from unexpected off-the-wall claims against your business. My main point here is that, unless you've decided to buy property in your own name(s), you need to organize your legal entity before you start looking for property so that you can close the deal quickly.**

PHASE TWO: SEARCHING FOR PROPERTY THAT MEETS YOUR CRITERIA

Once you have decided how you are going to hold title to the property you invest in, it is time to start looking for property. It's time to put in offers with sellers and make deals. It can be an exciting time, and some investors enjoy the search and the negotiations just like some people enjoy going to garage sales. However, as I mentioned earlier, finding the deals can be the least controllable process and the weakest link in the chain of necessary events on your way to wealth.

Real estate deals are not necessarily available "on demand" like a movie from a streaming service. You may be in the market and looking for deals all the time, but there will be stretches where nothing is worthwhile, and there will be times when you come across more deals than you can manage. **The key is to always be working a system or perhaps several systems that are known to yield results.** Sometimes you will find good deals as a direct result of your systems, and sometimes properties will seemingly just drop into your lap. You could call that luck, but, especially with real estate investing, I believe this is a special kind of luck. In this case I think **you can define luck to be *where preparation recognizes opportunity*.** The deal was out there, and maybe it was passed up by others who weren't looking and weren't prepared. But you knew what you were looking for, and you were ready to make an offer when you found it.

Notice that I said that you knew what you were looking for. **Knowing what you are after is the first step in the looking process.** If you know what type of property you want to buy it will narrow down the sources you go to with the systems you have chosen, and consequently your efforts will be more productive. This is not to say that you can't change what you're looking for over time, or that you can't have more than one specialty. I just mean that **it's better if you concentrate your efforts on a short list of types of property that you've familiarized yourself with.**

Having said that, before I get into how to find good deals, it's imperative that we discuss the different types of property you may want to consider. Through the process of elimination, you should be able to pick a few categories that interest you and which are practical for you. There are many types of property, but they all started out as undeveloped vacant land. It's not unheard of to buy vacant land and rent it to farmers or the government, and you can certainly buy vacant land and build brand new buildings on it for the purpose of renting the property to others. However, for the purposes of this book, we need to consider properties on which there is already a building, and which may or may not already be a rental property.

You first must decide who you want to have as customers or tenants.
Are you thinking of private individuals? In that case, the type of property you are
after is called residential. An overview of the types of residential property would
include:

- Single family homes (entry level vs. luxury)

- Two-unit duplexes (side by side mirror image apartments)

- Two-unit flats (up and down similar apartments)

- Two or more units of dissimilar floor plans in the same building

- Four or more-unit townhouses (identical or mirror image side-by-side
  2-story apartments)

- Apartment buildings with similar but possibly different sized apartments
  that are entered from a common lobby or hallway.

- Apartment complexes that have groups of the above-mentioned
  types of buildings around a common parking area with perhaps other
  amenities like a pool

- Condominiums that are perhaps a townhouse style or in an apartment
  building where each unit is owned separately, and the property line
  is in the wall between the units, while each owner has access to
  the amenities. Owners pay condominium association fees for the
  maintenance, taxes, and insurance of the common areas.

- Row homes (similar multi-story side-by-side units that are individually
  owned, but each owner is responsible for their own exterior maintenance
  with no association fees)

- Mobile homes on a lot that is rented from the owner of the trailer park

- Mobile homes on a private lot

- Mobile home parks where you rent the lot to the owners of the mobile
  homes, and you maintain the shared areas and amenities

Although this is not a complete list, these types of properties are the kind that are most easily rented out to long-term tenants who sign a one-year lease and often renew that lease year after year. Many residential rental properties are used for short-term stays, however. So, **that is your next decision...do you want to do short-term or long-term rentals?** Virtually any of the above types of properties could be used for either depending on your business plan. This is especially the case with the advent of the air B&B which can be booked on the internet. People who are going somewhere for a short stay sometimes find a stay in a single-family home, apartment, or condo to be more interesting than in a traditional hotel or motel. Technically, traditional hotels and motels are a type of residential rental real estate, but they are more in the realm of the hospitality industry and are beyond the scope of this discussion.

Most of those types of properties on the list could also be used for vacation homes or getaway destinations as well as long-term rentals. This depends a little more on location, of course, since the vacation home would be located in the midst of a touristy area, and the getaway home would be more or less the opposite with its location more remote and away from activity.

Sometimes the plan is to rent rooms or small apartments to local residents by the week or month. These tenants are typically, but not always, more transient with fewer possessions and perhaps uneven income. They are much easier to remove if they are not following the rules or paying their rent compared to tenants who have signed a long-term lease. Often the properties used for this purpose are located in more populated sections of town and are within walking distance of goods and services. A sample list of other types of residential property that is used for short-term rentals includes:

- Rooms in a larger house with a shared area in the house for all residents
- Apartments carved out of a larger house that have their own entrances
- Former roadside motels
- Groups of cottages or bungalows

Up to this point, I've been listing the types of structures that you can use for rental properties if you've decided that your customers are going to be private individuals who are looking for a place to stay. **Now you need to decide on the quality or condition of the structures that you are looking for.** There is a loose grading system used to classify the condition of rentals which uses A, B, C and D as a reference. To give a quick description of this system, "A" grade properties are essentially new or nearly new with the most desirable layouts, features and amenities and no deferred maintenance. "B" grade properties are a little older with some wear and tear but are still solid and are likely also to be of so-called *new style construction*. "C" grades are much older and probably need some major updating, but they are still viable in their current condition for some residents. They are likely of so-called *old-style construction*. "D" grades are more run down than "C" properties and are not likely worthy of putting serious money into (other than for keeping them safe) because they are not likely to appreciate in value much over time. For homes, new style construction essentially began in the 1950's as builders moved away from plaster walls to finished drywall with more standard framing techniques and leaner looks for interior trim wood.

Having said that though, **I believe that most properties can be improved to the point of moving them up from whatever grade you find them in.** This is dependent on whether the overall location of the property would support the move and whether the properties around yours are also being improved. As we will discuss later in this book, **you must always be mindful of the degree of return you are going to get from the money you spend to improve a property. Usually, you will get a greater increase in value than the amount spent. But sometimes, if you're not careful, you won't even get a dollar-for-dollar increase, and all you'll have is your own satisfaction of having made an improvement.**

Naturally, **property condition, location and features are primary determinates of what residents will pay for rent**. Ultimately, combined with the amount of regular attention that a property needs to operate properly (management), the net rental income (revenues less expenses) will determine the value of an income property. An A grade property theoretically commands the most rent per square foot and requires the least attention to maintenance issues, and the opposite is true for a D grade property.

As a generalization, an A grade property is likely to yield less cash-on-cash return than a D grade property. The simple explanation of this is that investors are willing to pay more for and to accept smaller cash flows from pristine properties that need less attention and are likely to appreciate in value over time because they will make their money on the back end when they sell. Investors in D grade properties pay less for the property and trade away the potential for significant appreciation for them as well. Also, in exchange for higher rents percentage wise compared to the value of the A grade property, the D grade property owner will have more management requirements. To illustrate this mathematically, let's say that a one-unit A grade property has a rent of $1000 so, using a rough calculation that says the monthly rent is 1% of value, the value of the property is $100,000. By contrast, the one-unit D grade property which also rents for $1000 may dictate that rent is 2% of its value, so you might be able to obtain that property for just $50,000. Consequently, the return on cash invested is greater for the D property than the A property assuming the same percentage of the purchase price was put down at purchase for each property. Of course, **if you manage to use a technique for buying the property using no money down, your return on cash invested is infinite.** But that's a discussion for another part of the book!

Personally, I like the middle. Although I believe in excelling at whatever it is you choose to do, I've always had certain connections to the middle. For example, I was raised middle class. My last name starts with "M" from the middle of the alphabet. My birthday is July 2nd which is the exact middle day of the year. I live in a medium-sized town. So, it's no surprise that I like the B and C properties, and I have found them to be very profitable with a reasonable amount of management. I guess you could say that I believe in excelling at being in the middle.

Moving on, **you may decide that your customers are going to be businesses as opposed to individuals.** In this case, instead of providing a place for someone to live, you would be providing a location for a business to run. This is called commercial property as opposed to residential property. Like with residential property, you must decide on the type of buildings you want followed by their condition and location. The types of commercial property are just as varied as residential property, but here is an overview:

- Free-standing multi-use property that is usable by many kinds of businesses for their storefront, office, warehouse, repair, or manufacturing facility, etc.
- Strip plaza with multiple retail storefronts entered from the exterior
- Commercial storefronts on ground level with apartments above
- Single-level or multi-level office building with common hallways and lobbies
- Single use building for a specific customer like for a franchise restaurant, post office, convenience store or car wash
- Light industrial or office park with multiple buildings containing single or multiple units that are adaptable for many types of business
- Shopping mall with interior and exterior entrances to retail establishments
- Heavy manufacturing facility
- Warehouse for commercial use
- Self-storage units for private use
- Hospital or long-term care facility that houses patients
- Developed land offered for lease to a tenant who will construct their own building on it

Just as with residential income property, the tenant pays you for the use of the property under a contract called a lease. But **there are some key differences between the leases for residential vs. commercial tenants.** Notice that I said that the leases are different based on the type of tenant, not the type of property. If you rent out a single-family home in a commercialized area for someone to use as an office, then you must use a commercial lease. Conversely, if you rent out a former storefront for someone to live in, you must use a residential lease.

When considering investing in commercial property, consideration must be given to what is happening locally in terms of the need for different types of business space. For example, demand for retail space is decreasing due to online shopping, but retail space is more viable when you can get stores as tenants that maintain both an online *and* physical presence. Similarly, office space demand is decreasing because more companies are allowing employees to work from home, so you must gauge the future demand in your locale.

Unlike residential properties, commercial properties are sometimes rented out with what is called a "triple net lease." In this arrangement, in addition to paying rent, the tenant is responsible for the taxes, insurance, and maintenance of the property. These are the three areas of expense that make the lease "net, net, net" or triple net. If there are multiple tenants at the same property, you would periodically bill them for their percentage (based on relative square footage) of these costs as part of your management of the property. Especially if they are the only tenant in a property, you must periodically do inspections to ensure they are keeping up with the maintenance on your building. Triple net leases can be especially good for single-use properties because the tenant is likely to be there for a long time, and the tenant would be absorbing the increases in expenses as they occurred. However, it is imperative you rent to established companies that are not likely to go bankrupt.

Dealing with large and established companies as tenants has its plusses and minuses. They may be able to guarantee the rent payments until the end of the lease, but they may not continue to occupy the space while still paying the rent. Sometimes there are corporate decisions to move or close locations while honoring their lease commitments. At first glance this sounds like a good thing for the landlord, but the downside is that their vacancy can kill off the smaller tenants due to decreased traffic to your location.

For residential properties, the landlord will certainly be supplying the lease the tenant is required to sign. It is likely to be uniform for all residents. However, **for a commercial property, the lease form is often custom crafted to express the deal that has been struck between the landlord and the tenant.** The landlord may have a framework for a lease, but the final document is unique.

Also, for larger tenants like chain stores, the tenant may be a larger company than that of the landlord. Consequently, because of so many specific requirements, the tenant might be the one providing the lease document for the landlord to agree to.

The first difference I would point out between residential and commercial leases is that, in order to follow state and local laws regarding evictions, **residential leases protect resident tenants to a much greater degree than commercial leases protect business tenants.** Evictions of residential tenants typically involve a sequence of events that are prescribed by law to ensure that people aren't being thrown out of their homes by overzealous landlords. The process likely starts with a written demand for the unpaid rent that is served on the tenant followed by a court hearing. The tenants then have a prescribed length of time to either pay the rent in full or leave. If they don't leave, then a government official (typically a constable) physically removes them. **Not allowed are so called "self-help" eviction tactics** such as changing the locks while the tenants are still living there. On the other hand, commercial tenants are not afforded near as much grace from the law. You very well may be able to change the locks on their storefront after proper notice without any help from the courts.

While we're on the subject of evictions, I know that the prospect of having to evict a tenant could be one of your major reasons for not wanting to invest in rental property. However, **please believe me when I tell you that, provided you learn to screen applicants sensibly before you even agree to show them your vacant apartment (we will cover this later), evictions are extremely rare.** When they do occur, they are a significantly less painful event for the landlord than you may be imagining. If you don't give the wayward tenant too much time before you act, and you follow the local rules, it shouldn't take an unreasonable length of time to get them out while they still owe you a small balance. So, please don't let this deter you.

There is one other angle you may want to consider for delineating the type of property you are seeking. **You can further define your residential or commercial tenants by a niche that you would like to serve.** Some examples of niche markets are:

- Senior housing

- College students

- Refugees

- Special needs (physically or mentally challenged)

- Section 8 or other government-assisted housing

- Pet owners

- Corporate housing

To sum this up, deciding on the type of structure you wish to buy is the first thing, but then you must decide on the condition of the property and the location you want to buy in. By location, I mean do you want to invest in specific neighborhoods in your own town, or do you want to invest in another city and state altogether? Putting these decisions in a list, here are some major considerations to think about before you begin searching for property that meets your criteria:

- Type of property

  - Residential
  - Commercial

- Structural type of the building

  - Construction style
  - Number of units or size
  - Type of building (flat, townhouse, apartment building, strip plaza, etc.)

- Condition of the building and surrounding land

  - Turn-key ready
  - Fixer upper
  - In between (updates to be done over time)

- Location

  - A town close to where you live or far away
  - The area of the town in which you will be investing
  - Local landlord/tenant laws

- Condition of the surrounding properties

  - What you prefer
  - What you will accept

Notice that these items are all points of consideration for the purpose of establishing your criteria for selecting properties to investigate. **If you examine the pros and cons as you see them for all the distinct types of property ahead of time, you can concentrate your efforts on finding the type of property you prefer.** You will likely find a suitable property more quickly that way as opposed to being too general in your search. When you are too nonspecific, you will waste time on properties you could have avoided.

Once you've decided on the type of properties you want to go after, there are still a couple of decisions to make to narrow down your search a little more.

- Affordability

  - General price range of the property
  - Type of financing you are prepared for
  - Cash flow vs. appreciation

- Management

  - Self-manage
  - Property manager

- Supply and demand of the type of property you want in the location you want

  - Current conditions
  - Market trends

Yes, I just mentioned the "M" word (management). We will be spending much more time on managing rental properties in upcoming chapters. **Deciding whether you are going to manage the property yourself or hire a professional property manager is a big "Y" in the road to navigate in advance of searching for properties.** Also, understand that management and maintenance are not the same thing. Maintenance is only a part of management. You could still, for example, manage your rentals but have someone else do the maintenance.

As I mentioned at the beginning of this phase, good real estate deals are not going to be available every time you get to the moment when you decide it's time for the next addition to your portfolio. You must keep working your systems and be prepared to evaluate the deals as they come up. Then you either proceed or walk away.

I recognize, though, that you will not have all your favorite systems set up right from the start. You will hone these systems over time. So, let me just state something that virtually every successful real estate investor will tell you with probably a smile and a chuckle. **Your first deal will be the hardest, but don't be discouraged because it keeps getting easier.** Don't give up because of all the seemingly fruitless searching, clumsy evaluations of properties, and disappointing rejections of offers at the beginning. **Sometimes you win, and sometimes you learn.** Win the deal or not, you will be learning tons of stuff in the beginning, and the momentum of your deal flow will increase with your knowledge. We are going to discuss financing properties later, but let me encourage you now by saying that **if you find a great deal, you will find the money to buy it. I will go as far as to say that finding the financing is easier than finding the deal.**

Once you have decided on the parameters for the property you wish to acquire, you must set about trying to locate the properties that fit your plan. The following is an overview of some of the best ways to find properties. The key is to decide what methods appeal to you and then **set up a system to routinely work these methods.** If something isn't working, then move on to another method and system.

- **Realtors.** Licensed Realtors are in the business of connecting willing sellers with willing buyers. They do this by finding sellers, compiling the information about the property and then "listing" the property for all to see on what is known as the MLS or Multiple Listing Service. Realtors work under a real estate broker who has a higher level of training and licensing. All the listings of a Realtor under their broker are visible on the MLS to all the Realtors working under all the other brokers. Brokers also advertise their Realtors' listings to the public in hopes of finding buyers. Some Realtors are better at obtaining listings that end up being sold by other Realtors, and some are better at helping buyers choose properties that others have listed.

  The system to work here is simply to have a relationship with one or more Realtors who routinely alert you to new listings of properties that you potentially would want to buy. If you're working primarily in one metropolitan area, you may not need more than one Realtor since all see the new listings simultaneously. Your Realtor must know specifically what type of property you are looking for so that you're not wasting each other's time. And the Realtor must know that you are ready to act if an interesting property comes along.

  Although most Realtors are mainly occupied with buying and selling single family homes that transfer from one occupant to another, some specialize in investment property. **My advice is to find one that has experience in the general type of investment property you are looking for in addition to their bread-and-butter deals.** Don't try to get a superstar top-producing Realtor whose success is in selling single family homes to owner-occupants to find you great investment property deals. Your ultimate goal is to become one of the primary investors, if not the only investor, with whom this Realtor works.

  Realtors will oversee all the paperwork necessary for the deal and watch out for your best interest as the deal moves toward closing. I would caution against inquiring about a listed property through its listing agent since their primary allegiance is to the sellers. Make your inquiry through your own Realtor. Both Realtors will split the commission on the sale which is typically paid by the sellers at closing.

You can certainly sell your property on your own and avoid paying a sales commission, but it is my experience that a Realtor will typically make up for their commission by finding a buyer faster and at a higher price than selling on your own. This brings me to the downside of trying to buy properties through a Realtor which is that, through the MLS, everybody else in the market is exposed to the property at the same time. Accordingly, you may find yourself bidding against other investors and having to pay too much or even getting outbid altogether. But working with a good Realtor is not a method to neglect.

- **Off-market deals.** If you're not buying through a Realtor, you are buying off-market. In other words, you have found a willing seller who has not listed their property on the MLS. **Generally, I will say that when you look back at your real estate career, you will notice that your best deals were off-market deals.** Deals that you find on your own where you are dealing directly with the seller offer the most flexibility in terms of meeting yours and the seller's needs for financing, price, timing of the closing, what items are included in the sale, etc.. If you are buying a listed property, you may never meet the seller unless it's at the closing, but with an off market deal you have the chance to meet with (or at least otherwise communicate with) the seller face to face and develop a relationship. It is through this relationship that the deal is forged for a win-win result for both you and the seller. You're not using a go-between Realtor to hammer out the deal. You ask lots of questions about the seller's motivation and their needs as well as building trust and a desire for both parties to help the other.

Many times, the terms resulting from an off-market deal are ones that would never have been arrived at had the property been listed. For example, the seller may start out thinking they just want to sell the property and get all the money at once, but you discover their property does not have a mortgage against it, and you negotiate a low-money-down deal where the seller takes payments from you over time. This arrangement would not have given the seller enough money at the closing to pay their Realtor's commission, so it probably would not have been proposed if it was a listed property.

So, the question is about how to find off-market deals. There are many techniques for this, but working a few of them diligently will get you the best results. **The primary advantage of finding an off-market deal is that you become the only buyer (or at least one of the few) the seller is dealing with** as compared to the many buyers they may be exposed to through the MLS.

The avenue for finding off-market deals is comprised of two lanes going in opposite directions just like with a real avenue. In one lane you are waiting for the sellers to come to you as the result of your marketing efforts, and in the other lane you are travelling toward where you know the sellers already are. More specifically, **in the first instance, your efforts are all for the purpose of getting a prospective seller to contact you directly instead of calling a Realtor. In the second instance you are approaching sellers** such as banks which have property to sell that they have obtained through foreclosure, or you are contacting other investors to see if they want to sell. Attending auctions is another example of going to where the sellers are. Here are some examples of how to get sellers to come to you:

o **Direct mail or phone calls.** This is where you are using a list that you create or buy to use to send something to (or call) a select group of property owners to tell them you may want to buy their property. You haven't seen their property before you send them the letter.

　　The methods of gathering the necessary contact information can vary by county, but the recipients could include borrowers in foreclosure, debtors in bankruptcy, all the owners in a certain subdivision or the executors of estates just to name a few groups you to whom you may want to send. **If you don't want to compile the list yourself, there are plenty of places where you can purchase professionally prepared lists which can be super specific** such as ListSource.com, PropSource.com and DealMachine. com's Driving for Dollars app. The term "driving for dollars" refers to the technique of driving around the area in which you wish to buy, and identifying properties that fit your requirements whether they are abandoned single family homes or nice apartment complexes. You then look up the owners and make your contact.

I know some investors who literally hand-write their letters to prospective sellers on notebook paper and then address the envelope themselves. This can be impressive in that the seller sees how much you've taken personal interest in contacting them about their property. Other investors print labels for the envelopes with their computer and send out loads of form letters. This can get results from the sheer volume of mail pieces.

I'm not going to give you a sample letter because you need to craft one to reflect your or your company's own personality, but here are the key things to include and the points to make in the content of your letter or mail piece:

- A nice company letterhead unless you are hand-writing the letter
- Your phone numbers, email address and website name unless they're already in your letterhead
- Your business card (assuming you are sending a letter as opposed to a post card)
- Professional/responsible-sounding language with proper grammar, punctuation, and spelling
- Appealing quality and layout of the printing
- Points to make include:

  ◇ Your personal name
  ◇ You're an investor, and any other credentials you may have
  ◇ You have an interest in buying their property (give the specific address if that's possible).
  ◇ You want them to call you to discuss the property and the possibility of them selling it.
  ◇ The fact that you can buy it with cash (if that's possible) and close quickly

◇ You are willing to buy even if the property is run down and that you will take the property "as is."

◇ A nice closing with your signature

o **Bandit signs.** These are the "WE BUY HOUSES" signs that you see everywhere. These can be an inexpensive way to get started, but there is some work involved in posting the signs and maintaining damaged or lost signs. They are called "bandit signs" because you are typically posting them like a bandit in the middle of the night in public areas like telephone poles where it's probably not legal to post them.

o **Internet advertising.** Creating an online presence as a buyer of real estate can be done inexpensively or by making an investment in an elaborate system for collecting and funneling deals to your company. The former can be accomplished by yourself through utilizing public forums such as Facebook, but you can grow it into the latter by creating your own website, posting videos, and utilizing paid third-party systems for deal flow. The opportunities for creativity here are endless.

o **Traditional advertising.** You could throw any type of advertising that you can think of into this category such as radio, television, or print (to name the most obvious ones) where you are paying another company to advertise the existence of your company to the general public. You must remember, though, that your target (when attempting to acquire property) is a motivated seller of real estate. This target is a very, very small percentage of the general population, so **efforts to reach your target more directly will pay off better than with traditional advertising** where you will be paying to reach people outside of your target.

o **Be a "friend of a friend."** Owners who need to sell property often discuss this with people who are close to them. If you can make yourself known as a buyer of real estate to attorneys, financial planners, accountants, elder care providers, hospice workers, funeral homes, corporate recruiters, animal control agents, and code enforcement officials, you can be the friend they think of when the matter comes up.

The following are some of the best ways to go directly to the sellers:

o **Networking with other landlords and investors.** Every property that is acquired must be disposed of at some point. **Active real estate investors are more likely from my experience to first attempt to sell an income property to another investor directly before they list their property on the MLS with a Realtor.** If you have a network of contacts with other investors, you stand a good chance of finding out when someone is ready to sell, and you will find a ready market when you are in the mood to sell.

   This would include those who wholesale properties to other investors. They work hard at nailing down a good deal with a seller (usually a distressed property from an individual), and then they arrange for a second buyer to pay them a higher price. The wholesaler either assigns their contract for a fee (and never takes title to the property), or sells to the second buyer at a back-to-back closing on the same day. Having a relationship with a good wholesaler can yield a steady stream of deals.

   At this point **I'm going to put in my plug for your local landlord association. This would be the professional organization of landlords and/or real estate investors in your area.** I was blessed for my whole career to be a part of a very fine organization called the Apartment Association of Northwestern Pennsylvania. It was started in the late 70's almost at the same time I bought my first rental, and we both grew together over the years. Later, I became a long-serving board member and one of its longest-serving presidents, having served as president for six years (and even longer as a vice president). We have monthly dinner meetings with guest speakers on relevant topics, and none of our speakers are selling a product; just educating us. We have a brick-and-mortar building with 3 employees who produce a monthly educational newsletter and serve our members with such benefits as running inexpensive credit reports and providing forms such as leases. We have an attorney under contract who is available for free phone consultations on landlord/tenant matters. Additionally, we schedule various seminars on requested topics, and offer what we call Landlord 101 classes. As one of the Landlord 101 instructors, I have the privilege of teaching our proprietary 4-session class on residential land lording that was written by one of our founding members, John Baldwin, whose family is in its fifth generation as one of the largest developers in our area. **With the majority of landlords in our part of the state, from the mom-and-pops to the biggest players, sitting all at the same table, do you not think we are becoming better landlords and that we are selling our properties to each other?!**

I can only hope that you have some sort of organization that serves landlords in your area. Some are non-profits, and some are privately owned. Some are affiliates of a national organization, and some are not. In any case, I implore you to join it no matter what it costs. You will make up the cost many times over.

o **Auctions.** I have made quite a bit of money with properties I bought at various kinds of auctions over the years. Primarily they were single family homes that we flipped to an owner/occupant after we rehabbed them. However, **I must say that in recent years it has become harder and harder to get good deals at auctions because of competition from other bidders...not the lack of properties being auctioned.** There have been numerous times when I was the only bidder, and I walked away with the property for just $1.00 over the minimum bid. Sometimes I was the only person in the room other than the auctioneer. Now the room is full.

In my view, the reasons for so many people bidding at auctions boil down to a convergence of two factors. One, following the financial crises of 2008 plus other factors causing companies to rethink their workforces, many capable people became unemployed, so they started their own businesses. In many cases, while possessing some degree of proficiency in home repairs, these people became contractors. They held themselves out as being available for general repairs, roofing, siding or whatever it was they were good at. However, in addition to working for others, they were willing to "buy themselves a job" by using their savings to buy properties (for cash at auctions) which they would work on themselves in between the commitments to their customers. Since they were not going to be paying third-party contractors for most of the work like I would, they could afford to pay more for the properties.

Secondly, the proliferation of TV shows about flipping houses, books on real estate investing (like this one), readily available information on the internet and real estate gurus have all been rather successful at encouraging a wider range of people to buy investment property. One of the places they end up, as you may well do also, is at an auction.

Despite the heightened interest in auctions, if you attend the right auction, there will still be deals to be found there. So, here's a breakdown of the main types of auctions:

- ◆ **Sheriff sales.** Generally, these are the sales conducted typically monthly by the county in which the property lies. The sheriff or a deputy is the auctioneer. They are held at the request of any lender whose loan against the property has not been paid as agreed. The borrowers/owners have been properly notified that they are in default, and they've been given ample time to bring their payments current. However, for whatever reason, the borrower has not paid up so, as a last resort, the lender has hired an attorney to foreclose on the property. Whatever costs the lender has expended to get to this point have been added to the loan balance along with unpaid late fees, etc. to arrive at the total the lender is owed. If nobody bids more than what the lender is owed, then the lender takes title to the property, whereupon they can sell the property at whatever price they choose. Any junior liens (liens that were recorded chronologically after the foreclosing lender's lien), like a second mortgage or a judgement for another unpaid debt, are wiped out by the sheriff sale, and they are no longer kept recorded as an obligation secured by that particular property. A junior lienholder, by the way, can bid in the amount of their lien although that does obligate them to pay off any creditors who are ahead of them. In that case, you would have to bid more than the total owed to the two creditors, in my example, to be the successful bidder.

◆ **U. S. Marshal sales.** These are similar to sheriff sales, but the auctioneer is a United States Marshal. U. S. Marshals sell property that has been seized by the federal government which may include real estate. However, in the case of foreclosures as opposed to siezures, the government does not yet own the property. The property in question would have been purchased using a USDA mortgage. Foreclosures on these properties are for the same reason in that the owner has failed to pay the mortgage, but the rules are such that the USDA must use the U. S. Marshals Service and not the sheriff's department. One difference, though, is that, if nobody bids what the government wants, the government will typically not take possession of the property like a bank would at a sheriff sale. Instead, the property is offered up again at a future auction. Also, auctions are held sporadically whenever the government has a group of them ready.

◆ **Bankruptcy auctions.** When someone goes bankrupt, the case is overseen by the federal bankruptcy court. The judge may rule that certain property is to be auctioned off to settle the debtor's obligations to creditors. This may include real estate like a personal home or rental property. These auctions are conducted by the court in front of a judge. Sales are sporadic.

◆ **Estate sales and liquidations**. Sometimes the executor of an estate chooses to liquidate the decedent's assets via a public auction. Typically, this is done at the location of the assets, such as the decedent's home, or at the various locations of any real estate being sold. Also, sometimes an owner will choose to sell their property by auction to close a business or otherwise just move on in life. These auctions are typically organized and held by a private professional auctioneer who is being paid by the estate.

♦ **Tax sales.** The features of these are all over the board around the country, but basically these are auctions that are held by each county once a year to collect unpaid real estate taxes on behalf of the county and the various municipalities and school districts. Around here, they have one auction where you buy the property subject to any liens connected to the property, but any properties not sold are offered in a subsequent "lien-free" sale some months later where you don't have to assume responsibility for any existing liens.

It's hard to get too specific about the mechanics of auctions because rules and customs vary from type to type, from jurisdiction to jurisdiction and from auctioneer to auctioneer. You need to investigate ahead of time as to what to expect. However, there are some common denominators:

◇ The USDA and the Dept. of the Treasury maintain websites that list the properties in their upcoming auctions at www. treasury.gov/auctions/treasury and www.resales.usda.gov respectively. The auction may be held at the property, but most likely, since multiple properties will be offered, it will be held in a designated room somewhere that is borrowed for the occasion.

◇ Sheriff Sales are advertised in the local newspaper or similar publications. The auction is usually held "on the courthouse steps" or in a room in the courthouse. The county may also maintain a website with the details of upcoming foreclosures.

◇ Public auctions of estates and other private property are also advertised in the newspaper, on the auctioneer's website, with yard signs, mailings to the auctioneer's list of regular bidders and whatever means the auctioneer company wishes to use.

◇ Tax sales, which may involve hundreds or more properties, are advertised by local rules similarly to sheriff sales. Perhaps a professional auctioneer will be hired to hold the sale in a venue large enough to accommodate the numerous bidders.

◇ Generally, you are going to have to pay immediately following the auction with cash or cashier's checks. Local rules, however, may allow you to go get the cash in a short period right after the auction if you leave a deposit and/or show evidence of the funds being available at your bank.

◇ Except for estate or private property auctions, you probably will not have an opportunity to examine the interior of the property before the auction unless you are somehow able to arrange access on your own.

◇ Lots of investigation and evaluation of the risks is necessary ahead of the auction so you know what you're getting into.

◇ You may be disqualified as a bidder if you don't follow the rules.

◇ Due to whatever bureaucratic procedures are in effect for the particular auction at which you were the successful bidder, you may not actually receive the deed for the property for weeks or months after the sale. However, you should be prepared to insure the property as of the day of the auction to protect your interest.

◇ Although you should always take steps to secure a property immediately (such as board up broken windows), it is debatable among investors as to what extent any improvements should be made until you have the deed.

◇ It is interesting to note that you can deal with the owner of a property in foreclosure right up to the day of the auction. If the owner can demonstrate to the lender that they have entered into a bona fide contract to sell their property for enough money to pay off the loan, the lender is likely to postpone the property's sheriff sale for enough time to get the deal closed.

◇ In the case of a property that has more owed against it than it is worth, instead of going through the whole foreclosure process just to get a property that they sell for a loss, the lender may agree to allow the owner to sell the property for less than would pay off the loan. The lender would agree to accept less than what they are owed, but they would still extinguish the debt. This is called a "short sale."

As long as I'm on the subject of auctions, I feel I should comment on a possible consequence of buying a property at an auction; **you may buy property that is still occupied by the prior owners or tenants.** If there are tenants there, you may or may not be required to honor the lease that is in effect depending on the language in the lease and state law. If you wish to end the lease and have the tenants move out, you would be doing so, again, under the lease terms and the law. If they refused to move after proper application of the lease and law, you could proceed with an eviction.

If the property is still occupied by its former owner, then an ejectment is the proper method of getting them out if they refuse to otherwise come to terms with you on a move-out arrangement. *Ejectment* is the term for removing people who do not have the right to occupy a property as opposed to *eviction* which is the term for the process of removing tenants who have violated a lease. Ejectments and evictions both come by court order, but people being ejected tend to have fewer protections under the law than tenants.

The best course of action with former owners still in possession of their former residence is to try to gently work with them to get them out. Remember, this has been an emotional time for them. Here are some tips if you must go down that path:

♦ Identify yourself as the property manager, not the new owner.
♦ Ascertain if they already have plans to move and when. If it seems like a good plan, go with it.
♦ If they fail to move by when they said they would, or if they seem to need some incentives to move (like they don't have the money

or are under the mistaken impression that they don't have to move) offer them several hundred "reasons" (dollars) to move in a few days. At the same time, give them a firm-but-not-nasty written ejectment notice to start the clock ticking for any legal requirements.

- ◆ Walk through the property with them and determine what they must do, clean up, fix, or remove from the premises. They're not going to get the money from you, of course, until after they're gone, and they've met whatever other terms you've decided on, including not causing any further damage to the property.

- ◆ Unless there is some compelling reason at your end of the situation, DO NOT allow them to stay there and rent the property back from you. That is not a hard and fast rule, but generally if they did not make good owners, they will not make good tenants.

○ **Lenders who have taken properties through foreclosure.** If a lender, such as a bank or credit union, has obtained title to a property as the result of a foreclosure, it has done so as a last resort in an attempt to get their money back by selling the property. After the auction, the property moves from the foreclosure department to what is known as the Real Estate Owned (or REO) department. The lender may do some minor work on the property such as clean out the trash or address immediate safety issues, but then it will offer the property to the public "as is." Usually, banks will routinely list their REOs with specific Realtors, but sometimes (especially in the case of local lenders like savings & loans and credit unions) they will sell them directly to investors and owner/occupants. **It is possible to develop a relationship with the people in the REO department so that you get a call when they have a new property.** You wouldn't necessarily have to be a cash buyer since the bank may be willing to finance the property with you based on your relationship. Sometimes you can negotiate with a lender while a property is still going through foreclosure. In this instance you would be informally agreeing to buy the property from them at a specified price should they get the property at the auction.

○ **Wholesalers.** When you begin networking with other real estate investors, you will become aware of some whose specialty is finding property, locking down its purchase at a significantly below market price, and selling the property to another investor for a profit. Sometimes wholesalers own investment property of their own while wholesaling to others, but often wholesaling is all they do. Typically, a wholesaler is paid a fee by the buyer at the closing when the property transfers from the seller to the buyer without the wholesaler ever entering the chain of title. Wholesalers maintain a list of potential buyers whom they contact each time they have an available deal. As a buyer, you must be prepared to follow the terms the wholesaler has arranged with the seller, which usually involves a cash purchase, and you must be prepared to close quickly.

○ **Word of mouth.** Let's wrap up this section by giving a nod to the best source of business no matter what business you're in...a recommendation from someone else. **Word of mouth can work both for you and against you, so it really depends on the reputation you build as you take part in life.** I will say that your general reputation will carry over into your real estate world. More specifically to your real estate activities, **you want to build and protect your reputation as a buyer, a seller, a borrower, a landlord, a customer, a rehabber or whatever it is you do.** This positive word of mouth is what will bring your name to the lips of people when they are in conversations with others who must sell their house, find an apartment, or decide about approving a loan. **It has always been my philosophy that I would rather give up some money than to give up any of my good reputation.**

It has probably occurred to you by now that these efforts to locate property are as much efforts to find sellers as they are to find real estate for sale. **Aside from locating the type of property you are seeking, you are trying to identify what we call "don't-wanters." These are owners who don't want their property anymore to a larger degree than you want to own their property**. You hear about distressed property that is run down, but not all distressed property looks like a dump. We are looking for an owner that is in a distressed situation because we will get better deals from people who <u>need</u> to sell. **It is my contention that it is the distressed seller who makes a property qualify as a distressed one no matter what condition the property is in.**

For both owner-occupied properties as well as non-owner-occupied investment properties, here are several typical reasons **why the owner may be distressed:**

- Divorce, bankruptcy, death of a loved one, health issues
- Job transfer, retirement, loss of employment, distance to work
- Behind on payments, financial reversals, owes back income or real estate taxes
- Estate issues, out-of-state-owner, too busy to take care of property
- Partners, neighbor troubles, fear of the future
- Over-extended, double payments, balloon payment due
- Overhead, negative cash flow
- Tired landlord, management problems, updates or maintenance needed
- Other preferred opportunities the seller wants to persue

The question then becomes about how to identify potential don't-wanters whose situation is on the above list. You'll find them through properties listed by Realtors, but you'll also find don't-wanters in both lanes of the off-market deals avenue. Some are obvious like the creditors who are forcing an auction on the property or the tired landlord that you find through networking, and, of course, your own advertising is aimed at getting the *don't-wanters* to call *you*. **Here is a list of where to find don't-wanters when *you* are willing to go to *them*.**

- For Sale By Owner ads (FSBOs) wherever these sellers are advertising such as online posts, classified ads or yard signs

- Word of mouth when you hear about someone's distressed situation. Sources could include friends, mail carriers, building inspectors, tenants, religious leaders, nursing home visitors and employees, and delivery people.

- Accountants and attorneys who are representing distressed clients

- Property managers who become aware of a change in the owner's situation

- Vacant properties in any condition

- Occupied properties that are in disrepair or have tall grass

- Houses advertised for rent by their former occupant

The overall point is that there are many sources for properties for sale by people who want to sell their property more than you want to buy it, and there are many reasons why people have arrived in that mindset. Some sources involve *you* going to *them*, and some involve *you* attracting *them* to come to *you*. I will conclude this section with one giant tip: **your success at buying a property from a don't-wanter will most likely hinge on whether you can solve their immediate problem, whatever that is. Your job is to find it!** That fact leads me to our next phase which is negotiating.

PHASE THREE: NEGOTIATING THE PURCHASE

Right now, let's move to the point at which you have identified a property that meets your preferred criteria. **The next step, then, is to negotiate with the seller on the terms of the deal for the purpose of arriving at the point where you either sign a contract to buy the property, or you walk away** from the deal.

Negotiating is one of those areas, whether we're talking about the real estate business or any other interaction in life, which lays more on the *art* spectrum than the *science* spectrum. It's not exact since the participants and the objects of negotiation are always changing as are the market conditions. As a result, there have been countless books, articles, seminars, and internet postings about developing negotiating skills. It would be impractical to try to teach it all here.

Some people are born with naturally good negotiating skills in their personality. Some people are oblivious to how poorly they negotiate. **My recommendation to you is to study the art of negotiating by using whatever source appeals to you with an eye toward finding several techniques that fit your style.** Then, work to perfect those techniques so that you can confidently pull out the right ones depending on the situation.

Perhaps the source material that you use will provide you with outlines of scripts that you can use with sellers or buyers, or you may learn skills such as overcoming objections or writing offers. You can find source material that will provide templates for contracts you can use if you are the buyer or if you are the seller. There would likely also be samples of nicely worded paragraphs to put into an offer to cover specific situations. Figure out what you're *not* good at and find material that will help you improve.

Instead of trying to teach you specific negotiating techniques, I just want to lay out the universal requirements of negotiating. **The requirements basically remain the same even when the techniques change.** It would be silly to not have certain objectives in mind when we enter negotiations, and it is equally silly not to understand that negotiating requires certain things in order to meet those aims. **The task is to make sure that we take the requirements that are specific to the deal at hand, and then match them up to the universal requirements** to make sure we've got all the angles covered.

Jayson DeMers is the founder and CEO of AudienceBloom, a Seattle-based content marketing and social media agency. He's written many articles for Inc.com, and I like the way he lays out seven universal requirements for successful negotiating in a 2015 article. The headings are his, but I will summarize his comments with a twist toward real estate.

- **Background information.** Walking into a negotiation blindly can ruin any chance you have at negotiating successfully. You need to know what comparable properties are worth, what the rents in the area can be, and what the market trends are, for example. Statistics or relevant information can put you in a stronger position.

- **A goal.** You need to know **where you're willing to end up** before you start making an offer. A goal will help you set the course of the negotiations.

- **A plan.** You also need to prepare a plan, complete with hypothetical scenarios and contingency plans, if you want to navigate unforeseen obstacles successfully. If you can **identify ahead of time the likely objections** that your opponent will have, you will be less surprised and more able to counter them.

- **Confidence.** If you appear to be confident when you enter into a negotiation, your claims will be taken more seriously. Consequently, you will get better offers from the other side.

- **Self-interest.** I agree with DeMers when he suggests that greed and self-interest should not dictate your life. But I only partially agree when he says that searching for a "win-win" scenario isn't an effective negotiation tactic because it's more of a form of compromise. I say this because, in the real estate world, finding a "win-win-win-win" solution for multiple parties involved (for example, you, the seller, the bank and the neighbors) is often the way we roll. However, **self-interest can make you bolder** in your requests and give you better deals in the big picture.

- **Practice.** Like anything else, the more you negotiate the better you get at it. The caution, though, is to not get robotic because that will give you the exact opposite effect you are after.

- **Objectivity.** Finally, you'll need to walk into the negotiation with an objective perspective that applies to everything in the process. This is the equivalent of looking at the negotiations from a third-party perspective, all for the purpose of evaluating the realistic outcomes and motivations of both you and your opponent. This incorporates the background information from point one. You want everything to go your way, and objectivity helps get you there.

Before you get to the point where you can make an informed offer to a seller, it is imperative that you get a lot of questions answered. **It is most important to find out the reasons <u>why they are selling.</u> This is the first step to crafting a solution to their immediate problem.** Here are some other questions that will help you get the full picture:

- How long has the property been for sale?
- How long have they owned the property?
- Have they had any other offers?
- Why have they not accepted any other offer?
- Why do they think no offers have been made?
- How did they arrive at the price?
- When and for how much was the last appraisal?
- What major improvements have they made?
- What major improvements need to be made?
- When do they need to close?
- What do they need the proceeds for?
- Are they planning any major purchases with the proceeds?
- What are the existing mortgages, liens, or judgements against the property?
- What are the terms of the existing mortgages?
- Are the mortgages assumable?
- Would monthly payments be acceptable instead of all cash?
- (in the case of an owner-occupant) Where will they move to?

It should be noted at this point that, if you are going to make an offer to a private seller who has not listed the property on the MLS, **your interest in buying their property is presented to them through what is known as a Letter of Intent or LOI.** If the property is listed on the MLS, the offer would need to be made on a standardized form, but if it's not listed you pretty much have to free-form it. To be clear, the LOI is used primarily when approaching the seller of an income property, especially a larger property. The terms within the LOI are non-binding on both parties. The LOI is just the opening of the negotiations, and an actual contract to buy the property would potentially evolve from the LOI. However, for a smaller rental property or with an individual homeowner, your negotiations may all be verbal during a face-to-face interaction. Then, after informally settling on the terms, you go right to the contract that everybody signs.

You can find sample LOI's online, but basically—aside from identifying you, the property, and its owner—your LOI spells out suggested price, earnest money deposit, required inspections, potential closing date, terms, and other typical aspects of a real estate offer.

There could be many fine points to negotiate when buying real estate (such as whether the appliances are included, or the date you will take possession), but when you're negotiating the purchase of an investment property with a seller who simply wants to cash out of the property, then the main point of negotiation would just be the price. However, **if you are making an offer to a seller who is open to taking payments for the property, the principal areas to cover are:**

- Price

- Down payment

- Interest rate

- The amortization rate upon which the payments are calculated

- Length of time until the balloon payment is due, if any

- Monthly payment

- A possible prepayment penalty (the amount and for how long until there is no penalty)

- Closing date

The amortization rate is the number of years that it would take to pay off the loan completely if the payments were the same amount each month. However, you and the seller could decide that the payment would be calculated as though the loan would be paid off in thirty years (to keep the payment low), but at the same time agree that after, say, seven years of payments you must pay off the balance of the loan all at once. Obviously, agreeing on one or two points can automatically dictate another point like how the interest rate and amortization rate will dictate the payment.

These are a few general tips for negotiating:

- **Be prepared.** Learn the negotiating techniques necessary for the type of deals you are involved with. Know the universal requirements of successful negotiating as outlined above, and incorporate the pertinent elements from the deal at hand.

- **Listen to what your opponent has to say.** Ask questions, and do not monopolize the conversation.

- **Put yourself in the seller's position.** Look at the proposal from the other's point of view and ask yourself if you would accept the offer you are presenting. If not, then why?

- **Attack the problem, not your opponent personally.** Focus the negotiations on solving the other's problem, and not on will-testing or personal issues.

- **Solve the seller's problems.** Property is sold more for the **benefits conferred on the seller** than for raw profit!

- **Solve the buyer's problems. People buy benefits more than features.** You must explain the *benefits* a buyer will have IF they purchase the *features*.

- **Find the "black swan event".** Swans are supposed to be white, so when a black one is found it is a surprise. A "black swan event" is the unpredictable or unforeseen event with extreme consequences that has come into a seller's life to turn them into a motivated seller.

- **Develop multiple solutions.** Let your opponent state their preference for one solution over another instead of offering only one solution which may be turned down. **But do not confuse the seller!**

- **Address multiple issues separately.** Attack them one at a time, and move on to the next topic once an agreement has been reached. Start with the easier ones to build agreement with your opponent, and then go after the bigger ones. **Ultimately, you must convince your opponent that the solution is fair and is in their best interest.**

- **Provide as many certainties as possible.** Don't leave your counterpart with any doubts about whether something will be done as promised or about how any part of the deal will work.

- **Negotiate with your immediate re-sale in mind.** Don't agree to buy a property when you must depend on something out of your control occurring in the future in order for you to make a profit.

- **Don't give in. Instead, trade off.** Don't just give in on something your counterpart is asking for without asking for something in return.

- **Find your opponent's most critical objection.** Zero in on reaching an agreement on that issue. The other issues will be resolved more easily.

- **Don't project enthusiasm.** Be positive and confident, but make the other party sell YOU.

- **Don't let on about the softness of your offer.** You don't want the other party to think you can do much better.

- **Never be a pig.** Let your opponent win some points; just win the important points.

- **Always deal from a position of strength.** Weakness will cause you to give up too much.

- **Never negotiate with yourself.** Don't change your offer just because you think the other party won't accept it. Wait for a counteroffer.

- **Don't give the other party too long to accept your offer.** You don't want them to use your offer as bait for better offers.

Here are a couple of what I call *axioms* of real estate negotiating which I can attribute to Tony Hoffman. Tony was an Al Lowry disciple who became one of the early "no money down" real estate gurus who sold cassette tape courses on late-night TV infomercials in the 1980's. Then, in 1996, he famously marketed the video that O. J. Simpson recorded with an interviewer following his murder acquittals where O. J. tells his side of the story. Sadly, Hoffman fell into legal and financial troubles as did many of his generation of "get rich quick" practitioners. So, I want to be careful here to point out that **I do not subscribe to the systems and practices that got these personalities into trouble.** However, Hoffman did author the book *How to Negotiate Successfully in Real Estate,* so I must give him credit for articulating these axioms as well as being the inspiration behind some of the negotiating tips listed above. **Effective negotiating techniques are universal**, but you must couple them with a good business plan and good character to achieve long-term success. **Good negotiating skills and a good business plan are two different things.**

- **The Golden Rule.** Not the one you're thinking of. This rule says, "**He who has the gold rules.**" This means that the person in control is the one who wins. If you control the item that your opponent wants to sell/buy more than you want to buy/sell that item, then you will negotiate in your favor. So, if your cash is the "gold" that all the sellers want, then you will be in control. Or, if your property is the "gold" that all the buyers want, then the same is true.

And now, here is my all-time favorite negotiating axiom. I believe this axiom is the summation of everything that's ever been expounded about negotiating including The Golden Rule. **If you just employ this one principle when dealing with your negotiating counterpart, you probably won't make any unfavorable deals.** You may inadvertently pass up an OK deal, but you are not likely to get burned on the ones you accept.

- **He who cares least wins!** When you don't actually care if you get the deal or not, you will make a better deal for yourself. If you're willing to walk away from a deal when you're not getting what you want to a greater degree than your opponent is willing to walk away, then it will be your opponent who will give in. Think about it. It's when you get it in your head that you must have something that you start making bad decisions like paying too much. **If you don't fall in love with a property, and you are willing to move on to the next one, you'll negotiate more boldly.**

Finally, I offer you one last tidbit that you can employ when opening negotiations to buy a property. **If your offer is not embarrassing, then it's too high.** If you can develop the skill and confidence to employ this technique while coupling it with the two axioms I mentioned above, you will do well.

PHASE FOUR: DOING YOUR DUE DILIGENCE

When you negotiate a deal to buy a property you are basically doing so by taking the information about the property, as provided by the seller, at face value. In other words, you are negotiating with the assumption that everything the seller has told you so far is true. You are combining that information with other information that you already know to be true (such as facts about the market or the availability of financing) which are not specific facts about the property in question. Then, you are using that amalgamation of information to come to terms with the seller. However, **the seller may not have told you "the whole truth and nothing but the truth,"** and it is up to you to check things out before going ahead with the deal. This is called *due diligence*, **which is known as the investigation or exercise of care that a reasonable business or person is normally expected to take before entering into an agreement.** You probably jump into your car and drive off without checking everything over, but don't do this with a real estate deal. Every income property deal needs to be inspected more like the way pilots inspect their plane *every time* they are going to fly it.

Due diligence is done with the understanding that, if the facts change or if new facts are brought to light, the deal may have to change. Depending on the size of the property, there is a set period prescribed in the original agreement for doing due diligence which may be a matter of days or a matter of weeks. This keeps the deal moving along, and there would be a certain date by which you either decide to go ahead with the deal, modify the deal, or walk away. If you haven't completed your due diligence and made your decision within the allotted time, you may not get your earnest money refunded. Sellers know that time kills transactions, so they want the due diligence period to be as short as possible. This is because buyers can become less interested (he who cares least wins) as time goes by, and they are more likely to ask for concessions as defects are discovered.

You may be familiar with contingencies that are part of a contract to buy a home. Typical contingencies are for a well test, a septic system test or a home inspection. The buyer has a set time to remove those contingencies by approving the results of the tests in question. If the septic system doesn't pass, for example, the buyer is not required to continue with the deal. These contingencies are types of due diligence, but they are only part of the due diligence you would do when buying an income property vs. your personal residence. That's because, **with an income property, you not only have to dive deeper into the physical property; you must also verify the financial information. Don't take any information provided by the seller, especially financial information, for granted.** Not that every seller is automatically out to screw you; it's just that honest mistakes are made, and certain things that don't matter to the seller may matter to you. Like Ronald Reagan said, "Trust, but verify."

In my view, the goal of doing due diligence is twofold. The first is to **accurately verify the financial information** on the APOD (Annual Property Operating Data) if the seller gave you one, or to create an APOD of your own. The APOD is essentially an income statement for the property in question with all its income and expenses listed by source or category. Good examples of APODs are readily available online, and some even allow you to enter the information into the form. Since income properties are essentially valued based on their net income from operations, you can see how important it is to have an accurate APOD.

Secondly, due diligence helps you **determine just exactly what it is you are buying and the condition it is in.** This takes in everything from the accuracy of the property lines to the remaining life of the HVAC systems to legal issues. This is a time to really get to know your new acquisition and to begin formulating your long-term plans for repairs and capital expenses.

Of course, once this information (both financial and otherwise) is gathered and/ or verified, it may be determined that there needs to be some adjustment in the deal to account for the new facts that have become known for you to stay interested in the deal. I am not advocating automatically using the due diligence results as a heavy-handed tool for hammering the seller. You need to remain honorable in your dealings and follow through with the original terms as much as you can. For this reason, **you need to make offers you are willing to stand by in the first place, assuming things are reasonably close to how they were originally presented. Don't use due diligence just to take advantage of the seller by trying to get a better price than you deserve.**

If you search "real estate due diligence checklist" you will find some nice templates to follow, but most will divide the inspections into similar categories. I will credit the following headings to Steve Steadele, the author of *Multifamily Millionaire*. The added comments are mine, but this is a good list of the typical areas to investigate during your due diligence period.

- **Books and Records.** These include, for example, such things as bookkeeping methods to judge the accuracy of the financial info, rent roll and leases to verify occupancy, bank deposits to establish the occupants are actually paying their rent and do not need to be evicted, plus inspection records to alert you of any violation history with the government. As a contingency, require that an updated rent roll be presented to you at closing.

  Keying in on inspection records, these are particularly important to ask about. A seller may not readily produce them unless you ask. Such reports can be eye-opening regarding violations that either have been corrected (the work that was done to correct the violation can be interesting to know about) or which have been left uncorrected, in which case there could be a red flag. For properties withing the city limits in our area, there is a rental inspection program which involves regular inspections of the interiors and exteriors of every apartment. The owner is given a paper copy of the inspection report that shows any violations. Some violations need to be corrected immediately or within thirty days. Others are given until the next inspection, possibly two years later, to be remedied. Many communities are enacting such inspection programs for the safety of tenants, so you would want to check. You would need copies of the latest inspection reports to determine if there are any violations you, as the new owner, would be required to make before the next inspection if the current owner hasn't corrected them. Keep in mind that, even if there is no regular inspection program, the seller could have been cited by the code enforcement office as the result of a complaint or a drive-by inspection.

- **Financials.** This is primarily the accuracy of the APOD. You want to separate fact from fiction. The seller may have given you a projected or sample list of income and expenses based on how things "could be." But you want to get to the actual numbers and then have them explain why they think those numbers are different from their projected numbers. Depending on how far into the current tax year you are at the time, you may demand what is known as the T12 which is the operating statement for the previous twelve months to date. One thing to look for is misallocated capital expense. If they are expensing capital expenses (long-term improvements), then the operating income will seem lower. If they are throwing all kinds of minor repairs into capital expense to be depreciated over time, then they are inflating operating income. Check the property taxes to see if the current owner is paying them at discount like you plan to do.

  It is up to the buyer to ask the seller for the necessary financial information and to ensure the data is accurate. Your purpose in doing financial due diligence is fourfold:

  o Confirm income and operating expenses
  o Gain leverage to negotiate your purchase price
  o Calculate the current and potential cash flow
  o Calculate the return you are likely to get on your investment

The sources of this data primarily consist of:

o The last two years of tax returns on which the current owner reported the operation of the property

o The rent roll and leases

o The past twelve months of income and expenses from the seller's books

  ♦ Copies of utility and tax bills may be helpful

Some of the most useful math calculations to determine the desirability of a rental property are included here for reference. There is no set standard as to where the results of these calculations must land for the investment to be viable. You must decide what you are looking for from your overall portfolio of properties and each property individually. Figures are assumed to be annual amounts.

o Net Operating Income or NOI

  ♦ Gross operating income less all expenses other than debt service

o Capitalization rate or Cap Rate (expressed as a percentage)

  ♦ The NOI divided by the purchase price

o Debt Coverage Ratio or DCR

  ♦ The NOI divided by the annual total of the mortgage payments

o Cash Flow or CF

  ♦ The NOI less the annual total of the mortgage payments

o Cash on Cash Return (expressed as a percentage) also known as the Return on Investment or ROI

  ♦ The CF divided by the amount of cash you invested in the property

- **Physical inspection.** This is, of course, when you look over the physical assets including the building and any equipment/appliances included in the deal. If you don't have the expertise to judge the remaining life of the roof or boiler or chimney, for example, hire someone who does, and get a written report from them. You may have walked through just some of the units or shared areas before making your offer, but **now is the time to walk every single apartment and nook & cranny of the property (no matter how long it takes)**. While you do so, make a list of needed repairs (both long-term and short-term) for use both in planning and negotiating.

    Joe Herbert is a successful real estate broker as well as an active rental real estate investor. He is a friend, and he served on the board of the Apartment Association while I was the president. This is his list for multi-unit rental property inspections.

    o Is there a natural and pleasing front entrance, or does the layout force you to enter through a side door or the garage?
    o Check the soffits, gables, and roofs for proper attic venting. Look for vents in the overhangs, roof peaks, and for either ridge vents or turtle vents on the roof.
    o Avoid properties with a slate or asbestos roof unless they are still well within their expected life. They last longer but are expensive to replace.
    o Avoid larger properties with a flat roof unless it is a newer rubber or similar synthetic roof. Flat asphalt or rolled roofing does not last without occasional coating.
    o Does the ground slope toward the building which could cause water problems in the basement? Is runoff from the neighbor's property a problem?
    o Are there any large trees that must be trimmed or removed?
    o Who owns any fences, and should they be removed or repaired?
    o Are the exterior bricks or chimney caps deteriorated, and are there areas where the mortar between them must be repaired?

o Thoroughly inspect all the sidewalk, driveway, garage, and basement concrete for needed repairs and to see if any surfaces direct water toward the foundation.

o Open and close all kitchen cabinet doors and drawers. Should the cabinetry be replaced, painted, or just cleaned with the hardware replaced?

o Does the plumbing run against exterior walls? This can cause frozen pipes in the winter if the pipes are not properly heated.

o Are there exhaust fans in the bathrooms?

o Are there GFCI electrical outlets in the bathroom and kitchen?

o What are the ages of the furnaces, boilers, and AC units? Does it have central air?

o Are any of the basement walls severely cracked or bowed?

o Does the basement footer water (from the French drains & sump pump) go to the storm system or to the sanitary sewer? Most municipalities require ground water to be kept from the sanitary sewer.

o Ask the tenants if the basement floor drains or sewer lines in the basement ever back up. This could be a sign that the sewer line going to the street or septic tank is collapsing or is full of tree roots. A sewer line camera inspection will tell.

o Is the main water line to the property galvanized? Is there any interior galvanized piping? At this point, it's been long enough since copper became the standard that any galvanized pipe you see is close to needing to be replaced. Turn on all the faucets at once, and then flush the toilet to get an idea of the water pressure.

o Do any of the rooms or stairwells appear to have low ceiling heights?

o Are the interior and exterior doors standard height, and are they opening and closing properly? Custom ones are expensive.

o Do the doors need new locksets, and will they accept standard hardware?

- o   Ask the tenants questions.

  - ◆ How long have you lived/had your business in this unit?
  - ◆ How much rent are you paying?
  - ◆ When does your lease end?
  - ◆ Will you be renewing your lease when it expires?
  - ◆ Are you happy with your apartment/commercial space?
  - ◆ Are there any problems that need to be taken care of?
  - ◆ Do you ever have any drains backing up or getting plugged?
  - ◆ How is the heating and air conditioning?
  - ◆ Do you get enough hot wat?
  - ◆ Do you have any electrical problems?
  - ◆ Are there any other consistent problems?
  - ◆ How would you describe the noise/activity level?

Whether or not the seller has promised to do something for you ahead of the closing like a repair or removal of an item, you should always schedule a final walk-through the day before or the day of the closing to make sure it is done and to make sure the property is in the condition you expect.

- **Marketing.** This is an examination of how the property is advertised to prospective renters. Will you be taking over a website dedicated to the property? What are the contractual obligations for the website and any other marketing tools connected with the property.

- **Management team.** If you are not going to self-manage or implement your own management team immediately, you will need to assess the existing contractors and employees. If there is no dollar amount for management in the APOD, you will need to plug in a reasonable amount to account for your time or the amount you will be paying your property manager.

- **Operations and Systems Management**. This is an examination of the systems the current owner has in place for the day-to-day through year-to-year operation of the property. What is their system for handling maintenance issues, and routine inspections (the ones done by the owners as well as the inspections required by third parties like for safety or equipment operation, emergency drills, and tenant complaints)?

- **Competition.** This is an assessment of the competition this property has for tenants and how your prospective property measures up in various aspects such as rent, location, attractiveness, condition, amenities, and marketing.

- **Residents.** You need to not only establish whether there are residents there in the first place, but you will want to know what sort of residents they are. Can you do a better job at screening for more quality tenants? Are the tenants happy and good payers? Basically, will you immediately have to set about getting rid of lousy tenants, or will you be striving to keep a building full of excellent tenants?

- **Legal Issues.** Pending legal issues with tenants, neighbors, the government, lenders, or partners can be a problem. Get them out in the open. This includes environmental concerns like the long-running battle with the township over runoff from the parking lot or thorny situations like the encroachment on the property line by the not-so-friendly landlord next door.

Doing due diligence may seem discouraging because it seems like a lot to do regarding things which, at present, you don't know much about. Don't worry. Generally, the smaller the property, the less due diligence there is to do. So, **for the properties you are likely to be looking at when you are starting out, the due diligence will just seem like a commonsense process of examining obvious features of the deal.** It may only take a couple of hours. You will probably always be able to describe it that way, because, **as you move on to larger and larger deals, your experience and comfort level will be following you.**

Before you start thinking you could get cavalier with doing due diligence, think of something Jim Rohn is credited with saying about due diligence. Jim said we can no more afford to spend major time on minor things (referring to investors failing to hire out extraneous tasks) than we can afford to spend minor time on major things (referring to failing to take adequate time going into a deal to check out major concerns).

Lastly, **I'll conclude this phase by embedding a gem of a concept that could have been dropped into any part of this book.** This is a concept that you will understand increasingly more as you gain experience in the rental real estate game. **That concept is that you make money on the day you buy your property if you buy it right. You will put that money into your pocket on the day you sell, but in the meantime the equity you earned when you bought the property is on your balance sheet.** On that day, or at least shortly thereafter, you acquire instant equity and cash flow. If you are a real estate *investor,* you are not relying on anything out of your control to happen before you make money. If you're buying property hoping the highway comes through, the water line gets laid, the shopping center gets built, the schools improve, the hoarder neighbor cleans up his yard or whatever, then you are not an investor. You are a *speculator*, and that is not what this book is about. **It's hard to do too much due diligence, and it could be what makes the difference between your solvency and insolvency, especially on larger deals.**

PHASE FIVE: FINANCING THE DEAL

Just like deciding how you are going to hold title to a property, having some idea how you are going to pay for your real estate purchase is something you need to be thinking about even <u>before</u> you start looking for property. However, I've opted to position this discussion as Phase Five in the sequence because it is not until this point that the activity shifts to making definite plans regarding financing a particular acquisition. In other words, it's not until you know certain details about the deal that you concentrate on how you are going to pay for it. Then, you need to assess what your options are for financing as though they were tools in your toolbox. When you're gearing up for a project that requires mechanical tools, you must consider which tools you already have in your toolbox, what they do, whether you know how to use them, whether they will do the job required, and whether you need to get some different tools before you start the job. Similarly, methods for financing real estate deals are sorted and selected for use.

Again, it is imperative to make the point that your financing tools must be placed in your toolbox *before* you start looking for deals so that when you find a deal you are able to act quickly. **Educating yourself on the various methods of paying for income property, and evaluating which of these methods is going to be available to you, is something that will be constantly evolving as you move through your investing career.** After you learn the basic ways, more esoteric or complicated techniques will present themselves which can be added to your toolbox should you choose. But familiarizing yourself with the typical methods ahead of time is required so that nobody's time gets wasted on negotiations on which you cannot follow through.

Just like with mechanical tools, not every financing technique works in every instance. Also, not every appropriate technique for a given deal may be available to you personally at the time. Your ability to employ a certain technique can be impacted by how much cash you possess to put into the deal, your credit score, your investing experience, your relationship with lenders along with your knowledge and comfort level with the technique, for example. On the seller's side, the possible techniques are influenced, perhaps, by the need for cash (or the lack of that need), tax implications of the sale, and the required time frame for closing the deal. **You must be able to quickly offer the best path for paying the seller, considering your tools and the seller's problems which need to be addressed.** It's worth noting that your knowledge of financing can come into play when you are the one selling a property because you may be able to suggest a technique to a potential buyer that holds together a faltering deal.

Let's now consider the main methods with which you need to familiarize yourself as you begin your real estate investing journey. These are the most common ways that the financing aspect of income property deals are structured. Basically, every technique will fall into one of two categories:

- Pay cash
- Borrow the money

Of course, it's more complicated than that. But it really is true that either you're going to buy the property with cash you already have on hand, or you're going to borrow all or part of the purchase price from a third party. We call that using "OPM" which stand for "Other Peoples' Money."

You may be approaching investing in rental real estate with a philosophy which dictates that debt is bad and that the best practice is to avoid debt as much as possible. Perhaps you hold that belief because, as the wise and disciplined manager of your family's finances, you have held things together nicely while not giving in to the urge to acquire everything for which you could qualify to make the payment. Maybe your aversion to debt (and its unforgiving commitments) is the very reason why you have been able to set aside the money to get you started in rental real estate. I get that, but household finance philosophies and income property financing philosophies are not a 100% overlay. Frugality, honesty, accuracy, thoughtfulness, and similar practices are certainly examples of crossover between the two. However, unwillingness to go into debt is NOT to be considered in the same light when investing in income producing property as it is with personal finances.

I'm here to tell you that responsible borrowing is the fuel for successful real estate investing. There is a substantial difference between accumulating consumer debt to purchase depreciating personal items and borrowing to expand your portfolio of income producing assets which are likely increasing in value while you hold them. The vehicles on the road to profitable real estate investing run on the use of responsible debt, and successful landlords both large and small fill their tanks with it as much as possible.

There. You've just read two of the most important paragraphs in the whole book. We call the use of debt/OPM by the term "leverage." Just as the leverage created by pushing down on the long section of a board that is pivoting on a rock allows you to move a heavy object with the short end, using OPM allows you to acquire (and profit from) a more expensive property than you would otherwise be able to buy using only cash you already have on hand. Yes, your net cash flow from a property on which you must make loan payments will be less than from the same property for which you paid cash and don't have any payments. But, expressed as a <u>percentage</u>, **the return on your investment (ROI) will be greater if you put a small amount of money down when you compare the amount you put down with your net cash flow after paying the loan. Also, borrowing money to buy a property increases the rate at which you will be able to acquire property** because saving for 100% of the cost of your next property will take a lot longer than just saving enough for your next down payment.

But let's be clear. Sometimes the best path is to pay all cash. When I say "all cash" I simply mean that the funds used at the closing to buy the property do *not* come from some sort of amortized loan that was arranged just for the purchase of the property in question. In the case of an amortized loan, I'm referring to a mortgage that calls for typically monthly payments that include both an amount toward the paydown of the loan (principal payment) and an amount to cover the interest the lender has earned on the remaining balance of the loan since your last payment. The buyers would have had to apply for this mortgage, to put it in brief terms, based on their ability to repay the loan as well as on the value and condition of the property. The buyers' requirement to follow through with the purchase would likely have been contingent on a financial institution approving their application, and if their application was not approved the deal would be cancelled.

When you "pay cash" for a property, then you are not relying on getting the approval for an amortized mortgage specifically for that deal, but you may be using funds that are borrowed to which you have ready access. You've arranged for access to these funds ahead of time, and the use of the funds is not limited to a particular property. These are funds that would be available to you on short notice for whatever investment you are about to make, without having to qualify the property or to re-qualify yourself for the deal.

Here are the most common sources of funds to use for paying all cash for real estate:

- **Money you have in your checking or savings account** from whatever sources of income you've had such as your job, business profits, pension, interest, stock dividends, or inheritance. Wherever it came from, it's simply your stockpile of available cash.

- **Your retirement account** such as a traditional or Roth IRA or maybe a 401 k. The rules vary regarding whether there's a penalty for taking money out of a retirement account when you are less than a certain age and whether or not the withdrawal is included in your taxable income, but sometimes it can make sense to deal with the consequences of the withdrawal in order to make a more profitable investment.

- **Selling something you already own** which is no longer adding value to your life and/or not producing as much income, if any, as will your new investment. Maybe you could sell some collectibles you don't enjoy anymore, a recreational vehicle you no longer use, or some sort of financial asset like stocks or bonds.

- **An advance on your inheritance.** Maybe it is already known that you are going to inherit some money from someone. Perhaps, if you can demonstrate that you're not going to be a "prodigal son" and squander the advance, your benefactor would be willing to give you a stake to get you started investing which would be subtracted from your eventual inheritance.

- **Money you could borrow that would *not* be secured by the property** you are buying such as:

  o **A loan against the equity in another property** you own such as your personal residence or another investment property. Unless you own that property free and clear, this loan would be in addition to the main mortgage. The lender, presumably a bank, savings & loan, or credit union, would have an appraisal done on the property to determine the maximum amount of the loan based on 80% (give or take 10% or so) of the appraised value less the amount of the main mortgage you already have on the property. Sometimes a lender will give you a "blanket" loan which is one loan that is secured by multiple properties. This could take two forms:

    ◆ **A home equity line of credit** or HELOC where you have the ability to borrow up to the prescribed limit at any time in any amount. You also have the right to pay it back down to a zero balance in any fashion as well. You just use the money for a given project, and then pay it back after you sell or refinance the project. In this case you are only paying interest monthly on the amount of money you have borrowed on the line, and the interest rate typically will be set daily based on the prime lending rate. You may have to agree to a set time for this line to exist, like maybe ten years, before there must be another appraisal on the property that secures the loan. Also, you may be required to show the lender your financial statements each year. Investors love HELOC's!

♦ **A home equity loan** where you are given all the loan proceeds at once, and you then have monthly payments for a set time until the loan is paid off. The amount of this loan would be determined by an appraisal process just like the HELOC above. Although this allows you to unlock your equity, the disadvantage of an amortized loan like this is that you do not have the option to pay back the money you are not using in between projects, and then re-borrow when you need to. On the plus side, though, your interest rate would remain the same for the entire length of the loan unless the agreement calls for it to be reset based on current market conditions every five years or so.

o **Credit card balance transfer offers** you receive in the mail for use with credit cards, typically Mastercard, VISA, or Discover, that you already have open. I have dozens more credit cards of this type than I need for making routine purchases, and I regularly take advantage of the better balance transfer offers they market. Sometimes they will offer you a balance transfer deal over the phone if you call them even when they haven't mailed you one. **I recommend you work hard to keep your credit score high, open new credit card accounts from time to time as you receive attractive offers (but not so frequently that it appears you are applying for credit too often), and then periodically ask the credit card issuer to raise your credit limit.**

Balance transfer offers come with a couple of checks that, presumably, the issuer is enticing you to write to another credit card where you are carrying a balance from past purchases upon which you are being charged a high interest rate. The bait is that you would have a much lower, usually 0%, interest rate on your transferred balance for a specific length of time. However, **the checks may be written to anyone for any reason; you don't have to be paying off a balance. Instead, the strategy here is to fund your bank account with a balance transfer check when you need money for purchasing a property or funding a rehab.**

Balance transfer offers have four components to consider. First, what is the interest rate to be charged on your unpaid balance during the promotion period? Second, when does the promotion period end? Third, by when must you use the attached checks to get the promotional interest rate? And lastly, what is the immediate fee for using the checks?

Usually, the promotional interest rate is 0%. That's a fantastic interest rate for a while, but then the rate would shift to their regular unreasonable rate after the last day of the promo period. So, the strategy is to pay off the balance before the promo period is over and the higher rate kicks in. Promotion periods are usually between ten and eighteen months, with the normal being one year. If you use the check not long after you receive the offer, you have plenty of time to complete a project, sell it or refinance it, and then use the money to pay off your full balance.

Invariably, though, the credit card issuer will require a one-time fee per promo check based on a percentage of the amount. Usually, the fee is 3% to 5%, but sometimes it is less. Balance transfer fees are charged in full on the first statement, and added to the balance for which you wrote the check. **This fee, combined with the length of the promotion period, yields the most important calculation for you to consider.** Essentially, the fee represents the total amount of interest you are going to pay on your advance. It's easy to calculate the annual interest rate if the promo period is one year and you use the promo check right away. However, let's say the fee is 5%, and the promo period is fifteen months, or five quarters of a year. Then, your effective interest rate is 4% expressed as an annual rate. If the fee is 3%, and the promo period is eighteen months, then the effective interest rate is just 2%.

Credit cards promotional offers are cheap money. If you have large credit limits on your cards, you can see how taking advantage of these offers can significantly impact your ability to raise cash for real estate investments. But you cannot be reckless. **Here are my rules:**

- ◆ Keep a chart of available promotions, and update the chart every time a new offer arrives in the mail.
- ◆ Only utilize the offer if you do not have sufficient cash on hand, and the effective annual interest rate is less than that of any other money you can borrow quickly.
- ◆ Be careful not to write the check for an amount that would create a balance greater than your credit limit once the promo fee is added. For example, if you have a $10,000 credit limit, and the fee is 3%, don't write the check for more than $9,708, or it will be rejected.
- ◆ Don't use balance transfers on accounts that you otherwise are carrying balances for purchases. Keep the cards you may use for a transfer free of any balance while you await offers.
- ◆ For the lowest effective annual interest rate, take advantage of the promo not long after you are offered it.
- ◆ Each month, make the minimum payment as shown on the statement to keep as much cash local for your use as possible. It is a myth that your credit score is lowered if you only make minimum payments. Your score is negatively impacted when you make a *late* payment (even if you are late making a payment of the full balance), or if you *miss* a payment.

- I have one exception to paying only the minimum payment. Pay the full amount of the promo fee on the first statement even though that amount is greater than the minimum. This way, in your bookkeeping, you can easily associate the payment of this fee as a stand-alone expense in the year you pay it, as opposed to it being lost in the shuffle when you eventually pay off the balance.

- Keep track of the exact date when the promotional interest rate will expire, and make sure you pay off the full balance by then. This could be a date that is in between monthly statements.

- It is OK to use a newer offer to pay off an expiring offer if you still need the money.

- The best practice is to write the check to your company, and deposit it into your company's checking account. Then, wait a few days for the check to clear, and start using the money.

- Another good practice is to make the check out to whatever financial institution holds a credit line with a balance upon which interest is being charged at a greater rate than the effective interest rate of the promo offer. Then, have the check applied directly as a principal reduction on your credit line.

- Refrain from writing the promo checks to vendors or mailing them to anyone. If the vendor doesn't cash the check before the date by which the check was required to be used, the check will be honored, but instead of having 0% interest during the promo period, you will automatically be charged the issuer's regular ridiculous rate. Also, if the check is lost, you may not have another check on hand to replace it, since you typically only get two checks that trigger the promotion if used.

- **Use every credit card you have at least once every year.** We use each of our cards for a minor purchase every January as long as it doesn't have a balance on it already, and we mark the date it was used on the envelope to be sure. If you have credit card accounts you keep open in case they send you a promotion you wish to use, there could be long times in between uses. If the card is dormant for too long, the issuer may close the account at will.

This not only removes it from your use, but it can negatively affect your credit score when the available balance of the closed card is removed from calculating the overall percentage of your available credit you are using.

o **A loan against your life insurance policy.** If you have a life insurance policy that builds up cash surrender value over the years, it probably also gives you the option of borrowing money for any purpose against the policy. You would not have to "cash in" the policy to get the money. Any unpaid loan balance at the time of your death, or whenever you might choose to cash in the policy, would be subtracted from the payout. Here again, you can repay the loan and reborrow the money as needed.

o **A personal loan** you can qualify for at your bank, savings and loan or credit union. Perhaps the relationship you already have with a lender would allow for an unsecured loan based your credit history and financial position. Terms for these types of loans can vary widely.

o **A new loan against a vehicle** or RV that you already own. Yes, I mean refinance your car.

o **A loan from a trusting relative or friend** who wants to see you succeed and who is willing to "take a flyer" on a personal loan to you.

o **An equity partner** who has cash from one of the above sources, and who is willing to give some of the equity to you in exchange for whatever it is you bring to the table. They provide all the cash for some of the equity while you provide, for example, the labor for the rehab. This would not be a loan. Nobody makes money unless there is a profit, which is divided by predetermined percentages.

• **Money you could borrow that *would be* secured by the property** you are buying such as:

o **A "hard money" loan.** Strap in, bear down and get ready to absorb as much as you can from this section. **Hard money loans are the honey pot of short-term funding for flips and "keeper" rental**

properties. Having a relationship with a hard money lender will supercharge your investing career. I have been actively making hard money loans to other real estate investors since 2018, and it is the most rewarding phase of the real estate world in which I have participated.

Hard money gets its name from the fact that the loan is approved more on the viability of the hard asset backing the loan (real estate for our purposes) than on the financial position of the applicant. Lenders making hard money loans to other real estate investors typically have personal experience investing in the type of property being offered as collateral for the loan, and they can evaluate the likelihood that the project is going to turn out the way the applicant is proposing. Consequently, **hard money lenders are the source for buying and rehabbing properties that banks will not lend against because the property, in its current condition, or you, in your current financial position, do not fit into the bank's comfort zone for making loans. Additionally, established investors may use hard money to take advantage of an opportunity that is only available to them if they can pay cash (no financing contingency in the offer to purchase the property) and close quickly (which the banks cannot do) even though they otherwise would have been able to finance the purchase with conventional lenders.**

To describe the framework of the hard money lending realm, the hard money lenders we are going to discuss here are likely to be private individuals or small groups of individuals right in your investing community. They may still be active landlords or house flippers, but they have accumulated enough cash above what they need for their own investing activities, and they are willing to lend that cash on a short-term basis to other investors. They are comfortable knowing that, if you don't repay your loan, they would know what to do with the property if it had to be taken to satisfy the loan.

To put it loosely, lending is termed "private" when the loan is not from a conventional lender such as a bank or any lender that falls under federal or state regulation. Private lenders can be anybody who is willing to make a loan using their own money and not that of depositors (like a bank has) or that of other individuals who do not have a say in where the money is lent. Hard money lending is a segment of private lending, but not all private lending is considered hard money lending. That's because some private lenders are more interested in investing in long-term amortized mortgages so they can lock in a monthly check for an extended period of time at a set rate of return. This contrasts with **a hard money loan which is typically for a short time—only a year or two—and which requires interest-only payments until the loan is paid off all at once.**

You can easily become aware of private companies on the internet offering hard money loans. I am sure there is some success to have there if you want to pursue hard money for your project, but I am going to give you my axiom for seeking hard money. **Your best experience with hard money lending will occur by dealing with lenders right in your own investing community who get to know you personally and who are familiar with the area in which you are buying.** One of the main reasons real estate investors seek hard money loans is to avoid dealing with the requirements of a bank and the time it takes for the bank to close the loan. The more out-of-town your lender is, and the less they are connected to you and your property, the more formal and involved your application will be and the more "bank-like" the process will seem to you.

Make no mistake; your hard money lender is not going to totally disregard your financial condition and history. In fact, those facts can be used to your advantage as can the extent of your experience with the type of project you are bringing to the table. But you probably aren't going to find yourself filling out a formal application, and the lender may never even run your credit score. Your lender will be interested in what you have done to educate yourself in the business and, in general, what your financial successes and failures have been.

Here are the common features of a hard money loan:

- **A set interest rate.** Being a short-term loan, the interest rate is locked in for the length of the loan.

- **Points.** In lending terminology, a point is equal to one percent of the amount being borrowed. You may be required to pay several points as a "loan origination fee" in addition to paying interest. Usually, all the points are paid when the loan is started, but your lender may allow you to add all or part of the points to the loan balance so that they are paid when you pay off the loan.

- **Amount borrowed.** This could be all or part of the amount you are paying for the property plus all or part of your closing costs and rehab budget or any combination of the above. If you are borrowing money for rehab costs, it is likely that you will get some of it at closing, but the rest would be made available to you in draws as you work your way through the project. Your lender wants to see that the work is actually being done, and that the materials are actually being bought.

- **Payments.** These are likely to be required monthly, but probably they will be interest-only with no principal included. Payments may be due on the first of each month, but also could be due on the anniversary each month of the day of the month when the loan began.

- **Length of the loan.** This would be negotiable to fit the project, but probably the loan would be just for a year or two. Loans for flips are usually for a year, but longer terms may be needed for a rental property project where there are multiple units to be rehabbed and you need time to remove existing tenants.

- **Soft landing extension.** Some hard money loans allow for the loan to automatically be extended for a set time—like six months— at the option of the borrower if the project is running longer than expected. The concession might be that you pay a higher interest rate during this period.

♦ **No prepayment penalty.** Sometimes long-term amortized loans require that a fee be paid if the loan is paid off in full more quickly than the full term. This is because the lender wants to enjoy the interest income for a while without having to figure out what to do with the money if it gets paid back. The hard money lender knows exactly what to do with the money, and is looking to loan it out again with a new set of points, so there is no penalty if you pay it back quickly.

♦ **Late fee.** If you don't make your payment by the monthly due date, you would agree to add an agreed upon fee to the payment.

♦ **Personal guarantee.** Although you may be taking the loan in the name of your legal entity like your LLC because that's how the property is going to be titled, all owners/LLC members are likely going to sign personal guaranties that allow the lender to seek repayment from any or all of you personally if your entity does not pay off the loan.

♦ **Mechanics' lien waiver.** If you hire a contractor to work on your property, and that contractor does not pay anyone who worked under him or her on your property (even though you fully paid the contractor), the unpaid party may file a lien against the property for what they are owed. An unpaid supplier of materials could do the same. The property cannot transfer or be refinanced unless this person's lien is paid. Lenders will require you to file a Mechanics' Lien Waiver at the courthouse at the time you take out the loan (before any work is performed) which puts everyone on notice that, if they work on your property and they don't get paid, they are giving up or waiving their right to put a lien on your property. This is for both yours and the lender's protection against complications when you are selling or refinancing the property to pay off the loan.

- **Deed in lieu of Foreclosure.** I'm sure you realize that a hard money loan is secured by your property just like a long-term mortgage. Mortgage holders can foreclose if the loan goes into default for the purpose of obtaining title to the property so they can sell it to satisfy the loan. A Deed in Lieu of Foreclosure is an actual deed that is signed by you which, if recorded, would transfer the property from you to your lender without the lender having to go through the time and expense (and, in your case, the embarrassment) of a full-blown foreclosure. Although this deed is prepared and signed by you at the time you close on the loan, it is held in escrow until the circumstances dictate that it be recorded. This would probably not be until after every effort has been made by all parties to satisfy the loan in some other way. It is interesting to note that, if the lender chooses to record the deed and take the property as satisfaction of the loan, the lender gives up the right to pursue you personally (remember the personal guaranty you signed?) for any deficiency between the amount you owe and the amount the lender ultimately realizes from the sale of the property.

- **Assignment of Rents.** This document gives the lender the right to require that any tenants renting the property which secures their loan pay their rents directly to the lender instead of to you, the borrower. This would be enforced if the borrower is receiving rents but not making their loan payments.

- **No entering into a land contract or lease option.** We did not require this at first, but eventually we realized it complicated the borrower's ability to sell or refinance their property when it came time to pay off the loan if they had entered into a lease option agreement or a land contract with a third party who now had a legal interest in the property securing the loan.

- **Attorney fees.** We require our borrowers to pay all the fees charged by our attorney for preparing the note and mortgage, deed in lieu of foreclosure, assignment of rents, etc. as well as any recording fees. This would include the eventual costs of preparing and recording the satisfactions of the mortgage and assignment of rents.

◆ **Title insurance.** You will need to purchase title insurance by the time of the closing to buy your property so that you and the lender have protection against issues that may come up later regarding the validity of the deed. You would get this insurance through the attorney you are using to represent you as a buyer in the transaction. However, if the borrower chooses to use our attorney to represent them as the buyer, then they can save the cost of title insurance because our attorney, who will then be the attorney examining the title history, will allow us as his lending clients to accept a "certificate of title" from him in lieu of title insurance since he personally examined the chain of title instead of a third-party attorney.

◆ **Proof of insurance.** Your hard money lender will need to be listed on your property insurance policy just like a bank would require. You will need to bring proof of this to the closing when you are getting the loan.

◆ **Proof you have paid your property taxes.** During the loan you will need to be able to show proof that you have paid the property taxes that have become due if the lender asks you to.

◆ **Inspections.** You will need to agree to allow the lender, with notice, to enter and inspect the property. This is especially true if you are getting draws on a rehab escrow that are dependent on your progress.

As we have discussed**, hard money loans are given primarily based on the hard asset that backs them up, but the lender needs to feel comfortable with *you* as well. Your payment history on owner financed deals or on any prior hard money loans will not have been reported to any credit reporting agency, so they will not be in your credit report.** Consequently, when you approach a hard money lender about a loan for your next project, you need to be prepared with certain information. If it's your first time borrowing from that lender, some of that information is going to be about you. But hard money lending is done on relationships. Once the lender is familiar with you, you will not have to cover the same ground regarding your personal and financial history. Just present an update. Examples of your background the lender would be interested in are:

◆ Do you have any outstanding judgements against you?

◆ Have you or any of your businesses ever declared bankruptcy?

◆ Are you currently a party to a lawsuit?

◆ Have you directly or indirectly been obligated on any loan which resulted in foreclosure, transfer of title in lieu of foreclosure, or a judgement?

◆ What real estate educational programs or coaching programs have you taken?

◆ What education do you have outside of real estate?

◆ How long have you been involved in real estate investing?

◆ Do you have any professional designations including any outside of the real estate field?

◆ Are you a member of any professional organizations relating to real estate such as the local group?

◆ How many rental units do you own or manage?

◆ How many flips have you done?

◆ What employment do you have, if any, outside of real estate?

◆ What is your credit score?

All these topics may be covered in conversation with the lender, or you may be asked to write things out on an application form. Either way, the lender is just trying to get to know you better to see if there are any red flags that need an explanation. **The full process, though, of evaluating the property and the borrower will not come close to the scrutiny, documentation, and long approval process of a typical bank.**

If you are not going to use all cash to buy your investment property, we can assume that you are going to use a mortgage from either a private lender or a financial institution. Here are the most common sources for mortgages:

- **Banks.** These are for-profit lending institutions owned by investors and which are subject to a ton of federal and state regulations.

- **Savings and loans or savings banks.** These are not-for-profit lending institutions owned indirectly by their depositors, but they are also subject to lots of federal and state regulations.

- **Credit unions.** These are similar to savings and loans, but they have some sort of a qualification for membership you must meet before doing business with them. In the past this might have meant that you had to be an employee of a certain company, but these days the requirement might be as broad as living in the area where the credit union has branches. They are owned indirectly by their members. However, credit unions may or may not make mortgage loans using their own funds. Depending on their size, they may only be acting as a mortgage broker where they are simply providing their services to originate the mortgage (take the application) on behalf of a group of lenders with which they have a relationship.

- **Mortgage brokers.** These are companies which, for a fee to the borrower, will present your loan need to lenders on your behalf. They may be one-person operations or larger offices, and they are skilled at packaging your deal and presenting it in the best possible way to multiple lenders. This increases the chance of your loan being accepted, and you may get better terms. Your deal may be presented to local banks that you already know about, but the broker likely has multiple connections with out-of-town lenders as well. In any event, unless you already happen to have a working relationship with a particular lender, your mortgage broker will have direct access to decision makers who may not be available to you. The broker can find out more quickly if a particular lender has an appetite for your proposal, which can save you fruitless time waiting for what turns out to be a rejection had you put in the application directly yourself. A good broker will work with you, if needed, to improve certain areas of your financial picture before presenting your deal.

- **Mortgage brokers may not restrict their connections to financial institutions; they may also place loans with area hard money lenders**. I am regularly brought into deals by my good friend Jeff Potts of NorthStar Erie, LLC, who has been a mortgage broker for decades. The scenario is typically that his client needs to make an all-cash offer on a property that will be a keeper rental property. After the property is stabilized, Jeff will then arrange permanent long-term financing for the client by utilizing his connections with over one hundred lenders. It is important to note that, **by the time Jeff brings this deal to me, his client has been so well vetted that I am far more comfortable making a loan to that client than if they had come to me directly.** The viability of the project from a hard money loan standpoint has already been evaluated, as has the likelihood NorthStar will be able to find permanent financing for the client to pay off my hard money loan in the allotted time. When my own clients need help getting their permanent financing I, of course, refer them to Jeff and his team.

- Mortgage brokers are subject to regulation by the same federal and state authorities as savings and loans, banks, and credit unions. Brokers are not making the loans; they are only connecting you with lenders, so this regulation refers to the oversight of their business practices and the integrity of the people operating their business, and not to the regulations imposed on the actual lenders.

- Mortgage broker fees are typically paid at closing, so there is no fee unless they are successful in finding you a loan source and getting the deal closed. Their fee may be a set amount or calculated as points (a percentage of the amount borrowed), but the service provided is worth the cost when you look at your big picture. In some instances, though, the broker's fee may be paid by the lender, so it's worth asking.

- **Pension funds and insurance companies.** I will mention these here for future reference, but giving mortgages on multi-millions dollar properties are often a routine activity for custodians of large pools of money that must be invested on behalf of third parties like pensioners and policy holders.

- **The seller.** We covered owner financing in PHASE THREE: NEGOTIATING THE PURCHASE. In this case, the seller is acting as the bank. The same documents are prepared to secure the mortgage with the real estate on behalf of the seller as are prepped for a bank, although the process of "qualifying" yourself for the seller will be far less arduous than for a financial institution. The property itself, of course, would already be well known to the seller, whereas part of the process of getting a mortgage from a bank includes presenting information about the property.

It should be noted that banks and savings and loans may, for an immediate profit, sell off a mortgage they make so that they don't actually use their own funds to close the deal. They just use their resources to process the application. Whoever they sell the loan to will make the interest income. But they may "portfolio" the loan, in which case they use their own money to fund the transaction, and the borrower makes their payments to the same bank. The bank is holding the loan as one of their own assets until it is completely paid off, and they are making the income along the way from the interest portion of your payments. In another instance, the bank may bundle together a group of mortgages they have had in their portfolio for a while, and later sell them off. In that case, you will get a notice to start making your payments to a different entity.

Any lender, with the possible exception of the seller in an owner financed deal, who would give you long-term permanent financing on a real estate purchase is not going to lend you 100% of the purchase price; they are going require a certain percentage down at closing. This ensures there is enough equity in the property in case the lender must foreclose and sell it to cover the debt. In the real estate investing world, the usual percentage down is in the 25% to 20% range, but the lender may require more under certain circumstances. Also, there are some lending programs the borrower could qualify for that allow for a much lower percentage down. Examples of these are FHA and

VA loans. **Right now, FHA and FNMA will do lower down payments on properties with up to four units, but the borrower must live in one of the units.**

In the case of a new purchase, the required money down would come in the form of cash from you. But in the case of a refinance where you are getting a new mortgage on a property you already own, the "money down" would be from the equity you have in the property. **Your equity is the difference between the loan balance and the value of the property.** Whether you are buying a new property or refinancing an existing one, the lender will require an appraisal from an independent party, which you will pay for, to establish the value. The maximum amount of the loan will be limited to a prescribed percentage of the appraised value. Even if the appraisal comes in at a higher amount than your purchase price, you will still be required to put down the set percentage. For a refinance, the amount of the loan they give you would be limited to the set percentage of the appraised value, but you would not be bringing the down payment money to the closing because you already have the needed equity. **Another way of stating the lender's required amount of equity is called the loan-to-value ratio or LTV.** For example, if the lender is requiring 20% down, they are requiring a maximum loan-to-value ratio of 80%.

Not every lender will have the same requirements for a loan on a given property. Their appetites for certain types of properties on which they will lend and for certain types of borrowers change over time for internal reasons only they would know. Here are the major points of negotiation for the terms of a mortgage, some of which are negotiable:

- Term or length of the loan
- Interest rate
- Points or loan initiation fee
- Prepayment penalty (the penalty, usually expressed as a percentage of the remaining principal balance, for paying off the loan too soon especially if you do so by refinancing with another bank) (this is a common, but not standard, feature—usually when the lender is planning to portfolio the loan)
- Maximum LTV or loan to value

- Type of appraisal (full appraisal paid to a third party, or a less extensive evaluation paid to a third party, or an internal estimation of value made by the lender's employees)

- Whether money reserved to pay property taxes and/or insurance is escrowed with each of your payments and then paid from your escrow by the lender when due

- The amount of time until a balloon payment must be made that fully pays off the loan (even though the monthly payment was calculated as though the loan was going to last longer)

- The amount of time between intervals (often five years) when the interest rate is re-set based on the then current rate of a prescribed index (like prime rate). The loan would continue on with a new payment amount based on the revised interest rate until the next re-set.

- The maximum amount the interest rate can change up or down when it is re-set. This is known as the note floor and ceiling.

- Other document prep or ancillary fees connected to originating the loan

- The closing date

Banks and similar lenders, because of the numerous state and federal regulations under which they work, coupled with their own internal procedures, require a substantial amount of documentation to get to the finish line when the loan is finally made on the day of the closing. This fairly rigid list of requirements can be broken down into two segments. The first segment would be the information needed for the bank to determine whether they would like to make the loan, and the second would be the documentation required after they have made a loan commitment to you while everyone is working toward a closing.

As I alluded earlier, different banks of varying sizes and philosophies have ever-evolving preferences for the types of loans they want to make. This will trickle down to the loan terms they offer, the requirements they make, and the service they give the applicant/borrower. This is where the disappointment with banks can begin. **The biggest complaints real estate investors have with banks are the pile of information banks require and the length of time it takes to close the loan.** Just when you think you've given them everything they need, they ask for something more. Then, after you've been told a closing date to count on, the bank delays it because they can't do the work any faster. Also, sometimes after you have dutifully turned over everything they've asked for, you find out you've been wasting your time because they decide they won't make the loan after they've already told you they would.

Don't let the distastefulness of dealing with banks turn you off to the greater good of investing in rental property! Borrowing money is unavoidable as you build your rental portfolio, so you just have to get used to this part of the game. **The bankers are not out to hurt you; they're just doing their jobs, and the better you get at helping them do their jobs, the more success you will have borrowing from banks.** If you pay your existing loans as agreed, and you learn to provide them with the information they require, the banker will be happy to see you come through the door with another loan request. They have quotas to meet, and they need good borrowers to help them.

You can certainly approach banks with a loan request on your own. They have representatives on the front line ready to meet with you. But **the issues I have just described are what drive borrowers to use hard money loans to get quick approval and a rapid close. Or, if permanent financing is desired, desiring to minimize these issues is what makes the case for utilizing the services of a good mortgage broker.**

This is not a complete list, but **some of the information required by a bank-type lender for them to decide if they would like to make a particular loan would be:**

- The loan amount you are requesting

- The loan to value you are requesting

- A personal financial statement (they usually provide their own form for you to fill in) covering your personal financial picture (see Chapter Eleven)

- Income statements and balance sheets for your business if a business is the source of your personal income, or if you intend to hold the investment real estate in an entity which already has other operating properties

  o These will be used to calculate the debt-to-income ratio (DTI) you have now and the DTI you would have after getting the loan. These will also indicate the sources of your income and your cash reserves.

- Tax returns for at least the past two years (probably three years) for you personally and that of any business entities per above

- Bank and/or brokerage account statements

- Pay stubs from your job and/or W-2's

- Your credit score (they will run a report with your permission)

- The property type, location, and condition including, perhaps, photos (although this information would be presented in detail if there is a paid appraisal done as a requirement for the loan)

- Whatever operating statements you can get on the subject property from the seller

- A "pro forma" statement which shows what you believe the income and expenses will be for the property once you own it. This statement may also include projections several years into the future.

- Whatever information you can give them regarding your experience and education, similarly to what we discussed under hard money loans above. Whatever you can do to impress them outside of the boxes they are trying to check off on their application forms is beneficial.

Then, **after your loan is approved, some of the things they may ask for include:**

- An appraisal of any property securing the loan

- A rent roll (list of tenants' names, addresses, and amounts of rent)

- Copies of existing leases to back up the rent roll

- A survey of the property

- Proof of property insurance that will go into effect on the day of the closing

- A copy of the organizational papers for your entity

- Your entity's federal tax ID number

- A statement of good standing for your entity from your state

- An examination of the chain of title for the property to make sure there are no issues with you obtaining clear title

- Title insurance in case something comes up later

- Proof the property is not located in a designated flood zone

- Flood insurance depending on the location

- Certification from an independent inspector that any water well or septic system on the property passes environmental and quality requirements

- Proof that any needed work required as the result of the appraisal has been completed, such as mold remediation, a roof repair, or other structural issues

Mortgage broker Jeff Potts notes that commercial banks and lenders do *not* issue pre-approval letters like you receive when applying for a residential loan for a personal residence. However, **your mortgage broker will provide you with a letter of pre-qualification after reviewing your key financial documents. The ultimate purpose of compiling this information is to help the lender follow what are known as THE FIVE C'S OF CREDIT.** This is the box lenders put borrowers into to determine the likelihood the borrower will repay their debt. **The Five C's of credit are:**

- **Character:** This measures your reliability and trustworthiness as a borrower. This is where your pattern of meeting your current and past obligations will come into play. Your credit score is a good indication of this. You can improve this by avoiding late payments, defaults, bankruptcy, and lawsuits.

- **Capacity:** This considers your ability to repay your debt from your net cash flow. You can improve this by paying off obligations that take up your cash flow.

- **Capital:** Lenders compare your level of debt to your total assets to determine your net worth and equity to gauge your access to capital. Again, paying down debt and increasing cash reserves and equity in your properties will improve this.

- **Conditions:** Current economic conditions for the industry in which a business operates will factor heavily. Lenders want to know what you will use the loan proceeds for and how well you are adapting to the current conditions.

- **Collateral:** Of course, for real estate investors, lenders want to know all about the property that will secure the loan. The nicer the property you offer for collateral, the more interested the lender will be.

Most lenders use the Five C's, but how they are weighted for a given deal varies from one lender to another. In any case, doing whatever you can ahead of applying for a loan to impress a lender in each of these areas will increase your chances of approval.

Beyond falling short in the Five C's, **some reasons banks turn down commercial loan applications are:**

- Competent or experienced management is not in place.
- The purpose for the loan is too speculative.
- The applicant has an insufficient track record in the business.
- The bank has too much loaned to the applicant already.
- The applicant cannot provide sufficient information about themselves or the property.
- The borrower would have insufficient equity in the particular property.
- The requested repayment period is too long, the requested interest rate cannot be offered, the requested closing time is too short, or some other loan terms (such as fees like points or document prep costs) cannot be met by the bank.
- The bank already has too many loans on this type of property

Learning how to finance your deals is second only to learning how to locate potential projects. Let me follow that by saying, if you find a good deal, you WILL find the money for it somewhere in your finance toolbox.

The more you do it, the easier it will be. I will tease you with this statement: You will find, as you get more experienced and you are getting involved with larger properties, **it is easier to borrow a million dollars than it is to borrow a hundred thousand dollars.** There is one simple reason for this. The representatives of the lenders of larger amounts are trained to be more in tune with your vision and needs than the reps at your local bank branch. The bigger the property, the more the lender is evaluating whether the property can support the debt service versus whether you personally can make the payment from the income you have from your job, as would be the case if you were applying for a mortgage for your personal residence. Mortgages on properties with more than a few units are handled by these specially trained execs in the commercial department, as opposed to bank branch managers. It is interesting to note that, like with owner financed deals and hard money loans, **your payment history on your commercial loan is not on your credit report.**

I know I said earlier in this section that you're either going to "pay cash" or "use a mortgage" to acquire rental property, but financing techniques are, in reality, much more varied than that. **I would be remiss if I did not touch upon the fact that there are more exotic ways to finance an income property,** and you will become aware of many of them as you move through your investing journey and network with fellow investors. Such techniques are exciting and interesting, but most of them are beyond the scope of this writing. However, many investors choose to become experts in certain methods, and they specialize in putting deals together when others would have to walk away. You can find specialized training from experts who will spend entire seminars teaching you how to properly do just one technique.

While I am not going to fully unpack any of these exotic techniques, I wanted to at least name and describe a few of the more common ones. I'm going to do this with the help of my good friend and fellow investor "Real Estate Steve" Szumigale. Steve is second generation in the real estate business, but the first in his family to be an active real estate investor. His mother has been my Realtor since the early 1990's, and she is consistently among the top producing Realtors in our area. Steve began as a Realtor in the same office as his mother, but (as he tells the story) he decided to investigate investing in real estate after observing the transactions I was doing with his mother. He dove in, started with nothing, studied everything he could, took coaching under Ron LeGrand where he eventually got a master's degree in real estate investing, and became a coach himself in LeGrand's organization. Using a toolbox full of techniques from paying cash with hard money loans, conventional mortgages, owner financing and a few specialized techniques, in their first six years Steve and his partner/wife Gina amassed a portfolio of beautiful properties valued at over $10,000,000. Steve is successful because he is a transactional engineer. When he is talking with a seller, he is already envisioning not only how to put the deal together to buy the property, but he is envisioning his exit strategy for when he will be selling the property. The more tools and knowledge you have, the more deals you will be able to close. Steve can employ alternate techniques to open up doors, whereas other buyers would walk away.

Steve is an unusual guy in a good way. The kind of unusual that puts a grin on your face when you talk to him or even see him. It's apparent in the way he markets himself as "Real Estate Steve" because he thinks his last name is too hard to pronounce. It's reflected in the invariably impeccable appearance of his clothes, his shoes, and his hair...no matter what the occasion is. The only time I see him in dirty jeans is when we ride four wheelers in the mud. It can be seen in his unflinching demand for positivity in his conversations, and in his seemingly endless knowledge of evaluating investment properties and structuring real estate deals. His vanity license plate says "CASH FLOW." His wife Gina is a perfect match, and an integral part of their business, so it can be a hoot when you are around both of them at the same time.

I've known Steve since he was a little kid, and I saw him overcome about a half dozen factors working against him becoming successful in the real estate business. I've seen people use just one or two of those challenges as their excuse for not even trying. So, I'm going to make a prediction that Steve may become the wealthiest person I know whom I also knew when they had nothing.

Having painted this picture of Steve for you, I think you would nod with understanding when I tell you the result of asking Steve to contribute to this section of my book. Remember, I wanted to name and describe a few of the more exotic ways to finance an income property with Steve's help. But it was not surprising to me, after I asked him to give me a couple of paragraphs each on some techniques of his choosing, he presented me with about twenty pages including graphics!

Consequently, instead of presenting them here, I have included an entire bonus chapter at the end of the book entitled BONUS FROM "REAL ESTATE STEVE" SZUMIGALE.

If the income-producing properties in your portfolio are the foundation of your rental property activities, as I stated at the beginning of this chapter, then financing is the mortar that holds the blocks together. Your business entity is the footer, the individual properties are the blocks, negotiating ensures the quality of the blocks, and due diligence ensures the blocks are laid nice and straight. Let's now look at the final stretch toward acquiring property.

PHASE SIX: PREPARING FOR A CLOSING

When all the parties of a real estate transaction meet to sign documents and disburse money, it's called a *closing*. All the maneuvers to transfer the title and pay the seller and anyone else who deserves money from the transaction come to a close. The buyer's lender brings the money to fund the deal, and the seller's lenders, if any, are paid off. Then the lawyers give everybody copies of pertinent paperwork and have all the necessary documents recorded at the courthouse.

Getting to the point of having this meeting can have some twists and turns because there are several groups of people with their own agendas who all have different jobs to do, and all of them are attempting to finish their jobs by the same time...the date of the closing. Everyone's aim is to facilitate the transfer of property from the seller to the buyer according to the terms agreed upon by the seller, buyer, lender, Realtors, title transfer company, title insurance company, lawyers, lawyers' assistants, property appraiser, property insurance agent, utility companies, any lien holders, surveyor, contractors, inspectors, property tax collectors, and maybe your accountant, to name the typical players.

Most of these parties will be doing their work behind the scenes as instructed by the people who are being paid to represent you. Primarily, this would be the Realtor, if any, and the attorney or title company you have representing you as a buyer, so **what I want to cover here are the tasks that will be left up to you.** You will need to concern yourself with:

- **Keeping in touch with your lender, Realtor and attorney** as to the progress

  o Staying engaged is important to pushing things along. If anything is going wrong, you want to know more sooner than later.

- **Signing or providing anything special** your lender, Realtor or attorney asks for

  o Sometimes documents appear that need to be signed or proof of something needs to be provided for things to keep moving, so do your best to respond in a timely fashion.

- **Making sure you have in your control any money,** such as your down payment, which needs to be brought to the closing

  o As the closing nears, you will want to move the money to a readily accessible account. This may involve liquidating stocks or requesting a draw on your retirement fund, so be sure to allow more than enough lead time for the cash to arrive locally and clear as a deposit in your bank account, especially in case everybody gets their work done early, and you are able to close sooner than expected.

- **Finish your due diligence**

  o This might include digging a little deeper into whatever financial and tenant records the seller can provide. Your lender may have already required a rent roll and copies of leases, but you may want to meet the tenants now, for example. Now is the time to dig into anything you want to know about which hasn't already been thoroughly investigated...especially anything that would be a deal-killer for you if it turned out differently than you expect.

- **Select an appraiser**

  ○ You probably aren't going to have an appraisal done unless it is a contingency for your lender to give you the loan. Like we talked about, the property must appraise for enough for the LTV not to be exceeded, but a paid appraisal may not be needed if you are paying cash. Although, as the buyer, you will be paying for the appraisal. Because of federal regulations, your bank will put the appraisal out for bid to several independent appraisal companies who are in a rotation on the bank's list. After the bank gets the bids back, you will be allowed to choose which one you want to go with. You can evaluate which one fits. You may decide to pay more for one that would be done more quickly. It could be that you want to accompany the appraiser during their visit to the property.

- **Hire the inspectors** that are allowed as part of the deal

  ○ **Many deals will hinge on the results of inspections, and the particular inspections of the property to be allowed are part of the negotiations between you and the seller.** It could be that your offer is an all-cash offer that waives all inspections, but especially if there is a lender involved, certain inspections may be required. Most inspections listed here would not be required by the lender, but you may simply have an interest in knowing the results. **You can only do the inspections agreed to in the sales agreement, and typically your contract with the seller will give you a set number of days to have the inspections done, review the reports, and approach the seller with any issues you have with the results. This is a point at which there could be some additional negotiations with the seller to account for the results.** If your differences cannot be resolved, then you would have a right to end the deal, if you have brought the problems found by the inspectors to the seller's attention within the allotted time.

The most common inspections are:

- **Home/property/environmental inspection**

  ◇ This is the common home inspection you hear about that is done on most owner-occupied home purchases. Once you develop expertise in spotting issues with a building, you may not need to do this on a rental purchase. But until you do, and you are comfortable making your offer without having a contingency for a home inspection, you will want to hire a certified home inspector. Accompany the inspector during the inspection, read over the nice report you will get, and learn as much as you can. Many facets of the property are within the scope of this inspection including structural, HVAC system, appliances, plumbing, electrical, roof, mold, fungi, general safety, hazardous substances (like asbestos), indoor air quality, and maybe wetlands.

- The following are specialized inspections that are not part of a standard home inspection, but which are employed as the situation dictates. **You can choose to do any of these even if you are not doing a full home inspection if you have a particular concern.**

  ◇ **Wood infestation**

    ➤ This is often required by lenders along with a home inspection. Typically done by an exterminator, the purpose is to spot the hard-to-notice presence of structure destroying insects such as termites and carpenter ants.

  ◇ **Deeds/restrictions/zoning**

    ➤ This is more of an inspection of paperwork and recorded documents regarding the property's compliance with (and the owner's obligation to follow) everything from homeowner's association bylaws and deed restrictions to municipality zoning restrictions. The homeowner's or condo association is required to give you their bylaws to examine, and your attorney will look over the deed restrictions and zoning compliance. This is also the place to see exactly what is in the deed regarding any shared driveways or other rights-of-way that may be of concern.

◊ **Water service/well**

> With a typical municipal water service, there is not much call for an independent inspection. However, if you suspect issues with the water service from the property owner's connection at the curb and into the structure, you would hire a plumber to check this out. **In any case, if the water supply is from a well, have the well tested for rate-of-flow and contamination by a specialist. DO THIS EVEN IF YOUR OFFER HAS NO OTHER INSPECTION CONTINGENCIES!** A structure that has no potable water supply is valueless for our purposes.

◊ **Sewer service/septic**

> Ditto here for what was said about water service and wells. **Always have a septic system tested. Do not buy a property with septic issues unless you have a viable plan to fix the problems and know the cost.** Often, residents have been living in a house for years with no knowledge of an improperly functioning septic system, so have the system checked regardless. Septic system problems may not be as easily rectified as a water well issue due to updated requirements on the part of the municipality for septic systems. These requirements may not be enforced on the existing homeowner, but whomever is faced with updating the system after problems are

found, would be forced to comply at great expense. Another situation to check is whether there are imminent plans on the part of the municipality to run sewer lines which every property owner will be forced to connect to, always at significant expense. This could be a good thing in an area with historical problems with septic systems, but you must account for the cost.

Another area for trouble is the lateral or main sewer line from the house to the street. Older ones, which are constructed of individual drain tiles laid end-to-end instead of a solid plastic line, may have collapsed or have tree roots. One municipality here requires all laterals to be replaced if they are the original lines anytime a property is changing hands. Again, this is something to address with the seller before finalizing the deal.

◇ **Radon**

▸ Radon is a colorless, odorless, tasteless gas that comes out of the ground and into basements through small cracks in basement floors and walls. It can filter throughout the house without detection, and it can cause cancer in people who are exposed over prolonged periods. There are companies that specialize in testing for radon and installing radon remediation systems if the gas is found over a certain level of detection. Radon systems are primarily just a fan that continually draws air out the basement through PVC pipes to the exterior coupled with sealing the cracks. They are not terribly expensive to install (around $1,500), and there is no requirement that they be installed even if radon is found. It's basically a matter of who is concerned about the radon presence. If the buyer is concerned, then a high radon reading could be cause to bargain with the seller to have the remediation system installed before the closing, or to credit the buyer with the cost of the system.

◇ **Property and flood insurance**

➤ **You will not want to own property for a moment without it having adequate coverage for property loss and liability.** If the government has designated the location of your property to be in a flood zone, you will want to buy flood insurance. **Property casualty insurance does not cover damage from floods.** Lenders will require you to have these insurances in effect as of the day of the closing, so obtaining coverage is one of your tasks leading up to closing. The point of mentioning it here is that you may need to arrange for an inspection by an insurance agent to determine the insurability of the property, especially if the property is in bad condition. Also, you may need to inspect the flood plain maps to see if flood insurance is required even if the seller says they don't carry it. Many a buyer has been surprised to find that an area which has not flooded in decades is actually in a flood zone.

◇ **Property boundaries**

➤ This inspection, of course, is called a survey. You would rarely have to order one of these, but sometimes there are concerns that come up while talking with the seller and neighbors that may make your antenna go up. In this case, you may feel the need to settle some disputes ahead of your ownership.

◇ **Lead-based paint hazard**

➤ Any structure built in the United States before 1978, when they outlawed the manufacturing of paint containing lead, has the potential to have been painted with lead-based paint. Ingesting lead from paint chips or dust (like in wood window jambs) or inhaling fumes from removing lead-based paint by heat can cause serious health problems, particularly in children up to six. When a pre-1978 property is sold, the seller must disclose to the buyer what they know, if anything, about the presence of lead-based paint. Generally, everybody says they know nothing, but if there has ever been any testing for lead or any remediation of a lead issue, the documentation of these events must be disclosed and turned over to the buyer for review. Then, the same is true each time the owner rents to a new tenant. If knowing the location of any lead-based paint is important to you, then you need to schedule testing sufficiently in advance of the closing.

- **Arrange to insure the property**

  o Ask your insurance agent to recommend the amount for which to insure the property. They have computer programs for this, and the amount you are paying for the property is not the only factor. Have them explain the difference between a policy that covers actual cash value vs. one that covers replacement cost. The former will be cheaper, but the amount it will pay if you have a claim will disappoint you. The latter is a little more expensive, but it will pay to restore the building to the way it was before the loss, and you will be much happier. You also need to know the difference between a policy that covers "named perils" and one that covers all perils. You'll be much happier with the latter if you have a claim that was not caused by some specific type of event that is listed in a "named peril" policy.

  Discuss with your agent what optional coverages are available. Income protection that pays you for the rents you would have received while a property is being repaired is a must for a claim where the property could not be occupied after an insured event. Other options include cyber protection for your data, sewer and drain backup coverage (not to be confused with flood insurance), siding/roofing restoration (which pays to replace *all* your siding or roofing if it can no longer be matched even though only a small part was damaged), "green" endorsements, and earthquake insurance.

If you have a lender for this acquisition, you will be required to bring proof to the closing that the insurance is in effect and that the lender is named as the mortgagee on the policy. This assures the lender they will be paid off in the event of a total loss, and they will be notified if the policy is ever in danger of being cancelled due to non-payment of premium.

Considering the amounts rewarded these days for liability claims, I urge you to discuss a commercial umbrella liability policy with your agent. This is a relatively inexpensive policy that is separate from the individual property insurance policies on your properties. It does not increase your property damage coverage, however it increases the limit given in your underlying policies for liability coverage. You do not need to have a separate umbrella policy for each property, nor does your umbrella policy need to be with the same carrier as your property coverage. Rather, you maintain one umbrella policy that increases your liability coverage by a set additional amount...often increments of one million dollars. So, if you already have this coverage, notifying your carrier of the existence of a new property is one of your tasks leading up to a closing.

- **Make sure you have an up-to-date government issued photo ID**

  o You will need to show this at the closing. The notary will need to see it, and the attorneys will make a photocopy for their files as required now by law to ensure the purchasers and sellers of real estate are who they say they are.

- **Obtain the locks you will use** to immediately change the locks

  o Change the locks on the day of the closing. These may not be the nice locks you eventually install after a rehab, but you don't want to leave the ones the sellers used no matter how many keys they turn over to you.

- **Open accounts with the utilities**

  o Call the gas company, the electric company, the cable company, and any other utilities that need to continue after you take ownership. Arrange to have them place these utilities in your name as of the date of the closing which, especially for the gas company, may involve making an appointment to meet them at the property so they can have access to the meter. This will automatically take the account out of the name of the prior owner, so they do not need to call. However, when you are on the selling side of this equation, be sure to call and check to see if the new owners have opened their accounts. If not, a message must be sent to your Realtor to have a reminder sent to the buyers. Since closing dates often get pushed back a few days, it's best to wait until a couple of days before the closing is locked in before calling the utilities so the changeover occurs on the proper day.

    It should be noted that, from my experience, the attorneys involved will make the calls to the local public water and sewer providers (and any other municipal utilities like garbage pickup) on your behalf. This is because they need to get an exact amount to use on the closing statement, including any back balances of the sellers. A new account will automatically be set up in the buyer's name as of the closing. Since an unpaid municipal bill can become a lien against the property regardless of who owns it at the time the lien is recorded, a small amount of the seller's proceeds will be held by the seller's attorney in an escrow account to use to pay the final bills which will come several weeks later.

- **Contact service providers**

  o If there are any companies that are working regularly on the property such as those that provide cleaning, trash removal, landscaping, snow removal, or pool maintenance, you need to discuss whether their services will still be needed after the closing date (the contracts need to be changed into your name). Otherwise, you must sign contracts with the new providers so that there is no interruption of services.

- **Do a final walkthrough.**

  o A day or so before the closing, make another visit to the property with the seller and/or your Realtor to make sure everything is as it is supposed to be. If it is not, you or your Realtor may call a halt to the transaction until things are remedied. You are looking to see that any repairs or other tasks (like trash removal) have been done that may have been agreed to as a result of any inspections or other negotiations. Test the appliances, the heating, the air conditioning, the water pressure, the hot water, and anything else that has a function that was supposed to be in working order when you take over.

- **Get a certified check** from the bank where your money is on deposit

  o If you are bringing money to the closing above what your lender is providing, such as for your down payment or other fees, you will do so in the form of a certified or cashier's check. Eventually, maybe only a couple of days before the closing, you will get notice from your attorney as to the exact amount and in what name your check needs to be made out. At this time, you may be shown what is hopefully the final version of the closing statement (or HUD as it is called in reference to the Dept. of Housing and Urban Development which prescribes the format of the closing statement if the buyer is borrowing money to purchase the property) so that you can review it and look for anything that is not the way you expected.

Hopefully, all the separate parties, including you, will accomplish their parts in a timely fashion, and it all dovetails together on the day of the closing. It is not at all uncommon for the closing date named in a sales agreement to be changed. The most common cause, from my experience, is the lender taking more time than promised to do their internal paperwork (which often generates more and more requests for information and documentation from you), and to give you final approval for the loan.

The second most common cause seems to be title issues which are not brought to light until the title is searched at the courthouse and then examined by the buyer's attorney. Some of these things are simple to resolve, but others are more complicated and take more time. Unpaid judgements and the failure to open an estate and pay estate taxes when a former owner died are two common findings. The judgements must be paid when the title transfers, and estate taxes may need to be escrowed for later payment after an estate has been properly opened on behalf of the decedent. All of this, of course, comes out of the seller's proceeds, but it can delay things while everything gets sorted out.

Eventually, the attorneys or closing agents are comfortable that everyone has properly contributed their work, and the closing date is locked down. Your representative will go over the myriad of documents with you at the closing, you'll turn over your money, the seller will give you the keys, and you can begin the next step in building your rental real estate portfolio which is preparing your property for your customer...a tenant.

3
PREPARING YOUR PROPERTY FOR TENANTS (FRAMING)

If the physical properties in your portfolio are the building blocks in the foundation of your rental property activities, then **preparing those properties for occupancy can be considered the framing.** Once you have a foundation in place, the structure can begin to take shape. When you are preparing your units for tenants, you are creating the framework for what you have to offer to potential residents. **Apartments must be fully prepared for occupancy before you show them to your applicants.** The art of selecting tenants will be covered in the next chapter, but now I will discuss how to get to the point of marketing your properties for rent. All your other rental property activities, from selecting tenants to managing your finances to maintaining your properties, are attached to the product you have to offer just like the finishes are added onto the framing of a structure.

If you are buying a vacant property, then what is discussed here will be employed immediately. If you are buying a turn-key property which is already occupied, then much of this would be used when the existing residents move out and you want to prepare the apartment to your own specifications.

By now you should have some idea as to the extent of the work you will do yourself. This can range from securing all materials and pounding every nail to hiring a general contractor who will do everything. Considering that most landlords fall somewhere in between, **having relationships with contractors and suppliers is paramount for being able to proceed quickly with turning around a property for new tenants.** Contractors and suppliers are two of the most important links in the chain, but be prepared for them to sometimes be among the weakest links.

Before you offer your units for rent, you will need to concern yourself with:

- Your repair and maintenance team
- Your suppliers
- Your office files and records
- Banking and accounting
- Physical preparation of the apartment for viewing
- Setting your rent rate

REPAIR AND MAINTENANCE TEAM

One of the categories of teams I listed in Chapter One was that of contractors. Unless you are capable and willing to handle every repair and maintenance issue yourself, you will need to call on others who are professionals to do the work.

When I started out, I tackled almost everything that came up at the apartments. I had a lot of help from my father who had skills exceeding that of general handyman. I learned as much as I could from him, but I never learned *everything* he knew. We just tore into stuff. Most of the time things turned out OK, but sometimes we didn't even know what we didn't know. It was a great learning experience, and I don't regret at all that those things took longer because I was doing them myself as I learned. This experience paid big dividends later as I applied my knowledge of "what should be done, how it should be done, how long it should take, and how much it should cost" to dealing with contractors. Now I joke that if I can't fix it with a screw gun, glue gun, duct tape, Goop Glue, or hammer, I'm calling someone else.

Most landlords don't get into the business to show off their handyman skills. Usually, the objective is to get to the point where you are hiring out all the work while you concentrate on putting deals together. But **there is no shame in doing things yourself for a while to familiarize yourself with what you will be asking contractors to do for you. As I pointed out, you don't have to know how to do everything; you just need to know the people who do. Not just one other person who says they can do everything, but relationships with multiple people who are skilled in specific areas.** Some people will be able to cover several related skillsets like, for example, carpentry, drywall hanging and painting. Others will be specialists like for tree removal or concrete installation. We call these individuals/companies contractors. **I would emphasize the importance of being able to call on more than just one provider for any given specialty so that you can always find one available in your timeframe or to get competing quotes on a project.**

You wouldn't need to have *all* these relationships set up before you bought your first property, but the need for routinely used contractors will become apparent as you begin to prepare your apartments for potential renters. **It's never too early to start developing a list of contractors** so that your team is somewhat in place when the need arises because, as you've heard, time is money, and you don't want any more time than necessary to pass until you can get a property producing rent.

Beyond confirming the skillsets offered by contractors for your list, you'll want to be sure each contractor is established in the community, reliable, honest, and trustworthy in addition to being reasonably priced and fully insured. Basically, **your objective with a contractor is for them to consistently be able to:**

- Do what they say they can do

- Charge you a fair price for doing it

- Show up when they say they will

- Finish by when they say they would

- Tell you the truth

- Not steal from you

- Treat your tenants and other contractors professionally

- Make things right if they do something incorrectly

- Have their liability insurance cover you if they really screw something up

You can sign a contract that states the amount you'll pay for a job along with when it must start and finish. You can get proof the contractor is insured from their agent. But everything else on that list is up for continual evaluation on your part. **Being able to plow through full rehab projects, turn around an apartment between tenants, or just do routine maintenance on your buildings will largely depend on your relationships with contractors.** They can become a weak link in your chain, or they can be glue that is holding everything together, to use a couple of metaphors. I've learned that contractors can move in and out of an acceptable degree of reliability as things change such as their personal life situations (especially health and finances) and their workloads. If you find a contractor who meets all the criteria on the above list, treat them well by showing them respect, paying them what they ask, and paying them on time. If they start falling short, be prepared to cut the ties and move on to another on your list. Don't let the contractor make you think you owe them a living just because you've been using them regularly for a long time. Your contractor list is fluid, and **some of the best places to find contractors to add to your list are:**

- Other landlords in the neighborhood or in your local association

  - These landlords can give you their opinions on contractors before you decide to approach the contractor.

- The pro desks at the big box stores and smaller suppliers

  o They see these people regularly and have impressions of them.

- Business cards tacked to bulletin boards

  o Sometimes suppliers have a spot where anyone who offers services can tack up their cards.

- Seeing the contractor's vehicle in traffic

  o Often their specialties and phone numbers are on their vehicles.

- Places you can search where the contractor has advertised

  o The Internet, the Yellow Pages, or the newspaper classified ads are examples.

- Places you notice where the contractor advertises

  o Start paying attention to radio, TV, billboards, and print ads.

Primarily, your list might be no more than a notebook or computer file with contractors' names, range of work, and phone numbers which you are continually adding on to. But once you start working with a contractor, your files on them will need to be more extensive. The basic pieces of info on contractors would include:

- Their real name and their DBA company name
- Their mailing address
- Their cell, office, and home phone numbers
- Their email address
- Their federal tax ID (Employer Identification Number or Social Security Number)

  o You'll need to send them a 1099 IRS form each January when you've paid them at least $600 the year before.

- A certificate of liability insurance from their insurer

  o It's better to keep all the different contractors' insurance certificates in one file that is separate from the individual contractor files. This is so you can continually see the policies that are going to expire soon which will require updated certificates. Check with your property insurance carrier to see if they require you to keep a current certificate on file for any contractor you are working with.

Don't let a new contractor start working for you without getting all the information on the above list...especially their phone numbers, their tax ID, and their proof of insurance! These items can be hard to obtain after they've been paid for the job.

When compiling your list of contractors, remember that contractors can be broken down into two groups. The first group contains those you need often and/or in a hurry, and the second is comprised of those you may use occasionally. Examples of the first group are:

- General handy person to cover a variety of typical repairs

  o Basic painting of walls and trim
  o Wall damage repairs
  o Light plumbing repairs like replacing a faucet, pipe, or toilet part
  o Screen repairs
  o Light electrical repairs like replacing an outlet or light fixture
  o Minor carpentry like replacing wood trim or installing a door
  o Door hinge and lock replacement
  o Just about any minor repair that comes up wherever people interface with buildings

- Plumber for more involved plumbing especially when a permit is required like adding a bathroom

- Sewer and drain opener

- Electrician for more involved electrical work especially upgrading a breaker box
- Heating and air conditioning technician for both repairs and installation of new equipment
- Roofer for both emergency repairs and roof replacements
- Glazier for glass repairs
- Cleaner for general cleaning
- Trash hauler
- Scrap metal recycler who will pick up scrap at your property
- Carpet cleaner
- Appliance repair person
- Carpet installer
- Landscape and mowing company for misc. planting, trimming, mulching, grass cutting, and edging

In the second group you will find:

- Exterminator
- Locksmith
- Roll off container provider (dumpster)
- Tree trimming and removal company
- Insulation installer (both blown-in and spray foam)
- Tile installer for floors and walls
- Fiberglass and cast-iron tub/shower refinisher
- Wood flooring refinisher
- Concrete and paving contractors for stairs, sidewalks, and driveways
- Window washer

- Carpenter/remodeling contractor for larger jobs

- Drywall hanger

- Drywall finisher (sometimes the hangers don't finish and vice versa)

- Plasterer if repairing using drywall is not appropriate

- Landscape design and construction

- Painter for exterior and whole house interior jobs

- Mason for brick and foundation repairs

- Siding installer

- Gutter installer

- Overhead door (garage door) maintenance and installation

- Kitchen designer

- Décor designer

- Social media assistant if you need help posting ads

Whether the contractor will be billing you pre-set charges for service calls, or if you need to negotiate a fee for a custom project, **make sure you know ahead of time what you will be expected to pay.** This is especially true when you are getting to know a new contractor, but it's great when you get to know and trust a contractor. Then you can just send them on a job and expect to be charged fairly without having to involve yourself much in the arrangements.

In any case, it's important that the expectations you and the contractor have for each other are laid out ahead of time. Clear expectations dictate whether you have a right to be disappointed and whether you have grounds for recourse. Some expectations to cover are:

- What quality of work you expect

  o This can differ from one property to another and can depend on whether the property is a rental where a lesser level of perfection is acceptable as compared to a flip where everything must be perfect.

- How you will be charged

  o This could be a set amount for the job or a set amount per hour for the time.

- How and when you will be invoiced by the contractor

  o Should you expect the bill to be mailed, emailed, or handed to you

- What, if any, partial payments must be made as the job progresses

  o If the contractor will receive draws for materials or labor as the job progresses, it must be clear what triggers the draw. Is it by date or by percentage of completion, which can be a judgement call?

- How long you have to pay the invoice once you receive it

- What methods of payment the contractor accepts

  o This could be cash, business check, certified check, credit card, ACH or other electronic transfer, or some other payment in kind.

- When the work is to begin

- Requirement, if any, for a Mechanic's Lien Waiver to be filed before any work begins

- The consequences if the contractor does not show up when agreed

- Policy requiring the contractor to contact the tenant if, for any reason, they will not be able to show up at the agreed-upon date and time

- Policy if the contractor shows up on time but cannot get access to the apartment

- When the contractor has access to the property for planning and for working

- When the work is to be completed

- The consequences if the contractor does not finish when agreed

- Honesty and trustworthiness

- Policy for answering phone calls and texts in a timely manner

- Policy regarding checking the contractor's work before payment is made

- Reporting screwups and problems accurately

- Cleanliness and organization of the jobsite

- Who is going to select materials

- Who is going purchase which materials

- How the materials will be delivered to the jobsite

  o Perhaps the materials can be delivered by the supplier, but otherwise either you or the contractor must pick them up.

- How the tenants, if the unit is occupied during the work, and other contractors on the job are to be treated

- Who is going to set the appointment with the tenant for work in an occupied apartment

  o My tenants call the office to initiate a service request. After fully discussing the problem with the tenant (which may involve a visit to the apartment), I decide who is going to respond. I then give the contractor the name, address, and phone number of the tenant. The contractor makes their appointment directly with the tenant. I also inform the tenant as to from which contractor to expect a call, and I give the tenant the contractor's number. I instruct the tenant to call the contractor directly if they haven't heard from them by a certain time. Tenants, when they move in, are given the numbers for the contractors we work with regularly for things like HVAC and appliance repairs in case they have an emergency and can't reach anyone in our office.

- What limits you have on what subjects may be discussed with the tenant

  o I ask my contractors not to get into any discussions with tenants about either their or the tenant's relationship with me or how we handle things, other than to reassure the tenants the repair will be done properly. They should not express their opinions to the tenant about anything else that needs to be done in the apartment, or on the work of any other contractors who have worked on the apartment. This could be a needed repair the tenant brings up or that the contractor discovers on their own. In those instances, the contractor should call me right then to discuss it (if it is something they could take care of while they are there), or they should report it after they leave the jobsite if it is something to be done another time. Similarly, contractors should report any perceived lease violations to the landlord without discussing the issue with the tenants.

The three desired elements of any product or service are "fast," "cheap," and "good." I have found that you can rarely, if ever, have all three. When it comes to the work you get from contractors, the best you can hope for is to experience only two of the three. You can have any combination of two out of the three, but you must decide which one of the three is the least important to you. If you don't care how quickly a job gets done, you can usually find someone to do it cheaply and well. If you demand that it gets done right away and at top quality, it will not be cheap. If you don't care about the quality of the work, you can get it done immediately at the lowest price. Keep these things in mind when you are setting your expectations for those whom you will allow to work on your properties.

SUPPLIERS

Preparing an apartment for a tenant, of course, is not all labor. There are going to be some materials involved. In the old days, we found what we needed at a variety of hardware stores, lumber suppliers, and other specialty shops. Nowadays, most of what we need can be found under one roof at the big box home improvement stores such as Lowe's and Home Depot. Each department there represents a type of specialty store, and you can typically find a version of an acceptable product for you project.

You will not always find *everything* you need at the big box stores, so it's important to familiarize yourself with resources for certain items just like you develop your list of contractors with different specialties. Some examples of local stores you may need to call on are:

- Specialty lumber supplier

  o Sometimes you may need to match a particular wood trim profile for a baseboard or window casing. The big box stores carry the most popular ones, but the custom builder lumber supply houses have the unusual ones too. They also carry (or can order) old style doors and hardware. You're more likely to get lumber cut to your specifications here as well.

- Hardware store

  o I'm referring here to one of those long-standing locally owned stores where the locals go because they "have everything." They are typically located in an older area of town compared to the big box stores in the outlying areas. Since their surrounding customers are maintaining older buildings, they tend to stock a lot of hard-to-find items and provide all the down-home services from glass and screen repair to electrical fixture repair to package mailing. They may also be able to fabricate a replacement section of screen or glass for a storm window or storm door.

- Paint store

  o This would be anything from a locally owned shop that sells several brands to a brand-name store such as Sherwin-Williams or PPG. This would be where to go when you really need to speak with experts who live and breathe their paint products all day every day. They will also keep track of what special color you used on a given project for future reference. It is possible that you could get better pricing here than at the big box stores if you open a pro account or belong to a professional organization that has a pre-arranged discounted price for members.

- Flooring store

  o What I just said for paint stores also goes for flooring stores, although they may not have as much of a selection in stock as you'll find at the big box stores, whereas a paint store will stock almost all their products. An added advantage, though, is that they may have installers on staff (either as employees or as subcontractors they can call on) with whom you can develop a professional relationship. Typically, installations can be arranged here with less formality than the process at the big box stores. You want to be the one the installers remember when someone cancels, and they can do your job instead.

- Flooring supply store

  o This is where the flooring stores and installers get their materials, but you may be able to buy there too. You may occasionally need a specialty flooring transition or unique color of caulking that is not available at the big box store.

- Window supplier

  o You can often find usable window sizes in stock in the big box stores, which is great if you are doing new construction. But unless you get lucky with the size that you need to replace an existing window, you will need to order in custom sized windows. **You can never have too many sources for custom windows.** Lead times for manufacturing windows have been very erratic over time. Window manufacturers tend to be regional, and their products might be offered through multiple outlets from Lowe's to locally owned home improvement stores in each area. Windows can be some of the first items you want on site because often many of the other tasks cannot be done until the windows are in place, so you will want to know where you can get windows quickly. The problem is that some manufacturers will be reliable for a time and then, due to anything from local labor problems to bankruptcy, will suddenly have an unacceptable length of time before they can deliver. So, you will need to quickly pivot to another supplier. Maybe you can come back to your original source later, but the point is that you will want to have multiple suppliers to check with who carry acceptable window products to get the fastest delivery times.

- Door and window hardware supplier

  o This is in addition to your local hardware or window supply source. Sometimes you take over a building with older windows or doors that have hinges, catches, locks, handles, or other hardware that is in disrepair. Parts may not be available locally, but if you can see who the manufacturer was, maybe you can order parts from them. Otherwise, you're going to need a good source for oddball hardware to save you from having to replace the whole unit. I recommend Blaine Window Hardware in Hagerstown, MD. They have a great research department that will figure out what the needed part is from your texted photos and measurements, not to mention a huge stock of parts for most window and door manufacturers.

- Glass company (screen repairs too)

  o You may be able to buy glass cut to size at the big box stores, but that would be for when you're going to do the repair yourself. You need to know where you can get a section of glass or screen (or the entire frame) replaced quickly by a professional. This could be a place like a locally owned glass company or that hardware store that "has everything" where you bring in the old frame with the broken glass or screen for them to fix for you to pick up and reinstall. But you also need to know who to call for instances where the broken window needs boarded up temporarily until the glass company repairs it on site.

- Locksmith

  - Locksmiths were mentioned above in the Repair and Maintenance Team. You may occasionally need one to do a service call at *your* building, but more often you'll use them for making key copies and re-keying locks at *their* shop. It's good to know which locksmiths have the blanks in stock for those hard-to-find keys.

- Used or scratch-and-dent appliances

  - In our area there are several companies with showrooms for used appliances. Primarily, they sell stoves, refrigerators, washers, and dryers. They have obtained their stock for next-to-nothing from private individuals, new appliance stores that took in trades, and manufacturers that don't want to ship back units that were replaced under warranty to name a few of their sources. They are skilled at cleaning and reconditioning appliances, and they are sold with a three- or four-month parts and labor warranty. The pieces usually have a few small marks on them, but often these appliances look and perform like brand new. I am a big proponent of putting used appliances in apartments (and in flips if they're nice enough) because they are much less expensive than new ones, and the amount of service calls on them are not appreciably higher than new ones. Plus, you can afford to replace them more often if the situation arises. Typically, these stores will deliver and set up your purchase, and they will take away your old ones.
  - We also have a store that sells nothing but brand-new appliances that have minor damage on the outside. These units are sold with huge discounts, and they still have warranties on their functionality.

- Electrical materials supplier

  - When you can't find a particular breaker for an old panel box or a not-so-popular cover for an outlet or switch at the big box store, you may have luck at the parts counter in an electrical supply store. Find one that sells to people off the street because you may not be making enough purchases here to have an account.

- Plumbing and HVAC supplier

  o You may want to open a store charge account with a good supplier of this type. Often, they will not sell to the public because this is the source for professional plumbers and heating & air conditioning contractors. However, you can probably open a business account as a landlord. I recommend this because you would then be able to purchase big-ticket items at wholesale prices. If you have a store charge, you can add your trusted contractors to your account so that they can pick up a furnace or hot water tank of your specification (and any other necessary hardware) on your account for an emergency install without you having to buy the items in person for the contractor. You would be paying the contractor for labor only in this case. **In addition to refrigerators, the most common emergency service calls will be for furnaces and hot water tanks. Most other service calls can be handled in due time during normal business hours.** Plumbing and HVAC suppliers may have an employee on call to open the store after hours for a contractor making an emergency call.

- Equipment rental

  o Some tools just aren't used enough to warrant owning them yourself. Unless you're hiring a professional for every job, occasionally you will need to rent a tool for a one-off task.

- Metal shop

  o This would be your source for custom metal items on occasion. One example would be the metal support bars you must attach to the underside of a countertop when the top hangs over the base cabinet to create an eating area or buffet. Another is a thin stainless steel splash guard cut to size to attach to the wall over the stove and below the vent hood.

Am I saying you need to have all these sources for materials locked down before you buy your first property? No, but **I'm recommending you start keeping your eyes open to their existence so you can start a reference list just like the one you will be building for contractors**. You could go quite some time before you need some of these contractors or suppliers, but if you stay in the business long enough, you are likely to need one in every category I've listed at some point.

As I mentioned earlier, much of your shopping will be at the big box stores. This is for both convenience and selection because the stores are typically in well-traveled areas of town, and you can usually find what you need under one roof. If they don't stock it, they have robust special-order programs. Additionally, they offer incentives to those like landlords and contractors who are, by nature, regular customers. **Such benefits come from opening a commercial store charge as opposed to a personal store charge. When you do this, you can have them provide you with extra store charge cards in the names of your trusted contractors or employees so your workers can buy items they need for your repairs without you visiting the store. Then, all purchases on your account contribute toward any rewards connected with your account. With some retailers, your purchase is automatically reduced by a percentage at the register whenever your commercial account is used.**

Some big box stores even offer a charge card connected with their brand that is issued by a major credit card company such as VISA, Mastercard, or American Express. These are true credit cards that can be used anywhere. You can request separate cards for multiple users, and every user's purchases are grouped separately on the monthly statement. Just like with their regular commercial account, a job name can be entered at the register, and the job number is shown both on your receipt and on the statement for each purchase. **Not only are rewards built up with each purchase whether the purchase was from the branding retailer or not, but some branding retailers may offer a percentage off automatically at the register when this card is used at their stores just like for a commercial account.** Getting that percentage at the register probably beats the reward you might be getting from your regular Mastercard or VISA, so there are many advantages to opening commercial accounts at the big box stores.

Whether you have a commercial account or not, the biggest savings at the big box stores—and even some specialty suppliers—will come from having them quote a price for a large list of materials for a project which you are willing to buy all at one time. Just turn over a list to the pro desk with a brief description of the item, the store's item number, and the quantity you need. The minimum full retail total for your list may only need to be $1,500. The pro desk will go through it on their own and call or fax you with your discounted price for each item. Then, **you can charge it to your commercial account and get the additional discounts and rewards that come with your account!** No worries about buying everything at one time because the store will deliver them to your job site for a minimal charge. Just check everything off the list at the delivery to make sure everything arrived. Also, I have found that they are willing to deliver items separately if you would not be ready for them all at once at the beginning of a job, like large appliances.

Developing relationships with team members and suppliers is a never-ending part of being in the rental real estate business. Knowing on whom to call or where to go is a big part of having the confidence to face any challenge when it arises, and you may even make some good friends along the way!

OFFICE FILES AND RECORDS

Beginning with when you make your initial offer on your first property, there are records that need to be kept. Record keeping is documenting the past so you can make decisions about the future. It keeps you out of trouble when memories aren't clear. Record keeping, whether it's done in file cabinets or in computer files, must be organized in a logical fashion and be readily accessible. Some records, like insurance policies and documents from a real estate closing, are provided to you by others for your reference. Other records, like accounting and tenant files, are created by you and need to be accurately maintained.

Generally, record keeping for income property falls into the following categories:

- Bookkeeping for the purpose of preparing tax returns and making financial evaluations and projections
- Tenant interaction including both financial and otherwise
- Property information which can include everything from the closing documents from when you bought it and when you sold it to the plans and special materials you used for the rehab
- Insurance policies
- Company documents

Of course, there can be many subcategories such as mortgage documents, appraisals, inspections, employees, contractors, advertising, and insurance claims to name some of the possibilities. But the five main categories mentioned above are the areas into which every record will fall before you decide whether it needs its own file.

You may grow large enough to warrant having an office in a location away from your residence, but probably you will start out utilizing a space in your home for doing your record keeping. You may decide to allow tenants to pay their rent in person at your remote office, but **I don't recommend interacting with your tenants at all at your personal residence. They shouldn't even know where you live, so I advise you get a PO box for any correspondence with tenants.**

Regardless of where you set up your office, you will need the typical equipment like a desk, computer with a printer, and some filing cabinets or boxes for paper documents. You don't need them on day one, but you'll want to work toward having a copier with fax and scanner capabilities, and a fireproof cabinet or safe for extra-important files and removable computer backup drives.

Personal taste and computer savvy will dictate the type of files you store as hard copies vs. computer files, but you must come up with a system that works for you. There is no "one correct way" to do it as long as the result is that you have accurate and secure files that are readily accessible to *you* for reference.

Keeping track of the money in and money out will be covered in the next section, but storing the documentation of those transactions falls into this section.

It's necessary to keep a ledger of the ongoing rent payments received from each tenant separately. Whether it's done in a property management computer program you buy, a spreadsheet you set up on your computer, or a paper form, your ledger must show each tenant's charges, payments against those charges, and their current balance. You may choose to keep each tenant's ledger inside a file that has your other documents related to that tenant such as their lease. However, I prefer to keep all my payment ledgers in one file. The ledgers are kept in alphabetical order by the tenant's last name for each property separately. Leases are kept in consecutively numbered files that also contain any other correspondence with the tenant. Each new tenant is given the next higher number, and their number is noted on their rent payment ledger along with other quick reference information like their phone numbers, the beginning and ending dates of their lease, and the amounts of their security deposit and rent. Additionally, **I find it useful to keep a "cheat sheet" on my desk which serves as a quick reference for who has paid their rent for the month.** Each address has a line on the chart, and there are twelve columns representing the months. When a tenant pays their rent, I mark in the date on the proper line in the corresponding column. It's an easy way to tell at a glance who's been naughty and who's been nice.

Rent payments will be your primary source of revenue, of course. There won't be receipts to file from receiving rent; you will just indicate the payments in your records. But there are lots of destinations for the money going out, and there will be receipts to file for those transactions. Whether you scan the receipts and store them digitally or file them in a box, you'll need to keep them organized. Most payments and their accompanying receipts will be attributable to individual apartments like a furnace repair, for example. Some will be for a whole property like for landscaping maintenance on a property that has multiple units. If you have multiple properties owned within the same legal entity, then you may have expenses that are attributable to the company as a whole such as tax return preparation. Consequently, **it's important to organize receipts in files by apartment, by property, and by company according to how they apply.** For example, if you have a four-unit townhouse building with four different addresses, don't have one stack of receipts covering the activity of all four apartments mixed with the grass cutting invoices.

Have receipts grouped by address and a fifth file for the exterior expenses that are common to all the units.

When you take rental applications from prospective tenants, you will be collecting private information including birth dates, addresses, and social security numbers. If you rent to an applicant, you will likely keep their application with their lease in their tenant file, but **ALL rental applications, including the ones you reject, must be kept on file for several years.** Consequently, because these applications (and related documents such as credit reports and background checks) obviously include information that could be used for identity theft, **it is your responsibility to keep all tenant files secure.** Depending on who may have access to your office area, this could mean keeping those files in a locked cabinet (or on a password protected computer) inside a locked room.

Separate from the bookkeeping and tenants' records, you'll want to **maintain individual files related to the acquisition, operation, and sale of each property separately.** Paid receipts and tenants' files are ever changing as you make entries, but files on the properties tend to be added to as you receive important documentation from other sources. Here, you would collect any legal documents or other information to which you may occasionally need to refer.

Insurance policies should all be kept together for quick access. You may have a separate policy for each property, and those policies may be from different carriers. You may have one master policy that covers multiple properties, or some combination of the above. In any case, keep your property casualty policies together with any other policies relating to your rental properties like a commercial umbrella policy, auto policy for business owned vehicles, general business policy, or insurance covering any employees. You don't want to spend any more time than necessary locating a policy folder when the need arises.

Maintain a file containing nothing but documents relating to the formation, operation, and dissolution of each business entity separately. This would include all your organizational and operating agreement documents along with any filings with your state. Any documents for transfers of interests, or from when a partner loans money to the entity, are also candidates for inclusion in this file. Basically, anything that affects the entire company is filed here.

It's wise to assume from the beginning that your company is going to grow and to organize your record keeping with a good system that will accommodate expansion. **It is far easier to spend a little time thinking through your filing system before you start accumulating data** than it is to undo and reorganize a poor filing system later. You don't want to be the only person in the world who understands your illogical filing system!

BANKING AND ACCOUNTING

There are two reasons for keeping track of all the income and expenses of any business.

- Tax return preparation as required by law
- Financial planning as necessary for you and your business

The most important thought to get across to you regarding banking is that you need to keep your business transactions separated from your personal transactions, and the most basic way this is done is to have a checking account dedicated strictly to your rentals. No rental income or expenses should run through your personal accounts! Not only does this give you clarity as to how much your rentals are cash-flowing because none of your personal money is in the account, but it is also a legal requirement if you are holding your property in any kind of entity. Certainly, you can see the importance of this if your entity is a partnership, but it applies even if your entity is a corporation or LLC, and *you* are the only shareholder or member. Entities, as well as a business you are operating in your personal name, must have their own bank accounts. This is just good accounting practice.

My good friend Jeff Potts has been a mortgage broker for several decades. Regarding mixing personal finances with business money, he told me the following. "I see this in over fifty percent of the loans we do for small companies. Owners use the business debit card for many or all their personal purchases. Some go as far as paying their mortgage and weekly groceries right out of the business! And then they write them off as a business expense. If you treat the business account like your personal piggy bank, it is not a 'business account'. Owners (of an entity) must be able to show a separation of business and personal expenses."

I bought my first few properties in my personal name. I was not married at the time, so I'll admit that I operated my personal finances, my DJ business, and my rentals out of one checkbook. This worked for a while, but eventually it became impractical. My personal finances became "family" finances when I married. Then I learned the necessity of holding property within a legal entity to create liability protection for my family finances. Rental property held personally was transferred into an entity, and new property was purchased within the entity. Over time, multiple entities were created containing distinct groups of properties. Each entity has its own checking account.

Note the importance of each legal entity having its own bank accounts. **Not only must you separate business and personal funds, but you must keep the funds from each entity apart.** I'm sure you can see how this makes tax return preparation and financial planning less cumbersome, but there's a legal aspect that comes into play. **When you create a legal entity like a Limited Liability Company (LLC), you agree to follow certain guidelines, such as distinct financial accounting and keeping records of company meetings.** This is what keeps a liability that was created within the operations of the entity from affecting your personal assets. If there aren't enough assets or insurance coverage within an entity to settle a claim, attorneys for the claimant will try to "unwind" the entity to get at the owners' personal assets. Their strategy is to prove the entity does not deserve its status because it did not follow the requirements the law prescribes, and therefore the entity did not actually exist in the first place. **The two most common requirements they can attack are 1) not keeping proper company organizational records up to date, and 2) mixing company finances with personal finances by paying company expenses from personal funds or depositing company revenues into personal accounts.** This is obviously a really bad outcome if you've gone to the trouble of creating an entity only to find out it offered you no protection!

You should be able to find a bank that offers free business checking, so maintaining several accounts is not an added expense. Also, **less transactions in an account that handles only one business makes it easier to balance the statement each month...something that should not be neglected.**

This is not to say that you cannot cover a business expense out of your personal funds in a pinch. You can, and assuming you are doing your accounting on a cash basis where income and expenses are accounted for only as money moves in and out of the company's possession, this becomes an expense to the company at the time the company writes a check to reimburse you. **Don't try to claim the expense on the entity's tax return because you paid the expense from your personal funds until the entity has actually made the expenditure by paying you back.**

When it comes time to withdraw profits from your entity, this also must be done in a way that leaves a paper trail. If you have a partnership or LLC, write checks to the owners according to your operating agreement. If you have a corporation, declare dividends, and write checks to the shareholders. If you own your properties as a sole proprietorship, and you keep your rental money in a separate account, write yourself a check to withdrawal your excess. As covered in the last chapter where we discussed entity formation, partners who work for the business are paid in the form of *guaranteed payments to partners.* However, do not combine a guaranteed payment in the same check for a distribution of profits or along with a reimbursement for a company expense that had been paid from that partner's personal funds (like a mileage reimbursement). The point is that **any expenditures of a stand-alone business operation must be accurate, complete, clearly understood, and easily referenced in the financial records. The same applies to any event where money comes into the business from revenue, loans, or investment by the owners.**

Presumably, you will be collecting security deposits from each tenant. I will cover the ins and outs of security deposits in the next chapter, but while we're on the subject of bank accounts, I must mention escrow accounts. **Since the money given to a landlord for a security deposit technically still belongs to the tenant, it is a good idea to keep it separate from the general funds of the business.** The tenant is trusting their landlord to hold their funds as security in case they owe anything at the end of their tenancy, so they expect the funds remain on hand to give back regardless of the financial condition of the landlord. This is easily accomplished with an escrow in the form of a checking account. As a practical matter, you can initially deposit a new security deposit into the company's general funds, and then write a check from the general funds to the escrow account. Then, when returning the deposit, you can write a check directly to the former tenant from the escrow account. If part or all the security deposit is being retained to cover a tenant's obligation, a check can be written from the escrow account back to the general funds to cover that obligation.

A key policy regarding opening an escrow account at a bank is to use the word "escrow" in the title of the account. In the event of the escrow account owner's bankruptcy (or when a creditor is making a claim against a borrower's assets), the tenant's money in the escrow account will be protected. In that instance, if you don't have "escrow" in the title of the account, you may have difficulty proving the funds are not part of your assets. For this reason, most, but not all, states have laws requiring escrow accounts be used for security deposits. **Even if your state does not require them, it is a good idea to set them up.** You may not be required to have a separate escrow account for each entity, so you may be able to use just one account with a title that does not tie it to the name of any specific business entity. In any case, accurate record keeping is paramount.

For those of you who just want to get out there and make deals or do rehab work, bookkeeping may not be your strong suit. You want to deal with the numbers as little as possible, and you don't want to spend any more time in the office than you must. You view keeping receipts and maintaining financial records as necessary evils. Congratulations! You've at least accepted that they are *necessary* even though you don't like to do those things!

Then there are those who like making deals, but your goal is to get to the point, as quickly as possible, where you can afford to hire out virtually all your maintenance and rehab tasks. You don't mind overseeing the work, but you would sooner be checking your financial position than swinging a hammer. As someone who has kept track of every penny I've earned and spent since I was an eleven-year-old paperboy (and then got a BA in accounting), I guess I fall into this group. I love logging income and expenses on QuickBooks all year and doing my business and personal tax returns. When I prep our annual financial statements for the bank, it's like my own personal Super Bowl where the sum of our efforts for the year is measured.

You may fall somewhere in between where you don't mind bookkeeping, but you don't feel comfortable preparing a tax return for a business. You may be OK with doing quick routine repairs, but nothing too complicated or time consuming. That's fine; you can pay someone to do the returns, but **you must keep good records for the tax preparer to use.** And you can draw on your list of contractors while giving up some cash to pay others.

Like we discussed in the last section, **it is imperative you have a good record-keeping system right from the start.** It doesn't have to be the fanciest system, but it must be able to be expanded to accommodate more properties over time while maintaining accuracy. Perhaps a more precise statement would be to say that **you must make up your mind to be diligent in your bookkeeping right from the start,** or find someone who will do this for you. It's *that* important. First, for the unavoidable tax returns. And second because **you can evaluate your financial future more confidently when you understand where you've been.**

Bookkeeping for income properties is simple compared to other types of businesses like retail or manufacturing. You may have ancillary income such as from coin operated laundry machines, but basically, your only source of income is rent. You'll want to identify where the rent came from by property and apartment, which is uncomplicated because there is only one easy-to-track transaction per apartment per month. There aren't that many areas of expense as well. Primarily, mortgage payments, property taxes, insurance, utilities, repairs, supplies, and leasing costs are the only categories of recurring expenses. That's not a very egregious list of accounts. Of course, you'll want to keep track of expenses by property and apartment, but some months there won't even be an expense for every apartment. I'm making the case that, **even for the inexperienced or disinterested bookkeeper, the challenge will not be that great to keep track of all your transactions for the average rental property business.**

In my view, **bookkeeping for a small business such as income property can be broken down into three phases.** They are:

- Noting the occurrence of any money-in or money-out event

- Entering these notes into a compilation system

- Creating reports from the compilation system for preparing tax returns and evaluating your financial position

For rental property, you simply must note the receipt of rent by recording the date, tenant, and amount. You may want to do this in more than one place such as the tenant's individual ledger, a cash receipts journal, and perhaps the "cheat sheet" that I spoke of in the last section. The tenant's ledger contains only one tenant's payments, but a cash receipts journal could organize cash received from all sources into one ledger.

Outflow is typically noted in a check register. There aren't many cash expenses in a rental property business, but if you maintain a petty cash system, the petty cash is replenished with a check. If you've charged expenses on a card, payment of the credit card statement would be noted in the checkbook.

As a side note, **I encourage you to use a charge card for all expenses** down to just a few dollars in amount. Your purchases will be automatically tracked, and you will accrue rewards from the card company. You could charge both personal and business items on the same card for maximum rewards. Just pay the personal and company charges from their respective accounts. **My strong encouragement is that you pay your full balance every month.** Charge card interest rates are ridiculous.

Find a comfortable way to note every transaction. Make it easy for you, because here's the requirement: **The notations of your money in and money out must be made every day on which a transaction occurs.** Don't get behind on entering a tenant's payment. Do it while it's fresh in your mind and especially before you deposit any checks. This ensures accuracy. As for money out, it goes without saying that you should not write a check without entering it into the check register at the same time.

Every receipt is saved as the documentation for any money out. Charge card receipts are collected throughout the month and then matched up to the line items on your monthly card statement. When the charges are paid, the purchase receipts are placed in the corresponding organizational files as described in the previous section on office files and record keeping.

Noting cash receipts and expenses in a journal and a check register will become routine. The important thing to grasp is that **you must keep after it on a regular basis or you will lose accuracy, and the task will seem daunting after many unrecorded transactions are piled up.** No matter how large your income property holdings get, the corresponding expansion of your bookkeeping system will be accomplishing nothing more than noting the occurrence of each money-in and money-out event. You can start by doing it manually and move toward a computerized system, but the ultimate purpose is the same.

Next, from time to time, the occurrences of money-in and money-out, which you have noted in your routine record keeping, must be transferred into an accounting system capable of summarizing the transactions in various accounts. Unless you've got just a few units, you are going to want to use a third-party accounting program like QuickBooks. Property management software is bridging the gap between noting transactions as they occur and plugging them into an accounting system by combining these steps into one action.

When you make entries to your accounting system, you will tell the program to which account the transaction relates. You would have a separate account for each apartment under each property under each company along with some income and expense accounts common to all apartments at the property like for vending income or insurance expense. On the expense side, each apartment would have their own list of accounts representing whatever are the usual categories of expense such as repairs and utilities. **Once entries are made into the various accounts, your individual notations of income and expense events can be viewed as a compilation of all similar transactions.** For example, all the repairs on a particular apartment are viewed together for whatever time frame you choose. This ability to compile your transactions is the purpose of the second phase of bookkeeping as listed above.

The third phase involves making use of the information compiled in the second phase. This is done by creating reports from the information in individual accounts or groups of accounts. These are the reports you would review in making decisions about your properties, such as valuing the property, increasing your cash flow, making improvements, selling, or refinancing, or how much profit you can safely pay out. The information needed to plug into a tax return is also extracted from these reports. You, or your bookkeeper, will be able to prepare reports used internally to make business decisions, but the preparation of your tax return might be the point at which you hand off to an outside professional.

In Chapter Five, I will discuss property management software. These web-based programs are all encompassing in the sense that they integrate everything from lease preparation to maintenance records. Included within them is a financial component for rent collection and the recording of income and expenses. However, if you are only looking for an accounting program tailored for rental properties, Dan Lane of the *Rental Income Podcast* told me he likes a reasonably priced subscription-based product called Rental Hero. I have not used it, but their sight says "Everything about of Rental Hero is custom built around the way rental owners track their income, expenses, and do their accounting. It works on single family homes, duplexes, multi-unit properties, short term rentals, Airbnb's, and storage units. You can even track everything on a per property and per unit basis, including the ability to generate separate profit & loss reports for each one." This is not an endorsement of their program, but **I have included this reference to demonstrate that programs like this are out there to come to the relief of the financial record-keeping challenged real estate investor.** If you were looking for such a program, you would want it to have the features just mentioned.

If you would like to look into the IRS rules for rental property, you can find them in Publication 527 entitled *Residential Rental Property (Including Rental of Vacation Homes)*. You can view this publication online at www.irs.gov.

If you take a step back from record keeping, it boils down to this:

- Keep your receipts
- Enter income and expenses into a bookkeeping system as they occur
- Enter your bookkeeping information into an accounting program as needed
- Review the various accounts to make decisions and prepare your taxes
- Hire someone to do any of the above which you don't want to do because getting it right is *that* important...especially when it comes to impressing lenders and paying your taxes

PHYSICAL PREPARATION OF THE APARTMENT FOR VIEWING

You can have your team, your suppliers, your record keeping, and your bank accounts all set up, but if you don't have a nicely prepared apartment for your prospective tenants, it will place unnecessary strain on the framing of the business structure while you are operating. Everything we have covered to this point is behind-the-scenes activity that is not something your tenants will intersect with on a daily basis. Now, however, I am moving to a discussion about the rental units themselves. The rental units are your actual "product," and your tenants (your customers) will see your products and use them every day.

As I stated in the first paragraph of this chapter, **apartments must be fully prepared for occupancy before you show them to your applicants.** This cannot be overstated. Prospective tenants are shopping for their new home, not a haircut. They buy the latter based on how the barber tells them it's going to turn out, but an apartment must be the way it's going to be right from the start. Hopefully, you have the vision when you are shopping for an investment property to envision what it will be like when you are finished working on it. But **it is my belief that most renters do not have the ability to picture the appearance and feel of a dwelling as it will be when you are done** with the painting and the new flooring, so it is a risk to allow prospects to see the apartment with work in progress. **You may inadvertently turn off a good prospect if you show the unit before it's in its final form.**

The general concept is that no repairs, cleaning, or decorating should be left undone before the apartment is offered for viewing. You may begin your advertising slightly before the unit is ready to line up showings, but even this can be a risk if things are not completed on the exterior of the building. This is because once you begin advertising and taking calls, the apartment's address will be made known to the prospective tenant, so they may drive by on their own.

The positive first impression someone has when they view the property from the street is known as curb appeal. Good curb appeal is very important because otherwise a prospect may just drive off without bothering to see the beautiful apartment you have prepared inside. Creating good curb appeal is accomplished by preparing the property as following:

- Grass is cut, and all pavement edges are trimmed

- No overgrown shrubbery

- No garbage or debris visible (unless it's garbage night and the bags are staged neatly for pickup)

- Siding, trim, mailbox, shutters, windows, and doors are in good repair without peeling paint

- Siding, trim, door colors are attractive

First impressions continue to be made as the prospect views any common exterior amenities like a pool, picnic area, or garage. Common interior areas such as common entrances, interior hallways, recreation rooms, and laundries are equally important. In addition to the cleanliness and appeal of the décor, the applicant begins to judge the level of personal security offered when they pass through the front door.

Once inside the unit, the prospect's scrutiny becomes even more intense. These are the features they will see for hours at a time as they enjoy their residence. Consequently, **my rule is that there should not be any visible imperfection or annoyance to catch their eye and lower their opinion of the apartment or of the landlord.** Usually, people won't even ask about such things; they will just wonder if there are issues they *don't see* which should be of a concern to them. **This is especially true of any visible incomplete or poor workmanship.**

Properties need to be presented as neat and clean, and nothing should be in disrepair. All hardware and equipment must work properly. Painting, flooring, appliances, door hardware, fixtures, and cabinetry must be of an appealing style and color. **The level of updates and quality of these items will vary from one property to another, but must be in line with the overall quality of the property and what a resident would expect who chose to live there.**

An important consideration is to not over improve your property. No apartment will be perfect; you just need to ensure you are not doing anything to turn off your target tenant who is likely to want to live there. Every rental unit has its upper limit on rent based on the general quality of the property and its location. You won't be able to charge more rent than this no matter how much you improve the property. **This applies to both rentals and the sale price of a flip.**

My process for navigating from an uninhabitable property to a residence worthy of being shown to a prospective tenant or buyer is the same whether you're turning over a recently vacated apartment or doing a full rehab of a new rental or flip. Organization of your team members and suppliers is key. Here is the order I find works best:

- Make a punch list

  o **Carefully examine every wall, floor, ceiling, fixture, piece of equipment, and hardware on the interior and exterior of the building.** Do this in an organized fashion, one room at a time. Make a note of everything that needs to be done. I used to do this by writing in a notebook, but now I dictate my observations using voice-to-text into the Notes app on my phone. I then email it to myself and clean up the text in a nice Word document. I make a note of every little task from "remove the old robe hook on the back side of the bath door" to the big jobs like "full exterior paint job." Only one task can be written on each line, so you don't have to wait until multiple things are completed before you check off a line as "done." **Don't rush the punch list creation. The more detailed the better** for the purposes I will explain. It might take me fifteen minutes to do this for an apartment turnover to several hours for a full rehab.

- Make a materials list

  o Using your punch list, go through it line by line and **give thought to whether the task on that line requires any materials.** Create a separate chart of required materials with only one item on each line. Indicate the quantity needed, size, and any color or other style specification with the name of the item. I typically have a few columns to the right that are headed by the names of the suppliers at which I am likely to shop for these items including an "Other" column for any specialty products.

- Make a contractors list

  o Using your punch list, go through it line by line and **determine what jobs will be done by contractors** and not by you. Make a plan as to which contractors you will approach about quoting the job.

- Shop for materials

  o Take your materials list to the stores on your chart, and **shop for your needed items.** I prefer a paper version of the materials list for this purpose because I need to hand write notes in the store column after each item to which I can easily refer on a moment's notice in the field. Write in the price, brand, and any other descriptive information necessary to help you remember the product. You may even want to write in the shelf and bin number if it may be difficult to locate the item again on the shelf. **Most importantly, write down the item number used by the store.** I do this in the margin to the left of the item's name so that it's clearer by not being jammed into the column with the item's description.

  o One tip here is that you likely will develop favorite items to use over and over. You can save time by transferring the information, especially the item number, for these items from prior lists onto your current list before you take your list to the store.

- Meet with contractors

  o Using your punch list, **visit with contractors at the job site, and call out everything on your list.** If you are going to do much of the work yourself, you may want to take the time to eliminate those line items from the punch list so that the list you show each contractor contains only the tasks you expect them to do. If you have created your punch list as a Word document, it is easy to cut and paste a punch list for a specific group of jobs. Give the contractor their own copy of the punch list so they can follow along as you walk through the project. They will make their own notes from your discussion as you point to the location of every task noted on the punch list.

Referring to the discussion about team members in the first section of this chapter**, it's important that the expectations you and the contractor have for each other are laid out ahead of time.**

It has always been my practice to *not* **have contractors quote jobs including materials** unless the materials are inherent in the job they are doing. For example, if I'm hiring someone to install custom glass block windows, I expect them to provide the glass blocks. Otherwise, I only have contractors quote the labor for a job. I provide the materials of my selection at my price.

Although I try to list every item that I think we will need when I make my materials list from the punch list, not everything will be known ahead of time. Certainly, I can list everything that involves a style or color choice, but I probably will not think of all the hardware pieces necessary to accomplish the job. Consequently, **the norm is to let trusted contractors charge hardware on my store charges.** As an alternative, they can buy hardware on their own and turn in the receipts for reimbursement, or they can include their purchases in their bill. In the latter case, I would need to see copies of the receipts, but they would keep the originals since they would be writing off the expense while including the entire amount I paid to them in their gross income. If I will be reimbursing them for materials purchases separately from their labor bill, I would write off the total of their labor and reimbursements, but they would only be including my labor payment in their income.

- Buy your materials

  o After deciding which materials you want and from which stores, per
    the discussion above at the end of the SUPPLIERS section of this
    chapter, **make a neat and easy to read list of the materials
    you need and get it to the pro desk at your favorite big box
    store.** Make sure you include each item number, quantity, and a brief
    description with only one item per line. Presumably, you can get most
    of your choices at one store, but you will need to eliminate any items
    on your list that you don't intend to buy at that store before giving
    them the list to avoid confusion.

    After getting your quote from the pro desk, comb through it to
    check for complete accuracy. Make adjustments as necessary, agree
    on the prices, and get on their schedule for delivery. You can always
    delay the delivery if needed.

    For items outside what you can have delivered, if you are supplying
    the materials, you will need to bring them to the jobsite for the
    contractor to use, unless you make prior arrangements with the
    contractor to pick them up.

- Select your contractors

  o **Sign written agreements with your final choices for
    contractors.** In some cases, for smaller jobs with contractors you
    trust, you can just make verbal agreements. Start to get everybody
    scheduled for their part of the project. Obtain each contractor's
    insurance certificate and tax ID number if you don't already have these
    in your files. File a Mechanic's Lien Waiver at the courthouse with any
    contractor who will be hiring subs or helpers.

- Do the work on the project yourself or have others do it

  o When you've got all the above sufficiently organized, it's time to
    tear into the job. Either you're going to spend your own time doing

the work, or you are going to leverage your time by using your bank account to pay others. It doesn't have to be all one way or the other. **You can choose to do the jobs you like and hire out the balance.** But if you have anyone else work for you, there is a certain level of supervision that will be necessary. You will learn to what extent you can trust different people or companies to work on their own, but the general rule is that people do what is *inspected*, and not necessarily what is *expected*.

There is debate about whether to put up a FOR RENT sign while the work is still going on. As I see it, the problem is that people will inquire about the apartment by approaching the people they see working there. **This goes against my rule about not showing an apartment until it's done.** I don't want prospective tenants to see the "before" version of the unit. Also, the workers may not be the best people to show the apartment. Consequently, I make sure the workers have my phone number to give to anyone who inquires with strict instructions not to let prospects inside. If I get approached while I am working there, I identify myself as someone working for the owner. I tell them to call the office at which time I will be able to screen them over the phone before I make an appointment to show it to them.

Having now laid out a step-by-step process for the attacking physical preparation of an apartment or flip project, I wanted to add on some practical tips to help you make decisions about the products and tasks you select for the project. Obviously, these tips do not necessarily apply to a special-purpose commercial building, but they are tried and true for your average residential property.

- Try to **use the same colors of paint** in as many apartments as you can. This takes decision making out of the equation, and allows you to store just a few cans of paint for touchup in multiple apartments. You don't have to use the same color in every room; just stick to the same color for the corresponding room in each apartment. Your favorite white trim paint can be used almost everywhere.

- **Diligently touch up marks and damage to paint surfaces between every tenant.** I am the king of touch-up painting! I typically go about twenty plus years between full interior paint jobs on an apartment. If you don't touch up anything that would catch someone's eye each time a tenant moves, it won't be long until you have convinced yourself you should just repaint the entire room. However, if you take a little time to dab some paint on every little nick, smudge, or repair, the apartment will look for years like it was freshly painted. This applies to walls, trim, cabinetry, and anything you have the touch-up paint for.

- On an apartment that is being freshened up between tenants as opposed to a full rehab, **I have the professional cleaning done first before the repair work is started.** The main reason for this is to be able to see where the paint marks are that need to be touched up. Typically, the cleaners are wiping every mark they see, so many dirt marks which you otherwise may have thought you needed to paint over would actually get cleaned away instead. Presumably, the repairs are not very extensive in this instance, so it's not hard to clean up after yourself, and you don't need the cleaners to come back again. You can roll right from the repairs to the touch-up painting without having to wait for the carpet cleaners. However, **make the carpet cleaners the last people out the door before you start showing the apartment.**

- Using the same color of paint from house to house for flip projects can work as well. Maybe use trendy colors in living rooms, kitchens, and baths but then stick to your usual color for the bedrooms. Leave the unused trendy colors with the house for the new owners.

- **The lower the paint sheen, the less imperfections will show.** The higher the sheen, the more washable the surface. My preference is to use eggshell sheen on every wall and ceiling of an apartment, but to use semi-gloss in baths, kitchens, laundries, garages...anywhere there is likely to be water in use or a greater instance of dirt. All rooms may be the same color, just different sheens. However, for flip projects, since the intention is to downplay imperfections in the surfaces when buyers are viewing a vacant home, I lower the sheen. In this instance, I use flat sheen everywhere except the kitchens, baths, etc. where we would switch to eggshell. Trim paint is always semi-gloss in apartments and either semi-gloss or satin in flips.

- With either rentals or flips, **don't move away from neutral colors to colors** you might enjoy at your own home. You do not want to lose a good renter because their furniture and décor preferences will not go with the colors in the apartment. Stick to either earth tones (like antique white) or neutral gray tones for walls and ceilings. Trim, if it's not unpainted wood in good shape without paint slopped on it, is usually white unless there's a good reason to use another color.

- **Exterior siding, whether painted or new, should also not be a color that makes the general public wince.** Look around the neighborhood and see what fits considering the style of the building. Shutters look nice in a third color compared to the siding and trim. Exterior paint is usually satin sheen. You can go glossier, particularly for trim, but you risk accentuating the imperfections in siding if it's too glossy. Never use flat paint on exterior siding or trim.

- Decks, railings, and similar features made of treated wood can be painted with latex solid wood stain. This is like paint, but it is technically a stain, and it works well when you have replaced some of the wood. Regular clear stains will not give a uniform color on the old wood compared to the new wood. Stick to medium or darker colors that complement the siding color. Light colors show too much dirt. Don't use an earth tone deck color with a gray tone house color and vice versa.

- Other materials, like cabinetry, plumbing and lighting fixtures, door hardware, flooring, siding, windows, doors, and roofing can all be used repeatedly from apartment to apartment and flip to flip. Adjust as necessary, but don't keep trying to "reinvent the wheel" unless the property is unique.

- Nail holes and other damage to walls and trim can usually be fixed by filling with drywall compound. I like the kind that goes on pink, but it is off-white when it dries, so you can tell when it's OK to finish it. If you're using an off-white color, you may not need to touch up a tiny hole.

- **Wiping off excess drywall compound with a damp sponge makes no dust compared to sanding it.** Drywall compound reconstitutes immediately with the moisture in the sponge, and you can easily clean it away down to a smooth surface.

- Sometimes natural wood surfaces develop bare areas from either rubbing or water contact. This is often found on kitchen and bath cabinets. These marks will easily disappear by rubbing oil base stain of a similar color on the affected area. It probably wouldn't be noticeable if you didn't apply any varnish afterward in small areas. Oak bath vanities that have gotten water stained, for example, respond well to rubbing Golden Oak colored stain over the marks.

- Light bulbs are almost exclusively of the LED type now. They last longer, and they use much less electricity. If you've got any CFL (fluorescent) bulbs in stock, use them in for out-of-the-way areas like attics and basements.

- Don't use CFL bulbs in any rooms where you need the light to be at full brightness as soon as you turn it on when you are showing the unit. CFL bulbs take a while to get to full brightness. Don't use too low or too high of a brightness of a bulb in any area. Generally, the brighter the better, but don't make it irritatingly bright.

- Don't fail to provide an adequate number of light fixtures in a room or bulbs within a light fixture. One theory is that **the brighter an apartment in terms of lighting and paint colors, the cleaner it will be kept.**

- Use a coded lockbox to keep a key on site for anyone who must come in to work when you're not there. Be sure to keep an extra key for yourself off site.

- **Change the locks for each new tenant.** If I'm concerned about the former tenant using an unreturned key to come into the apartment, I will change the locks right after the tenant moves out; perhaps using a temporary lock. Then, after all contractors are done going in and out, I will change the locks to the ones the new tenant will use.

- Locks can be moved around from one unit to another, or you can use battery operated locks that can be re-coded. If you create the system early enough, **a master key system can be handy so that you have one key that opens all your locks,** but the tenants all have different keys.

- **Kwik Set makes locks with their Smart Key system.** They come with a small tool that allows you to quickly re-key the lock to the key of your choice as long as you have the old key. Once you learn the sequence, it takes about fifteen seconds. This way, **you don't have to change the lock; you just change the key.**

- If you've forgotten your ladder, and you need to do something out of your reach like changing a light bulb, stand on a couple of paint cans placed side by side.

- Screws holding door hinges can sometimes get stripped out. Using larger and larger screws may not be the solution, especially if that means the flat screw head is too large to go flat into hinge. In this case, use plastic screw anchors in the old screw holes just like for hanging something on drywall.

- An easy way to lift a heavy door into position to line up the hinges, especially if you are working alone, is to use a pry bar under the door.

- **Use good toilets.** Using crappy toilets (pun intended) can lead to unnecessary repairs and wasted water. Toilets are, in fact, a common source of service calls, but they are not the stereotypical nightmare episodes uninformed people talk about. Movable toilet parts, like the ones inside the tank, do wear out, but they are easily replaced. A worn-out flap between the tank and the bowl can cause the toilet to keep running and thereby waste water. Cheap toilets may use more water to flush. My advice is simply to use *better* toilets, but not top-of-the-line, so they malfunction less often and use less water.

- **My favorite is the Stealth toilet made by Niagara.** It boasts an astounding .8 gallons per flush (half that of a regular toilet) and a fifteen-year warranty! As you might guess, the guts in the tank are unconventional, but they rarely malfunction, and they are easily replaced if they do. These may not be available off-the-shelf in your area, but the big box stores offer them as a special order. I might just grab a regular toilet from the store for a flip project, but these are wonderful for rentals and worth special ordering. Surprisingly, Stealth toilets are on the lower end of mid-range priced toilets.

- **Heaved sidewalks are always a concern.** They are tripping hazards that inspectors (especially the ones randomly sent by your insurance carrier when you have no warning they are coming) love to point out. You want to replace them, but pouring new cement can be costly. Also, if the sidewalk section is heaved up because of an adjacent tree, the concern is that you will kill the tree by digging out the roots to the extent necessary to get the new concrete level with the surrounding sidewalk. The solution is to **forget about pouring new cement.** Break out the offending concrete and **replace it with gravel.** You can curve it a little around the tree roots if necessary. But don't use gravel made from tiny rocks; **use what is known as 411 gravel** which is crushed limestone. The advantage is that it is comprised of various sizes of jagged irregular shaped pieces down to almost a powder. It compresses very well, and it doesn't move around like stones do. Then, over time and with moisture, it solidifies into a cement-like form. It works great in driveways as well.

- When trying to decide the extent to which to take your rehab, **give preference to safety-related issues even if they are not readily seen by your potential renter or buyer.** You may be tempted to spend heavily on décor, but safety issues (about which it can be said you should have known and should have fixed) can come back to bite you if left unaddressed. Of special concern are chimney flues, missing mortar or bricks from chimneys or walls, railings, steps, electric services and wiring, plumbing leaks, clogged drains, uneven concrete, window sashes that don't stay in the up position, broken glass, peeling paint (especially if it may be lead based), ruts in yards, and the lack of smoke and carbon monoxide detectors.

- **Use springy metal sash controls to keep windows in position after their counterweights have broken from their ropes.** You could open the casing around an old-style window to get to the weights, but this is unnecessary if you install a sash control in the window jamb. They are a curved, springy piece of metal about an inch wide, and they only cost a couple of dollars at the hardware store. Although they have a little burr on them that is supposed to hold them in place between the window sash and the jamb, be sure to put one screw through them into the jamb so they don't fall out.

- **Don't try to match up the joints when you lay wood or vinyl plank flooring.** Some installers try to have the joints be at the same distance from the wall on every third or so course. This is just another opportunity for imperfections to stand out. Randomly stagger the joints for a more interesting look.

- **Revitalize hardwood floors instead of refinishing or covering them.** You will often find beautiful hardwood floors under old carpeting. People love hardwood floors, so if they are in good shape, avoid the expense of new carpet if the hardwood still fits the décor...especially in a flip. Refinishing hardwood floors by sanding and applying stain and varnish is both time consuming and expensive compared to covering them with just about any other flooring material. However, if their condition is somewhere in between pristine and "beat up and paint slopped with uneven joints," **you can revitalize them for a cost about the same as carpet.** Inquire in your area to find a company that offers this service which involves a thorough scrubbing by a special machine. This is followed the next day by the application of three coats of a lightly stained conversion varnish. This material dries so quickly they can do all the coats in one day! Like traditional polyurethane, it lasts way longer than water-based floor finishes, but it doesn't stink for the three days like polyurethane does while you are waiting for it to dry.

- If you only have a small car right now, you may be wondering about what kind of vehicle to get in the future for tending to your rentals. It's not like you'll need to be driving around with a fully packed truck all the time. It is more the case that you will need to move larger items from time to time such as loaded trash cans, cabinetry, siding, or rolled flooring. These types of items are either too bulky or too long for a car. You can get by for a while having things delivered, but that means you're on someone else's schedule. You can rent or borrow trucks for a while, but you'll get tired of setting that up. The next move is a light truck, and the choice boils down to a pickup truck or a van. I come down firmly on the side of a van because it's an enclosed vehicle. If I'm temporarily moving valuable loose materials, I'd rather be able to enclose them from the weather and thieves. The only disadvantage of a van in my estimation is that there is a limit to the height of the item you can transport. But the only thing I've ever moved that was too high for my van was a refrigerator, which I moved with a utility trailer. However, the last time that happened was in the 1990's. Since then, I've always had the appliance stores deliver fridges.

- An appliance dolly is nice to have, if only to jockey appliances around in an apartment so you don't damage the flooring. It's one of those tools you will rarely use, but when you need it, you *gotta* have it.

- Fortunately, it is now possible to **watch a video on You Tube** about how to perform almost any repair or installation on a property. This is not only useful if you intend to do the work yourself, but you may want to familiarize yourself with the proper way to do a job that you are planning on having someone else do for you.

- As a final touch, I recommend placing a few plug-in air fresheners throughout the unit. Don't overwhelm the place, or people will think you are trying to cover up a bad odor. Cinnamon-apple is my favorite scent.

I could fill a book with nothing but tips on lesser encountered situations, but I wanted to address some of the more common issues that come up while prepping a dwelling for rent or sale. Hopefully, this input will save you from having to think too long about these things when you encounter them, and perhaps you will avoid an expensive mistake.

SETTING YOUR RENT RATE

Your final task before starting to seek tenants is to set the rent. I've talked about being careful not to over-improve your property because there is always a top limit to the amount for which an apartment can be rented. It may be your plan to try to get top rent, or your intention may be to shoot for something less. Different levels of quality will attract different renters in the same locale, as will different locations. Ultimately, **the rent you can charge will be determined by the market created by prospective tenants comparing your unit with other rentals competing for the same customers.**

People will pay what they think is fair, given market conditions. Like the one thing you joke about remembering from economics class, "supply and demand" will determine price. To set your rent for a new apartment you have coming online, or to determine a new rental rate on one you are turning over or renewing the lease, your mission is to keep a pulse on two things. One, you must **keep aware of how hot or cold the market is.** If quality applicants are claiming apartments quickly, it's a hot market. If it takes longer to fill a place than usual, and the applicants don't seem as good, then it's a cool or soft market. Over time, **the condition of the market will be continually apparent to you as you absorb what you are experiencing** with your existing rentals combined with news reports and networking with fellow landlords. In a hot market you can raise rents more aggressively. Not so in a soft market.

Secondly, **you need to be aware of what other landlords are charging for similar units.** This has become much easier now that virtually every apartment that comes on the market is advertised with photos and its rental amount on the Internet. Between the photos and the written description of the apartment, you can easily note the differences compared to your unit. You can compare everything from the number of bedrooms and baths to the square footage and location. Depending on the website, details as to the apartment's condition and many of its features may be listed. Working off an average rental rate for similar units, add and subtract in comparison to your property. **A similar process may be employed to determine the market value of a property you wish to buy or sell.**

This is also the time to consider whether you will offer a move-in special to attract applicants. This is typically only done in a soft rental market when you need to do something, other than offering a lower rent, to make your unit stand out compared to your competition. Examples are giving one month's rent free or gifting the new tenant with a TV or microwave. In the case of the month of free rent, the free month is usually the twelfth month of the lease, and it is credited to the tenant only if they have kept all of the terms of the lease up to that point. The purpose of move-in specials is to create an incentive for new renters, while keeping the monthly rent at a higher amount. This way, you are qualifying prospects based on their ability to pay the higher rent, and later when the market heats up, you don't have to jump a long-term tenant's rent as much to bring it up to the market rate. **Be very careful with offering incentives, and do not make them a normal way of doing business.**

Several websites offer the ability for landlords who are listing apartments, or tenants looking to rent an apartment, to gauge what the rent should be based on general information. The same or similar sites do the same for sale prices of homes. Essentially, they are attempting to ingest the information I was talking about in the last paragraph, and spew out a rental rate or property value. Their estimates can be worth considering, but their input data may not be as fine-tuned as yours would be if you researched it on your own. So, I wouldn't take their results as the final word.

In the last chapter you acquired your property, and in this chapter, you prepared it for occupancy. You've chosen your maintenance team, familiarized yourself with suppliers, set up your office and your banking relationships, finished any necessary rehab, and decided on your rental rate. You now have everything in place to begin interfacing with prospective renters or buyers in the case of a flip house. You are now finally ready to meet the people for whom you have been doing all this behind-the-scenes preparation...none of which was producing any cash. Let's reach out to some paying customers!

4 ACQUIRING TENANTS (ROOFING)

Once you have framed up your rental property activities by preparing your properties for occupancy, you need to install a roof by filling your vacancies as quickly as possible. The sooner your income exceeds your expenses, the sooner your obligation to take money from your own pocket will end. When you enjoy profits from an investment property, you can cover your obligations the same way a roof covers a building. In both instances, your assets are protected.

Acquiring the right tenants for your apartments or commercial spaces will make the difference in your rental real estate investments between a good experience and a bad experience. Most components of a rental real estate operation are not recurring enough to be upsetting. If you have made a poor choice in your insurance, record keeping, or financing, for example, you make the correction and move on. If a repair becomes necessary, you fix it, and it's done. You would be dealing with other professionals when addressing these issues, and none of these examples are likely to be something that would make you sorry you own income property. By contrast, **tenants can get under your skin.** They don't have a professional reputation to uphold in their dealings with you, and often they don't care about their personal reputations. Sometimes, ongoing issues with tenants are not as easily fixed as other problems, **so it is imperative to make good choices when selecting residents.**

An important point might not have been apparent to you when you were reading Chapter Two, PHASE TWO: SEARCHING FOR PROPERTY THAT MEETS YOUR CRITERIA. In that section, I was discussing the necessity to decide ahead of time what type of property you wanted to buy. You might not have realized, however, that I was simultaneously asking you to think about what kind of tenant to which you would want to rent.

It will be obvious to you that this chapter is written primarily for obtaining residential tenants. My assumption is that you are much more likely to begin your real estate investment journey with housing as opposed to commercial properties. However, it will not be hard to assess the interface between obtaining tenants for both types of properties as you read this, and you will be able to glean the parallel application of this information to commercial investing.

While teaching our Landlord 101 class, when we begin the section on tenant selection, I always ask my students to tell me at what point they believe tenant selection begins. They answer things like "when you're looking at their application," or "when you're talking to them on the phone." Both answers are certainly phases of tenant selection, but the correct answer is that **tenant selection *begins* with selecting the property.** It begins before you set the rent, and even before you prepare the apartment for occupancy. This is because **the general features and location of a building will be the first considerations to carve out a segment of the public who will potentially consider living there.** Every person in the world is your potential tenant until you say, "The apartment I have available is located in this building, in this neighborhood, in this city, in this country, and it is such and such in size with this floor plan." When these facts are known, you have made the first step in defining the group of people who could become your tenants. So, since these attributes are readily apparent when you consider a property for purchase, you are beginning the selection of your tenants at that point.

The point is that **you must be comfortable with the type and quality of tenants you will get for a property before you buy the property.** Beyond the general features and location, you can further *affect* the applicants from which you have to select by how the apartment is prepared and presented to them, but do not underestimate or overestimate what your eventual applicants will have to offer in terms of meeting your criteria for being approved to become tenants.

Your objective, when you have a vacant apartment, is to get it rented as soon as possible to the best qualified tenant. Once you have properly prepared the unit for showings, this objective will be met by navigating through the following phases:

- Marketing the available unit
- Screening callers over the phone
- Showing the unit
- Taking an application
- Processing an application
- Approving the applicant and offering them the rental unit
- Signing the lease
- Arranging the move-in
- Move-in day

To this point in the book, I have been discussing setting your criteria for the properties you will purchase. Now it is time to think about the criteria for the tenants who will occupy your units. **Your criteria, whatever they are, should be set before you begin to market your vacancy so that you can effectively screen prospects.** Your criteria are the screen through which you run your thoughts about the applicant.

It is my recommendation that you produce a page of written rental criteria because it will help defend you against illegal discrimination charges should a disgruntled rejected applicant want to go down that road with you. Your requirements may be different from that of other landlords, and they may change over time. Keep in mind, though, that only reasonable legitimate business criteria may be used. **You must apply the criteria fairly by asking the same**

questions of each interested party and using the same procedures to evaluate each applicant.

Having said that, here is my **Rule #1: Do not rent to friends, friends of friends, relatives, co-workers, or anyone whose relationship you are not prepared to lose if your experience with a particular tenant goes south.** You can make this part of your official criteria. It makes it so much harder to maintain fairness and impartiality, not to mention authority, when your tenant has a tool for leverage in your decision making...beginning with your decision on whether to accept their application.

Your criteria should at least cover the following general areas:

- Rental history

- Employment history

- Ability to pay the rent and required deposits & fees

- Ability to provide landlord, employment, and personal references

- Ability to show a photo ID

- Lifestyle choices such as pet ownership and smoking

- Credit history / credit score

- Desired date to take occupancy

- Criminal history

- Number of occupants vs. apartment features

If you are renting a commercial space to a locally owned business, you may be dealing directly with the owner of the company. In this case, much of the rental criteria listed above can be used to evaluate the applicant. Additionally, of course, you would find out what you could about their business experience. With a much larger prospective commercial tenant, you may not be able to get a personal guarantee from anyone, so you must research the company's history as best you can with public records in addition to the financial data they provide you.

PHASE ONE: MARKETING THE AVAILABLE UNIT

Marketing a vacant rental unit involves more than just advertising. It includes everything from the look, sound, and placement of your ads, to the appearance of the property. It also includes your personal appearance and demeanor when you show the apartment. Marketing **is any instance where your company and its products interface with your prospective customers to the extent that your prospects gain an impression or make a judgement about your operation.** Things do not need to cost money to be considered as marketing.

My good friend and author of the Landlord 101 manual from which we teach, John Baldwin, says, "Your goal is to expose your rentals to as many qualified prospects as possible. The key words here are 'qualified' and 'prospects.' Prospects are people who are now actively looking for rentals like yours. And qualified means they have good credit histories, good rental histories, and a reliable source of income sufficient to pay your rent.

You need to have your prospects in mind when you do your marketing, and this gets back to the fact that you begin selecting your tenants when you are selecting a property to buy. **Not only do you not want to waste time or money marketing to people who are not qualified prospects, but your marketing must be appealing when it reaches qualified prospects.** You do not want to fail to play up the features of your property once your marketing efforts have reached the prospects you desire. For example, if students are your likely prospects, you would advertise where students will see your ads, and you would point out the proximity of the apartment to the school. If seniors are your target, you would note that you have a ground floor accessible apartment.

Although you may have in your mind the description of the person to whom you want to rent, there is a caveat. **When you advertise your property, you cannot describe the person for the apartment; you must describe the apartment for the person.** In other words, you cannot say the apartment would be perfect for (fill in the blank with someone's job, hobby, protected class of any kind, etc.) because it could be interpreted that you don't want to rent to other types of people even if that is not what you meant to say. As you might guess, this can get you afoul of federal, state, or local fair housing laws.

You will discover many instances where your activities interface with your qualified prospects to the point that you can consider it marketing. In these cases, you must consider the message you are sending both intentionally and unintentionally. Now, though, let's consider some of the methods available for the *advertising* portion of marketing.

- FOR RENT sign (in window or yard)

  o This would be any sign you post right at the available apartment with a contact phone number. You may also want to post other information such as the number of bedrooms and amount of the rent to narrow down the callers. **Don't post this before the unit is completely ready to be shown unless you are comfortable with people walking in on the workers.** It may be possible to utilize a FOR RENT sign that covers multiple vacancies at one property.

- The Internet

  o **Posting your vacancy on the various websites created for this purpose is probably the most popular and effective method of free advertising available.** Sites allow for an ample description, **including the address,** of each apartment along with photos and videos. Some sites are free-standing in that all they are for is advertising rentals, but others are part of a larger site such as Facebook Marketplace. Ownership of sites can change as one acquires another, and in some cases, if you list on one site, the listing will automatically be picked up by others. The best sites to use are always evolving, so I will leave it up to you to do a search for apartment advertising sites, just as a tenant looking for an apartment would do, when the time comes.

    You can choose the method that interested renters can contact you once they view your posting. Although some sites may not allow your phone number to be visible in the ad, others will if that is your preference. In some cases, inquiries can be sent to you by email through the site, and in other cases they can email you directly.

Different sites have different ways of displaying the facts about the unit, so you need to take your time entering the information to get it right. However, once you have posted an apartment once, the ad can be saved on the site when you take it down. When you have the same apartment come available again, even years later, you can resurrect the ad and update the details.

Some sites offer more than the ability for prospects to contact you. They may offer, usually for a fee, the option for the tenant to fill out a rental application for you to review. Also, the site may sell you reports on the applicants such as credit reports or criminal background checks.

Unfortunately, sometimes scammers will lift the address and photos from an ad and make their own fake posting. This is not usually harmful to you since their objective is to extract deposit money from unsuspecting tenants who quickly find out they've been scammed. If you are alerted to one of these ads, just flag it on the website so it is removed.

Finally, you may want to consider developing your own website if you are a larger company. In this case, only *your* apartments are in view once you have driven the searcher to your site. This can be expensive, of course, but you could create your own way of presenting the information about a particular apartment as well as that of your company as a whole. Also, the way you collect information from the prospective tenant, like an application, can be customized.

Most importantly, though, whether you post on a free site or create your own, is that you need to keep your ad fresh. Most of the free sites will give you the opportunity to "refresh" or "renew" your listing every few days.

- Flyers

  ○ These paper handouts can be useful if you want to advertise the unit to people who already live in or visit the area. You can canvass a neighborhood with information about a vacancy by placing the flyer in public places where anyone interested can take a flyer or tear off a tab at the bottom of it with your number. Laundromats usually have a bulletin board. Places where students congregate is a good example of where to put flyers if you offer student rentals.

    You may want to make flyers available from a weatherproof box or envelope at the property. The more information you can provide ahead of time, the fewer calls you will get from parties who would not have called had they known certain facts ahead of time.

    If you are putting out any printed material, including a QR Code that links to a video or more detailed online description of the apartment is very effective.

- Place ads in a publication or website offered by organizations in the area

  ○ Putting a flyer on a neighborhood bulletin board is free, but perhaps larger employers, churches, or social clubs offer a newsletter or website where you can buy an ad for a minimal fee.

- Word-of-mouth

  ○ If the neighbors to your vacancy, whether or not they are also your tenants, are the type of individuals you also would like to get as your new tenants, it can pay to let them know directly about an upcoming available apartment. They probably will tell people like themselves, so if that is not who you want, don't mention it to them. You may even offer them a referral fee for an applicant you accept, and the same goes for your outgoing tenant.

- Newspaper classifieds and rental guides

  o With the advent of free advertising on the Internet, these methods
  are used less and less. Not only does it cost money to place these ads,
  but the qualified prospects you are trying to reach are not likely to be
  looking at them.

- Broadcast media

  o Radio and television advertising is not cost effective for advertising
  a single apartment, but you may consider it if you have a very large
  apartment complex, for example, that continually has vacancies.

PHASE TWO: SCREENING
CALLERS OVER THE PHONE

**While tenant *selection* begins when you are selecting the property,
tenant *screening* begins when you start to interact with the prospect.**
Traditionally, the aim of your advertising is to encourage qualified prospects to
phone you after they have perused your description of the apartment. Some landlords may prefer interested parties to jump through a few hoops before talking to
them. For example, the landlord may require them to provide certain information in
an online application before it is the landlord who then calls the applicant. Perhaps
this application form is offered through the website the tenant is looking at, but
it could be that the prospect is asked to email the landlord who responds with an
email. The landlord's email would contain a link for the landlord's customized
application. At some point, though, **you are going to start a dialog with the
prospect to determine whether you will take the next step of meeting
the prospect in person...presumably at the apartment for a showing.
The simplest way to begin that evaluation, known as tenant screening,
is to talk to people on the phone when they call you in response to
your advertising.** That said, let's examine the art of handling rental inquiries
on the phone.

- Choose the phone to which the calls will come

  o I love what my cell phone can do, but one of the things I don't let it do is receive calls from people inquiring about apartments I have advertised. That would be too many calls interrupting my travels. My preference is to have the calls go to a "land line" connected to an answering machine at my office. I don't mind answering the office phone while I'm there, but **I would rather answer voicemails left at my office at my convenience than get into conversations with prospects at inconvenient times.**

    There are sophisticated ways to utilize a separate phone number from your cell number in your ads with the result that the caller can leave a voicemail. An example would be Google Voice. One of these methods may work for you right from the start, but the simplest way when you are getting started is to do one of three things (all of which are cheaper than maintaining a second cell phone for inquiries about vacancies in case you were considering doing that):

    - Have an old-fashioned land line connected to a conventional answering machine. This is easy, but no longer the cheapest.
    - Get a phone line from your cable TV provider, and connect it to a conventional answering machine. You will now have a VoIP (Voice over Internet Protocol) phone line. If you bundle it with other services, it's likely to be cheaper than a land line from the phone company.
    - My preferred way is to buy an Ooma Telo device. Ooma is a state-of-the-art phone service provider that uses VoIP technology. To quote their own website, "Ooma is **a standalone device that does not require a computer**. There is no software to install and no need for a headset. Ooma replaces your current phone service and delivers clear, landline quality calling over your existing phone and high-speed Internet connection."

      There are a few different models of Ooma devices, but the main one seems to be the Telo. I suggest you check out www.ooma.com as well as read independent reviews before you make the switch.

Here is how Ooma works:

◇ Buy an Ooma device. You can find them online and in stores. They cost less than $100.

◇ Spend five to ten minutes on the Ooma activation site to choose your phone number, set up your 911 service, and create your Ooma account. There is no activation fee.

◇ If you wish to keep an existing phone number, there is a onetime fee of $39.99 to port your number. The porting process takes a few weeks, so do not cancel your land line account until Ooma takes over the number.

◇ With their basic service, which I have, Ooma charges you a monthly fee to cover the taxes they are required to collect. This fee is less than $10.00, and is less than a land line or a VoIP line through your cable TV provider.

◇ For an extra monthly charge, Ooma has premium options that provide more services like sending you an email every time someone leaves a message.

◇ Once you have completed your activation and number porting, connect a conventional phone to the Telo. I actually take the phone connection from the Telo and run it to the phone jack on the wall which then feeds all phones in the building that are plugged into a phone jack.

◇ Your phones will work like normal, and your Ooma device is now your answering machine. Messages can be retrieved remotely by calling into your number, and they are retained until deleted.

♦ There are hybrids of these systems, such as using a live answering service with a custom phone number that rings to a special phone. Whatever your choice is, **the objective is to maintain a way for you to connect with callers so you can begin screening them through a <u>conversation</u>.**

- Answer the phone or return a call

  o **All your prior efforts—virtually everything we have addressed in this book to this point—are done with the aim of getting qualified prospective tenants to inquire about your vacancy.** Despite your best efforts to the contrary, **you will have many inquiries from prospective tenants who simply are not qualified.** It is rare that one of your first callers after posting a new apartment will turn out to be the one you accept. **Your job is to spend as little effort as possible weeding out the callers to whom you do not want to show the apartment much less take an application from.**

     Screening on the phone is also important for the caller because sometimes, after asking a few questions, they can determine the apartment does not meet *their* qualifications. Somehow, your posting left something unanswered in their minds, but their phone call clears things up. Even so, there will be instances where you accept an application after showing the apartment to the prospect only to have them decide not to take the apartment—a huge waste of time not to mention the possibility of losing an alternate tenant while you thought you had it rented.

     All this points to the fact that you <u>must</u> develop a skill for talking to callers over the phone before showing them the apartment. That first phone conversation can tell you what you need to know before you take the next step of meeting the caller, but you must know what, how, and when to ask the questions. You also must know how to evaluate their answers, and when to just listen to information they are spewing out, even though you haven't asked. <u>Tenant screening over the phone is more an art than a science, and it is critical to your success in this business!</u>

     The key to successful phone screening is to ask the same questions of every caller in roughly the same order. This not only keeps you from anti-discrimination trouble, but also it aids you in organizing in your head the impressions the caller is feeding you. You want to be able to balance each call in the same fashion against the standard you have set for your new tenant.

Your questions must lead to establishing virtually everything important about the caller short of what you can only get from processing an application. Signed applications will give you contact information for personal, employment, and landlord references along with the permission to contact the references and run the applicant's credit report. I believe it is not only possible, but necessary to get as close to knowing ahead of time what the information will be that would be entered on their application should you show them the apartment. **You do not want to waste your time showing an apartment to someone whose application you could have known you will reject.**

If you market well, you will have fewer calls from unqualified prospects. If you screen callers well, you will have fewer showings with applicants you reject. My phone screening is so rigorous that I only have few showings for each apartment before I find an acceptable tenant. Often it is the first party to whom I show it that becomes our newest customer.

Even though each apartment in your portfolio may be unique, the questions you ask can be virtually identical each time you are advertising a unit. You may have a few special questions relevant to one property vs. another, and the answers you are looking for may change for standard questions, but basically you need to make evaluations in the same areas each time you are taking calls to fill a unit. For example, you may need to establish whether they are comfortable with a third-floor walk-up, whereas that would not come up for a first floor apartment. Also, you would be looking for a different answer regarding their income depending on the amount of the rent.

After first asking which property they are calling about, here are the main things you want to establish while doing your phone screening:

♦ **The number of occupants.** You need to make sure the caller isn't trying to put too many people into the unit considering how many and how big the bedrooms are. Familiarize yourself with any local regulations regarding occupancy, or if none, use the current federal guidelines. There are minimum square footage requirements for occupancy, and you may have too few square feet in a bedroom, for example, to allow for more than one person. Also, children of opposite genders must not be in the same bedroom after a certain age.

I am always wary when they seem unsure about how many people would be occupying the apartment. If they say they have a friend or relative who *may* want to take the apartment with them, I usually tell them to call me back after they have that figured out. You do not want to rent the unit to just one person only to find out more people have moved in about whom you know nothing in terms of names, contact information, or background.

♦ **Do they have any pets?** If you have a "no pets" property, and they say they have a pet, establish whether they have a pet you will accept. For example, you may not take cats or dogs, but you might allow a hamster in a cage. Otherwise, the conversation is over. If you allow pets, you will want to establish whether the one(s) they have meet your criteria as far as size, immunizations, spaying or neutering, maximum number, etc..

It is totally OK to require a higher rent from tenants with pets in addition to a pet deposit and/or a non-refundable pet fee upon move-in.

Some animals are not considered pets, and you cannot refuse to rent to someone because they want to bring one of these animals to live at your apartment. Specifically, I am referring to service animals and emotional support animals (also known as companion or comfort animals). Service animals are primarily dogs, and they are specially trained to help the owner perform a specific task or tasks. Think seeing eye dog. An emotional support animal, or ESA, is used to alleviate the symptoms of a wide range of mental health conditions such as depression, anxiety, and PTSD. An ESA may be something other than a dog or cat.

Service animals and ESAs can only be prescribed by a licensed physician or by certain counselors and therapists possessing the required professional designations. The landlord may require documentation of a tenant's disability and the disability-related need for a service or assistance animal, but only if the disability or disability-related need is not readily apparent or known to the landlord. Some tenants try to scam landlords with fake documentation, but you can require them to produce an ESA letter from a local provider (many ESA scams involve obtaining an ESA letter online) along with documentation from a vet regarding the health of the animal.

Therapy dogs are not ESAs. They are essentially pets of an owner who has gotten them qualified to make visits to nursing homes and other settings to provide therapy to those in attendance. Landlords are under no obligation to rent to therapy dogs.

As with all disabilities covered by the Americans With Disabilities Act (ADA) and the Fair Housing Act (FHA), landlords are required to make reasonable accommodations to afford the disabled tenant an equal opportunity to use and enjoy the rental property. If the reasonable accommodation entails making physical alterations to the property (like a wheelchair ramp), this is typically paid for by the tenant perhaps with the assistance of an agency with which the tenant is connected. Allowing an ESA in a no pets apartment is considered an accommodation. **In any event, tenants are responsible for the behavior of their animals** whether they are service animals or ESAs, and the landlord can establish rules regarding the animal. If the animal becomes a threat to others

190   Build Real Estate Wealth

or the property, along with a few other reasons, the tenant's accommodation can be terminated.

Landlords may not ask a tenant who has a service animal or ESA to enter into the same pet agreement a regular tenant would be required to sign. However, an agreement specifically for a service animal or ESA may be used to establish, for example, the rules for cleaning up after the animal, keeping immunizations current, or keeping a dog on a leash. Additionally, **landlords may not require additional rent, pet fees, or a pet deposit for a service animal or ESA.**

Making accommodations for people with disabilities makes sense, and the regulations will help you do this. ADA and FHA regulations are not daunting, and they need to be followed. This section is an overview of the concepts in the ADA and FHA rules, but you should take some time to research them on your own so you are prepared for the very occasional time you may encounter an applicant coved by them.

◆ **Are they smokers?** Smoking in an apartment will lead to odors, additional cleaning, more frequent painting, and the annoyance of other existing or future tenants. Good tenants may move out if they keep smelling smoke or seeing cigarette butts. Prospective tenants may refuse an apartment that smells like smoke from the prior tenant. Consequently, **I will not rent to people who intend to smoke** inside, and in some locations, outside the apartment.

On my first phone conversation with the prospect, I do not ask, "Does anyone smoke?" I ask, "How many smokers?" One of my landlord friends asks, "How many cigarettes do you smoke each day?" If you are going to rent to smokers, these questions will not matter to you, but otherwise you must evaluate the answer. If no one smokes, you move on to another subject. But, if there are smokers, you point out they may have missed it in your ad that it is a non-smoking apartment. They may argue they only smoke outside, so if that's OK with you, you must decide if you believe them.

- **Source and amount of income.** After I have established the answers to the prior three areas of questions, I then ask *what questions they may have* about the apartment after having seen the full description online.

    It is usually at this point that one common question may get offered up. It is, "Do you take Section 8?" If you do not, politely inform the caller that, unfortunately, this apartment is not involved with the Section 8 Program. If you will entertain a Section 8 application, now is the time to confirm the caller possesses an active Section 8 voucher and exactly how many bedrooms the voucher is for. If they say they are only on the list for a voucher, you may as well move on because there is no telling how long it will be until they receive their voucher.

    Section 8 is the name used to refer to the federal government's low-income rental assistance program. Applicants to the program qualify based on income and family size. Having a voucher means an applicant has been approved for the program, spent some time on a waiting list, and now they have the go-ahead to approach landlords to apply for apartments. Basically, the program pays landlords directly for a portion of the tenant's rent. The landlord agrees to a little more paperwork, and they wait longer to get a tenant moved in. There is also a habitability inspection before the Section 8 office approves the lease and at each lease renewal. In exchange, the landlord is assured of timely payment of the Section 8 portion of the rent, and the tenants know they can be kicked out of the program if they don't timely make their portion of the rent payment or if they otherwise fail to follow the lease. Landlords are under no obligation to be involved with this program, so allowing a Section 8 voucher holder to apply for your unit is optional.

Callers may have some specific questions, but usually they just want to know when they can see the unit. There is still a lot more screening to do at that point, so my next question is, "What is your situation as far as employment goes?" From there, you can establish:

◇ Whether they are full-time or part-time
◇ Whether they work for a legitimate employer
◇ What their job is
◇ How long they have worked there
◇ The amount of their typical take-home pay
◇ How often they get paid
◇ Whether their pay can be documented by paychecks or if it is "under the table"
◇ If they are self-employed
◇ How long they have had their business
◇ If they can document their income from self-employment with tax returns
◇ Whether their income is from a source other than a job such as Social Security or a pension
◇ The amount and frequency of income from other sources

Establishing whether the caller has the capacity to pay the rent is paramount. If they cannot pay the rent, it doesn't matter whether they meet all your other qualifications. If you take an application from them, they will have to provide documentation for whatever they tell you over the phone. But, if you can establish at this stage they will certainly not qualify, you can save yourself the time of showing them the unit.

I dig into their answers about income because I am looking for red flags. My enthusiasm for the caller wanes when I hear a red flag, and this can lead to ending the conversation. I get turned off when:

◇ They only have a part-time job. These rarely pay enough to meet our income standard unless added to another applicant's income.

◇ Their employer is a seasonal company, a temporary agency, a family member's business, a newly established business, or an employer that pays in cash.

◇ Their job is seasonal, barely legal, known for employee turnover, in another town or general area from the rental, or is paid with commissions or tips.

◇ They have not been on the job very long (usually a couple of months minimum for service type jobs), they haven't started the job yet, or they want to move to your town, and they are trying to find an apartment before they find a job.

◇ Their take-home pay (not their gross pay) is less than three times the rent (or less than two and a half times the rent when the rent includes gas and electric).

◇ They cannot guarantee they will produce their last few paycheck stubs or go to their employer's website to view their pay history on their phone when they come to the showing.

◇ They cannot guarantee they can show you their Social Security award letter or their documentation of income from sources other than a job at the showing.

◇ If their income is not documentable at all such as "under the table" income.

◇ They are legitimately self-employed, but not long enough to see what their profits are for at least two years.

◇ They want to pay the rent from savings.

◇ They want their application to be accepted even though they don't have a job right now, and **they offer to pay several months' rent in advance.** I need employment in place that shows how the rent will be paid.

♦ **Are they renting a place right now?** From here we can begin gathering information about their rental history or lack of it. Some rentals are well suited for a tenant's first apartment or house, but most are not. Past rental history can tell you a lot about what their future rental history will be, so it's very important to get as much of the picture as you can. If they are renting at the time, I will ask:

◆ **How long have they lived there?** The longer they have been in their current apartment, the better. I am always concerned when they have not lived at their current residence for at least a year because **that could mean they are breaking a lease.** You are assessing whether they like to move frequently.

◆ **Why are they moving?** Ask this, and let them talk. Most answers are just fine, like they make more money now, and they want a nicer place. But it can get really interesting when they start telling you about the problems they have with their do-nothing landlord, crazy neighbors, jerk roommate, abusive spouse, or their own health. Most of these are legitimate reasons to move, but **it's a red flag when they start running down their landlord or start enumerating the broken things in the apartment** "that have been like that since we moved in." You probably don't want to rent to people who whose decision-making abilities led them to accept an apartment like that in the first place.

◆ **By when are they looking to take a new place?** Sometimes people call even when they aren't looking to move in for a couple of months. In this case, I politely explain that the unit is vacant right now, and we are trying to fill it this week. I point out that, since tenants are only required to give one month's notice that they are not going to renew their lease, landlords do not know what vacancies they will have this far in advance. I may offer to keep their number, if they sound interesting, in case we have a vacancy for the month when they need to move.

◆ If someone wants to move in ASAP, and the unit is available, that's great. But, **if they say they want to move in <u>today</u>, that's a**

red flag. This request is usually accompanied with an offer to pay the security deposit and one or more months' rent in cash when they see the apartment. I explain we need time to process an application, and we would not take any money for rent or deposits until we have approved their application. There is always a story behind someone needing to move too quickly, and it's usually not a good one from a landlord's standpoint.

◆ **Have they looked at any other apartments?** This is when they might mention what they have been finding at other places that has not been satisfactory to them. It is your chance to point out that they will not find that to be the case at your property. For example, they might have been turned off by dirty conditions or small bedrooms. Certainly, though, if the same condition exists at your location (like small bedrooms), now is the time to admit that and thereby not waste everybody's time with a showing.

◆ **Did they apply for any of those apartments, and, if so, what happened?** These can be quite revealing answers because you may hear why they rejected a place after applying. Most likely, though, **you will hear the very reason why *you* are going to reject their application.** It could be that low credit score they just told you about or the past eviction in their rental history.

◆ **Do they have some idea what their credit score is?** These days, it is easy to find one's credit score online from a variety of sources like CreditKarma.com. Most people can tell you their approximate score, so their answer may trigger some discussion about your requirements. If you allow low credit scores to be mitigated by requiring the last month's rent or a double security deposit at move-in, now is the time to have the discussion as to whether the caller would be open to that. Better now than later.

◆ When are you (all) available to see the apartment at the same time? **It is a waste of time to show a rental to less than**

all the adults who will be on the lease. If the first showing goes well, you must have another showing for the absent ones to get their approval. Make it policy to meet every person, with the possible exception of children, who will live there. You want all the decision makers there at the same time.

PHASE THREE: SHOWING THE UNIT

Obviously, rentals must be shown to prospective tenants because people like to see and evaluate the apartment or house before they commit to a lease. It's a very big decision for them, just as it is for the landlord who is faced with selecting someone they just met to inhabit a property worth tens or hundreds of thousands of dollars without direct supervision for an extended period of time. Some tenants will take the first property they look at if it generally meets their taste, but most like to look at multiple properties until they settle on the best one for them. **Your job, as the busy owner of a vacant rental dwelling, is to show the apartment as few times as possible before finding an acceptable tenant. Again, I want to stress the importance of phone screening to narrow down the number of people with whom you are willing to set an appointment**. In accepting the appointment to meet at the apartment, the prospect has prequalified the apartment, and you have prequalified the prospect. You want this possible mutual commitment to either fall apart or click quickly. Either move on to another prospect or seal the deal with a lease signing as soon as possible. The elements of a successful showing are as follows:

- Set the appointment time and requirements

  - If a caller has survived my line of questioning during the phone screening, the final matter of business is to set up a time to meet. Set your parameters ahead of time as to when you will make yourself available. These parameters may be influenced by not only your other commitments, but by considerations such as the property's location and whether you will show it after dark or on Sundays, etc.

If the caller has indicated they have appointments to look at other apartments, **try to make your appointment to be *after* all their other appointments.** They are more likely to make the decision to apply for *your* apartment after they have seen the other ones. Or they will know for sure they do not want yours, and the showing will be over more quickly.

To save time, it is advantageous to schedule your showings back-to-back if you have multiple interested parties. Be sure to leave enough time in between in case any of them wish to do applications during the showing. You do not want others to hear your discussions when going through the application form.

Also, it can be a workable technique to set an open house and tell everyone to stop by the apartment during that time. I have never been a fan of this, however, because it would be inappropriate to get into the necessary questioning with individuals while others can hear. All you can really do is tell them to fill out the application and hand it back to you. Consequently, that could mean I leave an open house with a bunch of completed application forms from unqualified prospects to sort through. Also, it could mean that a better applicant than the best one from the open house never sees the apartment because they could not come during the open house times.

o Tell the caller what you need them to bring to the appointment so they will be prepared to complete an application. Explain that, if they want to do an application, you will take the application during the showing. I require:

   ♦ Their application fee in cash. Inform them of the amount of your application fee per applicant so they have the correct amount in cash with them. Carry some change just in case. Ask them if having the fee in cash will be a problem today. Believe it or not, I sometimes get to this point in the conversation and then must delay the appointment because the applicant would not have enough cash for the app. This is a red flag that they may be in the habit of spending all their money between paychecks.

◆ Personal references. Tell them to give some thought ahead of time to who they would use as personal references. You will need names and phone numbers, and the references cannot be relatives. It's helpful if they have this figured out ahead of time.

◆ Landlord references. They probably can readily provide their current landlord's name and number, but tell them you need the names and numbers of their previous landlords. They may need to dig these up, but explain that "the more of this sort of stuff you have, the stronger your application is."

◆ Income documentation. Require them to bring at least their most recent pay stub, but producing the two or three most recent ones is better. You do not need to keep their paystubs; you just need to see them for verification. Let them know that it would be acceptable if they can go to their employer's website where they can display their pay history on their phone for you during the showing.

◆ If their income is from Social Security, require them to bring their most recent annual award letter that shows how much they will be getting each month. Lacking the award letter, they could show you several bank statements which show the same amount being deposited on the same date each month. Similar documentation would be required for income from a pension, child support, insurance settlement payments, or lottery winnings.

◆ If they are self-employed, discuss what documentation they can offer to determine what would be acceptable to you. Usually, this would be two years' tax returns showing at least the net income they are representing they currently are relying on to pay the rent.

◆ Some callers may start to squirm a little at this point, and you may have to reschedule the appointment until they can gather everything. Remember, **income sources must be able to be verified, and you will need their documentation for the verification process.**

♦ Photo ID. If they don't have a government issued ID like a driver's license, I will accept a photo ID from their employer.

Before you hang up the phone, make sure you have each other's cell phone numbers, especially if they have called your land-line number from your ad. Then, state that you will be either calling or texting them about an hour or so before the appointment time to confirm. Tell them you will be doing this from your cell phone, so they should look for the call. Make it clear that **unless you get a confirmation back from them, you will <u>not</u> be there.** Some landlords like to require applicants to call the landlord to confirm, but I like to take control of the process and initiate the contact myself. Tell them to contact you on your cell phone if, for any reason, they have a change in plans, or they are running late.

- Meet your prospect at the apartment

  o Decide if you are going to wear casual business attire (and look like the owner or a Realtor from a management company), or whether you are comfortable wearing jeans or work clothes (so you look like the manager or maintenance person). Unless I am already dressed in nicer clothes for some other purpose, I prefer jeans or work clothes. In fact, **I identify myself as the manager (not the owner) if they ask**. Also, looking like a handy man subconsciously tells them the owners take care of their properties.

  o Intend to arrive a little early to make sure there are no surprises when the prospect views the unit like a mouse in a trap, the thermostat needs to be turned up, supplies were accidentally left in view, another resident's dog must be brought inside, or the like. If you are running late, call or text them to give them your ETA. It sets a good example for communication.

  o If they don't arrive within a few minutes of the appointed time, call them to see what's up. Do not text them, because they are probably driving. Even though people have confirmed, sometimes they don't show up. Being late for an appointment can be big red flag because it may portend how responsible they are at meeting obligations...like paying the rent on time.

- Greet your arrivals cordially, but **do not be overly friendly during the showing.** Give them the impression you are treating them neutrally—not with any favor, and not with any prejudice.

- Walk them through the unit, and **point out any positive features. Downplay any negative features**. If it is a small bedroom, say it is a bedroom. If it's not a small bedroom, say it's a "good-sized" or large bedroom. If something is noticeably worn or dated, don't mention it. If it's new or updated, like the paint, carpet, windows, siding, lighting, vinyl flooring, tub, appliances, then point that out. If there is more than one in their party, try to keep them together as they follow you through the unit instead of allowing them to wander around separately. For safety's sake, try not to let them get between you and the exit to a room or the main way out. Gesture with your hand for them to enter a room first, then stand by the door.

- **This is the time when a great deal of computing should be going on in your brain regarding how you feel about these people.** Watch their behavior closely to see if anything makes your antenna go up. Walk behind them to see if they smell like smoke after telling you they are not a smoker. Sniff for BO or alcohol; it gives you a clue as to what the housekeeping will be like.

- Ask open-ended casual questions to get them to open up. You're looking for their answers to get you leaning one way or the other about them. You need to determine how much or how little you want to encourage them to do an application.

PHASE FOUR: TAKING AN APPLICATION

My preference is to take their application during the showing, so I keep a supply of forms and pens in the apartment. As we discussed at the beginning of the previous section, some landlords require interested parties to fill out an application online before speaking with them. If that is what you have done, and you have printed out the application or you can view it on your device, now is the time to go through it with the applicant to make sure the information is accurate and complete.

In some cases, the prospect will ask if they can take an application with them to fill out and get back to you. People do this when they are unsure if they want the apartment, or as a polite way to say they don't want it. This could be a blessing if you've already decided you don't want to rent to them. **They may legitimately have other appointments set up, however, and they cannot decide yet. This is why you want to show them *your* place *after* they have seen the competition**. You can give them a blank form, but be sure to write on it the address, your contact info, and the rent. Keep in mind you will need to make another appointment with them to get the signed application, collect their application fee, and check their ID.

Getting back to taking applications during the showing, I do something that may surprise you. **I do not let the prospect fill out the form. Instead, after collecting their application fee and checking their ID, I ask the questions and fill in the answers.** This is an extremely useful technique because **the answers will be more complete and revealing if they are speaking the answers as opposed to writing them.** Prying into why they were only in their second-to-last apartment for a few months can tell you a lot of things you need to know. **Almost any innocent question on the application can lead to a revelation or back story that helps you decide whether you will accept the applicant or not.**

Another reason to fill out the form yourself is that you can ensure the writing is legible. This is especially true if you are going to be turning over the application to a third party to have them obtain a credit report. Neither you nor the applicant will be around for the person inputting the data to ask for a clarification.

One protocol I need to highlight is that **I never indicate I know a person the applicant is giving me for any landlord, employer, or personal reference.** Not even if I know their emergency contact who may be their closest relative. This is because I do not want to get the applicant thinking they have some sort of an advantage or that I "owe it to them" now that they know we have a connection. Also, I do not want the applicant to tip off their reference to expect a call from me.

I believe I will get more truthful answers when I surprise the reference with my questions without them having been prompted by the applicant.

Our application form not only is designed to collect specific personal information, but it also gives the applicant an additional opportunity to reveal things which may influence me. I use the form developed by the Apartment Association of Northwestern Pennsylvania, and it has a "Remarks" section near the end. It reads, "If this application initially appears acceptable, the landlord will verify the information provided, and may obtain additional reports and information, including the applicant's credit report, previous rental history, criminal background check, and similar information to determine whether the landlord's rental criteria have been met. If you wish to provide additional information to help the landlord understand and evaluate any such information or reports, you may explain below:"

Since I am the one writing on the form, I do not have the applicant read that statement; I read it to them. I actually change the last words to "now is your chance to explain," and then I look them straight in the eye and say, "This is usually where people start telling me about something on their credit report or criminal history I should know about." Then I shut up. They may have nothing to mention, but otherwise it can get interesting. Now that they know we may be doing a criminal background check, I have had people bring up convictions from everything from shoplifting to murder. They want to take this opportunity to give their side of the story instead of me just seeing their criminal charges on a rap sheet.

As interesting as all this can be, don't get distracted and fail to have them sign the application form. **You cannot process an application without their signature**.

If an application seems to be looking good, and you think you will be approving the application, you may say to them, "If everything on this application turns out to be the way you say it is, I can tell you this application will be approved. I should be able to get back to you within twenty-four hours depending on how quickly I can reach the people you have given as references." This can deter them from continuing to look at competing apartments if they believe they are going to be approved.

At this time, you may want to go over with them your move-in requirements and the sequence of upcoming events. For example, you may need to tell them that, **in addition to the gas and electric services needing to be in their name**

by the day of move-in, you will also require a renters insurance policy to be in effect. You may discuss how you will only charge them a pro-rated amount of rent for their first month if they are not moving in on the first.

This would also be the time to make clear your requirement that they pay their security deposit and first month's rent in full by move-in. **DO NOT agree to "work with" an applicant for the payment of their deposit. If they ask to do this, it is a huge red flag**, as it probably indicates the prospect is low on cash and bad at handling money. If you are otherwise interested in the prospect, you need to investigate why they would ask you to do this. Even if their explanation is satisfactory, explain the owner's policy is that the deposit be paid in full before you are permitted to hand over the keys. If you agree to this request, the next thing is that they will be asking you some month to "work with them" on the rent.

I would caution you against taking any kind of deposit from an applicant before processing their application. Such deposits are typically taken in cash, so if you reject their application for some reason, you will then need to return the cash. They probably would not want you to mail them a check, so this would require meeting up again with the applicant—something to be avoided.

Finally, give each party a copy of your Tenant Selection Criteria to take with them. If they look it over, they may see themselves as someone who will not qualify which will soften the blow of your rejection. Or they may perceive they will qualify, and consequently stop looking at other apartments while they await your call.

As you may be sensing by now, **the design of my tenant screen process from the first phone call to taking the application, is to give the prospect every opportunity, to use some slang, "to blow themselves in" by revealing something that would cause me to reject them**. It is better to be thorough, and reject an applicant whom you initially believed would be a qualified prospect, than to be disappointed later. **I would rather have a vacant apartment than rush to fill a vacancy only to be stuck with a losing situation that could have been prevented.**

PHASE FIVE: PROCESSING AN APPLICATION

After taking a signed application from a prospective renter, the focus shifts to the verification of whatever is on the form which could not be verified when the application was being taken. John Baldwin says, "Be cautious and suspicious." Primarily, this will be in six areas:

- Current and prior landlord references

- Employment references

- Personal references

- Criminal background check

- Credit report

- Other specialized reports

Your purpose for taking an application is to have an organized representation of the information you are using to determine if the applicant meets your criteria. When you are processing the application, **you need to determine two things:**

- Is the information on the application form truthful?

- Does the truth qualify or disqualify the applicant?

Sometimes the entries on the form will tell you right away the applicant is not qualified, but in another instance, you may believe you would accept an applicant as soon as you see their application. It is still necessary, though, to check the information. Even though the facts of your investigation, at face value, present a picture of someone you would accept, **if there were discrepancies between what was put on the application and the truth, this could be a red flag**.

Obtaining the contact information for current and prior landlords is one of the core parts of an application form. This is because, **even more than all the other information on the application, landlord references will give you the best indication as to what experience you will have from the tenant in every aspect of their tenancy.** The landlords prior to their current one may give a better perspective than the current one because their current landlord may shade their comments depending on whether they are trying to help a bad tenant move out or trying to keep a good tenant. Hopefully, though, the current landlord is being truthful and not reluctant to give you an accurate picture.

If I must leave a voicemail for a landlord, I will typically say my first name only and that I am calling because someone has given them as a *past* landlord reference. I say *past* even if the landlord is supposed to be their current one. If I say *current* landlord, the landlord may know exactly who I am calling about because they are aware of who is moving out. Some landlords are afraid of retribution from a bad tenant who doesn't get approved for their next apartment based on their current landlord's truthful reference, so I believe I have a better chance of getting a callback if the landlord does not think I am calling about a current tenant. This is sad because it indicates the landlord has lost control of the tenancy.

Some of the items you may want to discuss with landlord references are:

- Verify the address of the rental unit

- Verify when the tenant moved in

- Which tenants are still living in the unit? (Does this match with who your applicant says will be moving into your unit?)

- Did the tenant ever have additional people move in who were not on the lease?

- Do the tenants have any pets?

- Are any of the tenants smokers?

- What was the tenants' payment history?

- How would you describe the tenants' interaction with other people?

- How did the tenants get along with the other tenants or neighbors?
- How often did the tenants call with complaints? What type of complaints?
- How would you describe the tenants' housekeeping?
- Did the tenants respect your rules?
- Did you ever have to open a Landlord/Tenant action with the courts for these tenants? With what result?
- What was your overall experience with these tenants?
- **Would you rent to these tenants again?**

Employment reference interviews usually do not get too deep because employers are so cautious about what they say about employees. If we have examined the prospect's most recent pay history at the time the application was made, we can establish where the applicant works and how much their pay is. What you want to ask the employer is:

- Is the applicant still an employee?
- Confirm how long they have been working there.
- Confirm the job title and approximate pay.
- Are their chances for continued employment good? (Is the job seasonal or otherwise going to be eliminated, and are they in a probationary period?)
- How would you describe their interaction with others?
- How would you gauge your employee in terms of responsibility, being on time, and following rules and instructions?

Talking with personal references can be very revealing as well. When talking to the applicant's friends, you are trying to deepen your understanding of what type of person your prospect is. **Listen for comments that would raise red flags.** The line of questioning can be similar to that of the landlord references. In addition to whatever seems appropriate from the landlord's list, you may want to discuss the following with a personal reference:

- *How* do you know the applicant? (You want to make sure you haven't been given a relative as a reference, even though you required non-relatives.)
- *How long* have you known the applicant?
- Have you ever visited the applicant where they live? (Note if there are any locations mentioned that were not on the application.)
- Confirm the location of the applicant's current residence by asking the reference to say where it is. (They may not know the exact address, but you want to make sure it is not some other location entirely from what is on the app.)
- What can you tell me in terms of whether I should rent an apartment to the applicant?
- Verify your information about smokers, pets, and housekeeping
- Has the applicant ever mentioned to you anything about problems with their landlord or neighbors?
- How would you describe the applicants' interaction with others?
- Who do you know to be living in the applicant's household? (You are looking for people who have not been named in the application.)

Sometimes, at the end of the phone interview with a personal reference, they may ask the location for which their friend is applying. DO NOT GIVE IT! It is my protocol to say something like, "Thank you for being so truthful with your answers, but **it is our policy to let the applicant let everyone know their new address.**" I learned to do this after a reference, to whom I had told the address, talked an applicant out of taking our apartment because the reference did not like the area.

When I must leave a voicemail with an employer or a personal reference, I say something like, "Hi, my name is Joel. I am calling you because someone you know has given me your name as a reference on an application, and they would very much appreciate it if you would call me back at your earliest convenience." Notice that I do not say what *kind* of reference and *for what* the reference is. **I am trying to get them to call back as soon as they can by making them curious**. If I give the name of my applicant, they may waste time contacting the applicant to see what this is all about. If I'm trying to reach an employer, they may call back sooner if they think it's regarding a personal reference for one of their friends as opposed to just an employee. I keep them wondering as to whether it is regarding a job, apartment, credit, college, or some other nature of reference.

Criminal background checks can be useful for uncovering history that the applicant has not brought up on their own. I find this especially true if the applicant has admitted to a criminal past while doing the application, because often the whole story involves more than just the charges they have mentioned. Nationwide criminal background checks can be purchased online directly or, as in my case, through the local professional association of which I am a member. Probably, your state has a portal where you can go to online with the applicant's name and birth date that will show you any arrests and convictions in your state.

Credit reports, or at least credit scores, are much easier to obtain now for everybody. Like criminal background checks, credit reports can be obtained for a fee from a number of websites either independently or as part of certain real estate management software packages. Reselling credit reports from TransUnion to our members is the primary source of income to our local professional organization, and we charge our members much less than the online sources. Being able to run credit reports on prospective tenants inexpensively through our organization is one of the main reasons landlords join, and perhaps this is offered through your area group.

Instead of, or perhaps in addition to, charging an application fee, some landlords prefer to require prospects to pay for and obtain their own credit reports. Prospects are told what website from which to obtain their report using a credit card, and then the prospect provides the report to the landlord before the application goes any further.

I could go into a long explanation of how to read a credit report, but **I have found that credit reports can be quickly referenced for just two bits of information. First is the credit score** which essentially boils down all the information on the report to a bottom-line numerical rating of the person's creditworthiness. All three major credit reporting agencies (TransUnion, Equifax, and Experian) use very similar rating systems, and generally their scores will all break down as follows:

- 800 – 850   excellent credit
- 740 – 799   very good credit
- 670 – 739   good credit
- 580 – 669   fair credit
- 300 – 579   poor credit

You must decide what the minimum credit score is that you will accept for applicants on a property-by-property basis. The average credit score considered acceptable by my peers here is 650 for your typical apartment. **Often, but not always, a credit score is an indicator of the overall experience you will have with a tenant...not only how they will respect the due date for the rent, but also how well they will respect you and your property.** Consequently, a higher score might be required for a super-nice house, and a lower score might be accepted for a not-so-nice apartment.

As I'm sure you know, credit scores are greatly impacted by late payments, missed payments, balances written off by a creditor, and accounts turned over to collection agencies. If a low credit score is due to any of these black marks, and the creditor is a typical creditor like a credit card, utility, or bank (especially a mortgage or car loan) for example, it means a lot to me. However, I look at a low score caused by issues making payments on medical bills and school loans a bit less critically. Having a medical problem or getting socked with student loan payments is not necessarily a stupid life choice as can be buying a consumer item you can't afford. So, if the other items on their credit report look good, a low credit score may not rule that person out.

Secondly, credit reports show the subjects' past known addresses.
This can make things interesting when an address pops up that is not one of the
prior addresses listed on their application. This could be an address they did not
want you to know about where they had some trouble with the landlord. There
are lots of explanations as to why a related address shows up on someone's credit
report, so it is worth a call to the applicant to give them another opportunity to "help
you understand why the information on their application is not entirely accurate."

**There are other specialized reports you can buy to help you evaluate
a prospective tenant.** One report, which is automatically included with any
other report our members might order through our association's office, is what we
call the Landlord/Tenant check. This report tells us if the applicant has ever been
involved in a Landlord/Tenant action (either as a plaintiff or defendant) at the
District Judge level. There is a national version of this report available for an extra
fee. The purpose of this report is to reveal if the applicant has ever been evicted or at
least had a judgement placed against them by a landlord. It shows the amount of the
judgement, the date, and the landlord's name. Many landlords automatically reject
an applicant who has an eviction in their past, especially if it is recent. There can be
explanations for such things though, the most common being that they were on a
lease with a bad (maybe abusive) roommate, and they moved out. The remaining
roommate messed up, and everyone on the lease was named on the complaint
with the District Judge (as is proper for the landlord to do). Your applicant, who
no longer has contact with their former roommate or landlord, was never notified
of the court action against them, so this is a surprise to them.

It is often the case where a landlord goes to the court to start an eviction due to
non-payment of rent, but the tenant does not get evicted. The landlord would be
awarded a judgement against the tenant, but the tenant would be allowed to stay
if the judgement is paid within an allotted time. The judgement would show up
on any future reports even if it is paid, so you deserve an explanation of this from
your applicant and the landlord.

You should also be wary of finding a Landlord/Tenant record where the tenant
has sued the landlord. Do you really want a tenant who is likely to sue you in small
claims court when things don't go their way?

Landlord/Tenant actions in an applicant's past are most certainly a big red flag because they are evidence of a past failure in the same type of arrangement the applicant is attempting to get into with you. You will even see repeat offenders with the same or multiple landlords, so be especially concerned with these. However, the longer the time that has gone by since the eviction and/or judgement, the less weight should be given to them, but most of the time they are recent enough to give you pause. Predictably though, most prospects will attempt to hide any past Landlord/Tenant actions while hoping you do not run a report that brings them to light, so **it is a prudent idea for you to determine if such a report can be obtained in your area.**

Other types of specialized reports include your state's Megan's Law register for sex offenders, terrorist watch list, and the most wanted list. All of these are available through various government portals.

Once you have processed through the information on the application form, you must evaluate your findings and make a decision to either reject or accept an applicant. Applicants deserve an answer in a timely fashion, but you owe it to yourself to be thorough and thoughtful.

PHASE SIX: APPROVING THE APPLICANT AND OFFERING THEM THE RENTAL UNIT

If you reject an applicant, contact them, and let them know. Keep the conversation/text/email as brief as possible. Give them a specific explanation if appropriate (You didn't tell me your current landlord is evicting you.), but otherwise tell them you had multiple applications and, unfortunately, you have chosen one stronger than theirs. If you truly would reconsider them, you may be able to suggest they apply for another unit you currently have or will have open soon.

If you reject someone due to reasons other than their credit report, you do not have to give them their rejection in writing. However, **if you reject someone due to information you found on their credit report, you are required to send them a statement** that says:

"In reviewing your application, we received information from the Consumer Reporting Agency listed below. The Consumer Reporting Agency's role was to provide us with character background related information about you. Therefore, they will be unable to supply the reasons why an apartment cannot be offered to you. You have the right to request a copy of your consumer report free of charge, within sixty (60) days from the date you receive this letter. You also have the right to dispute the accuracy or completeness of any item on your consumer report.

For your convenience, the Consumer Reporting Agency's address is listed below. You may contact the agency by mail or by telephone. If you contact the agency by mail, please include your full name, current address, social security number, date of birth and a copy of this letter."

If you have decided to accept an application, contact the applicants ASAP. Let them know their application has been approved, and you are excited to have them as your newest residents. (You will find that I like to use the word *resident* when I am speaking or writing to tenants. I believe it sounds like we value them more than the word *tenant*.)

Perhaps, though, you are willing to offer them the apartment under certain conditions, so you are calling them to discuss whether they will accept your requirements. These requirements could be anything from agreeing to a move-in date that is different from what they first requested to requiring them to produce some documentation that is still missing. **The most common contingency, however, involves mitigating an applicant's weak financial picture by offering them different terms** from what you would normally offer to a stronger prospect. Of course, this would only be done only if all the other aspects their application make them a desirable tenant.

There are generally only two scenarios where you would consider offering terms that would give you the necessary comfort level to accept a financially risky tenant. Assuming you otherwise like the applicant, you might consider this if:

- They have a great credit score, but their level of income is just under what you normally require. In this case, you are banking on the tenant's ability to handle money as demonstrated by their credit score, recognizing that the rental payment could be a stretch for them. You would be hoping history repeats itself regarding their bill paying habits.

- They have a low or non-existent credit score, but they have significantly more income than your minimum requirement. Here, you are counting on them being capable of paying their rent because they make more money than the average person would need for that size of a rental payment. You would be hoping that their history of poor bill paying habits does *not* repeat itself, at least when it comes to your rent.

Commonly, in these instances, you can do one of two things to counter the risk you would be taking by renting to a financially borderline applicant:

- In addition to the first month's rent and a security deposit equal to one month's rent, require them to pay their final month's rent at move-in.

- In addition to the first month's rent, require them to pay a security deposit equal to two months of rent at move-in instead of a security deposit equaling only one month's rent.

Because the same amount of money would be given to you (three month's rent), it may not make much of a difference to you which is done. In either case, you are getting one month ahead on the money than you would be under normal circumstances where you only collected the first month's rent and a one-month security deposit. You are mitigating the possibility of losing money if the tenant gets behind in their rent.

The applicant is saying they can handle the rent, so you are asking them to "put their money where their mouth is" by requiring more cash at move-in. It may make a difference to the applicant, however, as to how you term it. Since many tenants believe landlords never give back security deposits, they sometimes balk at the thought of paying a double security deposit. They think it is automatically money lost. They would be required to make full rental payments through their final month of occupancy, and their landlord would have twice the normal security deposit out of which to recover damages. In the other scenario, they know they would not be obligated to pay their final month's rent, and their landlord would be left with the standard security deposit equal to one month's rent.

There are some subtleties to consider when you take extra money from a new tenant to mitigate their weak financial condition:

- Some states have laws that prohibit a landlord from holding onto more than an amount equal to one month's rent after the tenant's first year in the rental. This would mean you would have to credit the extra amount toward the rent for the first month of their second year.

- While your state's law may not allow you to keep a double security deposit after the first year, it may allow you to carry the tenant's final month's rent forward indefinitely until their eventual departure.

- Security deposits are not counted as income for income tax purposes, nor are they counted as an expense when you refund them. Assuming your accounting system is on the cash basis (as opposed to accrual basis), funds collected as the final month's rent *are* counted as income in the year you receive them.

- You must turn over to the next owner any amounts taken as a final month's rent when you sell the property just like you would a security deposit. Funds collected as final month's rent, since they were counted as rental income in the year they were received, are deducted against the current year's rent if they are turned over to a new owner.

- If you receive an amount at move-in designated as the tenant's eventual final month's rent, give them a statement making it clear that, if their rent is higher when they move out, they will be required to pay the difference at the beginning of their last month, or it will be taken out of their deposit. Keep a copy so there is no confusion later.

- Your state's law may require you to credit the extra security deposit only if the tenant has complied with *all* the terms of the lease. So, if the tenant has been messing up, you may be permitted to continue carrying it forward.

- It does not have to be an either/or decision as to whether you require a single or double security deposit. On a number of occasions, I have only required an extra $150 or so on the security deposit for an "iffy" applicant. This would be enough to cover my court fees if I had to initiate a Landlord/Tenant action.

What I have been describing is part of the "art" of being a landlord because the approval process involves some level of subjectivity. However, some landlords prefer to use a scoring system to objectively determine an applicant's acceptability. The idea is that the applicant will be considered further only if they score a minimum amount on a preprinted checklist form. Some of the yes/no items regarding the applicant that are commonly used on such a list are:

- On time for appointment
- Brought all required documentation and application fee
- Application was filled out completely and signed
- All information was able to be verified, especially income and employment
- Able to pay full security deposit and first month's rent by move in
- Take-home pay or other income is sufficient
- Income is stable and the applicant has been with the same employer long enough
- Satisfactory credit score (perhaps extra points for each increment of, say, fifty points above 500)
- Is not breaking a current lease / proper notice given to current landlord

- No prior or current evictions

- No issues with prior landlords including lease violations

- Criminal history, if any, is acceptable

- No pets (if the property is not pet friendly)

- Willing to provide documentation of pet shots, etc. if property is pet friendly

- Is willing to pay higher rent and deposit if property is pet friendly

- Non smoker

This is not an exhaustive list, and you would need to decide your own scoring criteria, but this gives you a place to start.

Once you have confirmed the applicant wishes to take the apartment with any contingencies you have expressed, the next step is to meet with them to sign the lease.

PHASE SEVEN: SIGNING THE LEASE

When an applicant has verbally agreed to take an apartment, I like to instill a sense of urgency to the process. I tell them we need to meet ASAP to sign the lease and collect their security deposit, and by that, I mean later that same day or the next day. **You want to stop taking applications for the vacancy, and the only way to do that is to get the lease signed.**

By this point, of course, you need to have crafted your lease form. Laws vary from state to state regarding what is required to be in a lease or what is not allowed in a lease, so I am not going to attempt to include a usable lease form in this book. Certainly, though, your lease is a legally binding contract for both you and your tenants, so it must reflect the law. I would not advise you to come up with your lease form on your own. Instead, you can obtain a lease suited for your locale from your local professional group, or your attorney. Online resources for lease forms, though usable, may not be as specific or as customizable as you want them to be.

I do not always demand the full security deposit be paid when they sign the lease, but I start out asking for it. Of course, as discussed earlier, the full deposit must be paid before move-in, but it may be reasonable to accept only a substantial part of the deposit when signing the lease. It should be enough to dissuade them from giving up their deposit and changing their mind about taking the apartment. **Whatever is agreed on as the amount toward their deposit that they will pay at the lease signing, require it to be paid in cash or money order. You are not yet ready to start accepting checks from your new resident.** You do not want to accept a deposit check from a new tenant only to find out it bounced after they take possession. Also, if an applicant decides not to take an apartment after signing the lease, you will be entitled to monetary damages which can be taken out of whatever deposit they gave you. **If they stop payment on a check they used for their deposit, you will have nothing to keep for damages.**

Especially if they only paid part of their deposit when they signed the lease, you may want to require the balance of their deposit as well as their first month's rent be paid in cash at move-in. Explain that they can pay their rent with checks or other methods going forward, but it is policy to collect all charges in cash before taking occupancy.

Once you have established exactly how much cash they must bring to the lease signing, set the appointment at everyone's earliest convenience. ALL adults who will be moving in must sign the lease, and ALL of them must be present at the lease signing. The timing could be dictated by the sequence it takes them to gather the cash, such as needing to go to the bank to make a withdrawal. Remind them to call or text you if they are running late or if they have any change in plans just like you asked when setting up their appointment to see the apartment. Especially if the lease signing will not be until the next day, confirm with them an hour or so ahead of time. **You may want to decide to stop taking appointments for showings at this point, but do not pull down the ads yet. Instead, start making a list of prospects you will contact if the deal falls through.**

Since lease forms do not take much time to fill out, I tend to wait to do them until the lease signing appointment has been confirmed. Do your prep when you feel comfortable, but make sure you assemble a complete set of all other needed documents and two copies of the lease. In addition to the lease, some other items to provide the tenant at the lease signing include:

- The *Protect Your Family From Lead in Your Home* booklet as provided by the EPA. This is required if your property was built before 1978.

- Any rules and regulations for the property including your office hours. You may want to have them initial they received and understand this form.

- Emergency contact numbers and procedures for initiating a service call.

- A list of your cleaning requirements at move-out. Explain they will get another copy of this list when they are preparing to move out, but you wanted them to get an idea now what has been done for them and what will be expected from them later.

- Instructions for utilizing the various methods you offer for them to pay their rent.

- Their Roommate Agreement. If the residents will be a married couple, they can sign the lease with no further agreements between the two of them. Married couples have certain legal obligations and privileges if they split up, but **if the residents are not married to each other, it is a good idea to have all sign an agreement to make sure everyone is on the same page as to their obligations** if one of them wants to move out during the term of the lease. Although you require it to be signed by the tenants, this document is not a part of the lease, and you do not sign it.

  I'm not going to provide you with a ready-made form, but here are the main points your Roommate Agreement should cover:

  - Name the roommates, and state they have entered into a lease agreement as tenants for the address of your unit.
  - State the name of the landlord, the lease dates, and the amount of the rent and security deposit.
  - State that each roommate agrees to promptly pay an equal share of the rent, security deposit, and any other charges when due under the lease agreement.
  - State that any roommate who moves out shall continue to pay their share of the rent until a replacement roommate approved by the

landlord is found, but that a replacement roommate will not relieve the roommate who is leaving from any of the obligations of the lease agreement.

o   State that all replacement roommates must be approved by the landlord and other roommates before moving in, and that they must sign onto the lease agreement and Roommate Agreement.

o   State that any roommate leaving during the term of the lease will give a forwarding address to the landlord, and will settle the security deposit with the remaining roommates because **the landlord will return the security deposit only to whichever roommates are remaining at the termination of the lease.**

o   State that **each roommate is 100% responsible to the landlord for paying the rent**, deposit, and any other charges up to the full amount even if other roommates do not pay.

o   State that any roommate required to pay more than their share, due to failure of another roommate, may bring legal action against that roommate to recover damages.

o   Give them a place for all to sign.

If you don't have a business location where you can meet your new residents to sign the lease, either meet them at their new apartment or at a public place where everyone can sit down. **Do not have them come to your home!** My go-to "mobile office" is a nearby bookstore or café with tables where patrons can hang out.

At the lease signing, before I start going through any of the paperwork, I collect the cash they have brought for their deposit, and write them a receipt. Next, I give them any handouts as mentioned above except for the Roommate Agreement, which I will have them sign with the lease. I want to instill in them that we are a rental company with procedures, practices, and expectations. We provide good customer service, and we operate as a business, not a hobby. In return, we expect cooperation and responsible care for our property.

Then, I place a copy of the lease in front of them. My practice is to go through the entire lease with them paragraph by paragraph, so they have a better understanding of what they are signing rather than just asking them to "sign and initial where indicated." **I believe the more a tenant understands our expectations, the better experience we are both going to have.** I point with my pen at each part of the lease form for their reference as I give a summary of the meaning. I encourage them to stop me and ask questions if they have any.

Lease forms can vary as long as they get the job done, but any residential lease should be considered "plain language" so that it meets what the courts like to see in terms of being simple, understandable, and easily readable. Most leases place the spaces to fill in the pertinent facts (like names, rental address, landlord payment address, lease dates, security deposit, which party is paying each utility, etc.) on the first page. I spend some time on those sections to make sure they understand how and where to pay the rent, what the due date is, what the late penalty is, and what the fines are for bouncing a check or getting a pet—all before I move on to the preprinted paragraphs in the body of the lease form.

At this point, **I would like to discuss an important technique you can use to encourage the on-time payment of rent**...or get paid extra if the rent is not received in full by your specified due date. First, I will point out that I have all leases start on the first day of the month, so the rent is due from all tenants on the first of each month. This makes it easier to keep track of who has paid on time, and who is has not. The following explanation of the aforementioned technique assumes the rent is due on the first of the month.

We offer a "prompt payment discount" to the tenant when we have their rent in full by the first of the month. The amount of this discount has crept upward over the years, and we may use a different discount depending on the amount of the rent, but let's use twenty-five dollars for this discussion. Here is how it works:

- We want to get a fair market rent of $700 for the unit.

- We advertise the unit at a $700 rental rate.

- The lease is written with a $725 rental rate.

- The lease clearly says, in a box right next to the box with the $725 rent, the prompt payment discount is $25.

- We require a $725 security deposit which is the "face amount" of the rent.

- So that the applicant does not assume the security deposit is $700, it is explained to them ahead of time (usually when going over our move-in requirements with a solid prospect while still at the showing) the required deposit is $725.

- The tenant pays $700, the amount for which we advertised the unit, if we have their rent in hand by the first day of the month.

- In another box on the front of the lease form, it states that, if the rent is not received in full by the tenth of the month, there is a $25 late fee added to the face amount of the rent.

- At the lease signing, it is clearly explain that they could pay $700 (if they pay by the first), $725 (after the first to the tenth), or $750 (after the tenth). In any case, though, I emphasize that we expect them to contact us by the first day of any month, if we will not be receiving their rent in full by the first, to inform us as to when we can expect their payment.

- I remind them they must mail their rent or start an ACH transaction about five days before the rent is due for us to receive it in time for them to take the discount. I point out they can always send a post-dated check well in advance, so we have it to cash on the first.

- I assure them we will not give them an eviction notice if they contact us by the first of the month to tell us they "will be paying on the fifth which is payday." As long as they pay when they say they will, and don't try to take the prompt payment discount, all is well.

- If the date on which they say they are going to pay is too far into the month (I typically use the tenth as the cutoff), I thank them for letting us know, but I inform them we will be giving them a Notice to Vacate to "start the clock ticking" in case they don't pay when they are saying they will. Our lease states we can give them just a five-day notice to move out before we initiate eviction proceedings due to non-payment of rent. I assure them that, if they pay when they say they will, the notice will go away.

Using the technique of offering a discount if the tenant pays by the first of the month accomplishes several things. First, it allows you to collect a slightly higher security deposit compared to the normal amount of rent. Secondly, it draws an earlier line for when you expect the rent to be paid before there are consequences. This is in contrast to having the rent be the same amount until a late charge is added on, say, the sixth of the month after a five-day grace period. In that model, you will find a lot of your rent gets paid on the fifth of the month. Next, you can still set a late fee to kick in to establish another point after which there will be further consequences. Lastly, the extra income from the disallowed discounts and the late fees is a nice bonus.

Returning to the lease signing, after all parties initial each page and sign at the end**, the government form known as *Disclosure of Information on Lead-Based Paint and Lead-Based Hazards* must be initialed and signed if the building was built before 1978.** The form covers what you, as the property owner, know about the existence of any lead-based paint hazards in the dwelling, and whether you have any reports from the dwelling having been tested for lead paint. If you do, in fact, have any such reports, you must give the tenants copies. The tenant must initial that they received these reports along with the *Protect Your Family from Lead in Your Home* booklet.

Next, move on to initialing any special forms you have such as the Roommate Agreement or Pet Agreement. Remember, both you and the new residents (as a group) each end up with one signed original of all documents at the conclusion of the lease signing appointment. However, in the case of the Roommate Agreement, each roommate in entitled to their own copy with original signatures, and you keep a copy for your tenant file even though you are not a signatory.

PHASE EIGHT: ARRANGING THE MOVE-IN

Rarely is it going to be the case where you give your newest residents the keys at the conclusion of the lease signing. Typically, there will be a subsequent meeting at the apartment on move-in day because there are arrangements that need to be made beforehand. Phase Eight begins as the lease signing appointment is ending, and the date of the move-in is discussed. **Once their desired move-in date is set, they must be given clear instructions as to what their tasks are between now and the move-in.** Here is what I require:

- The gas and electric accounts must be opened in the tenant's name, with the change of service set for the agreed upon move-in date.

- They must obtain a renter's insurance policy effective as of the move-in date.

- They must obtain the required funds for their security deposit balance (if any) plus their first month's rent and, if it is in the agreement, their last month's rent. Additionally, any required utility deposit must be paid by move in. I make it clear as to whether payment will be accepted by check or if cash is required.

If they are taking occupancy part way through the month, typically I will prorate the rent required at move-in to represent the remaining days of the month. However, I would still have the lease term begin with the first day of the upcoming month. This reduces the amount of money required at move-in, but I remind them they will have a full month's rent due a short time later at the beginning of the next month. If their move-in is during the last week or so of the month, I will require them to pay the full rent for the upcoming month at move-in along with all other charges.

There is preparation on the part of the landlord as well. There shouldn't be anything that needs to be repaired or cleaned in the apartment, because, as I have stated, you should not be showing an apartment that is not move-in ready. However, **you must check on what the new resident is doing.**

At the lease signing, I instruct the residents to inform me when they have opened their utility and insurance accounts, so if it is getting close to the move-in, I will call them about this if I haven't heard from them. **It is imperative that you call the utility companies and confirm the change of service as of the move-in date.** The utilities may not confirm the names of the customers into which the account is being changed, but they will confirm the date of any planned transfer.

Often, utilities provided by the municipality such as water, sewer, and possibly garbage collection, must be kept in the name of the landowner. In this case, if the tenant is responsible for these charges, you must bill them for reimbursement. However, some municipalities will allow these accounts to be placed into the name of the tenant. They will send a bill directly to the tenant, and they will copy the owner with a duplicate bill so that you can see if the previous bill was paid. Ultimately, though, property owners are responsible for municipal utilities, and unpaid balances can become a lien against the property. So, if the municipality will do direct billing to the tenant, **it is your responsibility to inform the municipality of the change-of-service date and the new tenant's name.**

If tenants will be responsible for paying any utilities, regardless of whether the tenants will be billed directly by the utility provider or be billed by you for reimbursement, **it is prudent to require a reasonable utility deposit in addition to the regular security deposit.** While the security deposit would be used to cover unpaid rent and/or damages, the utility deposit would cover the tenant's final utility bills. Any unused balance must be returned, but that balance could be applied toward charges for unpaid rent or damages in excess of the security deposit. Similarly, utility charges in excess of the utility deposit could be covered by the security deposit. You would want to talk about your utility deposit requirement when you are outlining the move-in obligations with the applicants. **The utility deposit must be paid in full by move-in.**

It is also a primary concern to verify your soon-to-be-tenants have obtained renters insurance with your required coverage. I will not let someone move in without renters insurance in effect, and I require the tenant to list our company on the policy. I also prescribe the minimum amount of liability coverage they must carry. Despite all the instruction about this ahead of time, often times they obtain the wrong amount of coverage, and they forget to have their agent put us on the policy. If we are not listed, the agent cannot talk to me about the policy when I call to check, so I must waste time contacting the tenant to have them inform the agent to put us on before I call a second time for verification.

At this point, you may be asking, **"Why is renters insurance so important?" Please read on carefully, because understanding renters insurance is a key part of prudent tenant management.**

For those who have never rented, or if you did rent, and you never purchased renters insurance, let me first describe the coverage I am referencing. Renters insurance offers coverage nearly identical to homeowners insurance, except that it is meant for people who rent their residence as opposed to those who own their home. Renters insurance is much less expensive than homeowners insurance, though, because it does not cover the building. The landlord's policy covers the building, but it does not cover the tenant's possessions from theft, fire, or any other peril. Consequently, the renters policy covers a tenant's possessions (at the level of coverage they choose) along with other benefits such as paying for a temporary place for a tenant to live while their unit is being repaired after a fire or storm. A renters policy may only cost the tenant a couple of hundred dollars per year, but the premium is likely the same no matter where the tenant lives. However, the landlord's policy on the property costs much more, and the premium is based on the value of the building among other factors. Property casualty insurance on a rental also includes, along with other coverages you can choose, payment for rent lost while your property is being repaired after a covered loss while the tenants cannot live there.

From a landlord's perspective, the most important part of a renters insurance policy is the liability coverage afforded the policyholder...your tenant. This is the part of their policy that will cover them for obligations they would have to their landlord due to an accident or the tenant's negligence. Tenants seldom have the money to pay the landlord for big-ticket damage, so the claim ends up as a claim on the landlord's property policy. **Claims are to be avoided on your policy when possible, because the number of claims you have (not necessarily the dollar amounts of the claims) is what determines whether your insurance company will renew your policy and what your new premium will be if they do renew it.** So, if a tenant's child sets your apartment on fire with an unattended candle, their renters policy will cover the rebuild, and your insurance company doesn't even need to know about it!

Some insurance companies offer renters policies that cover virtually every peril a tenant can accidentally or negligently inflict on their landlord's property, but most only offer coverage if the event involves fire, smoke, or explosion. In addition to an outright fire, those events include, for example, things like cigarette burns on a carpet or countertop, smoke damage from a fire on the stove, and cabinet damage from a toaster oven. **A policy with liability coverage for more than just fire, smoke, and explosion is better, but you cannot dictate to the tenant where they buy their insurance; you can only require them to get the insurance and you can set some coverage requirements.** As a catch-all for smaller miscellaneous claims, renters policies typically have a section called something like "Damage to Property of Others" with a much smaller limit of only $250 to $1,000. I have gotten claims paid under this section for events not otherwise covered by the main liability section of the policy such as water damage from a burst pipe when the tenant left the furnace off during a winter vacation.

Another reason to require tenants to carry renters insurance is so they will receive money from their policy to replace their possessions under a covered loss. Quite frankly, my concern is that the tenant can buy a replacement for their stolen television without having to take it out of the rent money.

Here are my protocols with residents regarding renters insurance:

- The new resident must acquire (or transfer) a renters policy that is in force on the property they will be renting from me as of the day of move-in.

- I recommend they begin shopping for renters insurance from the same carrier with which they already have other insurance such as their car insurance. Having more than one policy can get them a multi-policy discount on all policies. However, with a little shopping, they may find a better deal from another carrier despite the potential multi-policy discount savings.

- **I require them to list our company on the policy as something like "Additional Interest," "Certificate Holder," or "Third Party Interest."** This requirement is similar to how your lender requires that it be listed on your property policy if you have a mortgage.

  I used to believe there was an advantage to being listed as "Additional Insured" on renters policies because of the added protection in a case where the tenant became liable to a third party due to an occurrence on your property. The tenant's carrier (as opposed to your own property insurance carrier) would then be obligated to defend you along with the tenant if the claimant named you along with the tenant in their suit just because you own the property. However, after learning a shocking lesson when a tenant's carrier refused to pay a routine claim for cigarette burns on the carpet, **I no longer have us listed as "Additional Insured."** The way the insurance company got out of paying the claim was to point out that the tenant *and* our company were *both* considered to be *Insureds* on the policy, and the policy clearly states that it will not cover a liability that arises between parties insured by the policy...even though it was obvious we were the landlord. If we were an "Additional Interest" instead of an "Additional Insured" they would have paid the claim!

Any sort of listing of our company on the policy will accomplish what I am trying to do. **I need to be listed on the policy so that I will receive a notice from the insurance company if the policy is going to be cancelled for any reason.** The tenant may decide to switch carriers, but the most common reason for this notice (which the law requires be given to all parties on the policy) is non-payment of premium. When you receive a notice to the effect that your tenant's renters policy is going to be cancelled as of a certain date, you have time to contact the tenant regarding their plans to bring their account current, and **prevent the policy from cancelling**.

- **I require their liability coverage to be the standard limit offered by the carrier which is closest to what it would cost to rebuild the property if they totally destroyed it.** The difference in premiums for the tenant is very minimal between standard levels of coverage. Do not let them get a policy with the smallest standard level of coverage offered by the carrier, because that is likely to be only $50,000 or $100,000.

- I instruct them to inform me as soon as they obtain their policy. They must provide me with their agent's name and phone number, or as in the case of insurance purchased online or over the phone, they must provide the carrier's customer service phone number (which may be different from the number used to purchase insurance) along with their new policy number.

- **I call the agent and verify** our company name and address is on the policy, and that our information is spelled correctly with the proper address (sometimes tenants get this wrong). I also confirm the limit on the liability coverage. For policies they have purchased online or over the phone, I use the customer service number and the policy number combined with information from the tenant's rental application to work my way through the phone menu to get to a live person. I ask for proof of insurance to be faxed or emailed that day.

- **I require the insurance to remain in force at all times** as long as the residents are in control of the apartment.

- If I get a notice of cancellation from a carrier due to non-payment of premium, I wait one day, and then I contact the tenant. I wait one day because it is likely they received the same notification from their carrier on the same day I did, and I want to make sure they have seen it. Hopefully, when I call, they have already made up their late payment.

- If they have not brought their account current, I try to get a commitment as to when it will be taken care of. I make a note of the date they give me. Each state has a law that dictates how quickly an insurance company can cancel a policy due to non-payment. Often it is thirty days, so there is ample time to reverse the cancellation status by paying the past-due premium.

- If a resident has told me they have already made up their payment, or if they give me a date by which they will do so, I call their insurance agent (whose name and number will be listed on the cancellation notice), and ask whether a payment has been received since the cancellation notice went out.

- If the resident has not, in fact, made the payment they said they would, I relentlessly repeat this process until I get confirmation from the insurance company that the policy is no longer in danger of being cancelled.

- If a resident allows a policy to lapse, it is a violation of the lease. I would give them a notice to vacate per the terms of the lease. It is *that* important. **I would rather have a vacant unit than an occupied unit with no renters policy in force.**

Once the renters insurance coverage checks out, and the necessary utility accounts have been opened, we can proceed with confirming the time of the move-in. This is an exciting time for the new residents, so I try to keep the interaction upbeat.

PHASE NINE: MOVE-IN DAY

When confirming the time of the move-in, I make sure they are clear on what the dollar amount is for them to bring, and the forms acceptable for the payment (cash, money order, cashier's check, or personal check). The move-in meeting should occur, of course, at the apartment where you can show them any particulars about their new residence.

Especially if it has been more than a few days since the last time I was at the unit, **I try to arrive several minutes in advance of the appointed time to check things over.** I look for any "surprises" I don't want the new tenants to see such as a spider in the tub or a smoke detector that needs a new battery. There should be nothing that still needs done in the apartment at this point. Even the locks should have been changed by now to avoid any issues with keys or lock hardware in front of the tenant.

After collecting their balance, and writing them a receipt, now is the time to show your newest residents anything special they need to know. You want to head off unnecessary calls, plus you want to ensure they know how to operate any equipment. Here are the typical things I cover:

- How and how often to change the furnace filter (Be sure to point out how the arrow on the filter must face the furnace.)

- How to check and change the batteries in smoke and CO detectors

- Where the fire extinguisher is located

- How to operate the triple-track storm windows (This includes the placement of the window sections and the screen in the winter position vs. the summer position, as well as how to remove the sections for cleaning.)

- How to change the screen position on a vinyl replacement window as well as how to tip in the window sections for cleaning

- How to turn on the gas valve for the dryer hookup including where to store the plug or cap I have at the end of the pipe when they hook up their flex line

- How to determine which breaker has popped, and how to reset it

- A reminder about keeping a screen for hair over the tub drain

- How to operate the main shutoff valve for the water

- An introduction to neighbors, if appropriate

- Call in any required meter readings to the utility companies

Some landlords find it to be an effective practice to fill out a Move-In Checklist form during the walkthrough. The purpose is to document the condition of the unit when the new resident takes possession. Have them sign and date the form, and place it in their file. The same form can be used at move-out for your reference in determining any damages for which the tenant is responsible.

Finally, it is time to turn over the keys. I bring my copy of their lease with me because I have them initial the number of keys I am giving them. **My practice is to provide one key for each adult plus one extra key. I inform them the extra key is for them to hide outside or give to someone to whom they have twenty-four-hour access. I look at them and say, "If you lock yourself out, DO NOT CALL ME, because I don't do lockouts!"** I tell them

I would recommend a locksmith if they called me when they are locked out, or if I am even available to come and let them in, I would have a hefty charge.

Now is the time to leave your excited residents to themselves. Before you leave, make sure you take down your FOR RENT sign, and remove the lockbox from the doorknob.

At this point, you have completed another tenant selection process. Your selection journey began when you first considered the type of property to buy, and it continued through preparing, marketing, screening, showing, applying, processing, approving, signing, and moving in. You now have permission to pull down your ads for this unit.

When I teach our Landlord 101 class, we cover tenant selection in the second session. I stress the importance of stringent applicant screening, and we spend a lot of time on the techniques. At the beginning of the third session, after I've drilled into them the importance of eliminating weak prospects in the prior session, I read them the following essay I wrote about what mindset you must maintain when choosing who will occupy your property.

Your success and happiness as an investor in rental real estate is dependent directly on tenant selection. Unless your game is to buy land and hold onto it until you can sell it at a gain, at some point you will have to select a tenant. **Tenant selection began when you were contemplating investing in rental real estate**, and it continues through evaluating prospective properties, purchasing the property, preparing it for occupancy, marketing it, screening interested renters, and evaluating applications. At that point, you must make a decision about the rental application you have your eyes on. Some decisions will be obvious when it comes to whom to turn down, and some will not be. Your mission is to eliminate every person in the world until you end up with someone who is likely to pay the rent on time and not beat the place up. You are going to let this person occupy and use something you own that is worth tens of thousands—perhaps millions—of dollars without your direct supervision for an extended period of time. **Don't work to qualify an applicant. That's *their* job. Your job is to keep trying to disqualify them until you run out of things that would eliminate them.** Then, you *may* have a good applicant, but only time will tell.

Now that you have cash coming in from an occupied unit, you must not only manage your money...you must manage your property and your residents. In the next chapter, I will take on the "M word."

5
PROPERTY MANAGEMENT (UTILITIES)

You must begin to install the utilities in a structure once the roof is completed. Utilities, such as electricity, natural gas, and plumbing to name a few, form the connection to systems that allow the occupants to make use of, or get utility out of, the building. Utility systems are relied on to routinely do their jobs the same way every time, as we need them. We don't think about them much until they are suddenly off, and then we must focus on alternative means of continuing to get use out of our building until the systems are working again. For example, we may use a generator when the electricity is off or a space heater when the gas is off. In extreme situations, we would abandon the building.

In the last chapter, you protected your investment by installing a roof over your rental property activities in the form of acquiring tenants who provide the cash flow to meet your obligations. **In the same way that utility systems make a structure habitable, management systems keep you in the rental real estate business.** Certainly, you must be prepared to pivot to an alternative way of doing things if a system becomes outdated. But when your systems fail, it will make you want to give up and abandon what you have been building. **Real estate operators must stay connected to good management systems that are routinely employed the same way, every time.**

It is my guess that the prospect of doing property management and tenant management is where you have the most self-doubt. Other phases like property acquisition and financing, which have a beginning and an end, can be stirred up at will when you become interested in a property. Management, on the other hand, goes on every day you own property. Just like with the "back office" management of the paperwork and bookkeeping, **you must consistently employ good management techniques, or you will find yourself selling your property to another investor at a "don't wanter" price because the property and the tenants got the best of you.**

Notice I have been mentioning property management and tenant management separately. In the big picture, they are inextricably intertwined since one is continually affecting the other. As long as you have both a property and a tenant, you will be doing both at the same time. **If you want to keep a nice property, you must manage your tenant. If you want to keep a good tenant, you must manage your property. However, property management and tenant management are separate sets of tasks done on independent schedules.**

As the rental real estate business progresses through the Internet age, **entrepreneurs are continually creating online based programs that integrate property and tenant management.** The use of these programs is subscription-based for a fee, although there are some free ones out there. They are something to consider as you buy more and more units while balancing the cost with the convenience and time saving they offer. The best programs combine the keeping of tenant records (leases, payment accounts, and other documents), the ability for prospects to apply for vacancies online, an online rent payment platform, a maintenance request portal, and a bookkeeping system for the owner. At this writing, some of the popular ones are AppFolio, TenantCloud, RentRedi, TurboTenant, Buildium, and RealPage. I hope they are as good at doing what they promise as they are at putting a capital letter in the middle of their name! Innago is for smaller landlord operations, and it is free.

For our purposes, let's say that property management refers to the activities related to the physical upkeep of your property including repairs, upgrades, regular maintenance, expansions, and the like. **You selected your property because you believed you would be proud to own it, so you manage your property to keep it the way you want it.** Tenant management, on the other hand, points to handling your interactions with your tenants on matters like maintenance requests, lease renewals, rent collection, problems with neighbors, and enforcing the lease terms. **You selected your tenants because you believed they could be the kind of tenants you want, so you manage your tenants to keep them from becoming the tenants you don't want. The more skillfully either side of the management equation is performed, the less the other side will need attention.** After we tackle both areas of management, we are going to have a little "heart-to-heart" about management philosophy.

PROPERTY MANAGEMENT

The physical upkeep of your properties involves both planning and reacting. Some of what you do to keep your properties looking and operating like the place where your tenants want to live will be either planned as an optional one-time project, or planned as required routine or recurring maintenance. Your remaining efforts in this area will be unplanned, but necessary, repairs that you either discover on your own or that are reported to you by your tenants. **Both sources of upkeep activities require systems to be in place to minimize getting behind on things needing to be done regularly and to eliminate panic from emergencies.**

When you have good systems in place for addressing the regular needs of real estate properties, the result will be that lists of daily, weekly, monthly, and yearly requirements will generate schedules. **Knowing the schedules in advance will allow time to arrange for the right people to perform the work and for the right materials to be acquired.** Cash flow planning is a part of this, so that the money is there to pay for the projects when they are completed. Discussing the routine needs of a property with whomever is selling it to you is helpful, but as you operate a property, you will develop your own lists. Your established systems can be blended into a new property to create the lists that work best for you. Your objectives with your routine management lists are:

- Accomplish regular maintenance tasks before they become urgent, and certainly before tenants notice any issues. You want to **stay in the "plan to do it" zone and out of the "must do it soon" zone.**

- Level the workload and cash needs through thoughtful scheduling. **The more you stay in control, the less of a weight on your landlording experience.**

When you have good systems in place for addressing unplanned repairs, the result will be the immediate implementation of set procedures and protocols to handle the situation. **Knowing what to do, who to call, where to get the materials, and what to tell the tenants without having to "wing it" will not only take the anxiety out of the unexpected service call, but it will also impress your tenants.** Again, you will want to establish your own systems as you go along, always looking to improve, refine, and simplify. Your objectives with your unplanned management lists are:

- Attack newly discovered repair issues quickly, commensurate with their perceived degree of urgency, with the least disruption to the tenants' lives.

- Make sure everyone who may be involved in the sequence, from reporting the need for the repair to reporting the completion of the repair, knows what to do.

- **Tenants must be instructed at the lease signing as to what to do if they have a maintenance issue,** and they should be reminded of your procedure from time to time—perhaps along with other communications you send to your tenants.

- Contractors also must be educated on your procedures, expectations, and on what to say to tenants.

- **Anyone, such as any staff who would be taking a communication from the tenant, must be knowledgeable of how to put the wheels in motion with a response to the tenant and a call to the right person to perform the repair.**

Essentially, **handling planned and unplanned building repairs/maintenance/improvements involves integrating the list of contractors and suppliers (as discussed in Chapter Three) with schedules and protocols.** My procedures for service calls are detailed at the end of the REPAIR AND MAINTENANCE TEAM section of Chapter Three, so I won't repeat them here.

Some items on your list of required periodic maintenance on your buildings will come from physical inspections. An example would be the roof, which you will replace on an as-needed basis, not on a set schedule. However, at some point in the roof's life, the act of inspecting the roof periodically should be a line item on your schedule. Other periodic maintenance on your list makes it onto someone's schedule on a set interval. An example of this would be the spring cleanup of landscaping.

This is a sampling of elements of rental property maintenance that generate regular entries on your schedule or that of contractors working for you. Again, some are at set intervals for predetermined individuals. Some are routine, but done as needed only after you give the go-ahead to a contractor. Remember, unless it's an emergency, you must give tenants reasonable notice before entering their dwelling—typically 24 hours.

- Interior and exterior painting

  o It would be rare to do interior painting while a unit is occupied. This would most likely be done between tenants. However, any paint exposed to the elements will need repainted from time to time, but probably not on a set schedule. **If you are planning to keep a property for many years, it pays to use the best paint you**

can find because increased durability will allow more years in between paint jobs. Also, especially for interior paint, cleaning marks off walls and just touching up the dings in between tenants can keep you from doing a full paint job for decades.

- Updating of old windows with vinyl replacement windows

  o Tenants will be impressed with modern windows. Unless your building has really decent original wood windows coupled with modern storm windows (with ALL the storm and screen sections in place), I recommend updating them with vinyl replacement windows. This is most easily done between tenants, but existing tenants will put up with the disruption because new windows are such an improvement for them. Window replacement is most likely a one-time event for you, and it can be attacked gradually.

- Roofs

  o While roofs can go decades between replacement, even new roofs can develop problems from storm damage. Springtime (or post weather event) inspection from at least ground level should be routine.

- Gutters and downspouts

  o Proper functioning gutters and downspouts are paramount to keeping basements and certain exterior areas dry. They may last as long as your roof, but they also must be checked for damage at least annually.

- Install aluminum or vinyl siding over existing siding

  o This is always a great update. While I may replace the windows without doing the siding, I never recommend doing the siding without replacing old-style windows. The window trim will need to be capped with aluminum when the windows are replaced, and it is such a nicer job if this is done before new siding is applied.

- Capping soffit, fascia, and trim with aluminum

  o If you have nice original siding, but your soffit and fascia are in bad shape, covering these areas with (usually white) aluminum will sharpen the curb appeal even if the siding remains the same. Typically, you would replace the gutters and downspouts at the same time.

- Deteriorated mortar between bricks on chimneys and house exteriors

  o Brick exteriors and chimneys can go several decades before this may need to be addressed, and there is typically plenty of notice that things (usually in a specific area, and not the whole exterior) need attention. Missing mortar can cause walls to shift and not be weathertight. Bricks can fall from chimneys, either onto the ground or into the chimney. In extreme cases, chimneys can topple. Mortar can be dyed to match the older mortar, so your repair areas don't stand out.

- Rotted wood in decks, railings, and steps

  o This is not only an appearance issue; this could be a safety issue for the tenant. To reduce liability, **steps and railings must be repaired at once when an issue is discovered, even if it is not a permanent fix.** If you do a lot of wood replacement, you can unify the color with a latex solid deck stain over the entire deck. This product is in between regular paint and tinted stain in that it looks and applies like paint, but it absorbs into the wood for protection like stain. The colors are "solid" as opposed to tinted stain, so the grains and imperfections in the wood are covered.

  o Presumably, pressure treated wood that resists deterioration was used to construct your decks, railings, and steps. Be sure any treated wood used for repairs is reasonably dried out before applying any paint or stain.

  o Unstained treated wood can be pressure washed when it weathers and appears too gray. The wood remains viable for many years, and pressure washing can bring it back to its initial beauty...perhaps to the degree that repairs done with new wood will be barely noticeable.

- Deteriorated concrete or asphalt driveways, parking lots, sidewalks, and steps

  - Not only is pavement unsightly when it is chipped, cracked, rutted, heaved, or shifted, it can be a safety issue. So much so that if your property insurance carrier ever sends a random field rep by your property for a surprise exterior evaluation, you may get a notice to repair it if they think it is a tripping hazard, or they will cancel your insurance. Asphalt can be patched, repaved, sealed, and re-striped. Concrete can be skim-patched, dug up and re-poured, and even large cracks or gaps can be filled with self-leveling caulk.

  - Cement steps, sections of cement sidewalks, and even whole poured decks that have sunken unevenly can be leveled. This is done by companies that drill small access holes, inject their special product hydraulically under your uneven concrete to raise it, and then fill the holes like it never happened. Way less expensive than digging up and re-pouring the concrete.

- Gravel in parking areas

  - These areas get rutted over time, and weeds can grow in the untraveled areas. An all-vegetation killer/pre-emergent spray works best because it not only kills the existing weeds, but it prevents new growth for up to a year.

  - New gravel must be spread over existing occasionally. Some like to use pea gravel or marble chips, but I like #411 gravel. This is crushed up #57 stones combined with rock dust. Over time, with weather and traffic, it hardens almost like concrete, and it doesn't shift around as much during snow removal. By comparison, pea gravel and marble chips never stop shifting around.

- Filters of any kind (HVAC, water, pool)

  - Furnace/air conditioning filters must be changed regularly, not only for efficient heating and cooling, but a severely clogged filter can damage the furnace. **I make it clear to tenants it is their responsibility to regularly check, purchase, and change the furnace filters just like they change their own lightbulbs**. I point out that this is to their advantage because, after all, it is their heating bill that will go up if the furnace is working too hard to move the air, and they don't want to be responsible for a furnace repair caused by a severely clogged filter. **A demonstration of how to change the filter is part of the move-in process**. Also, in September we send out a letter to each tenant reminding them about the importance of changing the filter, along with any pertinent news.

o If you have any in-line water filters in your plumbing system, you probably will need to put them on your maintenance schedule. Replacing these regularly is probably beyond what you can demand from tenants. Same with pool filters, especially if it's a community pool.

- Pools

  o Pools, of course, need daily monitoring of chemical levels and temperature. But regular checks of the mechanical components of a pool are important as well. This includes not only the moving parts like the pump and the heater, but also the stationary features like ladders, slides, and lights.

    In the larger picture, repainting concrete pools or the replacement of liners must be planned for, along with the replacement of solar covers and winter covers.

- Water wells and septic systems

  o Wells must be chlorinated by dumping bleach into the well to kill germs now and then, and septic tanks must be pumped out on a schedule. You can do the former, but call a professional for the latter.

  o Another practice you should put on your regular schedule if you have a septic drain field is to regularly flush a yeast product down a toilet. This product helps promote the necessary process in the system of breaking down solids. Doing this can pay for itself by improving the operation and longevity of the system.

- Electrical fixture and service updates

  - One of the easiest things you can do to give a mini rehab to an apartment is to update the lighting fixtures along with the switches and outlets. New colors become popular, while older ones can make a place look dated. Of course, in between tenants, replacement of broken shades, outlet covers, etc. is a common task.
  - Updating the electrical service (replacing the fuse box with a breaker box) should be on your long-term list along with eliminating ancient knob-and-tube wiring. Check with your local authorities as to any permit requirements.

- Plumbing fixture updates

  - What I just said regarding electrical fixtures also applies to faucets. Like replacing fuse boxes, eliminating galvanized water pipes, and replacing them with copper or PEX (Cross-Linked Polyethylene), should be in your master plan. PEX is a godsend for quick and easy water line replacement—especially when you've got to snake it through an offset or hard-to-reach cavity. It is reinforced plastic, and it comes in colors with a system of connectors that can also be joined to other types of existing piping if necessary.

- Tree and shrubbery trimming, removal, or additions

  - Naturally, these items are constantly either growing or dying. Not only must they be on a regular maintenance list for trimming and spraying, but they must at least annually be evaluated for removal or replacement. Even if your lease requires your tenants to do all the lawncare, you probably must keep the trees and shrubs in your own purview.
  - Periodic inspections may reveal dead branches that could damage property when they fall, or live branches that must be cut away from buildings.

- Landscaping seasonal maintenance

  - Mostly, this refers to the annual spring and fall cleanups. But on your list should be any necessary mulching, re-seeding, fertilizing, or aerating.

- Lawn damage

  - This can refer to a sudden event like a car going off the road and making ruts in the grass, or it could be when grass has died due to lack of water or accidental over-fertilization. Either way, if Mother Nature isn't going to take care of it, you must.

- Mowing and snow removal

  - If you are renting out a single-family residence, it is reasonable to require your tenants do their own mowing and snow removal. Early on, I tried to get residents at our two-unit properties to figure out the mowing between them. In some cases, I required them to have their own mowers, and for others, I tried supplying the mower for their use. Eventually, I decided the better route was to include lawncare in their rent and hire a lawn service. It eliminated communication with the tenants about whose turn it was to mow the overgrown grass and rake the leaves, and the properties looked nicer with their nicely edged lawns provided by the mowing service. Obviously, with larger properties, you must provide lawncare.
  - Responsibility for snow removal from tenants' own steps, sidewalks, and driveways can more easily be shifted to the tenants than mowing, even at multi-unit properties. However, snow removal from common area sidewalks and parking is the landlord's responsibility. This is true not only from a practical standpoint, but also from a liability concern. People slip and fall on snow and ice, so you want to control the conditions as much as you can.

- Fences

  o Fences are not a high-maintenance item, but when they, or any
     moving parts like gates, get broken, they cease to function, and they
     are unsightly. Periodic inspections are list worthy.

- Tree root preventative maintenance in sewer lines (chemical
  applications)

  o One of the more common maintenance calls is for opening a clogged
     main sewer line between the building and the street. This *can* be
     caused by something the tenants put through the drains like grease
     or a solid object. In even rarer instances, the sewer line has collapsed
     or been damaged by careless digging. But most likely, if there's a tree
     over the sewer line, the clog will be caused by tree roots combined
     with normal things in the line that have built up a blockage against the
     roots. Trees like to seek the water source in the lines, and they weasel
     their roots in through the joints between the sections of drain tile.
     Newer lines are typically solid PVC, so they do not get roots unless
     broken.

  o If tree roots are a recurring issue, the solution is annual treatments of
     problem sewer lines with a tree root killer. Reaming out the lines with a
     machine solves the immediate problem, but the roots will grow back.
     Chemical application of a good root killer will persuade the tree to look
     elsewhere. In the past, copper sulphate granules dropped or flushed
     into the line were the go-to process. The granules lay in the line and
     slowly dissolve while you hope the now-poisonous liquid splashes
     against the roots which are entering the line from the top down.
     Now, the best treatment is done with products that foam when they
     combine with the water in the lines and coat the roots immediately.
     You can buy bottles of foaming pellets off the shelf, but the best
     product I've found is a two-part product called Rootx. The container
     has two powders divided by a partition. After removing the lid, you
     dump the powders into a funnel they provide to mix them. Then, you

open the small end of the funnel to dump the mixture into the sewer line. You can buy individual containers online, or order a box of twelve directly from Rootx.

- Carpet and other flooring updates

  o It's hard to replace flooring in an occupied apartment, so you're only likely to do that for a very long-term tenant. Otherwise, every time a place turns over, you should assess the flooring for possible replacement. Like paint colors, use the same flooring over and over. Scrap pieces of carpet can be saved for future jobs, particularly for use in closets and on stairs.

  o You must develop your preferences for where you use which type of flooring. The major groups are carpet, rolled vinyl, luxury vinyl planks (LVP), and tile. The main considerations are:

    ◆ Do not use carpet anywhere there is water or the possibility of spills such as in baths, kitchens, or entries.

    ◆ Good carpet padding helps carpet last longer, so don't go too cheap here. The bonus is that you may find you can reuse viable padding when you replace the carpet.

    ◆ Balance durability and quality against the overall quality of the unit and the type of tenants you will get. Do not install too high quality, but put in the best that you can justify. Go for durability and cleanability with attractive colors and patterns, but keep it relatively generic to go with just about anyone's décor. You do not want to use the cheapest flooring you can find, or else you will end up changing it out too often.

    ◆ Stick to darker colors to hide dirt.

    ◆ For rolled vinyl, use models that are fiberglass-backed with as thick of a wear surface you can justify. This material releases dimples from furniture legs and appliances easily, and can be loose-laid *or* glued.

    ◆ Consider using LVP instead of carpet in living rooms and bedrooms for a trendy look to eliminate carpet cleaning and stains that will not come out.

- ◆ LVP and rolled flooring must almost always be laid over underlayment that evens out the imperfections in the existing floor and adds resistance to flexing. Otherwise, any imperfections will "telegraph" through to the wear surface over time.

- ◆ LVP comes either glue-down or click-and-lock. The glue-down type is more tedious to install, but it is necessary if you are going over a subfloor that is uneven or flexes. Click-and-lock planks require a level and stable installation, or the tongue in the interlocking system will break off leaving the plank unattached.

- ◆ Most LVP is based on a wood pattern and color, so be careful not to choose a style that clashes with any adjacent wood trim.

- ◆ Floor tiles are mainly made of various composite materials, porcelain, or ceramic offerings. With the possible exception of certain composite materials, tiles most certainly are glued to rigid underlayment (like cement board) because they are rigid and have grout seams.

- ◆ To me, using tile comes down to more of a décor selection than a purpose necessity. Carpet, LVP, or rolled vinyl can likely by used most anywhere you could also choose tile. Tile *can* be more expensive than the others, but tile offers the greatest opportunities for creativity. With all the different shapes, materials, colors, installation patterns, and grout combinations, tile has a lot to offer the imagination.

- ○ It is advantageous to develop a relationship with a source for flooring and installation that can give you a "landlord discount" and not offer you the same prices as Joe Homeowner would get. Ideally, this supplier should have multiple installation crews at their disposal because the more crews they have, the more likely you will be able to get your job scheduled soon. Also, if you must push back a scheduled installation, they won't be too unhappy to give your spot to someone on the waiting list.

- Countertops and cabinetry updates

  - Counters and cabinets dictate the overall feel of baths and kitchens as much as the paint and flooring. But, since they tend to last a long time, it is best to stick with colors, patterns, and styles for rentals that are more classic than trendy (unless you are prepping a flip property for a big wow factor with the latest products).

  - Cabinet quality is truly a good-better-best world. You can get everything from cheap particle board construction to all wood (some pieces may be a laminate like plywood or Luan) to solid wood. Quality levels also exist for drawer glides, hinges, handles, and finishes. All cabinets look and operate great when they are first installed; the question is how long they will last. Choose the best value.

  - Cabinets come in 3" width increments, and you can buy fillers that can be cut down to fill a gap. Unless you have a need to order in a custom color or door style, you can usually select what you need off the shelf. Ordering cabinets can take time that you do not have, considering cabinetry is often not able to be installed until near the end of a job.

  - Likewise, laminate countertops (think Formica) can usually be found cheaper in stores than the custom prices, and in a selection of the most popular colors in several lengths. They can easily be cut down to size, and you can buy them with pre-cut forty-five-degree mitered ends for corners.

  - One instance when you would be forced to pay for custom cabinetry, and possibly professional installation, is when you have any kind of oddball shape or contour that cannot be accommodated using a standard depth counter that has an attached backsplash. An example of a piece that would need to be custom made would be a buffet top.

  - The cheapest counters are the laminate ones, and they are the only ones you can install yourself. If you are willing to pay more for the material and the required professional installation, you can get into granite, soapstone or marble (natural materials), quartz (crushed engineered material), or solid surface (formed from resins—think Corian). Ceramic tiles can be considered for bath counters, and there are places for wood butcher block tops in kitchens.

- Appliance updates

  - Appliances can last a long time, and they typically are replaced only when they totally break down, or if they look outdated or worn compared to the apartment in general.

  - If you have a reputable store that sells reconditioned appliances in your area, I recommend checking their stock each time you have a need. Prices are drastically less than brand new, and the pieces probably come with a warranty. This store could also double as an appliance repair company, so sometimes the process can be seamless when you send them for a repair in an occupied apartment, and they discover the appliance in question is not worth repairing. They will deliver your replacement appliance, and take away the old one.

  - If you prefer to buy new appliances, the key is to have a reliable source for in-stock selections that can be delivered quickly at reasonable prices. Perhaps your local professional association has a prearranged discount benefit. Use the same appliance models routinely so you don't waste time shopping.

  - My advice is to use gas ranges whenever possible. They have fewer parts that can wear out as in the case of the burners and the drip pans on electric stoves. Tenants prefer gas ranges, and they are easier to clean. So, if plumbing a gas line is possible, I routinely replace electric stoves with gas ones.

- Furnace, air conditioning, and hot water tank replacement before failure

  - I'll admit, most of the time these items are not replaced until they fail...often at the most inconvenient times for both you and the tenant. That's an example of when you need reliable sources in place for quick responses from suppliers and installers.

  - However, particularly between tenants, having a practice of evaluating the possible replacement of these big-ticket components is good practice. Unlike kitchen appliances, with rare exceptions, HVAC and hot water tanks are replaced with new ones, not used.

- Door and lock hardware updates (interior and exterior)

  o Locks and other door hardware such as knockers and hinges rarely wear out, but often they get worn looking due to scratches and slopped paint. At that point, since the front door is a big part of your applicants' first impression, changing them out is a quick and easy update. New doorknobs and hinges can really sharpen things up on interior doors as well.

  o Landlords are getting into new products such as battery-operated locks with easily changed entry codes. Some of these can even be monitored with cell phones, which is a great idea for short-term rentals. I do not prefer battery operated locks for long-term rentals because the batteries are a maintenance item.

  o Locks must be changed out for each new tenant for their safety, so that means physically switching out all the locks unless you can re-key the lock in place. And the answer is...Kwikset Smartkey locks. These look like the Kwikset locks we all know, but they are upgraded to contain a process (tiny tool included) where you can re-key the lock by inserting the tool into a tiny slot while the old key is in the keyhole. Then you pull out the tool and the old key, insert the new key into the keyhole, and lastly turn the new key. In ten seconds, I can have a lock ready for a new tenant!

- Elevators and escalators

  o If you find yourself owning a building that has an elevator or an escalator, you will be on a regular inspection program with a third-party. However, breakdowns are a possibility for maintenance calls, so they are mentioned here.

Many physical components of a property are subject to suddenly expiring or getting damaged by an accident. Sometimes you will have to sort out culpability later, but the repair must be made at once. (I'm amused when tenants say, "The fill-in-the-blank broke." when everyone knows it didn't break itself—someone had to have broken it.) Your established protocols would dictate whether you do one of the following:

- Go to the unit prepared to fix it yourself based on the tenant's report.
- Go to the unit to assess the repair, and either fix it yourself or call a contractor.
- Send someone else to assess the repair and report to you.
- Send someone else to fix it immediately based on the tenant's report.

The following statement is key to "enjoying the journey of rental property investment." Tenants often make things seem more urgent or a bigger problem than is actually the case. My theory is that it is because they are often unknowledgeable about home repairs. Or they may believe they need to make things sound alarming so their landlord will do something about it more quickly. I do not think I have ever repaired something (or sent a contractor on a service call) in the middle of the night. **I usually have experienced a strange phenomenon which is that repairs/situations usually turn out to be far less of a concern than the inexperienced tenant made them out to be.**

The following are elements of rental property maintenance that, when suddenly broken or malfunctioning, commonly generate unplanned repairs. Your aim is to have procedures in place for you or your staff to respond according to the urgency of the matter by bringing together contractors, suppliers, and tenants to "make it like it never happened."

- Toilets (I put it first because you probably expected to see it there)
  - The whole toilet repair scenario is an iconic myth. Toilets rarely break, and if they do, it is seldom an emergency. They have a few parts that occasionally wear out, but which are easily replaced with new ones from any hardware store. It wouldn't be an emergency. And regarding plugged toilets, at least in our rentals, those are the tenants' responsibility just like all the other drains in their apartment. The residents stopped them up; they can unplug them!

- Furnaces and air conditioners

  o The usual complaint is either "not heating" or "not cooling" even though the air is blowing. This issue is typically caused by one of only a few possible malfunctions, and technicians can fix it quickly at a reasonable cost.

  o If the unit is not turning on at all, it may be something as simple as the thermostat needing new batteries...which is a reason to avoid thermostats with batteries.

- Appliances

  o The most urgent repairs involve refrigerators because of the food, and the most common complaint is that the fridge and/or freezer is not cooling enough. Even so, losing the ability to cool is usually a gradual process. The fridge is typically still keeping the food cool to a reasonable degree when you finally hear about the situation, so it gives you time to act.

  o Repairs to appliances are usually either reasonable, or the unit is dead and not worth fixing.

- Clogged drains

  o My advice is to use DRAIN-NO, which means, "No, we do not open your drains." I make it clear when signing the lease, as well as on my handout that lists some companies they are welcome to call if a drain gets clogged, that all the drains work fine at move-in. If one gets clogged, it is because they put something down it, so it is their responsibility to get it opened (except for with tree roots, as explained earlier). This, of course, includes toilets. The cause may be something as innocent as hair and soap, so I recommend they keep a screen over their tub drain. Tenants are instructed not to allow feminine products to be flushed even if the box says they are "flushable."

  o Unlike for sink and tub drains, I do not expect the tenant to call a company on their own to open a basement main drain. I want to take control of that situation. However, as I explained earlier, the tenant is responsible for the cost if it turns out to be something other than a collapsed line or tree roots as the cause.

o   Technicians that snake out drains are rather good at being able to show the tenant (and report to you) what the cause of the clog was, so there should be no argument when requiring the tenant to reimburse you.

- Plumbing pipes (both supply lines and drain lines) and gas pipes

  o   The most common leak reported will be in the drain under a sink. The P-traps can get bumped and lose their seal. Usually, this can be remedied simply by hand-tightening the connections, but sometimes a replacement is called for.

  o   Leaks in water and gas supply lines develop at spots where pipes are joined together. This is usually not an emergency because they develop so slowly, although there are very rare instances where pipe connections come apart rapidly. Tenants should be instructed on how to turn the water off at the main valve (if one exists inside their apartment), but they should exit quickly if they smell gas.

  o   Frozen pipes that burst can cause a lot of damage, but usually this is preventable if you are aware of a situation that exists that would allow a pipe to freeze given the right weather conditions. If, during very cold weather, a tenant reports that their water has stopped flowing, you will have time to get the pipe thawed before it bursts. Then, efforts can be made to prevent a reoccurrence by re-routing or insulating the pipe, closing off the breach where the cold air is coming in, or applying electric heat tape to the pipe.

  o   In a properly designed piping system, there must be a shutoff valve just upstream from any appliance or faucet/toilet so the device can be isolated for replacement or repair without turning the gas or water off at the main shutoff.

- Electrical fixtures/breakers/switches/outlets

  o Though they have few moving parts, all these items can become damaged from normal wear and tear, abuse, or corrosion. Look for bulbs that flicker in their sockets, breakers that trip too easily, switches that move too easily or make a sound when they contact, and outlets that no longer grip the prongs on plugs.

  o The good news is that these are all easily replaced. Sometimes, the solution is to simply tighten the wire contacts.

- Smoke detectors and carbon monoxide detectors

  o While you may be relying on your tenants to change the batteries in detectors when the batteries get low, eventually detectors can go bad. The tenant will report to you that a detector keeps alarming even though nothing is wrong in the apartment, or it beeps like it needs a new battery even though they just replaced the battery. You will need to get them a new detector ASAP.

- Door hardware including locks

  o These are also items you can easily learn to repair or replace. Locks and hinges function great...until they don't. So, sometimes they must be replaced quickly.

  o Locks should be lubricated whenever the key turns with resistance.

  o Whenever the bolt from a lock does not rest perfectly in the hole in the strike plate, the plate must be shifted slightly because you will not be able to change the travel of the bolt very much. One trick, especially for old-style interior locks, is to use a Dremel tool to grind the strike plate until the bolt rests properly.

  o When hinges work loose from the door jamb, the screws must be tightened. Otherwise, problems will develop with the swing of the door. The issue is that often the screws holes are stripped, and you can't get screws tight enough. One possible solution is to use a thicker or longer screw, but only if the flat screw head recesses enough into the dimple on the hinge. I like to put a plastic screw anchor (yes, the same kind that are used to attach things to a wall) into the stripped holes in the jamb, and then use a drywall screw which will match nicely with the hinge dimple.

o If the flooring under a door is changed, be prepared for the bottom edge of the door to need trimming. Of course, you must take the door off its hinges by pounding out the pin (or unscrew the hinges altogether). One trick for getting the fingers on the hinges to match up when you are reinstalling the door is to use a flat prybar under the door to jockey it into position.

- Steps/railings/decks

  o Although the tenant may not report an issue until it becomes annoying, problems with these items can be a safety hazard, so they must be attacked quickly once discovered. Short of something catastrophic, like being hit by a wayward car, the problem is most likely one piece of wood gradually coming detached from another. Unless the wood is rotted to the point of needing to be replaced, you just need to reattach them.

  o When building or repairing exterior weight-bearing structures like steps, railings, and decks, ALWAYS use deck screws. NEVER use nails or other fasteners that are not specifically rated for deck construction. Deck screws *look* like regular drywall screws, but they resist the corrosion that other screws are prone to. Corroded screws will eventually fail, perhaps creating an unnecessary liability.

- Windows (both broken glass and functionality issues)

  o If a pane is only cracked, you have some time to make the repair. But if glass is broken out, you must act fast by at least boarding over the window. If one pane of a double pane (insulated) window is cracked or loses its seal, the space in between the two panes will get fogged up. A new insert can be ordered just like glass can be custom cut for a single pane window.

- o Old style window sashes become dangerous when their ropes break, and the weights drop in the cavity inside the wall. If sashes will not stay up, fingers and children can get seriously hurt when they drop unexpectedly. If you really want to, you can open the trim and tie new rope to the weights. But the easiest thing to do is install sash controls in the window jambs so the gap is smaller between the sash and the jamb. Sash controls are very inexpensive, especially compared to reattaching the weights. They are simply springy metal with a bow in them, and they slide into place. My advice is to put at least one screw through the provided holes to hold each one in place. Otherwise, they can fall out, and tenants will rarely put them back into place.

- o Sash locks prevent the window from being opened by clipping the upper sash to the lower sash, and they can become loose or broken. Any moving part of a window can break or get out of adjustment, but repairs are easy whether they are old style or modern vinyl windows.

- o If triple-track storm windows and screens are being used to add insulation over old-style windows, be sure each window and screen section is in place in the tracks and in good repair. Do not rent out an apartment with broken or missing storm windows or screens. Sections can be fabricated to match if necessary.

- o Tenants must be educated at move-in as to the proper operation and seasonal positioning of storm windows and screens. Also, if you have modern windows, show your new tenants how both the top and bottom sashes tip in so they can clean the outsides of the glass from inside the room.

- Gutters and anything that comes loose from the structure

  - o Gutters or anything attached to a structure can come loose or detach completely during a sudden event like a storm. While typically not an emergency, if gutters or downspouts get out of position it can make all the difference as to whether you will continue to have a dry basement or not. Consequently, this is not the type of repair you can let go very long. The same is true with siding, awnings, lighting fixtures, shutters, or anything that appears unsightly...especially if it is a safety concern.

o Most of the time, repairs are only a matter of reattaching the item using either larger screws in the same screw holes or more screws.

- Trees

  o Trees have so many benefits like beautification, supplying shade, and making oxygen out of carbon dioxide. However, the ones in your yard can produce a lot of annoying droppings, and even average sized trees can cause considerable damage when they fall. A fallen tree or branch is an example of unexpected maintenance.

- Pool equipment

  o Pools are inherently a safety concern. Aside from routine maintenance, filtration systems and equipment like ladders and slides can generate a surprise maintenance call, but these are rare if the routine maintenance is kept up.

- Water well and septic system equipment

  o Wells and septic systems are more examples of areas that will not generate many unplanned calls if routine maintenance is done. However, pumps and other moving parts rarely give you any advance notice before they fail, so there can be instances when you must spring into action quickly with a call to a professional.

- Elevators and escalators

  o These will be on a service contract with a certified company, and the same company will respond to any emergency. Your involvement will likely be limited to some phone calls.

Obviously, a weather-related event or a natural occurrence like an earthquake can cause damage to any property that otherwise wouldn't break or wear out quickly, and that situation may leave you "making it up as you go along" when it comes to following your protocols. But you probably won't face that test very often.

If you have the skills and desire to perform property maintenance yourself, that's great. You will save some money (providing you don't make the problem worse with your DIY efforts), but you will give up your time and take on the related aggravation. **I encourage you to learn *how* many of the common repairs are done as you encounter various maintenance issues, but *you* do not necessarily need to become *skillful* in performing these tasks yourself.** You can learn from watching and talking with contractors, from DIY videos and publications, and from the people who sell you the supplies used for the job. Learning what the choices are in approaching a repair/improvement/update and how those things are done properly (including experts' shortcuts) will help you make better choices in hiring other people to do them. **If you can "speak their language", even if you are not capable of doing the job yourself, you can better determine if the right fix is being proposed, if the job was done properly, and if you are paying a fair price.**

As a rule, **I do not allow tenants to perform maintenance or repairs on their properties** other than simple things like changing a lightbulb or furnace filter. I want to control how and when work is done, as well as who does it. Occasionally, if I know for sure a tenant has the skill to perform a small task, I will grant special permission, and they can deduct the cost of materials from the rent. However, **I never make deals with tenants to perform work for an ongoing or one-time reduction in rent.** This is not only for the same aforementioned control requirements, but also for liability considerations in case their work brings harm to others or their property.

I have joked that if I can't remedy the situation with an electric glue gun, GOOP glue, duct tape, a screw gun, or maybe the occasional wrench, I will be calling someone. **I want to make a point that you can be successful in the rental real estate business even if that is the extent of your skillset as well.** At the very least, though, if you are going to own just one power tool, make it a battery-operated drill/screw gun. It will serve you well!

However, if you want to prepare for the basic, most common repairs encountered when turning over an apartment **I can give you a list of tools to have at your disposal. With these tools, you can accomplish the vast majority of what typically comes up when preparing a unit for tenants.** It does not take long to develop the skills to tackle the usual quick repairs using these tools. Major rehabs, of course, require more tools and skills, so **you must forge the line between what jobs you will routinely attack yourself, and ones for which you will call a contractor.** You could make your loved ones aware of the following gift list:

- Basic tools like hammer, screwdrivers, measuring tape (minimum 15'), saw horses
- Battery powered wall stud finder
- Vice grips and assorted wrenches and pliers
- Screw gun/drill
- Basic painting tools like brushes, roller, rolling pan, gloves, scrapers, drop cloths
- Drywall tools like box cutter, drywall saw, applicator blades, sanding block
- 25' extension cord and 3-prong adaptor
- Plug-in tester for electric outlets
- Dremel tool
- Hot glue gun
- Electric hand saw
- Upright vacuum and battery powered hand vacuum
- Step ladder
- Flat pry bar
- Scissors, wire cutters, and sheet metal shears
- Miter box and hand saw
- Basic gardening tools like rakes and shovels

- Level

- Cleaning tools like a mop, bucket, sponges, coarse scrubber

- Lockbox for keeping a key on premises

Even if you are not planning to do much of the maintenance or repairs yourself, **the subject of stockpiling supplies must be addressed.** This is for two reasons. First, whether you or someone else performed the work on the project, **there may be materials left over** that are worthwhile saving. Secondly, **there are some routinely used materials which are prudent to keep on hand**, so time is not wasted by having to buy them each time they are needed.

The assumption with holding onto left over materials is that you are likely to use the same color/size/shape/brand on a future project. The general rule, though, is that **anything that can be returned should be returned; only large pieces of nonreturnable materials should be kept.** At lease because I do both residential rentals and house flipping, I have found it useful to **keep the following items when they are left over** from a project:

- Flooring and installation materials like padding, glue, transitions, and trim pieces

- Cabinetry trim pieces

- Partial sheets of plywood, drywall, and Luan (minimum one quarter sheet)

- Aluminum coil stock

- Siding trim pieces and large pieces of siding

- Regular and treated framing and decking wood of all dimensions (at least 4' long)

- PVC and copper plumbing pipes of significant length

- Rolled and rigid insulation

- Countertop pieces at least 12" wide plus end cap kits

- Floor tiles and wall tiles along with installation materials like grout and adhesive
- Window, door, and baseboard trim
- Hard-to-find trim from older homes that is likely needed to match something later
- Wire shelving at least 30" wide
- Gutter and downspout materials
- Drop ceiling panels and installation materials
- Oddball heat and cold air return vents
- Shingles and roofing installation materials like ice & water shield
- Paint (leave one-time-use custom colors at the property for the next owner)

Those items would be considered for storage as they present themselves *following* a project, but **some materials are wisely stockpiled *ahead* of time**. You will find that certain supplies are needed repeatedly, so it is easier to have some on hand to cut down on trips to the store. Here are some of the more common ones:

- Cabinet knobs and hinges
- Smoke and carbon monoxide detectors
- Window sash controls, and sash locks for both old and modern windows
- Interior and exterior doorknobs/locks
- Drop ceiling panels
- Your go-to paints
- Drywall compound
- Golden oak stain for oak cabinet touchup
- Goof Off for paint removal
- Goo Gone for sticker residue and gum removal
- Paint thinner

- KILZ oil-based stain killer in aerosol spray and regular can
- Assortment of nails and screws, especially drywall type screws
- GOOP glue in a squeeze tube
- Wood glue
- Kitchen sink strainers
- Toilet flush valves and flappers
- Outlet and switch covers
- Romex electrical wire, 14-2 gauge
- Electrical outlets (3-prong and 2-prong), GFCI outlets, switches, pull-chain sockets
- Ceiling and wall light shades
- Plug-in air fresheners
- Doorbell chimes and buttons
- 9 volt, AA, and AAA batteries
- Furnace filters
- Kitchen and bath sink faucets
- Towel racks, TP holders
- Duct tape
- Doorstops
- Storm door repair parts like closers and handles

The bottom line—and this is key to believing you can enjoy the journey of rental property investment—is that you do not have to know how to do everything that comes up with property management; you just need to know who to call.

6
TENANT MANAGEMENT (DOORS AND WINDOWS)

Property management is about the upkeep of land and improvements, while tenant management is about relationships with people. Tenant management is like the doors and windows on a building because it is what you use to allow the good elements to enter and to keep the bad elements out.

Specifically, it's about interacting with the tenants/customers with whom you are entrusting not only the use but also the occupancy of your valuable assets...with little supervision...for an extended period of time...and you hardly know them...gulp! But **with proper application of well-learned, tried-and-true principles, your experience with tenants will most likely be a positive one...both from a personal standpoint and a financial one. In the preponderance of instances, tenants will pay their rent on time, keep your property in decent shape, return it to you reasonably clean when they move out at**

the end of their lease, and not bother you unnecessarily along the way...
if you do your part as their landlord. They are not going to respect you
and your property if they don't sense that you respect them.

In the big picture, tenants are "managed" for the purpose of getting
them to behave properly so that you can operate your business within
the systems you have set up. Presumably, you have set up your systems for the
purpose of making a profit renting out housing or commercial space while maintaining your properties, running your office, and generally keeping things pleasant
with whomever you must interface in the process. You need your tenants'
cooperation to accomplish this!

In a sense, tenant management becomes a tool in your property
management strategy when you see that the better you manage your
tenants, the better they will take care of your property. And the better
your tenants take care of your property, the less maintenance you will
need to perform. In other words, spending time, effort, and money on
good tenant management doesn't cost...it pays.

As with most interpersonal relationships, you can get cheerful
cooperation if people believe you respect them. Sometimes you can get
cooperation because you know more than someone else, but, as they say, people
won't care how much you know until they know how much you care. One of the
ways tenants know you care is how you keep your property. Another way is how
you treat them when it comes to the ongoing business between the two of you
such as rent collection, lease renewals, inspections, maintenance requests, and rule
enforcement.

You may be thinking I am suggesting you have a close personal relationship with
your tenants to get the cooperation you need, but I do not at all advocate that.
Before we develop landlord/tenant relationships, let me put Rule #2 out there:
Be friendly with your tenants, but not friends. This ties in with Rule #1
from Chapter Four regarding not renting to friends, friends of friends,
relatives, co-workers, or anyone whose relationship you are not prepared
to lose if your experience with a tenant goes south.

You show respect to your tenants when you:

- Perform routine maintenance in a timely fashion and a quality manner.

- Handle unexpected repairs properly in a reasonable time frame with as little disruption to the tenants' enjoyment of their dwelling as could be expected.

- Have easy paths for tenants to reach you or your staff for maintenance and business concerns.

- Have good policies regarding pets, vehicle parking, trash, lawncare, snow removal, noise, outdoor grilling, smoking, and any actions or responsibilities of residents and/or guests that affect what other tenants see or do.

- Resolve disputes with fairness *and* firmness.

- Enforce the lease and related rules & regulations consistently.

- Acquire good neighbors for your existing tenants by applying your tenant selection criteria uniformly.

- Charge a fair rent with reasonable rent increases.

- Interact with residents in a courteous but confident manner.

- Make sure the tenant understands you have comprehended any concerns or input they bring to you even if you cannot accommodate their request. (To be understood is perhaps everyone's greatest need.)

Like property management, tenant management has tasks that are routine as well as those that are unplanned. It is just as imperative that policies for decision making, protocols for acting, and systems for operating be set up for tenant management as it is for property management.

Landlord/tenant laws are unique for each state, so I will speak in generalities. Such statutes cover landlords' *and* tenants' rights, and they dictate certain requirements regarding the lengths of time for providing the other party with various notices. Of particular importance are your state's laws about evictions, so you must learn them and follow them, or you will put yourself at risk. **Some of the routine**

activities related to tenant management, once your tenants have taken occupancy, which should be on your schedule are:

- Rent collection

  ○ Rent collection is the most regular activity in the rental real estate world because it occurs every month for every rented unit. No other contact with your tenants or your property will occur more often unless you are counting pool maintenance, grass cutting, or snow removal if applicable. By the term "rent collection," **I am *not* referring to personally going to your tenants' residences or businesses to pick up their rent. That should never happen.** I am referring to everything related to a landlord getting paid including:

    ◆ Keeping records as to who to expect a rent payment from, for how much it should be, when it is due, and what any late charges are
    ◆ Logging the receipt of the payment into your accounting system
    ◆ Contacting the tenant if their rent is not received in time

  ○ The first two bullet points above are done invisibly to the tenant, and I have discussed record keeping extensively earlier in this book. If, however, you get to the third point, tenants must be contacted, and that is when your tenant management skills will be called upon. **Your protocols should include a contact via phone call, text, or email (which may originate automatically from your property management program) within a day or so of the rent being late to ask the tenant as to when you can expect their payment. The tenant should be reminded that they have passed the deadline for taking advantage of any prompt payment discount, and the amount of the rent due now should be stated.** Make a note as to when they say they will pay, and follow up if you don't have it by then.

    ◆ **Tenants must be trained to contact your office by the date any rent is to be paid if, for any reason, they will not have their payment in your hands by that day.** Whether they have contacted you first, or whether you had to call them to ask about it, if you have developed some trust with them, you can assure them you will not give them an eviction notice while you wait for their rent. However, **if the time they are giving you for payment is too far in the future, kindly explain to them that you must give them a notice to vacate due to nonpayment of rent** immediately so that the clock starts ticking on the time between your notice and the point at which you could open a landlord/tenant case with the District Judge. This notice would be given in case they didn't pay in the allotted time, but it will "go away" if they pay.

- Lease renewals/rent increases/changes to the lease

  o **Unless your lease is going to automatically renew for another term (presumably one year) with no changes, you will need to present an offer to your tenants if you want them to remain in the apartment.** For example, if there were no predetermined increases in the original lease, or if all the increases have been exhausted, you will need to approach the tenants with a proposed increase. Any changes to the lease must be in writing, so it is best to send them two copies of the proposed changes with instructions for them to sign both copies and return one to you by a set deadline. If the changes are spelled out in your letter, it becomes an amendment to the original lease once all parties have signed. A new lease form does not need to be signed.

  o **If there are no changes in any terms of the existing lease, and if you accept a rental payment after the final month of the current lease term, all the terms of the existing lease are automatically renewed for another term of the same length as the one ending.** A one-year lease renews for a full twelve months; it does not switch to a month-to-month lease.

  o Tenants will be required to give you thirty days written notice if they do not wish to remain in their rental beyond the end of their lease. Consequently, if you wish to make any changes to their lease, such as a rent increase, **you must present them with any changes with a reasonable amount of notice** so they can decide if they wish to accept your proposal. I typically mail them a letter about ten days before the beginning of their final month so that they have time to respond with a thirty-day notice if they are not going to renew.

○ **Approaching a tenant about a rent increase can be one of the most uncomfortable conversations**, but there is a way to avoid it. From the landlord's perspective, your aim is to keep your units filled, so your concern is that good tenants will move out if you increase the rent. The tenant is concerned they will not be able to afford the new rent, or that the apartment is not worth the new rent, so they will have to move. A move-out for the landlord will cost money in lost rent and turnover expenses, and a move-out for the tenant is costly and stressful as well. **The uncertainty of all this can be eliminated by telling the tenants ahead of time what their rent will be for several renewal periods. This can be done as an attachment to or a notation on the original lease when it is signed before their move-in**. If a set amount is listed, and the tenants do not notify you by the beginning of their final month, then you can assume they are staying. In this case, you would simply send them a reminder about a week before the rent is due for the first month of their renewal period about how their rent is increasing per the terms of their lease.

○ **The amount of a reasonable rent increase can be determined by making comparisons to the rent being charged for similar units** using the same process for setting the initial rent as described earlier. Eventually, you will get a feel for typical increases for your type of units in your market.

○ **During and after the COVID 19 pandemic, the housing market saw dramatic and erratic increases** in the sales prices for both owner-occupied homes and residential rentals. The same was true for rents for apartments and single-family homes where rents were increasing at astonishing leaps that represented much greater jumps in rent than we would normally have the courage to offer to existing tenants. Even greater jumps were the norm whenever an apartment was being re-rented to a new tenant. This was caused by a perfect storm of inflation and lack of inventory (supply of homes for sale/ available rentals vs. demand) among other things.

o While we were stuck with rent increases that were prescribed in leases that were signed before entering this atmosphere, **renewal rates for long-term existing tenants became hard to calculate.** They were certainly beyond the normal increases, but by how much? This led to a technique I had never employed before where I began sending a letter about six weeks before the expiration of any lease if the increase was not locked in by the original lease terms. I would point out that rents have been increasing dramatically during the pandemic, and that **the purpose of the letter was to ask them to think about how much they would like to pay for rent if they renewed.** I told them what we had rented similar units for, but they were asked to do their own research, which I knew would surprise them with what they would need to pay for a similar place if they moved. **I asked them to contact me with an offer of a rent increase, and <u>invariably</u>, they would suggest an increase far beyond what I would have imagined under normal circumstances.** I pretty much accepted all their offers, and nobody moved due to the rent increase. Whenever someone moved for normal reasons, I re-rented the units for even more than I was accepting from the renewals.

o The market conditions I just described were an anomaly, but I wanted to describe the technique I used for getting the tenants to suggest their own rent. **It may be employed effectively, even if market conditions are closer to normal, for the purpose of getting greater rent increases than you would have felt comfortable offering.** After all, if the tenant is suggesting a change in their rent, they must be happy with it. **The downside, of course, is that it requires you to have the rent increase conversation on your schedule,** whereas having the increases prescribed in the original lease will eliminate that if you would rather go that route.

o If you are increasing the rent, be sure to **require the tenant to send an addition to their security deposit equal to the amount of the increase in the rent** so that their deposit always stays the same as their rent. You do not want to have a long-term tenant move out leaving you a deposit of perhaps hundreds of dollars less than their current rent.

o **You must overcome your fear of losing tenants when you raise the rent.** Tenants expect reasonable rent increases. In the long run, you are hurting yourself by allowing people to rent from you at a below-market rate. You will not only give up the lost rent along the way, but your property will be worth less because income properties are valued by the net income they *are* producing...not so much on what income they *could* produce. **A fair question from prospective buyers is to ask why *you* are not charging the rent *you* say *they* could get if they took over your property.**

o In today's economy, none of the underlying costs of operating your property (such as property taxes, insurance, maintenance, and overhead) are ever headed downward. **Rent must continually be increased to cover these costs, and small increases each year are easier for tenants to manage.** If you wait years to raise the rent, and the increase must be a large jump to catch up all at one time, not only will you have lost all the rent you could have had in prior years from small increases, but you also run a greater risk of losing the tenant. **Rent should be raised for every tenant, every year. Period.**

o In some instances, **the original lease form can be altered by having all parties initial the changes.** An example would be a change in the minimum liability coverage the tenant is required to carry on their renters insurance policy.

o **Some changes in a lease may also require additional forms to become part of the lease agreement.** An example would be if you agreed to allow the tenant to get a dog. There would be a Pet Agreement with accompanying documentation of the dog's veterinarian records as well as any related rules and regulations.

o Pet agreements, lead-based paint disclosures, resident rules and regulations, and roommate agreements, are technically *addendums* to the main lease form because they are *added*. Changes to the original lease form, such as a new rental rate, are *amendments* because they only change something already in the lease.

- Interior inspections

  o While exterior inspections can be done anytime without notice to tenants, **interior inspections must be arranged ahead of time.** Interior inspections may be in order under several circumstances. Some may be on your schedule, and others would be sporadic. In any case, the rule of thumb is to give residents at least twenty-four hours' notice before entering their home. **The notice is not necessarily to make sure the tenant is home for your visit; just that you are going to enter whether they are home or not for a certain purpose.** While some tenants may prefer to be home when you are there, you must build trust with tenants so that this is not a concern for them. Especially when you are lining up visits to multiple apartments at the same location, you may need to be firm with certain tenants regarding your right to enter with proper notice. They would need to understand you are not going to make a second visit to the property for the same purpose just to come into their unit when it is convenient for them to be home.

  o If things are going normally, you may prefer not to do regular inspections where you look for things to fix like I described for exteriors. However, you may want to develop an initiative where you are systematically going to perform certain interior updates. This might come about for properties you have owned for a long time, or perhaps with a newly acquired property that is behind the times.

  o Interior inspections that would be scheduled only on occasion include appraisals when you are refinancing or when you are selling, showings to potential buyers of the property, and whenever you suspect your tenant is abusing your property or otherwise violating the lease. **If your tenant has been a good housekeeper, you may feel the apartment is presentable enough to show it** to prospective tenants during the last month before a moveout.

o Some interior inspections must be on your calendar regularly such as if your locality has an apartment safety code inspection ordinance. In this case, the inspector probably will be telling *you* when the inspection is, and you will have to inform the tenant as to when you will be accompanying the inspector in their apartment.

- Periodic tenant information updates and other forms

o **For many years I have found it beneficial to annually send an update form** to all tenants on which they are asked to fill in the names of all adults and children living in the unit; their current personal and work phone numbers; the make, year, color and plate number for all vehicles at the premises; and names, addresses and phone numbers of two people who can be notified in case of an emergency. I do this in January when we have the highest occupancy.

Can you see the benefit of this?! For the most part, the information provided does not change from year to year, but occasionally we find out about a new cell phone number, a different car in the reserved parking spot, or a change in their emergency contact. I have even had tenants reveal that they have obtained a roommate who, of course, must be put on the lease. **All these things are key to identifying or tracking down tenants who may owe you money after they have moved,** and I would not have this new information if I had not asked for it.

This form can be sent to the tenants via snail mail, email, or management software. The tenant would then return the form in the same fashion, so consequently, your contact with the tenant will not be personal. However, if something is uncovered, like an additional resident, it would trigger direct contact with the tenant.

With the update form, **I also send a form for one adult resident to sign signifying they have tested each smoke and CO detector,** that they have replaced any low or missing batteries, and that each detector is affixed to its proper location. They are instructed to report any detectors that need to be replaced.

I also enclose our current list of emergency numbers including the contractors with which we work regularly. There is **also a reminder about checking their furnace/AC filters** to see if they need to change them.

I ask the tenants to return the forms along with their February rent, or send it separately by February first if they are paying online (or if the form is to be returned by email or through a property management program). Not everyone remembers, so the forgetful tenants must be reminded until you get their form, but **the payoff from doing this annual mailing is significant.**

- Communications to tenants about rental community events, work to be done in common areas, office contact info updates, and rules and regulations (for reinforcement and changes)

  - **Occasionally, residents must be informed about special occurrences or changes** in things that normally do not change such as phone numbers or rules. It should be clear that the information contained in your communication is an update of earlier facts.

- Move-outs

  - Most likely, **your lease will require tenants to notify you in writing at least thirty days before they intend to move out.** Presumably, this is by the first day of the final month of their lease term, unless they are exercising a clause in their lease which allows them to terminate their lease early. When you receive such a notice, **it will set off a series of events** leading up to what is perhaps the last time you will see this tenant.

o **Your first decision is whether to begin advertising the unit and conducting showings before the current tenant is gone**. This would be based on your relationship with the tenant in terms of how much they will mind the disruptions, and the condition of the unit.

o I hate to say it, but it is rare that the current tenant keeps your place in decent enough condition for you to show it, not to mention leave it clean enough for you to turn it over to the next tenant the day after the prior tenant vacated. It *does* happen, but even on the nicest of units with the best tenants, I plan on just waiting until it is vacant before advertising it for showings. **I want to be absolutely sure the unit is prepared to my standards before any prospective tenant sees it.**

o Your next decision is regarding **whether to plan any major changes or updates** once the unit is vacant. This may involve an inspection to help you make your plans. Materials and labor can then be lined up so that work can begin as soon as the tenant turns their apartment over to you.

o If none of the above is the case, the next thing to do is **send the tenants a list of your cleanup requirements** for them to follow. I usually do this so they receive it about a week to ten days before they have indicated they will move. Note that some tenants will inform you they will not be staying all the way until the end of their final month. The cleanup list contains a reminder that **they have an obligation to leave the utilities on in their name all the way to the end of the month even if they are leaving sooner** than that. It is a nice bonus if people leave early because you can get started on the turnover perhaps in time to get it rented for the beginning of the next month.

o As the time draws closer to when they are supposed to move**, contact them regarding the status of their moveout.** Try to pin them down as to whether they will be in there until the last possible day, or whether they may be leaving early. Remind them to follow the cleanup requirements, and ask them to keep you in the loop as to exactly when they will finish their cleanup.

You are probably thinking I am leading up to scheduling a final meeting with the tenant to do a walk-through. The tenant may be thinking that as well. However, when the tenant calls to say when they will be completely out, **I tell them to just leave their keys on the counter along with their new address where I can send the security deposit. I do this because I believe it is a bad idea to meet with tenants on their way out.**

Deducting legitimate charges from security deposits is a large part of good tenant management. When you meet with tenants who have just spent hours, if not days, moving their items and (hopefully) cleaning their former dwelling to *their* standards, **you are setting yourself up for arguments about what damage and cleaning will be deducted from their deposit.** Not only is this awkward, but you may feel pressured to agree not to deduct something reasonable while face-to-face with people who have different ideas as to the definition of normal wear-and-tear and who can't remember how clean their apartment was when they moved in.

So, unless your rental is very high-end and requires a detailed checklist at move-out, or you have some other compelling reason to meet with your tenants on their way out of the door, just do like a motel and let them leave without an official visit to the front desk. **If you truly believe it beneficial to meet right at the end, I recommend a surprise visit during their last few hours** just to point out things they still need to do. Do not make promises you do not want to keep about security deposit deductions. Then, tell them to leave their keys when they're done.

- Returning security deposits and collecting balances

  o **Security deposits allow landlords to have a fund to draw on if the tenant causes monetary damages** by not fully complying with all the terms of the lease. These damages could be either out-of-pocket costs incurred, or they could be unpaid rent. If the tenant owes you less than their deposit, you must send them the difference. If they owe you more, you send them a bill.

○ Tenants are asked to supply their new address during the move-out process, and most tenants will readily provide it to you. But if they do not, **you must prevail on them in the days immediately following their departure to provide it** so that you "know where to send their security deposit statement." I suggest you do this by text. You may already know that they are not getting back any of their deposit, but you still need their address as I am about to discuss. The words they will notice most are "send their security deposit," which may prompt them to respond even if they are assuming they are not getting any money back.

○ **Your state laws dictate how much time you have to send former tenants their security deposit** and/or a statement detailing any deductions. In Pennsylvania, we have thirty days from the date we know they have fully vacated their unit (which may be a date sooner than the scheduled expiration of their lease if, for example, they skip out or if they turn over the keys several days early because they have completed their move-out) to send an accounting of a security deposit. If we exceed that time frame, we risk the tenant successfully suing us for double the amount of the deposit with no deductions allowed. I'm sure other states prescribe similar time limits and penalties.

○ If there are not many charges, and the amounts of the charges are readily determined, you should easily be able to send the net security deposit refund in time. If you cannot calculate the exact total of the deductions within the time limit (for example, if repairs of damage caused by the tenants are extensive), it is likely the charges will exceed the deposit. In this case, be sure to send a statement to that effect within the allotted time to avoid possible consequences. In this case, you would indicate the deposit is being kept, and that you will soon provide the tenant with the full amount they owe you.

○ **Some examples of charges against a security deposit are:**

  ◆ Unpaid rent, late charges, pet fines, or other fees
  ◆ Out-of-pocket legal fees, court costs, bad check charges

- General and carpet cleaning charges paid to third parties or a reasonable amount for having done the necessary cleaning yourself, including trash removal
- Unpaid utilities for which the tenant was responsible
- Repairs of damage caused by the tenant, either through abuse or by accident, paid to contractors or a reasonable amount for having done the repairs yourself
- Anything else the tenant owes you per the lease terms

○ **Ordinary wear and tear cannot be charged to the tenant**, but if an item is damaged so that its life expectancy was unreasonably shortened, and it must be repaired before the next tenant could take occupancy, you have every right to charge the tenant. Good examples are broken windows, holes in walls or doors, ruined flooring, broken door and cabinet hardware, broken or missing appliance parts, plus damaged or missing electrical fixtures including outlets and switches. I also ding tenants for having to remove their stencils, stickers, and wallpaper (the application of any of these is against the lease), as well as for needing to paint over any defacing of the walls or trim.

○ If your statement shows that the tenant owes you money over the deposit you are keeping, **ask them to contact you within a certain time (maybe ten days or so) to make arrangements to pay the balance.** This first request can be made in a non-threatening tone, but if no plan to pay has been arranged in the time you allow, another letter must be sent with a firmer appeal. Give them some added time to either pay in full or set up a payment plan, or else you will turn their account over to a collection agency. Reinforce that by pointing out this will immediately go onto their credit record, which will make it difficult for them to lease decent apartments, obtain credit, secure loans, and get certain employment.

○ On a side note, **make sure the address shown on your checks is not your home address**, especially if your tenants are given an alternate address for correspondence. In other words, don't make the mistake of having your supply of checks display your home office address when you also have an alternate address like a PO Box for tenants to use. Otherwise, when your former tenant is perhaps angered by only getting part of their deposit back, the tenant will now have your home address.

○ **Send the security deposit and/or statement to the new address the tenant has given you. If they have not supplied an address, your only choice is to send it to their former apartment.** In the latter case, either the envelope will get forwarded by the post office (if they have put in a change of address), or it will be delivered to their old address. When you find the envelope in their former mailbox, fish it out and place it in their tenant file unopened to prove, via the postmark, that you mailed it in time. **If, in fact, there is a refund check in the envelope for them, now is the time to redouble your efforts to get a forwarding address** while assuring them "there really is a refund check" you are trying to send them.

○ In addition to sending the security deposit statement to their former apartment if they have not given you their new address, **you could also send it to their emergency contact** (from their rental application form, as updated per your annual request). Presumably, their emergency contact would give it to your former tenant, but since this would not be the tenant's new address, **it would not count as having been sent directly to the tenant.**

○ **If you received a call from a landlord who was processing a rental application on one of your current tenants, make a note of the landlord's name and number**. This will enable you to use the technique where you call that landlord and ask if they rented to your former tenant, and if so, would they kindly give you their new address so you can send the deposit.

○ **If, after all your local efforts, former tenants fail to pay you their balance due over the amount of their security deposit, it's time to bring in the big guns from out of town. I am referring to a collection agency.** Collection agencies charge a percentage of what they collect in exchange for employing professional techniques to collect debt. Any business, including individual landlords, can open a relationship with a debt collector. You don't have to do a huge amount of business with them. Once the relationship is established, simply fax in the information about your tenants and their balance owed, and let them go to work.

Your initial inclination is probably to open your account in your company name, but I do not suggest you do this. Whatever name is on the account is the name that will appear as the creditor on credit reports. **I want any landlord who is evaluating an applicant's credit report to see there is a collection account from a past landlord.** Consequently, my account is called **Landlord Joel Miller**. Often, company names do not indicate the business is a landlord, so the collection account may not be given much weight by a landlord who is reviewing a rental application. However, other landlords, seeing that a prior landlord had been stiffed, will take that into consideration. Also, **if the creditor/landlord's personal name is recognized, perhaps a contact can be made which would help the investigating landlord avoid a problem tenant.** Titling your collection agency account "Landlord Your Name" is a terrific way to pay it forward in your real estate investor community.

Immediately after turning over an account for collection, **it will begin appearing on the credit report of all individuals connected with the debt** (including each tenant on the lease as well as any cosigner) as a collection account. This will negatively affect their credit reports going forward, and collection efforts will begin. **You do not need to have a judgement against a former tenant to turn over their account for collection.** You simply must have a legitimate uncollected balance on someone's account like any business that uses debt collectors such as utilities, healthcare providers, and credit card companies.

I will be the first to tell you that actually getting any money from collection agencies is rare, but putting a collection account onto a former tenant's credit report can sometimes be satisfaction enough...

especially when it warns future landlords. Sometimes tenants eventually pay up with the agency's efforts, but usually it remains a negative factor in their report. Then, occasionally, when a long-ago tenant is cleaning up their credit to impress a lender for a home loan, for example, you will get a call about paying off their balance.

Instances of unplanned tenant management tasks would include:

- Lease violations
  - There are as many ways for a tenant to be in violation of their lease as there are sentences in the lease form. **Good tenant management includes not only doing the routine things the tenant expects you to do; it includes doing what the tenant does not expect you to do which is call them out when they are off track with following what they agreed to when they signed the lease. There are three caveats.**

    - Do not ignore lease violations.
    - Give notice shortly after becoming aware of the violation.
    - Enforce lease terms fairly among tenants.

    If you ignore lease violations, human nature says the tenant will believe you do not care if the violation continues. It opens the door for the violation to get worse and for different violations to occur. Soon, especially if the infraction is readily seen, the situation will be out of control as other tenants copy with their own version of the violation.

    The longer a situation continues after you have become aware of a lease violation, the harder it will be to correct it, and the more the tenant will question "why you're making such big deal about it all of the sudden." Tenants must be approached quickly about violations either verbally, in writing, or both.

    Especially when tenants live near each other, as in multi-unit properties, they will see when other tenants violate the lease.

And they talk to each other about the landlord and how they are treated. It is obvious that lease terms must be enforced uniformly among tenants, or there will be discord not only between you and the miffed tenants, but between neighbors. This can lead to decisions not to renew leases that did not need to be made.

○ Depending on the nature and severity of the violation, **you must determine whether it is appropriate to notify the tenant verbally, in writing, or both.** A cordial talk with a resident about how they need to cut their grass more often may do the trick, but a lack of response from the tenant would call for an official written notice. If you are planning to take the tenant to court over the matter, your state probably requires a notice to be in writing such as with a notice to vacate the property due to non-payment of rent.

○ **You must be able to prove you gave the notice.** Sending a notice in regular mail is problematic for obvious reasons. Sending it certified can work, but only if the tenant signs for it. In some cases, email or text will suffice because you have a copy of what was sent as part of a chain of communication. Mostly, though, **the best practice is to post the notice in a sealed envelope on their entry door where they can't miss it.** Then, take a photo of the envelope on the door. This will provide a time stamp and the location.

○ **Some typical lease violations to look out for are:**

- ♦ Rent is not paid
- ♦ People living on the property who are not on the lease
- ♦ Not keeping their renters insurance in good standing with their carrier
- ♦ Getting a pet or having more pets than the lease allows
- ♦ Not paying required utilities
- ♦ Smoking in a non-smoking area or unit
- ♦ Damage or unauthorized changes being caused to the property
- ♦ Behavior disruptive or dangerous to neighbors
- ♦ Operating a business at a residence

- Not following rules and regulations specific to the property such as for a pool, playground, parking lot, or laundry
- Failing to do lawncare or snow removal
- Too many or junk vehicles on the property
- Refusing to allow entry to the unit for the landlord or contractors even with proper notice
- Drug activity or a conviction for a drug offence during tenancy
- Refusing to supply their new phone number

o **Notices to tenants should clearly state the following:**

- The nature of the violation
- Why the violation is a problem
- The fact that this is an infraction of the lease
- What they must do to cure the default
- The length of time before you will take further action
- What the consequence will be if the violation is not corrected within the allotted time.

  For example, "You have a junk car in your front yard. This is unsightly, and we could receive a citation from the city's code enforcement office. The lease states in Section 13 that no junk or disabled vehicles may be parked in or around the rental unit. Please remove the car within five days. If it is not removed by Saturday, the 15th, we will be forced to take this matter before the District Judge, which could result in the termination of your lease."

  If the cause of the default is nonpayment of rent, which is the most common breach, you would want to show the total amount past due, including any late fees and forfeited discounts. Spell it out so they can see how you arrived at your total.

o Tenants rarely move out in the time given in the notice. After all, if they do not have the money to pay you, they don't have the money to move. However, **I want to assure you that, most of the time, tenants will catch up on their rent at least by the time given in your notice. In fact, if you have called them about the rent a**

couple of days after it was due, they will probably pay it before you choose to give them written notice. Do not worry that every time a tenant is late it will lead to a written notice, much less an eviction.

o **Learning how to recognize lease violations, how to interact with tenants regarding the default, and how to proceed— particularly during the time in between when the default occurs and when it is time to give written notice to cure the default—are some of the most important landlording skills to develop.** You must learn how to be firm and how to maintain control while not alienating your customers who need to shape up. Your overall purpose is to protect your investment, either by getting what is required from your existing tenants, or moving on to new tenants.

- Evictions

  o **Tenants can be evicted from a rental dwelling for any violation of the lease contract,** and aside from possible differences in the required lengths of time between giving a tenant a notice of a violation before filing an eviction with the court, the procedure for getting someone out is the same no matter what the violation is. Much of each state's landlord/tenant laws are centered around the eviction process to bring order to an emotionally charged situation. While recognizing that property owners deserve relief from a tenant who has gone too far, the law wants to protect renters from heavy-handed self-help on the part of frustrated property owners. Even so, state laws may allow the tenant to waive certain rights by agreeing to the change when signing the lease, such as a shorter time following a notice before the landlord can go to the court.

  o Before I go any further, since this book explores both residential and commercial rental real estate investing, I must point out that **the laws governing evictions from where people live are vastly different from those covering evictions from where companies do business.** The basic difference is that residential evictions, which follow landlord/tenant statutes, require the following of strict procedures while protecting certain rights of tenants. One the other hand, commercial evictions, which follow contract law, allow landlords much more freedom to pull the plug on uncooperative business tenants.

Since you can pretty much just change the locks on a commercial tenant that has not paid their rent (after giving whatever notice agreed to in the lease contract), the point I am making is that in these pages I'm not going to dwell on commercial evictions. Suffice it to say that **the ease of getting a mom-and-pop store out of your strip plaza is much easier than getting mom and pop out of their home.** This can be considered an advantage of commercial rental property over residential.

o **Learning your area's residential eviction procedures in advance, or at least knowing who to ask if the situation arises, is imperative.** If you are in this business long enough, at some point you will need to evict a tenant, and **you will want to know the steps to take without wasting time before you act.**

Some states' laws are more pro landlord, and some are more pro tenant. I can only present an overview of the typical steps in a residential eviction, and give you some pointers to help keep you headed in the right direction.

o **If you want to go the eviction route, the first step is to let the tenant know this by giving them a notice which states they are in default of their lease**, explains what the violation is, what they need to do to cure the default, and gives them a set number of days to either comply or move out. **This sort of notice must be in writing**, and the clock starts ticking when you conspicuously post this notice on the leased premises. Normally, laws do not allow this to be a verbal notice for the clock to start. Once you serve the notice, the ball is in their court to contact you and/or cure the default. Do not contact them and ask them how they feel about the notice or what they are going to do about it. **Just wait for the allotted time to expire.**

- o **If the tenant cures the default within the allotted time, the process is over.** If another default occurs later, you must give a new notice, even if it is the same default.

- o If, during the allotted time, the tenant contacts you and offers to pay all or part of the past due rent (or to otherwise remedy the breach) in a timeframe *after* the allotted time, **you have a decision to make about whether to accept their plan or take the matter to court**. The answer will depend on your history with the tenant, and how much you want to keep the tenant.

- o If you hear nothing from the tenants, and you are sure they have not already moved out, it is time to **turn up the heat by taking this matter before a District Judge**. On the day after the time has passed for them to fall back in line, you can file for an eviction. You will probably pay a court fee at that time, and it will set off a chain of events starting with the court notifying the tenants.

- A sudden event has occurred that affects the tenant's normal enjoyment of the property

  - o What comes to mind here is **something that affects the habitability of the property** from either a physical standpoint or a situational standpoint. It could concern solely their dwelling, or a larger region. Examples are:

    - ◆ A fire, smoke, or explosion
    - ◆ A natural disaster like flood, earthquake, storm, landslide, volcano
    - ◆ Long-term power outage
    - ◆ Mass violence
    - ◆ Safety evacuation order from local authorities
    - ◆ Fallen tree
    - ◆ Vehicle collision into the building
    - ◆ Crime event on the property

- **Renters insurance will pay to temporarily house tenants due to any of these occurrences,** but any such occurrence will trigger an unplanned interaction with your customers. Severe damage to your property or a community-wide change in habitability will challenge your operational systems along with your labor and material resources. These things will also challenge your personal skills in both asset management and people management.

  I am not going to lay out a step-by-step action plan for handling surprise disruptions to rental properties, but I will say that **with every disaster comes opportunities.** One of those is the opportunity to shine in the eyes of your tenants with the way you manage the situation, and another is the valuable education you will get when you go through such a thing.

- The tenant wants to make a change in the lease

  - The changes *you* want to make in the lease, such as a change in the rent, can be on your regular schedule, but sometimes tenants come up with requests that require some unplanned attention. The good news is that **these requests are more likely to come from better tenants who want to do the right thing,** as opposed to ones who proceed with a lease violation while planning to ask for forgiveness later if they get caught.

  - Usually, though, a change in a tenant's life is not reported to their landlord unless it somehow impacts the status quo with the lease, and **it is rarely a good change for the landlord.** Often, it affects the tenant's ability to pay the rent or perhaps even stay in the apartment. The obvious life event of this sort is the loss of a job, but it could also be the death or breakup with someone who shared the apartment with them. The remaining tenant may not be able to afford the rent, or even if the rent is not an issue, they simply cannot remain in the apartment or possibly in the area.

Alternatively, life could be going in a happier direction with an impending marriage or birth of a child which leaves their current living arrangements impractical. The big news could be a job promotion that comes with a transfer. Maybe a close relative needs to move in with them for health or financial reasons, or vice versa. Undeniably for everyone, life is what happens when you're busy making other plans (John Lennon).

○ When you are surprised by a request to change something in a lease, you may find yourself in a discussion you were not prepared to have with the tenants in question. It is usually a good idea to hear out the tenants, but do not make a decision right then. From my experience, my first reaction in my head to their requests is usually a "no", and I am looking for the words to deny them. But "no" might not be the best answer, so my recommendation is that you **assure the tenant of your understanding of their request. Then, tell them you will get back to them after you consider it**.

Sometimes, after careful consideration, I have found that I can accommodate their request without being unfair to other tenants or detrimental to my business. In fact, **their request may be an opportunity to raise the rent.** For example, just like how you may agree to do an upgrade in the apartment in exchange for a higher rent (which would *not* necessitate a change in the lease other than a notation of the new rental amount), you may agree to allow a pet for a raise in the rent (something that *would* require the lease to be altered).

If you cannot accept their request, you must be understanding, but firm. However, if you are going to consent to a different reality from what is stated in the lease, **you must put the updated terms in writing**, and have everyone involved sign to indicate their agreement.

○ If the change is minor, it could be that handwritten changes may be made to everyone's copies of the original lease form with the changes being initialed. An example would be agreeing to extend the length of the lease for a month to accommodate a soon-to-be-moving tenant's closing date for a home they are buying. This would be called an *amendment* to the lease because you are simply changing an existing part of the lease without adding any new subject matter.

If the change is significant in that it involves documents or side agreements being added to the lease, those documents are referred to as *addendums* because they become attachments to the lease. The government's Lead Based Paint Disclosure form is an example of an addendum, although it doesn't change any part of the lease.

Some instances when a tenant may come to you with a request for a change in the existing lease terms would include:

- Adding or removing a spouse or roommate
- Adding a pet
- Adding a service dog or emotional support animal
- Cutting or extending the lease term
- Altering a responsibility such as for cutting the grass
- Changing the day of the month their rent is due
- Transferring the lease to different tenants
- Operating a business at the property
- Erecting a storage shed or above-ground pool
- Installing equipment that would require an alteration

You may be able to access forms online or from your local landlord association which can be used as addendums to handle some of these lease changes. An example would be a Pet Agreement that spells out all the additional responsibilities and expectations for tenants who have pets. Same for service and emotional support animals. **Otherwise, you will need to compose your own document** that clearly states that, although it says something different in the lease, all parties agree to the stated change. The signed documents would then be attached to each party's original lease.

- Death of all tenants on the lease
  - This is rare, although obviously more possible if you are renting to only one person in the apartment. Of course, if this happens, you will

be dealing with the representatives of the deceased estate. Be very careful how you proceed at this point, because **there is a whole other set of state laws that come into effect to combine with the landlord/tenant laws immediately upon a tenant's death.**

- If not all the adults on the lease die, then your business continues as usual with the remaining tenants. However, if all the tenants are now dead, **the most important law to remember is that you must not allow access to the apartment to anyone except whoever can prove to you they are the court-appointed representative of the estate of the deceased.** This would be the duly sworn executor or administrator of each estate.

If people got in there before you became aware of any deaths, you cannot help that. But once you know, you must change the locks and open lines of communication with the emergency contacts so the executor is aware of how to contact you. This is not to preclude, however, meeting with someone who needs clothes of the decedent for the burial or to retrieve important papers to get the estate settlement rolling. This would be done under your supervision, and no other items could be taken on this visit. **The main legal concept here is that people who, under the decedent's will, are not entitled to the personal property of the decedent are not given an opportunity to come in and remove anything.**

Once the executor has emerged, you can allow them access to the apartment on their own. Perhaps you will not receive upcoming rent payments as scheduled while the estate has control of the apartment, but you will become a creditor of the estate, and you will eventually get paid before money is distributed to any heirs.

The main premise of this book is that you can invest in income property while you maintain a commitment to another source of income. Your goal could be to grow your real estate business to the point you can quit your W-2 job, or you may choose to balance both indefinitely. Either way, employing systems, procedures, and protocols for property and tenant management will keep you in the game with your power turned

on. Utilizing your predetermined resources for building your team, acquiring property, preparing your property, choosing your tenants, and the ongoing management of your properties and tenants will help you keep your family life, work life, and investing life separate and in balance. It will help you make better decisions by bringing order to chaos so you can focus on what is most important at the time. You will learn what is important at the moment, and what is not. You will not be tricked into someone else's poor planning becoming your crisis.

I promised I would end this chapter with a little "heart-to-heart" discussion of tenant management. Here are summaries of my key philosophies:

Most tenants are good people and will treat you and your property with reasonable respect. But not *all* will, and you cannot let it bother you. **If you are a decent landlord, and the tenants are not living up to your expectations, it's *them,* not you.** It is the opposite of the Seinfeld breakup catchphrase, "It's *me*, not *you*."

Part of how you keep from taking tenant issues personally is to not get personal with tenants. Simple, right? Be friendly yet firm with tenants, but not friends. Recognize that when tenants do crazy things, it's not about *you*. **If it were not for people who don't have their lives together, or are in transition, we would not have tenants for a good percentage of our units**. People who are not in a position to own their own home or place of business create our customer base to a large degree. There are reasons why people rent instead of own, and we are here to meet their needs and reap the benefits. Otherwise, unless they truly prefer to rent and not own, they may be out there buying property in competition with us.

Being firm with tenants means that you enforce the rental contract fairly and collect all rent due, and you are willing to end the rental contract (evict) without guilt when tenants don't pay or they otherwise break the lease. **When tenants don't pay, they are essentially turning you into a social service agency that benefits *them*.** When tenants try to make *their* drama *your* drama, or when they unload on you with the hardships they are experiencing (i.e. give you reasons why they can't pay the rent), they are attempting to turn *you* into a charity. But when you are fair and firm, then YOU decide which organized charity gets your free will contributions from the profits of your operation, and when that charity gets it...not the tenant and their own "disorganized charity" chipping away at your bottom line. **I'm not saying to never give a tenant a break. I'm saying that paying the rent in full is non-negotiable.** Give your tenants a break some other way if you want.

No tenant will be perfect, but that is no reason to forsake the benefits of the rental property business. If you are mature enough and capable in life of embracing an imperfect spouse, a disappointing child, a friend that lets you down now and then, a job you are not ecstatic about, a car that sometimes needs to be repaired, a movie that doesn't blow you away, or a vacation that wasn't as cool as you thought it should be, then you can deal with the unevenness of owning enough rental properties to make you rich.

Allow me to employ some double negatives here to make a few points. You don't *not* get married, have kids, have friends, work at a job, own a car, go to the movies, or go on vacation because of the potential pitfalls you have heard about. You don't *not* do these things even because you do not have all the information. No, you still do them despite the problems others have had in similar relationships even though you do not have much information in some cases. Marriages, kids, friends, jobs, cars, movies, or vacations do not exactly come with detailed instruction manuals (except for a car, but who reads it?), but you dive into these things anyway despite the negatives and uncertainty.

Here is the difference. **The rental real estate world has an expansive array of instruction manuals (this being one of them). I believe this gives you more of a chance to be successful** at this type of investing than at any of those other things I mentioned in the last paragraph that you are likely to do anyway without much instruction. About half of couples divorce, and everyone who stays married knows of something they would change about their spouse if they could. All kids disappoint you occasionally. Friends are not always around when you need them, jobs suck at least part of the time, cars break down, and the things you do for entertainment do not always meet your expectations. But you do them anyway. So, why not rental property?

Just like in most aspects of life, things will go wrong with rental property. You will have a tenant you must evict, damage to fix, messes to clean up, or some sort of suboptimum situation to deal with. **But with instruction manuals like this one, you can learn to relax when issues come up**. How do you relax when you've got a vacancy, a property needing repairs, or a problem tenant? By doing the following:

- Educate yourself with pertinent instruction manuals like this.
- Maintain the correct "big picture" perspective (proper attitude). Believe you are going to "get rich slow" (or maybe even faster), and move on from problems.
- Keep money aside for opportunities and emergencies.
- Have a good team, and know who to call.

Fix the apartment, find a new tenant, and get back to cash flow and increasing your wealth. If you sell out during discouraging times, you will be selling to another investor at a "don't wanter" price. That investor will gain the wealth and income you could have had because that investor "gets it" and does not care about the problems that have gotten under your skin at the property. They will be taking over with new energy and new optimism for that property without a care for the experiences you have had there. So, step back, take a breath, focus on the positive, and "sell" your property (or maybe even your entire portfolio) *back* to *yourself,* and move on.

7 THE AUTHOR'S BACKSTORY

At this point, I am going to take a break from making an analogy between the subject matter of each chapter and a phase of construction. Let's get back to my comments in Chapter One about not having to know everything before you get started. When my wife and I got married, she moved in with me at the house I already had owned since before we even met. In her eyes it was *my* house and not *our* house. I recognized that view, and we soon set about evaluating the possibilities. We quickly realized we were both enthusiastic about building a new home. Not just a home chosen from a slate of floor plans and constructed by a home builder, but a custom designed one. And not just a custom designed home proposed by an architect, but one designed by US! And not just a home we designed and had built by a builder, but one WE general contracted! Holy cow! Although I had been in the rental property business for twenty-two years at that point, and my wife worked for a real estate brokerage in their office, neither of us had ANY experience with building design or new construction.

But we were determined. First, we threw ideas on the table as to what features we wanted our new home to have so that it would be our home for a long time into the future. I literally made the first sketch of a floor plan on a napkin while

I was sitting on stage playing dinner music during a Christmas party at which I was DJing. Once we knew the approximate footprint of the house, and where the garage and doors were going to be, we began looking for building lots that would accommodate our design. After searching all over the parts of the county we were considering, unbelievably we bought a lot in a new subdivision that was being started about a hundred yards from our current house! That was in May after drawing out the house on a napkin in December. At that point, we bought a house design computer program at an electronics store and made a detailed drawing that an architect employed to make the renderings necessary for contractors to bid on and follow during construction. The lot was cleared on Labor Day, and the shell was weathered in by winter. My wife took some vacation days here and there as we ran around town selecting materials. The interior was finished over the winter, and we moved in mid-April.

People joked that the general rule was you should not try to build a house with your spouse until you've been married at least 10 years. We did it in about 2 ½ years from wedding to move-in. Not only are we still together, but we still live there to this day. When our son was born, the house was perfectly suited for raising him. As we have moved through various phases of our life together, every once in a while I am struck by how well suited this house has been for us as a result of the forethought we gave the design and the location we chose...even though the final layout of the house turned out to be not much different than that original sketch on a napkin at a DJ gig.

What?? Did I say DJ gig?? Yep. You just discovered it. **I got rich slowly by pursuing two passions simultaneously.** One was performing as a mobile DJ, and the other was rental property. I did both, and **I want you to believe it's OK to add rental real estate to some other source of income that you don't want to give up.**

I guess it's time for my bio. After having a neighbor who was a DJ on the radio and then an older kid in the neighborhood who built a low wattage pirate radio station in his house where I got to be on the air occasionally, I got interested in being a radio DJ while still in grade school and junior high back in the 1960's. Back then, there was no such thing as a mobile DJ, so I assumed the only way to live out this passion I had developed for popular music—and wanting to play it for other people to enjoy—was to do it over the airwaves. I guess I should point out that, unlike my mother who could read music and play by ear since she was a child and who sang solos in our church choir until her voice gave out in her eighties, I discovered I couldn't play any instrument very well or sing a note in tune. But, even in junior high, I had a deep voice, and I could read aloud well. So, DJing it would be for me instead of playing in a band like every other kid who saw the Beatles on the Ed Sullivan Show wanted to do.

The other thing that was going on in my life during junior high and into high school was that I had a newspaper route in our neighborhood. I started with just one route when I was eleven, which we kept in the prior carrier's name until I was twelve when the newspaper allowed me to have it in my own name. Then, I added a second adjacent route a while later. I was quite successful at adding customers and, over the years, I won several prizes in contests the newspaper ran to increase its circulation. One prize was a bus tour to Washington DC and another to New York City. One year, though, I won the largest annual contest they had, which was cosponsored by Parade Magazine, which our paper included in the Sunday edition. It was called the *Young Columbus Contest*, and each year they took the winners to countries that Columbus had visited. I went with over a hundred other carriers from across the nation to Tunisia and Italy for 10 days. This was the "holy grail" of newspaper carrier contests!

Although I added many customers that year from among the families who lived in the existing houses on my paper route, I was aided by another significant event that occurred in our neighborhood. An investor built four four-unit townhouse buildings right on my route, and I was able to get most of the new occupants to subscribe. But the real significance of this was that it was the event which first made me start thinking about rental property. Our neighborhood was a subdivision of single-family homes, so the introduction of multi-family homes in the area was a curiosity. They were constructed on the last undeveloped lots at the edge of the subdivision. As I watched them being built on my daily paper route trek, I began to ask questions of my parents (who had rented in the past) and others about how rental property worked. I have a distinct memory of being in my bedroom and "doing the math" for how to make money with apartments (to whatever degree a fifteen-year-old could figure this out). So, at that point, **a decision was made to invest in rental property in the future in addition to the disc jockey path I was forging.**

So, after gazing at the vacant lot of the radio business and dreaming about what the possibilities were, I snapped back to reality and took my first steps toward preparing for an opportunity to actually work as a DJ on the radio. In 11th grade I co-founded, with my best friend at the time, a nonprofit organization called the SPRING Foundation. It stood for Students Promoting the Return of Integrity to the Now Generation. The Now Generation was a term that was bantered around in the media at the time in reference to our segment of the Baby Boomers. The Free Dictionary by Farlex describes the Now Generation as "A generation of (typically) young people described as wanting everything to be given to them as quickly as possible in return for as little effort or sacrifice as possible." Obviously, we weren't getting much respect for that, so I thought it was time to bring back some integrity. The purpose of the SPRING Foundation was the production and distribution of radio public service announcements (PSAs) that dealt with the pressing social issues of youth. Our PSAs addressed subjects such as drug abuse, ecology and brotherhood.

What I did was interview virtually all the rock acts who were coming to town and playing at the colleges and the local concert venues. The promoters were just local people or college organizations, so I literally just called them up or chased them down and asked if I could go backstage to interview the bands. I would lug a portable 7" reel to reel tape recorder into the dressing room and ask band members to make comments about drug abuse, for example, while I held a little microphone in their face. I had a blast! I interviewed Poco, Rare Earth, Sha Na Na, the Beach Boys and the James Gang to name a few. I always laugh when I think about talking with Joe Walsh when he was still with the James Gang. I asked him to make a comment about drug abuse, and he responded with his trademark dry humor in that special unique Joe Walsh voice that has a restricted tightness to it which is in full contrast to his fluent and full-sounding guitar playing. He said, "Well, you can play a guitar really fast on speed, but not for long." Joe, as you may know, went on to live the life of a full-fledged rock star stoner...but not for long. Joe has been stone cold sober since the early 1990's before the Eagles reformed. He is reported to be an amazing Alcoholics Anonymous speaker, and if you ever have a chance to hear his two-minute elevator speech on TV about recognizing that you have a substance abuse problem and straightening out your life, it will bring a "wow" to your lips and maybe a tear to your eye.

After the interviews, I would take the raw tape to the production studio at any one of about four different local radio stations where I had somehow successfully pestered the management to give me some instruction on how their studio worked, and to let me in there alone to create. What was in it for them? Well, as you may know, broadcast facilities are required by the FCC to air a certain number of minutes of "public service time" along with their regular programming and paid commercials. At that point, they mostly had dry, government-sounding PSAs talking about things like joining the armed services or being a good driver. Those PSAs did not sound like their normal programming and stood out as un-cool. What I would do was edit the comments of the rock stars into snippets, with their popular songs playing in the background, into thirty or sixty second spots. My own announcer voice would be at the open and close, and the subject matter qualified the final product as a PSA. The stations loved them because they utilized music from the artists whose music they were already playing, and they sounded like they belonged in the stations' top forty formats.

What was I doing here? I was clearing the weeds on my vacant radio business lot by asking a lot of questions of the on-air DJs and of the management and owners at the stations. I was finding out many of the things I would need to know if I became a DJ and clearing up a lot of my preconceptions. Also, I was breaking ground on some DJ skills by practicing audio production and announcing...all in advance of even spinning my first record on-air during my first radio show that would become the foundation of my DJ career.

I did the SPRING Foundation thing throughout high school, and then it was time to go off to college. For a major, I was attracted to accounting. My father was a career excise tax auditor for the IRS, and he sometimes lent his bookkeeping skills to organizations and small businesses he had a connection with outside of work. Additionally, my older sister's husband was an accountant, and both he and my father influenced me in the areas of money management and record keeping starting with my four-and-a-half-year career as a paperboy in our neighborhood. Please don't judge, but I've kept a record of every dollar I've earned and spent since

I was eleven. I enjoy it, but some would joke it's a sickness. However, **being willing to pay attention to the details of money in and money out has served me well over the years.**

A degree in accounting can be used in any industry in which you choose to work. My plan was to enter the broadcasting industry as a radio disc jockey, maybe move around to some big stations in major markets, and then, armed with my degree in accounting, work my way up through management. Eventually, then, I would move into an ownership position in a radio station. In addition, along the way with my extra money, I would invest in apartment buildings. So, with that in mind I began a quest to find a college with not only a good accounting department but also a decent college radio station.

I didn't have to look too far. About 75 miles down the interstate was Grove City College, a nationally recognized medium sized Western Pennsylvania private college that is routinely ranked as one of the country's top colleges by *U.S. News & World Report* and *The Princeton Review*. The head of their accounting department wrote textbooks! AND they had a well-established student organization that ran their TWO radio stations...an AM and an FM! Grove City College is actually part of world radio history. The first scheduled radio broadcast was from the campus of Grove City College in April of 1920. The audience was the New Castle Rotary Club in a neighboring county who sat and listened to their "guest speaker" (the then president of Grove City College) on a strange box in the front of the room called a radio. The college's AM station continued regular broadcasting from that point on. Now, I know some of you (particularly those of you from Western PA) are raising your eyebrows because you've always heard that KDKA in Pittsburgh is the oldest radio station in the world. Well, it *is* the oldest *commercial* radio station in the world, but KDKA did not go on the air until November of 1920 when it began coverage of the Harding-Cox presidential election, and it has continued regular programming since then. The AM station on the campus of Grove City College had been broadcasting for six months by then, and when I got to the campus in 1972, they had a three-inch-thick binder of memorabilia from their 50th anniversary a couple of years before. There was a very nice letter of acknowledgement from KDKA in there. And there's a classy historical marker in downtown Grove City.

They told me typically freshmen were not on the air; they aided the upper classmen while learning the ropes. Also, freshmen rarely arrived on campus with their FCC license, so part of being involved with the radio club was to learn how to pass your FCC exam. Back then, even the DJs had to get a Radio Telephone Third Class Operator Permit by taking a test at a Federal exam site. This is so the Federal Communications Commission was sure that you, as someone who may be the only one on duty at a broadcast facility, had knowledge of certain rules and regulations like knowing how to power on and power off a radio transmitter.

I was determined to have a radio show as a freshman, so I studied independently and went to Buffalo, NY and passed my FCC exam over the summer after high school. Then, coupled with my experience with the SPRING Foundation and my freshly minted FCC license, by the second week of my first semester I was the only freshman on the air. I had an album rock show on the FM, and by second semester I had two shows...a Top 40 shift *and* the album rock show for which the college gave me an annual award. Also, during my first semester, I became the part-time weekend guy at the commercial radio station in Grove City. That was an FM station owned by the mayor (!) and, being a beautiful music station, there wasn't a whole lot of live announcing. But I learned a lot, and listeners occasionally commented favorably about my music choice. By the end of freshman year, I was named Program Director of both the AM and the FM in addition to doing both of my shows. The foundation for my broadcast career had been laid.

After a while at Grove City, I started sending "air checks" back to the Program Directors at each of the radio stations in Erie where I had done the editing for the SPRING Foundation PSAs. Finally, during Easter break of my sophomore year in 1974, I was offered the position of the weekend part-timer at WCCK, Erie's most powerful station...a 50,000-watt FM with a Top 40 format. They told me I could start as soon as I got home for summer vacation and then either return to Grove City or stay. I chose to transfer to Mercyhurst College (now University) in Erie where I finished my accounting degree over the next two years while continuing at WCCK.

Then, another life-changing event occurred. In March of my senior year of college the evening DJ left, and I was offered the full-time air shift of 7 p.m. to 1 a.m. Monday through Friday. Next, a few weeks later, one of the other DJs asked me to fill in for him at a school "sock hop" he was not going to be able to do. Listeners, particularly schools, would occasionally call the radio station and ask for a DJ to make a personal appearance and play records for dancing. I could never do this because I, being the weekend guy, was usually on the air. But on Saturday, April 3, 1976, I did my first mobile DJ event in the gym at a little school just over the border in New York called Clymer High School. I got paid $75, and my life was never the same.

While I was at WCCK I was part of the first group of on-air personalities that finally toppled the long-time reigning AM station from Top 40 ratings dominance in the Erie market. My full-time evening show had the highest ratings in our market for virtually every daypart and age group in our market survey, and I became Production Director. But the lure of performing live in front of people became increasingly intriguing. So, I began promoting my availability for "record hops" as a WCCK jock outside of my on-air work. My first business cards said, "DISC JOCKEY FOR RENT."

It's time to fast-forward this story. Over the next year, as I built up my mobile DJ business, I quickly found out I could make more in one night than I was making all week at the radio station. So, in June of 1977, I left to go on my own. The radio people said I would starve because they thought one had to be connected with a radio station to get appearances. This proved to be wrong, however, because within five years, none of the popular mobile DJs had ever even worked at a radio station. Without a role model, I set about pioneering the mobile DJ business and became the first full-time professional mobile DJ in our part of the country. I developed the largest lighting, sound system and special effects show for mobile DJ use, and, after lobbying General Telephone for years, a heading for Disc Jockeys was finally created in the Yellow Pages with me as the first advertiser. When the newspaper started an annual top-of-the-mind survey (there were no nominations...readers sent in their votes by writing in their favorites in a variety of categories) called the Erie's Choice Award, I routinely came in first place. This was significant because it was just a "disc jockey" category and not a "mobile disc jockey" category, so the people that followed me on the list were primarily radio DJs. Ultimately, over a little more than thirty-five years I did 5051 appearances...nearly all of them individual "one-nighters."

Why have I laid out my mobile DJ career bio in a book about real estate investment? Because **it's my personal testimony as to the viability of the premises of this book which is that it's possible to add rental real estate to your otherwise busy life and not regret it.** I wanted you to see that I really did have something else going on that I was passionate about while I was getting rich slowly. Obviously, being a full-time mobile DJ for thirty-five years took up a lot of my time, energy, and brain power. But, in keeping with the other part of my school-age plan, I bought my first rental property in January of 1978 barely a year and a half after my first mobile DJ appearance, and I just kept slowly adding on after that. Eventually, in 1991 I began rehabbing and reselling single-family homes before the TV shows taught everyone that this was called "flipping". By the time I retired from DJing (and the money stopped) in 2011, I was flipping two to five houses a year, and we had a very nice portfolio of one- and two-unit properties. We (my wife and I) have added some even nicer properties since then, and everything cash flows nicely. Plus, we still flip a few houses every year, and now we do hard money lending. I am glad we did all of it.

So, there it is. My condensed version of how I added rental real estate to my life which already included other things. **It is my belief this is a possible path for you and that you should consider it.** Also, I wanted to illustrate how the steps I'm laying out for rental property investing were also evident in my path to a disc jockey career. First, I saw the possibilities as a youngster, and then I educated myself and learned some hands-on skills before I got to college where the foundation of my DJ career was laid when I finally got on the air. Now, granted, I did not stick with broadcasting, but the mobile DJ career turned out much better. **No matter what the plans are that we make, we must be willing to pivot when a better way comes into view. We must be ready for luck. By the way, when you're working your way through a plan, there's no such thing as luck. In those instances, "luck" is more defined as preparation meeting opportunity. But don't just wait for opportunity; create your own opportunities. Take the initiative, and control your own destiny!**

OK, let's go back to the story about when we built our house. The point I wanted to make about our experience is that we embarked on something we had never done before without knowing absolutely everything about it. We imagined the possibilities and then we educated ourselves enough to get started. We hired contractors to perform the different trades, and we hired an experienced contractor friend to be a project manager to make sure things happened in the right order. He also suggested other contractors who could handle work when we did not otherwise have a contact. We selected materials as we went along, and made other decisions as needed. I want you to grasp that, **if "not knowing everything ahead of time" is keeping you from investing, then please let go of that self-imposed restriction!**

While some people fail to act due to thinking they will lose because they do not know enough, **there are some who do not act on something that would be beneficial because they think they know it all,** and what they "know" is telling them not to do it. Or they mistakenly think they know so much that their overconfidence leads to failure. Author, professional speaker, and trainer T. Harv Eker is credited with saying **that the three most dangerous words in the English language are "I know that…"** He says those words can be troubling because they signal closed-mindedness. His point is that most successes did not result from a set plan, rather that they are surprises resulting from something you *didn't know.*

I believe it's better to tackle something new knowing you don't have complete knowledge but having enough preparation so that your inter-section with opportunity will result in "luck." Then, commit to working hard. That tact is better than failing to act because you don't know everything there is to know, or acting recklessly because you think you *do* know everything.

For example, I didn't know much when I started the SPRING Foundation or when I did my first mobile DJ job or when I bought my first rental. I also didn't have it all figured out before I flipped my first house or when we designed and general contracted our home. The same was certainly true when I made my first hard money loan. I was truly surprised by the degree of success of some of these things, particularly the mobile DJ business. The other things had all been done before by others, just not yet by me. However, the mobile DJ business was not a path that was already known by anyone. I literally thought it would last a few years, and then I would probably head back to broadcasting!

General Colin Powell is credited with stating that you should make your decision when you know 70% of what there is to know about a situation. Interesting...a guy who led the most powerful and successful military in the history of the world was making decisions without knowing absolutely everything in advance. **You don't have to wait until you know 100% of the facts before getting into real estate.**

I will conclude this chapter by emphasizing that, because I took the time to educate myself to a reasonable degree before I bought my first property, I had the confidence to move forward. Although I did not know "everything" about it, I was, however, knowledgeable beyond the most basic phase you can be in before you do something new. That basic phase is called the "I don't even know what I don't know" phase. That is when you really are going into something blindly. *You* have *this* book and many other resources. **Absorb the information, and you will have enough to get started. Experience will fill in the blanks as you go along.**

In the next chapter, I am going to address house flipping as a parallel investment activity to rental real estate. There are many similarities between rental properties and "flipper properties" when it comes to acquisition and rehabbing, but the exit strategies are completely different.

8
HOUSE FLIPPING: AN OVERVIEW

I am going to continue my departure from analogous chapter titles by presenting this chapter on house flipping. Everything up through Chapter Three was fairly general in the sense that we explored your mindset, education, property acquisition, and the preparation of your property for either a tenant or a buyer. Chapter Four assumed you wanted to find some tenants, so you may have noticed there was a "Y" in the road after Chapter Three. **Renting your property to tenants is *one* of the paths to take at that point, and the other is selling your property to another investor or owner-occupant.** So, this chapter could have followed Chapter Three just as easily.

"Flipping" a property refers to buying a property, holding it for a relatively short period of time (typically less than a year) during which you may or may not improve the property, and then re-selling the property (presumably at a profit). The slang comes from the act of "turning over" the property rapidly to another owner. The "flip" begins with the process of searching for a property to buy, and it ends with the closing to sell it to the next owner. Some erroneously refer to rehabbing a property as doing a "flip," but this is incorrect because the rehab part is only a portion of the flipping process, and a sale to a new owner is required to officially call it a "flip."

When you operate rental properties, your objective is to build monthly income. Your intention is to enjoy the cash flow until you sell to the next investor. This could be for many years, and most likely the sale will net you a big check in the end. Flipping is an entirely different business model, however, because you are only going to get one check. There is no steady monthly income, only the check from the sale. The model requires a steady stream of properties. There is no more income until the next project is completed, but the attraction is that **the profits from flipping can be not only immediate, but significant.** It could take many years of rental income from the same property to equal the lump sum profit from selling it right after you finish the rehab.

After about thirteen years of owning only rentals, I did my first flip. I would have done it sooner, but it wasn't until then that I had the resources to buy a property for cash. Those resources were in the form of two friends who put up the money while I found the property and did the labor for the rehabs. One friend was a real estate attorney, and the other owned a mortgage brokerage. Both were familiar with the business, but they lacked the time and expertise to do my part of the deal. We split the profit three ways on our first two deals. On my third project, I only partnered with my mortgage broker friend, and we split the $32,000 profit (big money in 1993) fifty-fifty, again with me doing the rehab. An interesting sidenote is that I sold that property myself with one ad, one phone call, one showing, in the middle of a January snowstorm. Sounds crazy, right? Read on.

On my next deal, which was bought at a Sheriff Sale while the former owners were still living in it, an investor/friend and I each put up half the cash. Our intention was to split the work and split the profit after a minor rehab. We sold the property while the people who lost the house in foreclosure were still occupying it. We had someone replace a window in the bathroom, which was the extent of the rehab. My partner swept the garage floor after the former owners moved out in advance of the sale to our buyers, and I removed the ping-pong table from the basement. That ping-pong table was in my basement for many years. We split about a $20,000 profit.

An offshoot of this story is that, while we were offering the property on the market ourselves, a long-time friend who had just become a Realtor brought us a buyer in exchange for half the regular commission (the property was not on the Multi-List). Margel became my Realtor for every property I sold on the Multi-List from then on, and she brought me many of the deals I purchased. She is the mother of Steve Szumigale, who contributed the bonus chapter to this book.

After those initial four house flipping deals, I have been on my own with no partners other than my wife. Over the ensuing decades I have flipped well over one hundred houses. So, as you can see, I have travelled both paths from the "Y" in the road. Both have served a purpose, with rentals contributing steady income, and flips providing chunks of cash. We withdrew some of the profits from each source to augment my wife's job income and my DJ income, but mostly we kept the money in the business to use for down payments and rehabs on rentals. The profits also allowed us to rely less on credit lines while conducting multiple flip projects simultaneously. We also paid off our personal residence (the construction of which was recounted in the chapter on my backstory) in about ten years, and now our home stands as security for one of our credit lines with a credit limit of several hundred thousand dollars.

I wanted to tell you those stories not only to inspire you, but to emphasize two points. **The first point is that the financing for a flip project is usually different from that for a rental property you intend to keep long term.** Short of the technique where *you* are the wholesaler who is selling the good deals you find to other investors for a small profit, you are going to need some cash. Everything through the first three chapters—right up to preparing the property for a tenant or a buyer—can be utilized universally whether you are interested in income property or flip property...except **it is impractical to use amortized loans (mortgages from banks) to buy property you intend to flip**. You may be able to arrange amortized seller financing to buy a flip, but not likely a mortgage from a bank.

The second point is that you are not likely to have the opportunity to apply nearly as many qualifiers on a flip property for which you are negotiating with an individual seller (or bidding on at an auction, for example) as you would for a rental property from another investor. You may need to take the property with no inspections, and you probably cannot require the seller to fix anything before the close. To tie these points together, **the theme with flip projects is to buy a property "as is" at a bargain price by offering cash and a quick close.** Then, you will also need more cash for the rehab.

House flipping can generate large chunks of cash in a matter of months if you have access to cash for the purchase and rehab. I refer you back to Chapter Two where sources of cash are discussed, and **I want to reiterate the usefulness of a relationship with a hard money lender.** There are no guarantees you will make a profit in the end, though. **The mistake of putting too much money into an income property can usually be erased by holding the property long enough to mitigate your misjudgement, but since the holding period is so short for a flip, you don't have much room for error regarding your expenses and your resale price.**

This book, however, is about confidently adding *rental* real estate to your life. So, I'm going to leave you with just a taste of flipping information at this point. But, if you would like to explore house flipping in detail, **I am providing the QR code below which will link you to bonus material** on my website. Some of the points made there are also covered in the earlier part of this book through Chapter Three, but **I wanted to have a stand-alone tutorial on flipping to which you could refer if that is your path.**

The flipping process shares much with that of preparing a new property for use as a rental. The big differences in the business models between flipping and renting, as I pointed out earlier, are in the financing and the way you make your money. **Do you want paid in a non-recurring chunk in a matter of months from selling a flip, or would you rather have a monthly cash flow from an income property, followed by a big chunk (or monthly income from a mortgage you hold) when you sell a rental property?**

Operating either type of business requires steady deal flow, especially for a flipping business. Even though the money stops until you complete your next flip, you may be tempted by the potential big checks from flipping houses because you are not sure how rapidly you could get to where you want to be regarding your net cash flow from rental properties. To that end, in the following chapter, **I am going to lay out a hypothetical journey from zero to a net monthly cash flow of $10,000 per month** from adding rental real estate to your life... and not regretting it!

9
HOW TO GROW FROM $0 TO $10,000 PER MONTH NET CASH FLOW FROM RENTAL PROPERTIES

At about the time I began writing this book, Dan Lane contacted me to guest on an episode of his *Rental Income Podcast* (Episode #349 1/11/2022) where we would explore **what it would take to get to $10,000 of net income from residential rentals, and how long that journey would be.** The idea was not to tell the story of how this person or that person accomplished this; it was to map out a hypothetical path that could be followed by anyone intent on meeting this goal. Dan and I did our best to cover the outline I came up with in the allotted time, but we were not able to elaborate on some of the details.

Ten thousand dollars per month was picked not only because it is a nice round number, but because it represents an amount of income that is greater than most "real" jobs and greater than the net profit of most sole proprietor small businesses. Also, it's an impactful amount for most people when added to their income from existing sources, and it may be enough to cut the ties with one's W-2 job if that is their desire. Yet, at the same time, **it is an attainable amount in a reasonable length of time in an industry open to anyone who wants to be a player. It doesn't rely heavily on market conditions, developing technology, product preferences, luck, or multi-level marketing downlines being developed.** We're talking about places to live. Something everybody will always need. It's "not rocket science." **It's just a life decision to acquire assets that produce income derived from renting out a universally desired product.**

What follows is a refinement and expansion of the outline Dan and I used for the podcast. I am going to take you step-by-step, purchase-by-purchase, on a hypothetical investing story with a happy ending. I want to say that anyone can do this, but to be candid, we must make some supporting assumptions about the investor regarding background and life habits. However, these are basic assumptions that you would likely make if you were to describe anyone who you believed had the potential to succeed in life. So, **if you see yourself in the following description, zero to ten grand a month is possible for you!**

It will be assumed that the following is true about our hypothetical investor:

- They have identified their "why" or reason for wanting to take action. **Without motivation, there will be no action, and without action, there will be no change.**

- They believe that investing in rental real estate is a viable path to improving their financial position. **Without belief, there is no interest in a particular path.** (These first two points reflect the reason why so much attention was paid to establishing the proper mindset at the beginning of this book before we got to the how-to parts.)

- They have spent some time and effort on obtaining some education about purchasing and operating income properties. They are not expecting this hypothetical scenario to become reality for them if they haven't studied how to buy property and what to do with it after they own it.

- They have connected with other real estate investors in the area through a professional organization, and they are beginning to develop relationships with Realtors and other professionals related to the business such as contractors, attorneys, and lenders.

- They have maintained a good reputation in the community for being a person of integrity, reliability, and fairness. They make good decisions, follow through on what they say they are going to do, and treat people properly.

- They have developed a credit history which shows a good credit score of at least 620. Also, lenders will require they have no delinquent federal debt or judgements, tax-related or otherwise, or debt associated with past FHA mortgages.

- **They have developed good financial habits beyond those reflected in a credit report in that <u>they have the discipline to live below their means. Being able to save money beyond just meeting their obligations is key to progressing financially.</u>**

- They have demonstrated the ability to maintain steady employment without too many changes of employer. In our example, they need only have verifiable income of only $40,000 annually.

- They are willing to put $1,000 out of their job income toward their housing expenses (exclusive of utilities) and/or savings each month which will be added to the net cash flow from their income properties. No cash flow from the properties will be withdrawn for several years, but will instead be used to acquire more property.

- They do not own the property in which they live now.

- They have saved (or have been gifted) about $6,000 for the down payment and closing costs on their first property in this example.

As a preview, the course of this journey is to first purchase a multi-unit property, and live in one of the units. Then, more units are purchased using different methods. Eventually, a nicer single-family home is acquired after which the first residence is kept as a rental. More and more units are added by utilizing the cash flow from existing units. Obviously, there are as many variables as there are people and properties which could impact how long it would take to get to $10,000 net per month, but I believe **this is a good illustration of how to build cash flow from rentals.** Also, for purposes of illustration, we are assuming all tenants are paying for their own utilities including gas (or propane of fuel oil), electricity, water, sewer, and garbage. Consequently, the costs for any utilities are not included in expenses for any of the properties. If it were necessary to include any utilities in the rent, it is assumed that the rents used in the examples would be commensurately higher to cover them.

STEP ONE: Buy a $100,000 2-unit property, and live in one unit while renting out the other.

A $100,000 cost for a 2-unit property, less a $3,500 down payment, with a $96,500 30-year mortgage at 4%, leaves a mortgage payment of $461 per month. Assuming this mortgage is FHA, $44 would be added to the mortgage payment for a mortgage insurance premium (MIP). The MIP is paid to FHA so they can ensure that the lender (a bank, not the government) would be paid off in the case of a foreclosure.

$800 rent from one unit less a $505 mortgage payment (including the MIP) leaves $295 to put toward the other costs of owning the property or $3,540 annually.

Let's assume annual expenses of $750 for insurance, $3,000 for property taxes, and $600 for miscellaneous repairs for a total of $4,350 per year.

Annual expenses ($4,350 less $3,540 net income from rent after the mortgage is paid) leave a negative cash flow of $810 or $68 per month. This is taken from the $1,000 monthly commitment to housing and savings. The negative cash flow is not an issue at this point because the property is also providing our investor with a place to live, essentially for far less than paying for rent or meeting a mortgage payment on a single-family home.

The illustration here assumes the property being purchased is not a fixer-upper requiring time and capital to get the property to move-in condition. The property may not be pristine with lots of updates, but it is acceptable for this stage of the journey. The investor could choose to purchase a fixer-upper, but that would increase, over and above the $6,000 used in the example, the amount of cash needed to get started. Also, it would add to the number of months to get to the $10,000 goal due to the delay in collecting rent from one of the units and/or the investor not being able to occupy the other unit.

The strategy here is for the investor to take advantage of a 3.5% down program. The requirements (such as minimum credit score, debt-to-income ratio, and income along with ancillary requirements) and sources for these programs change over time, so I am not going to get into the weeds about how to qualify for them or where to find them. The point is they are always out there, and our investor is likely to qualify.

As you can see, there is a requirement for some savings to be accumulated before the first purchase is made. This requires discipline, but if the investor meets the assumptions outlined above, this should be attainable in a reasonable length of time. Also, some programs, such as those offered by the Veterans Administration, require zero down. So, the requirement of accumulating $6,000 to start may be overcome another way.

The investor now settles into enjoying their new residence with the help of a tenant to pay the bills. The task at hand is to continue putting $1,000 per month toward housing expenses and savings for the next property. At this point, $68 per month is going to negative cash flow, and $932 toward savings.

> Cumulative rental units: 1 (This number will always exclude the investor's personal residence in this example.)

STEP TWO: Buy another 2-unit with seller financing.

This and the next step are the most difficult ones because they involve finding deals where seller financing can be utilized. These will most likely be off-market deals, so more effort will be required than just perusing the listed properties as provided by a Realtor. However, **we are assuming our investor is now networking with other investors, which greatly increases the opportunities for finding off-market deals.** Other investors are constantly buying and selling properties, so our investor would have more sources for deals than trying to find individual sellers who are not connected with the investment community. To be clear, random sellers who only own a few properties and who are not active investors are out there, and they should be pursued. Sometimes they offer the best deals. Whatever the source of the seller, the objective is to seek properties that are held free and clear of any encumbrances where the seller is in a position to hold the mortgage with a small down payment. **The investor would point out their excellent reputation, credit score, education, and their active involvement with the local investment community while developing a relationship with the seller.**

A $100,000 2-unit, purchased from a private seller with a $5,000 down payment and 6% interest on a 30-year amortization schedule, would require a monthly payment of $570. Also, the buyer could agree to pay off the remaining balance after several years of payments if the seller demands a balloon payment. This payoff will come from refinancing the property (unless our investor wants to sell it then), which will be easy to do considering the likely eventual financial picture of the investor.

Let's add $2000 for closing costs, which brings the total needed to get into this to $7000. If our investor is saving $932 per month, let's round it up to eight months that it would take to have the money.

If each unit rents for $800, the total income for the year would be $19,200. Once again, let's use $750 for insurance and $3,000 for taxes just as for the first property. However, this time we will use $600 per unit per year for repairs for a total of $1,200. When insurance, taxes, and repairs are added to twelve months of mortgage payments, the total cash out for the year would be $11,790. With total income at $19,200 and cash out at $11,790, the net cash flow would be $7,410 or $618 monthly.

Read this calculation carefully. Between the two properties, our investor's cash flow from rental property ownership is now $550 per month when the $68 negative cash flow from the first property is balanced against the $618 positive cash flow from the second property. The investor has a place to live, and now the monthly commitment of $1,000 for housing and savings can be added to the $550 of overall positive cash flow for a total of $1,550 instead of just $932.

> Cumulative rental units: 3
> Cumulative elapsed time: 8 months

STEP THREE: Buy a 4-unit with seller financing.

This four-unit is not going to be as nice overall as the prior 2-unit properties, but it is going to be livable without much rehab work. The lower rent these apartments command is accounted for in the lower purchase price of $150,000.

A 5% down payment of $7,500 along with $3,000 in closing costs requires saving $1,550 for just seven months, so our investor must get to work looking for this deal as soon as the dust settles from the last deal. At 6% interest, the mortgage payment will be $854.

For this property, the rent will only be $700 per unit per month for a monthly total of $2,800, and a yearly total of $33,600. If taxes are $4,500, insurance is $1,500, and repairs are $2,400, the total cash out will be $18,648 including $10,248 for the mortgage. This leaves a net of $14,952 or $1,246 monthly. This, added to the cash flow of $1,550 prior to purchasing this property, yields $2,796 monthly which can be saved toward the next property.

> Cumulative rental units: 7
> Cumulative elapsed time: 15 months

STEP FOUR: Buy a 2-unit using conventional 20% down financing from a bank.

Once our investor has made it this far, the obstacles to acquiring those first three properties have been hurdled. Investment momentum is really going to pick up. By the time the investor has saved up the down payment for this property, over two years in the business will have passed, and they will be looking rather good to a conventional lender. Depending on which month they purchased their first property, the investor can probably now show two years of tax returns that include the activity from three rental properties, and they will be seasoned with a successful track record.

For this fourth property, our investor is going to purchase another 2-unit flat or duplex using conventional financing from a bank. Perhaps the property will have been listed with a Realtor, but it may be an off-market deal from another investor. Let's say it needs some repairs, but it's in a stable neighborhood. It is not in such bad condition that the bank does not want to lend on it. The plan is to put 20% down from savings.

With a purchase price of $80,000, the investor will need $16,000 down plus $3,000 for closing costs (including a paid appraisal). Additionally, $5,000 of repairs are planned, so the total amount needed to enter this deal will be $24,000. With savings at a rate of $2,796, it will take nine months to accumulate the necessary cash.

A $64,000 mortgage at 5% for 20 years has a payment of $459 per month, or $5,508 annually.

With these units not being as nice as prior units, they will rent for only $700 per month for a total of $16,800 annually. If insurance is $700, taxes are $2,500, repairs are $1,200 (in addition to the $5,000 spent right after acquiring the property), and debt service is $5,508, the net cash flow from this property is $6,892 or $574 per month. When added to the prior amount of monthly savings of $2,796, the new amount of monthly savings is $3,370. Keep in mind, this amount includes an extra $1,000 per month that is still being contributed by our investor from other sources of income. Hopefully, our investor is making even more now from their job. But even at just $40,000, a $1,000 monthly outlay represents only 30% of gross income. Considering this outlay is essentially in place of any housing expense because the investor does not have rent or a mortgage to pay in addition to this $1,000, 30% is well within the norm of expectations as to whether our investor can save that much every month.

Cumulative rental units: 9
Cumulative elapsed time: 24 months

STEP FIVE: Buy a better personal residence and rent out the original one!

Our investor has been diligent at growing their income while putting off gratification in hopes of a better future, and it's time to start planning to "make it real" by buying a nicer place to live. The plan would not require that the 2-unit in Step One would be sold. Instead, it would be kept, and the investor's former unit would become a rental.

The investor sets their sights on a $200,000 single-family home in a nice area. With a good credit score, and the income now being generated, it will be easy to qualify for any type of conventional loan for a personal residence with a down payment of 5%, 10%, or 20%. This would be up to the investor, but the amount needed for the down payment would dictate how long it will be until the investor can close on this deal.

For our purposes, let's say it is going to be a 10% mortgage. The investor will need $20,000 plus closing costs of around $5,000 or $25,000. With the current savings rate at $3,370, this will take eight months to accumulate.

A thirty-year fixed rate mortgage at 5% has a payment of $966, plus since the down payment is less than 20%, a mortgage insurance premium of around $34 will be required for a total of $1000. At this point, the investor can add $800 per month to the cash flow from renting out their former residence. However, now that there are tenants in that unit, let's add $50 per month to the repair budget just like the $600 we are using annually for all the other rental units. We can now adjust the net monthly cash flow upward by $750, but we also must adjust it downward by the $1000 per month needed for the new mortgage on the personal residence. This leaves $3,370 + $750 - $1000 or $3,120 for housing costs and savings going forward.

There are other considerations, however. Our investor is now responsible for payment out of pocket of the property taxes and insurance on their personal residence. Let's say those amounts are $6,000 and $900 respectively. Normal household repairs are taken out of the investor's regular disposable income (as was the case for their unit when they lived in their first property), so we will not count those here. The taxes and insurance will require another $575 of the investor's monthly cash, so instead of $3,120, the investor/homeowner is now actually back to $2,545 (still including their $1,000 contribution from personal income) for investing going forward. One way to look at it is that the net rent from their former residence is covering about half of the mortgage on their new single-family home. The other half is covered by some of the income from their rentals (combined with their monthly contribution) with plenty left over to save toward their next investment property.

Realistically, though, since (1) the mortgage on their personal residence must be paid from personal funds, and (2) both the mortgage and their historical monthly contribution to the plan are both $1000, let's just end the monthly contribution and use it for the mortgage. The extra $575 per month for the taxes and insurance on their personal residence would be covered by a withdrawal of profits from the rental property operations. In either case, the result is that we will now use $2,545 per month as the cash available to plow back into expanding our investor's rental real estate portfolio.

Cumulative rental units: 10
Cumulative elapsed time: 32 months

STEP SIX: Buy a vacant fixer-upper 2-unit with a hard money loan.

The objective here is to build equity by forcing up the value of a property with a rehab. Then, the investor will get permanent financing from a bank based on a new appraisal after renting out the two new units.

The investor finds a vacant 2-unit owned by a tired landlord, and negotiates a cash deal for $50,000. The entire property is in need of repair, so a cash deal works best because the seller knows banks are not enthused about approving mortgages for this type of property. Repairs and carrying costs (interest payments, insurance, taxes, and utilities) are estimated at $30,000. The investor has developed a relationship with a local hard money lender who will lend most of the money to purchase the property as well as the rehab money as long as the investor, as a new client of the lender, puts down $10,000 toward the purchase and the closing costs. Consequently, our buyer can confidently make a cash offer with no contingency for financing because there is no mention of the hard money lender in the buyer's offer. It is a cash offer in the eyes of the seller.

Needing to save $10,000 for this deal, only four months will elapse before a closing can occur. Closing costs are estimated at $6000 including points (loan origination fees) paid to the hard money lender, so the lender agrees to loan $76,000 on this deal. The investor brings $10,000 to the closing, and the hard money lender allows $55,000 to be released at the closing for a total of $65,000. After the $50,000 cost plus $6,000 in closing costs are paid, the buyer leaves the closing with $9,000 to get started on the rehab project. The remaining $21,000 from the lender is held in an escrow account to be released as the investor progresses through the project.

The rehab takes four months, during which there is no income from the units, but net cash flow of $2,545 continues from the other properties. After four months, both apartments are quickly rented for $850 each, and an application is made for permanent financing on the newly renovated property. The process takes two more months during which a paid appraiser says the property is now worth $110,000. Another two months of cash flow accumulates.

The bank is willing to loan 80% of the appraisal, or $88,000. At 5% for 20 years, the payment will be $581. Let's say taxes are $3,000, and insurance is $800. But this time, since the property has been newly renovated, repairs will only be budgeted at $800 total for the year for both units. Total annual debt service of $6,972 plus $4,600 annual expenses equals $964 monthly, When this is taken from the monthly income of $1,700, this property will contribute $736 to monthly cash flow bringing the new total to $2,545 plus $736 or $3,190.

At the end of six months of rehabbing and dealing with a bank, at the closing for the refinance, the hard money lender is paid back the $76,000. After $2,000 in closing costs for this $88,000 loan, the investor leaves the closing with their $10,000 (their down payment) back in their pocket. **Our investor now has zero money invested in this property, and it has a $736 per month net cash flow. The return on the buyer's investment is mathematically *infinite*!**

And the investor now has gained $22,000 in equity (net worth) as represented by the difference between the $110,000 appraisal and the $88,000 mortgage. **The tenants are going to provide the money to pay down the mortgage, while the property appreciates in value!** I love real estate!!

> Cumulative rental units: 12
> Cumulative elapsed time: 42 months

Something is different this time before we go on to the next step. Instead of starting out with zero cash available for the next deal, after needing to use all savings to fund each deal so far, our investor now has a war chest of cash from the income during the rehab and the tax-free funds from the refinance loan. Cash accumulated for six months during the rehab project and refinancing period at a rate of $2,545 per month for a total of $15,270. Also, the two new units came online at $850 per month each, which adds $3,400 for the two months. Technically, we should subtract $767 from that to cover the average expenses for two months based on our $4,600 annual figure. (There was not yet a mortgage payment to be made during those two months, and all monthly interest payments to the hard money lender were part of the initial $30,000 budget). Then, $10,000 is added from the refi closing bringing the war chest to $27,903!

STEP SEVEN: Keep buying more and increasing cash flow.

Things are really starting to pick up steam for our investor with savings for investment of $27,903 and a monthly cash flow from investment properties of $3,190 after the necessary amount is withdrawn to pay the taxes and insurance on their personal residence. The investor is still paying $1000 from personal funds for the mortgage on their upgraded personal residence, but they are now almost one third of the way toward our goal of $10,000 per month net cash flow from rentals.

Note that the original challenge did not include taking ownership of a new personal residence along the way. This, of course, has slowed down the process because money was taken from savings for the down payment, and the personal mortgage payment takes away from savings. But since living in their own single-family home in a nicer neighborhood is so often a goal, I wanted to illustrate that this could be accomplished more sooner than later as an encouragement to those starting this journey who are not already living where they would be content to live for many years into the future while they were building their real estate portfolio.

To get us to where we are now, I have illustrated a variety of types of properties and ways to finance them. However, our fictitious investor is now tasked with acquiring more properties for their portfolio in more of a cookie-cutter fashion. Using the average amount of net cash flow that can be added from a typical 2-unit property, I will extrapolate how many units and how long it will take to get to our goal of $10,000 per month. This type of property is common, so it is reasonable to use it as the cookie cutter. I did not want to weigh down this illustration with more text just for the sake of variety.

Our model is going to be a $100,000 2-unit (flat or duplex), like the property in Step Two, with gross rents of $800 per unit or $19,200 yearly. Insurance and taxes will remain $750 and $3000 respectively with repairs at $600 per unit annually or $1,200. This puts net income at $14,250 before any cash out for debt service. Monthly, this averages $1,188.

The only question is how these properties will be financed because that will dictate how much must be saved for each purchase, and how much the net cash flow will be. I believe it is fair to say that, by now, **our investor is actively engaged and connected in their local real estate market, and that they are known to both Realtors and other investors. They have been researching other possible lenders, and they may be working with a mortgage broker. As a result, it is likely they will be finding their deals in both listed properties and off-market offerings.** Most of these properties will be financed with conventional mortgages with 20% down, but some of the others may involve seller financing with a much smaller amount down. To be conservative with this illustration, I am going to present the math as though the investor must save for a 20% down payment plus $2,500 for closing costs for a total of $22,500 for each purchase. The object will be to buy a new property as soon as the cash flow from existing properties has generated another $22,500 in savings.

An $80,000 mortgage for 20 years at 5% has a payment of $528. Per above, the average income before debt service is $1,188, so the monthly net cash flow from each of our properties will increase by a net of $660 with each property brought into the investor's portfolio.

With $27,903 in the bank after the refinance of their last 2-unit, and $3,190 in monthly net cash flow, the investor is ready for the next property. We are going to assume they have been making offers during the two months while the refinancing was being processed, and they need just one more month to close the deal. Another $3,190 will be added to savings that month, and then $22,500 will be removed for the closing, which leaves $8,593.

> Cumulative rental units: 14
> Cumulative elapsed time: 43 months
> Resultant cash flow after this purchase: $3,850
> With $8,593 left in savings after the last purchase, another $13,907 must be saved for the next property. This will take four months.

> Cumulative rental units: 16
> Cumulative elapsed time: 47 months
> Resultant net cash flow: $4,510
> After this purchase, all savings have been used, and it will be necessary to accumulate $22,500 from cash flow before the investor's next acquisition. This will take five months.

> Cumulative rental units: 18
> Cumulative elapsed time: 52 months
> Resultant net cash flow: $5,170
> Our investor is more than halfway to $10,000 net per month. It has been nearly four and a half years since the journey began, but it will not be that long for the second half. Only four months are needed to obtain the cash for the next property.

Cumulative rental units: 20
Cumulative elapsed time: 56 months
Resultant net cash flow: $5,830
Another four months, and the investor has another property.

Cumulative rental units: 22
Cumulative elapsed time: 60 months
Resultant net cash flow: $6,490
Four more months, two more units.

Cumulative rental units: 24
Cumulative elapsed time: 64 months
Resultant net cash flow: $7,150
This time, only three months are needed.

Cumulative rental units: 26
Cumulative elapsed time: 67 months
Resultant net cash flow: $7,810
Three months again to the next one.

Cumulative rental units: 28
Cumulative elapsed time: 70 months
Resultant net cash flow: $8,470
Three months again.

Cumulative rental units: 30
Cumulative elapsed time: 73 months
Resultant net cash flow: $9,130
Since our investor has some money left over after the last few purchases, only two months are needed for the next deal.

Cumulative rental units: 32
Cumulative elapsed time: 75 months
Resultant net cash flow: $9,790

One last time, only two more months when combined with leftover cash.

> Cumulative units: 34 (plus the single-family personal residence)
> Cumulative elapsed time: 77 months. Less than six and a half years!
> Resultant net cash flow: $10,450

Success! **Our fictional investor has exceeded the goal of $10,000 per month net from rental properties, and it has happened in less than six and a half years.** I assumed in the model that none of the rents were raised over the years, but this would not normally be the case. So, it's likely the investor met the goal even sooner because gross rents are probably around $1,000 per month higher than what was used in the last couple of years in the model. Yes, expenses may have risen due to the inevitable increase in taxes and insurance among other categories. But mortgage payments stay the same, and **rent increases usually far outpace rent increases.**

And there is a bonus. **We haven't brought it into the discussion yet, but equity (property value less any debt) has grown significantly** from the original $3,500 put down on the first property. By my rough calculations, the investor's equity has grown to around $200,000 from increased property values and mortgage principal paydowns.

Just like icing on a cake, **there is an additional bonus that adds sweetness to the main ingredients of cash flow, mortgage paydown, and property appreciation. That is the extra bonus from expensing depreciation on your tax return.** Depreciation is not a cash-out expense, just a mathematical calculation. The result is a reduction of the taxable income from the property, which means some of the cash flow becomes tax free. More on this later in the next chapter on taxation.

Think about this. **Beyond the initial money used for the down payment and closing costs on the first property, all the flow and equity growth has come from tenants' payments and naturally increasing property values.** When you grasp that the monthly contributions from the investor were in place of housing costs the investor would have had anyway, you can understand that, had the investor made no investment at all, they would still have needed to expend the same money each month for a place to live. Ultimately, **they have not taken any more money for investments out of their disposable income than they would have otherwise, but now our investor's financial picture has improved dramatically!**

Wealth is created by utilizing OPM (Other People's Money) to buy income-producing assets.

Of course, nobody will actually achieve this goal exactly like my illustration. There are too many variables, but **the illustration shows the framework of how a residential rental portfolio can be grown.** The most obvious variables are:

- Interest rates and other mortgage terms and qualifiers change continually.
- The rate of rent changes is not a straight line.
- The market for real estate prices has its ups and downs.
- Deals may not be as readily available when the investor is looking for a property as the model assumes.
- Unplanned larger expenditures can derail savings.

Those variables are generally out of the investor's control, but if you were in the place of our investor, **there are some variables you could control.** For example:

- You may have a beginning income of more or less than $40,000 as in my example, so you could commit to more or less than $1,000 per month for your contribution from personal funds from the start. Or your monthly commitment could grow or decline over the years based on personal income.
- You may already live in a home you are happy with, so your journey could move faster since you do not need to divert money to a new residence as in my model.
- You may choose to contribute chunks of money from sources outside your investing activities to speed up property acquisitions.
- Large chunks of money could be arranged from selling and taking the profits or from refinancing some of the earlier properties.

I have seen quite a few of my colleagues grow their rental property businesses in the fashion of my model to where they left their W-2 jobs. Some have taken it way beyond $10,000 per month in a shorter time using effort and techniques beyond the scope of this book. Many simply added significantly to their income and net worth without leaving another job, but perhaps they retired early. Some, of course, sputtered along, but they still made a positive impact on their financial future. **Some crashed and burned, but almost invariably because of lack of effort, discipline, or education...not for lack of opportunity.**

One of the beauties of adding rental real estate to your life is that you can do it to whatever level you wish at whatever pace you would like to go. If you own and operate a retail store or restaurant, for example, you are committed to being open the necessary hours and going through all the other motions whether you are busy and making money or not. It's a full commitment of your time, and the same is true for many other types of businesses. **With rentals, you can commit to whatever level you want to be at in terms of time and effort. You can "get rich slow" at your own pace. It is easy to add rental real estate to your life and not regret it!**

10
TAX IMPLICATIONS FROM OPERATING RENTAL PROPERTY (FRAMING AND DRYWALL)

With this chapter, I am going to get back to making an analogy between the subject matter of the chapter and a phase of construction. **When you have income and/or expenses from your business, presumably you will have financial information that is required to be reported on tax returns.** Earlier, I talked about how the two main purposes of financial record keeping are to 1) determine the numbers that must be entered on your unavoidable tax forms, and 2) evaluate the performance of your income-producing assets for decision-making purposes. If you have a profit, the government will separate some of your money from you in the form of taxes. It becomes apparent that your money gets splintered into several parts...the one part you get to keep, and the parts you send to Uncle Sam and other agencies. You will not see specifically what Uncle Sam does with *your* money because there are dividers with doors through which your cash is delivered to various distinct taxing bodies in a seemingly never-ending flow. So, for our purposes, let us consider taxation to be like the framing and drywall that create the rooms in a structure. Certainly, the rooms created by the walls can be used for a variety of purposes. But for this illustration, they represent the different tax compartments into which some of your money is headed. **Consideration must be given to each type of tax when evaluating the profitability of a property.**

We will touch on the various types of taxes you may encounter while owning and operating an income property. Some taxes are the kind where the taxing body sends you a bill, and you pay the amount on the bill. But **what everybody thinks about when it comes to rental real estate is the unique ways it can impact any taxes on one's income.** In these cases, you are reporting your income and expenses using your own accounting records, and then they tell you how much of your net income they want you to send in instead of giving you a bill for the set amount of a tax. **You may have heard correctly that there are tax advantages afforded to operating rental property. In my opinion, those tax advantages come primarily from three sources:**

- Depreciation (where the cost of the property is expensed over a set number of years via calculations dictated by the IRS). Depreciation is subtracted from your income just like any other expense in arriving at your net taxable income, but your yearly depreciation deduction is not a cash-out expense. It is possible that a property will appear to be operating at a loss for tax purposes, once the depreciation is included in your expenses, even though it has a positive cash flow. So, in effect, **depreciation can "shelter" some of the property's cash income from taxation.** Additionally, with some dollar limitations, **a loss from a rental property can be netted against income from any other source including not only other investments or businesses, but also your W-2 job.**

- Capital gains. Just like stocks or any investment, any gain on the sale of real estate is eligible to be counted as a long-term capital gain if there was at least one year and one day in between when you bought it and when you sold it. **Long-term capital gains are added to your income from all other sources on your tax return, but they are segregated and taxed at a lower rate.** Short-term gains from assets held one year or less are taxed as ordinary income the same as from your job. Again, with certain limitations, **should you have either a short-term or long-term capital loss, it can be netted against other capital gains or ordinary income.**

- No Self-Employment Tax. Unlike any other business not operated by a straight corporation (C Corp) which pays tax on its profits based on a whole other taxation system, **net profits from the operation of rental real estate are not subject to Self-Employment Tax.** This tax, which is paid on net profits by all business owners in addition to regular income tax, is the equivalent of Social Security Tax paid by employers and employees because it is paid into the Social Security System to the credit of self-employed workers. Currently, both employees and employers each pay 6.2% of an employee's gross wages into the Social Security System each paycheck until the employee reaches earnings of $160,200 for the year. It then ceases until the beginning of the next year. Self-employed taxpayers have the burden of paying both halves of the tax paid by employers and employees, or 12.4% on up to $147,000 of the figure arrived at after multiplying the net profits by 92.35%. This is a bit of a break for those with earnings from self-employment.

    You do not need to know any of this, and the percentages and limitations change over time. But I have taken the time to unpack it to highlight the magnitude of the benefit from not having to pay 12.4% self-employment tax on top of your income tax on your earnings from your income property business. **The operation of rental properties, though technically a business, enjoys the benefit of not being viewed as self-employment by the tax law**, although the net profits are otherwise included in ordinary income. I think this benefit has been protected for so long because so many members of Congress own rental property!

In addition to the Big Three just mentioned, another tax favored aspect of real estate is what is known as the 1031 Exchange where **the capital gains tax on the sale of a property can be deferred indefinitely.** This technique involves using all the cash from selling a property to buy another property within a prescribed length of time, and not withdrawing the cash from the sale. **The cost basis, on which the gain would be computed by comparing it to the sales price, of the first property would be rolled over to become the cost basis of the next property.** The next property can cost more than the sales price of the prior property, in which case its cost basis would be increased accordingly. This can be done with a chain of properties so that the last property sold, presumably years later, would have a large taxable gain based on a very small cost basis. The tax would be paid in that year, after having been deferred to that point. Virtually any piece of real estate can be exchanged for another. **The proceeds from the sale of the first property are held by a third-party agent until they are used to buy the next property** so that you do not touch the cash. You could take money out of the transaction, but you would be taxed on part of the gain in that tax year. In some cases, **the last property owned could be inherited by someone who receives the then current market value as their new cost basis** for the property. In that case, even if the heir sells the property right away, the gains from all the properties in the chain never end up being taxed!

Section 1031 exchanges are a sophisticated technique, but they are used routinely. A full discussion of them is beyond the scope of this book, but I wanted you to know about them because they are a significant part of the tax aspects of real estate ownership that you may want to explore in the future. I do not know of any other asset class that offers this opportunity for deferring, or perhaps completely avoiding, capital gains tax.

I have begun this chapter by pumping up the favorable tax treatment of operating a rental real estate business, but let me throw in some philosophy before we go any further. **It is tempting to assign a lot of weight to tax implications when considering whether to invest in real estate in general or, perhaps, whether to invest in a particular property. However, tax considerations** are only a part of the whole picture. **DO NOT invest in real estate pri-marily for the tax advantages!** If you are showing a loss at the level of investing targeted in this book, you are probably doing it wrong.

My objective here is to boost your taxable income by boosting your overall income. Some of it will be sheltered by the depreciation deduction, and you will not be paying Self Employment Tax on your rental business income. But do not forget that the principal part of any mortgage, although a cash expenditure, is not deductible. Only the interest part of a mortgage payment is a deduction from gross income for tax purposes. Consequently, while some of your income is sheltered by depreciation, some of your cash flow goes to nondeductible principal payments.

I have often said that there is no harm in paying taxes if you actually made the income. While I do not want to pay any more taxes than necessary, **I do not believe the driving force behind your rental real estate investment decisions should be the tax implications. Just get out there and generate revenue, then let the tax chips fall where they may. Report all your income hon-estly, but take every deduction to which you are entitled without fail.**

The importance of financial record keeping and how to do it, either manually or with a computer program, was discussed extensively in Chapters Three and Five. I remind you that you do not have to do this yourself any more than you need to install your own furnaces. **You can hire others to do your bookkeeping and create reports for you.** The same is true for the preparation of your personal and business tax returns. **It is likely that your bookkeeper will not be the same person who prepares your tax returns, so the objective is to organize your records to show the data required on the IRS forms.** This way, your tax preparer can easily pull the information from your statements and transfer it to your return.

SECTION ONE: TAX FORMS

My intention in this chapter is to give you an overview of the IRS forms typically used for reporting rental property operation. The sources of the entries for the usual types of income and expense will be discussed along with the proper characterization of certain cash inflow and outflow transactions.

If you are an American taxpayer, you file your personal tax return on one of several versions of IRS Form 1040. This form funnels information from a myriad of other IRS forms down to a single number on which your income tax is computed. Once your income tax is computed, other taxes, tax credits, and prior payments are accounted for to arrive at the amount of your refund or your payment due.

If you own your properties in the same name as one or both taxpayers filing the 1040 (or if the property is held in a single-person LLC, which is a "disregarded entity" by the IRS), income and expenses from operating your rental property would be reported on SCHEDULE E (Form 1040) for "Supplemental Income and Loss." Form 4562, "Depreciation and Amortization," would be used to calculate the depreciation deduction entered with the other expenses on SCHEDULE E. Then, the net from all your properties would be transferred to SCHEDULE 1 (Form 1040), "Additional Income and Adjustments to Income," where it is combined with other entries to arrive at a final figure that is transferred to the "Other Income" line of your Form 1040.

If you own your properties in the name of an entity (and that entity has multiple partners/members/shareholders), then that entity must file its own tax return, typically on Form 1065, "U.S. Return of Partnership Income." Unless a Limited Liability Company (LLC) has elected to be taxed as a corporation, or an entity disregarded as an entity separate from its owner by applying the rules in Regulations section 301.7701-3, the LLC will also use Form 1065. An S Corporation would use Form 1120-S. These entities would report their rental property activities on Form 8825, "Rental Real Estate Income and Expenses of a Partnership or an S Corporation." Form 8825 is very similar to the part of SCHEDULE E where individually owned rental properties are reported per my last paragraph. Interestingly, the same Form 4562 for depreciation is used in all cases.

Any information that would be needed by a partner, LLC member, or S Corp shareholder to prepare their individual tax return is reported to each owner on what is known as a K-1. This form does not show any of the calculations used to arrive at any of the entries, but instead lists the individual partner/member/shareholder's pro rata share, based on their percentage of ownership, of any numbers that would impact their personal returns. Additionally, any guaranteed payments unique to that individual are shown. Income from rentals makes its way from the K-1 to Part II of the individual's SCHEDULE E, then to their SCHEDULE 1, and finally to their Form 1040.

As discussed in Chapter Two, **whereas C Corporations pay income taxes, no income tax is paid by a partnership, LLC, or S Corporation when filing their annual Form 1065 or Form 1120-S.** These are what are called "information returns" for pass-through entities. The information is "passed through" to the individual owners via the K-1, and any taxes are paid by the individual owners when filing their personal Form 1040.

That gives you an idea of the mechanics of the pertinent tax forms, but for our purposes, I want to expand on the reporting of income and expenses for rental property. **Although you may have a third party prepare your tax returns, being able to hand over accurate and useful information to the preparer is the central purpose of your internal bookkeeping efforts.** To that point, it is helpful to know the various categories of expenses that are provided on SCHEDULE E and Form 8825. **If you use the same categories for your internal record keeping, it will be easy to transfer the totals in each category onto the tax form.** There are, of course, opportunities on the forms to name your own "other" expense categories if needed.

SECTION TWO: RENTAL INCOME

Both SCHEDULE E and Form 8825 make the assumption that the only source of income from rental properties is, in fact, rent. They do not have a line for you to enter any other sources of income beside Gross Rents. Consequently, miscellaneous income such as from on-site coin operated laundries would be lumped with the normal rental income. However, **if you have anything out of the ordinary, for example, such as royalties from a gas well on the property or from services for which you get paid outside of the rent, you should consult with your tax advisor on where to report that income.**

Presumably, **you will be operating on the "cash basis" of accounting.** This means you report income in the year it was received and expenses in the year they were paid. The alternative is the "accrual basis" where income is reported in the year it is earned, regardless of when the income was received, and expenses are booked in the year the liability to pay the expense was created, regardless of when the payment was made. Obviously, cash accounting is much simpler, and for most businesses it more accurately reflects net income for any given period. Accrual accounting can be useful for some applications, but I believe it is not best used for a rental property business.

Operating under cash accounting, only the rental income received in a given period is included on any internal reports or tax returns. So, if a tenant pays their January rent before the end of December, then the rent is counted in December... not in January.

Though you are on a cash basis, **money received for a deposit, such as a security, pet, or utility deposit, is NOT counted as income** no matter when you receive it. Technically, it is still the tenants' money, so it may never end up being counted as income. Although the money from when the deposit was paid is included in your "cash on hand," the deposit is carried as a liability on your internal books until it is returned to the tenants. Then, when it is returned, the liability is removed. **Returning a security deposit is NOT an expense.**

Your net capital on your balance sheet is not affected by the receipt or return of a deposit. Net capital equals your assets minus your liabilities. Consequently, the cash (which is an asset on your balance sheet) from when the tenant paid the deposit is balanced out by the deposit carried on your books (which is a liability), so the result is a "wash" having zero impact on your net capital. The same is true when the reverse happens if you return a deposit in full. In that case, the reduction of the cash from giving back the deposit is netted out by the elimination of the liability.

It is important to note, however, that **if you keep a security deposit when a tenant moves out, the deposit must be converted on your books from a liability to one of two things.** First, if the deposit is being kept strictly to cover unpaid rent, the deposit liability is eliminated, and the amount of the deposit is added to the rent from that property in the year you kept the deposit. Now it is your money. Because you did not refund their deposit, no cash is expended, so it is your internal bookkeeping that would convert the former liability to rental income. At that point, you have increased your net capital by the amount of the deposit.

Secondly, if the deposit is being kept to repay you for expenses, your rental income for the property will not be increased as in the prior paragraph. However, your expenses for the property will be reduced by the amount of the deposit, and the liability from the deposit will be eliminated from your books. Again, since it is now your money, your net capital then increases by the amount of the deposit.

To drill a little deeper into the bookkeeping for keeping a deposit to cover expenses, let's say a tenant has a $1,000 security deposit. When they move out, you pay a cleaning company $400 for general cleaning, a carpet cleaner $250, and a repair person $350 to fix some damage caused by the tenant. In this example, you have spent a total of $1,000 to pay for things for which the tenant is responsible, and for which you need to be reimbursed. When the $1,000 security deposit is kept to cover these expenses, your gross rental income is not increased by $1,000, but rather your expenses are reduced by $1,000. This is a better reflection of the operation of the property because only the actual payments for rent by the tenants are included in your gross rental income, and the tenants' expenses (the cleaning and repairs for which they were responsible) are backed out of the property's expenses, leaving only your real expenses of operation. This gives a more accurate picture of the income and expenses for the property.

If a deposit is kept *partly* for unpaid rent and *partly* for expenses, the deposit must be split to convert partially to rental income and partially to a reduction in expenses. In the more likely scenario where only a portion of the deposit is kept to cover some expenses, only the amount not returned to the tenant would be converted internally to a reduction of expenses.

Finally, another "cash in" source that is not counted as taxable income is the cash received from a loan. **Loan proceeds, like from when you refinance a property and leave the closing with money, are not taxable** because you have not sold anything, nor have you performed a service. You have simply obligated yourself to pay back a loan. The same is true when you draw on a line of credit secured by real estate. Conversely, **repaying a loan is not a deductible expense**.

Pulling the equity out of a property tax-free by refinancing the debt is a great way to reward yourself with cash when you have a property you intend to hold long-term. A continually increasing value, coupled with the steady paydown of the current mortgage, can create untapped net value. You may choose to refinance a property multiple times over your ownership to take advantage of better prevailing loan terms and/or a significant difference between its market value compared to the existing mortgage balance. **The payment on the new mortgage may even be lower than the current payment**, so you may increase your cashflow in addition to putting a chunk of tax-free cash in your hands. However, there is a caution. On a property you have held a very long time, you are likely to have a low cost basis on which your gain is calculated when you sell. This can yield a significant tax bill, so you must be careful not to have such a high mortgage balance in the end that the sale does not generate enough cash to pay the capital gains tax.

SECTION THREE: EXPENSES

While the sole source of income for your property is likely to be from rent, there are quite a few categories of expenses for rental property. Your objective with your bookkeeping is to properly characterize any cash out and to break down expenses into their correct accounts. **Not all cash expenditures are, in fact, an expense for tax purposes.** As discussed in the prior section, **returning a security deposit is not an expense, and when you pay a mortgage payment, the part that went to principal is not a deduction for tax purposes.** Only the interest portion is deductible.

I have already mentioned how deducting depreciation expense is one of the major tax benefits from operating rental property. With depreciation being an allowable expense, but not a cash expenditure, **I want to take the mystery out of the concept of depreciation and how it is calculated.** So, let's focus on depreciation expense before moving on to cash-out expenses.

When a business buys a large asset that will last a long time, the IRS says that **the cost of the asset must be divided up and expensed over a number of years** which the IRS prescribes based on the type of asset that it is. The IRS does not want the entire cost of the asset to be deducted all at once in the year the asset is purchased. **In the case of residential rental property buildings, the depreciation period is 27.5 years**, and the usual procedure is to deduct an equal amount each year for the entire 27.5 years. This is called "straight line" depreciation because, if you graphed the yearly amounts of depreciation, the graph would look like a straight line. **Non-residential rental properties are depreciated over thirty-nine years**, so substitute "39" each place you see "27.5" in the following paragraphs, because the same rules apply to both types of property.

There are a few special things you need to know about depreciation, however. First, **only the buildings that are permanently attached to the land can be depreciated...not the land** itself. So, if you purchased a property for $100,000 (including any costs to purchase that were capitalized and added to the sales price), and $20,000 of that was attributable to the land, then you would calculate your depreciation expense by dividing $80,000 by 27.5 years. Secondly, though, the IRS only allows you to take a depreciation deduction for the portion of the year that remains after the month that you put the asset into service. So, if you bought a building that was already in use as a rental property on October 1st, you could only take 25% of a full year's amount as your deduction the first year. After that, you would get a full year's deduction until the year you sell. In that year, you would get a deduction only for the portion of the year you owned the property.

As a side note, the accepted way to calculate how much of your purchase price should be attributed to the land is to use the same ratio as shown on the property tax bills. Land and buildings are assessed separately for property tax purposes, and their respective amounts are shown. So, if the property you purchased in the previous paragraph for $100,000 had an assessment of $13, 237 for the land and $62, 950 for the building, the land represents 17.374% of the total assessed value. Consequently, you would use $17,374 for the value of the land on your books, and you would depreciate the building beginning with a purchase price of $82,626.

The next interesting thing about depreciation is that **the 27.5-year period starts over and over again every time the property is sold.** It is not like you only get to deduct depreciation for 7.5 years if you buy a building that is 20 years old. Even if you bought a 100-year-old building, you would still be entitled, in fact required, to depreciate it over the next 27.5 years. Also, **the amount that is used for calculating your depreciation deduction is based on what YOU paid for the property**, and it has nothing to do with what any prior owner paid. If you own the property for more than 27.5 years, then you are not entitled to take any more deductions for that property. Also, it is important to note that

you would have to begin a separate 27.5-year schedule of depreciation for a new addition you built onto your original building.

Without getting too far into the weeds, I will add that **there are choices you can make regarding depreciation.** The Internal Revenue Service (IRS) allows building owners the opportunity under the Modified Accelerated Cost Recovery System (MACRS) to **depreciate certain land improvements and personal property over a shorter period than 39 or 27.5 years.** Certain land improvements can be depreciated over 15 years at 150% declining balance (DB), with certain personal property depreciated over 7 or 5 years at 200% DB. Identifying such land improvements and personal property (like, for example, appliances) is done via a cost segregation study.

With a very broad brush, I will say that new mechanical components that are installed in an already operating a building could be written off 100% in the year they are purchased subject to limits and other rules. Or you could choose to depreciate them over a shorter period of time than is being used to depreciate the building because they are considered personal property as opposed to real estate. An example would be when you replace a furnace. Also, when you buy a *new or existing* building, you could choose to **have a cost segregation study done** to assign a portion of the purchase price to the various components of the building so that those components could be depreciated at a more rapid rate than the building, as described above. In this case, the segregated value of those components would be subtracted from the depreciable basis of the building just like the value of the land is segregated from the purchase price. The segregated components and the building would have separate depreciation schedules.

The other area of choice regarding depreciation is **whether to use an accelerated depreciation method** where the deduction taken is either 150% or 200% of what the deduction would have been if straight line depreciation was being used. Each year, the extra depreciation that was taken the year before is used to arrive at a declining balance (book value) of the asset. That ever-decreasing amount is used to calculate what the straight-line depreciation *would* have been for that year, and that amount is multiplied by one and a half or two depending on whether 150% or 200% DB is being used.

I am telling you this to point out that **there are ways to get larger depreciation deductions in the early years of ownership** than those yielded from depreciating all parts of the building equally using the straight-line method. Accelerated depreciation methods, writing off depreciable assets one hundred percent in the year they are purchased (also known as making a Section 179 election), and cost segregation will all yield a higher depreciation deduction while not increasing cash out. The result is lower taxes in those years due to lower reported income.

Before this sounds too exciting to you, **there is a downside I must point out. That is the dreaded recapture of depreciation.** The IRS says, "When you dispose of property for which you claimed a special depreciation allowance, any gain on the disposition is generally recaptured (included in income) as ordinary income up to the amount of the depreciation previously allowed or allowable for the property, including the special depreciation allowance." Special depreciation means anything beyond straight-line. In other words, when calculating your gain when you sell a property, **any amount of depreciation taken over and above what the straight-line deduction would have been is taxed at whatever your tax rate is on your regular income.** Only the gain outside of the recaptured depreciation is taxed at long-term capital gain rates. **There is no recapture of depreciation when calculating the gain on a property that has only been depreciated using the straight-line method.** I will point out, though, that you can choose to use straight-line depreciation instead of an accelerated method on the separate depreciation schedules resulting from implementing cost segregation.

Your tax preparer will know how to handle the depreciation on your property, but I wanted to raise your awareness of the mechanics of depreciation as well as some of the choices connected with reporting depreciation to help you open a discussion with your preparer about what is best for you. These are not one-time choices. **You can decide on your preferences for each property independently from all your other properties to suit your needs at the time.**

Let us move on now to delineating the categories of expense you are likely to experience. As I mentioned, using the same categories employed on the tax forms makes it easy to transfer the numbers from your internal reports to the forms. **You may have sub accounts that help you evaluate a property's performance, but a summary of expenses in the same category is entered on the tax form.** For example, you may keep track of repairs for each individual apartment in a multi-unit property, but the total for all the apartments would be entered under "repairs" on the tax form.

As discussed in SECTION ONE, income and expenses from operating a rental property are reported on SCHEDULE E (Form 1040) for individual filers and on Form 8825 for business entities. The expense categories named are roughly the same on each form, and there is space to write in "other" expenses. There are a few things to know, though, before you start compiling your numbers.

- The IRS wants you to use a separate column for each property.

- You can attach multiple forms to accommodate more properties than there are columns.

- While properties titled only in one spouse's name can be entered on the same SCHEDULE E with properties titled in the other spouse's name or properties titled in both spouse's names, **each separate business entity must file separate pass-through information returns (typically Form 1065) utilizing its own Form 8825 even if the partners/shareholders/members are exactly the same for each entity**.

Here are the expense categories offered on the SCHEDULE E and Form 1065:

- Advertising

  o Enter the cost of advertising materials as well as what you paid to place ads online or in other media.

- Auto and travel

  o I do not think it is a great idea to lump these expenses together in your internal books because they are two different things. The first represents the cost of using a vehicle in your business (either the actual costs, including depreciation of the vehicle, or the business miles multiplied by a mileage rate which covers all expenses as provided by the IRS). The second refers to travel expenses related to your business. Examples would be a plane ticket, meals, and lodging on a trip to visit your far-away property. So, keep these expenses separate in your own books to better evaluate what is being spent in these categories, but you can add them together for the IRS.

- Cleaning and maintenance

  o Your cleaning expenses may be easy to identify, but maintenance costs may be hard to separate from repairs unless you want to include only recurring activities such as janitorial, mowing, and snow removal here. Again, I would want all these expense categories to be separate in my internal books.

- Commissions

  o Typically, this refers to fees paid to Realtors to find tenants, and not for selling your property. (Expenses such as a Realtor commission and attorney fees when you sell a property are considered to be "costs of sale," and they increase your cost basis in the property when computing your profit or loss. Cost of sale are not deducted as operating expenses.)

- Insurance

  o You may have a blanket property insurance policy covering multiple buildings. However, since the IRS wants you to enter this information on a per-property basis, ask your agent to give you a schedule that shows how much of your annual premium is attributed to each property. Multiple types of insurance premiums may be totaled here.

- Legal and other professional fees

  o Mostly this is for attorney fees *other* than for purchasing or selling a property like for an eviction or a lawsuit. Bookkeeping, accounting, and tax preparation fees are also entered here, although you may have separate accounts for each of these in your own books.

- Management fees

  - Interestingly, they want you to list these separately from commissions only on SCHEDULE E, and not Form 8825. So, if you have it broken down in your books, you can make the entries. Otherwise, just lump them together on this line, and leave the line for commissions blank.

- Interest

  - If you have a blanket mortgage covering multiple properties, breaking down the mortgage interest per property can be difficult. You could just enter the total interest under one property, and write a note on that line that indicates the figure is also for the properties in Column B and C, etc. If you pay balance transfer fees on a credit card offer or interest on a charge account related to purchases for your rental, you can enter it here.

- Repairs

  - This would include not only the materials, but the labor paid to repair anything on your property. Not included here would be the materials and labor to create any asset that is going to be capitalized and depreciated as opposed to expensed in the current year.

- Supplies

  - This line is only on SCHEDULE E, but not on Form 8825. Unless you have kept a separate account for supplies, I would lump this together with repairs.

- Taxes

  - This is not where any kind of income tax that you paid is entered. I would not even enter payroll taxes here. This is for taxes directly related to your property where the taxing body has sent you a bill, and you paid the amount on the bill. Some examples of this are:

- ◆ Property taxes
- ◆ Streetlight or similar assessments
- ◆ Annual business registration taxes

- Utilities

  - ○ You may have a purpose for keeping the costs for each type of utility separate for each apartment in your local accounts, but you can put their sum here.

- Depreciation

  - ○ This is where you enter the amount calculated on your attached Form 4562.

- Other

  - ○ Form 8825 gives you four lines for expense categories not already named on the form, whereas SCHEDULE E only gives you one. If necessary, you can attach your own schedule of "other" expenses, and put the total on this line.

There is one last subject relating to the taxation of rental properties that I would like to cover, and that is **the qualified business income deduction under section 199A** of the Internal Revenue Code. Referred to as the section 199A deduction, this is the result of a new law in 2017 that allows the owners of qualified businesses (sole proprietorships, partnerships, S corporations, trusts, or estates) to **deduct twenty percent of their taxable income attributable to their business before calculating their personal income tax. This is one huge simple tax break for business owners!** There are some limitations and restrictions as is typical, but basically you just calculate what your taxable income would be like normal, and then only pay tax on eighty percent of it.

At first, there was some confusion as to whether the section 199A deduction would apply to rental real estate, but in 2019 the IRS issued **Revenue Procedure 2019-38 that specifically permits a "rental real estate enterprise" to be treated as a trade or business for the purposes of the section 199A deduction.** For the purposes of this Revenue Procedure, a rental real estate enterprise is defined as an interest in real property held to generate rental or lease income. The individual taxpayer or passthrough entity must hold each interest directly or through an entity disregarded as an entity separate from its owner, such as a limited liability company (LLC) with a single owner.

This is another wonderful example of the preferential tax treatment given to real estate investors just like not having to pay Self Employment Tax on our profits. In the first instance, our profits are treated like trade or business income so we can take the section 199A deduction. In the second instance, our income is considered passive, so we do not pay Self Employment Tax like a trade or business owner. It's a beautiful thing! **Our government *wants* people to be in the business of providing housing for its citizens**.

Though the IRS wanted to allow the section 199A deduction for rental real estate enterprises, they recognized that such operations are a little different from a trade or business. So, **they rolled out four requirements** that must be met by taxpayers and/or relevant passthrough entities (RPE) to qualify.

1. **Separate books and records** are maintained to reflect income and expenses for each rental real estate enterprise.

   o Not a problem. This would be the necessary procedure for preparing separate tax returns for each entity anyway.

2. For rental real estate enterprises that have been in existence less than four years, **250 or more hours of rental services are performed each year.** For other rental real estate enterprises, 250 or more hours of rental services are performed in at least three of the past five years.

   o **The 250 hours of rental service activities may be aggregated** amongst your eligible properties and entities. You do not need to have 250 hours for any one entity or, in the case of property held jointly by spouses, for either spouse.

- Eligible services include time spent on maintenance, repairs, rent collection, payment of expenses, and activities to obtain tenants.
- The IRS indicated that **the eligible services do not need to be performed only by you as the property owner. <u>You can count the hours spent on these services by employees, agents, and contractors.</u>**

3. **The taxpayer maintains contemporaneous records** which include time reports, logs, or similar documents, regarding the following: hours of service performed, description of all services performed, dates on which such services were performed, and who performed the services.

   - This is key to utilizing the section 199A deduction, and it is probably the only requirement that adds any work to what you are already doing. **Just get in the habit of keeping a running log** of what you did, where you did it, and how much time you spent on it for any date you did some work on your rentals. You can keep additional records for time spent by others, and then add the hours together for everybody at the end of the year.

4. **The taxpayer or RPE attaches a statement** to the return filed for each tax year the section 199A deduction is relied upon.

   - Make up a statement with something like "QUALIFIED BUSINESS INCOME DEDUCTION STATEMENT for John & Suzi Taxpayer Form 1040 Per Section 199A of the Internal Revenue Code" at the top. Then, list each rental property for which you have accumulated hours, and which are personally owned by you and/or your spouse who are directly filing the 1040, and those that are in your business entities. If your properties are owned within an entity, list the name and Federal Employer Identification Number (EIN) for each entity along with the addresses of the rental properties within that entity.
   - Add a couple of sentences at the bottom of the statement to the effect that "All of the above entities are grouped together and considered to be one rental real estate enterprise. The requirements of Rev. Proc. 2019-38 have been satisfied."

○ **You are not required to attach any of your logs or records** that show how your enterprise cumulatively spent at least 250 hours on rental service activities that year. Keep those with your tax preparation records in case you are audited.

Passthrough entities that have income from rental real estate must inform each partner/member/shareholder of their share of that income on each K-1 schedule. **There is not a pre-named line on the K-1 for income to be considered for the section 199A deduction**. However, the entry can be made on Part III, Line 20 of the K-1 where "Other information" is to be provided. For income to be considered in the taxpayer's calculations for the section 199A deduction, **the letter code "Z"** is placed in the column on the left, and the dollar amount is entered to the right of the "Z."

For example, if an entity has net rental real estate income, that amount would be entered on the K-1 in Part III, Line 2. The same amount would then be entered on Line 20 next to a "Z" code. When the taxpayer is preparing their Individual 1040 return, the information on Line 20 would be transferred to either Form 8995A Deduction for Qualified Business Income or Form 8995 Qualified Business Income Deduction Simplified Computation.

The 8995 and 8995A forms are fairly complex, but **if you are doing your personal tax return using a program like TurboTax (as I recommend you do), the program will utilize all the correct forms, and make all the required computations.** The program will first ask you if you have any income from rentals. This refers to rentals held in the name of any of the taxpayers filing the 1040. If you do, provide the program with the income from your own records. The program will also ask you if you have received a K-1. If you answer yes, it will ask you if you have an entry on Line 20 of a K-1 with a "Z" code in front of it. Enter the amount, and the tax prep program will do the rest.

I realize bookkeeping, accounting, and tax return preparation are not as interesting to most as whatever their chosen business is. However, if you do not do these things yourself, you must accept someone else doing them for you. Those tax returns must be filed because, as the saying goes, taxes are the only sure thing other than death. **The better you are at keeping accurate financial records for the**

normal transactions in your business, the less hours your accountant or tax preparer will need to charge you for. Also, with clear records, your tax bills will be as low as possible, while the likelihood of an audit will be minimized. Additionally, you will have better information at your fingertips for evaluating what is going on financially with your properties.

With what I have covered in this chapter, you should have a running start at preparing your own tax forms if you choose. Even if you do not prepare your own tax returns, what I have covered is most of what you need to be familiar with for a rental real estate enterprise like the one I hope you build. At the very least, this information will help you have a more productive conversation with your tax preparer. Let us move on to a discussion about how to manage the wealth you are going to grow after you have paid the taxes on your profits.

11
THE IMPACT OF WEALTH (PAINT)

After you have laid a foundation, framed a building, and closed in the workings with a roof and interior and exterior walls, the next consideration is to turn the surfaces into the form that anyone entering your building will see. I know there are varieties of products you can use to cover a wall, but let's generally identify this as applying paint. Visitors will not see what is inside the walls, nor will they ever know all the hard work that went on behind the scenes. But they will make judgements when they see the paint. In the same way, like it or not, **people make judgements about you when they see your "paint" or the visible part of your life**. They will not likely have the details about how you got to where you are, so they will draw their conclusions based on what they can see. To a large degree, **how you handle your money is a primary ingredient in the image others maintain of you. The impact from incorporating whatever level of wealth you have into your life is like applying paint to your life for all to see.**

Yes, it is easy to say that you do not care what anyone else thinks about you, but the fact is that they *are* thinking. Lenders, who have yet to meet you, are judging you based on your credit report. Others, who will never see your credit report, including even the people living in your personal residence, are getting their own impressions. **Though this may sound like a buildup to making a case for caring what other people think about you, it is not! This will be a chapter about what *you* think about *you*. My objective is to make you think about what wealth means to you, and how you want to handle it.** My belief is that, **if you have a healthy view of money, you will be happy to do things the right way** for yourself as well as for society as a whole. It will naturally flow that you will not have to care how others see your "paint," but you will rest assured that their image of you will be favorable.

When I was putting this book together, the title was *Get Rich Slow*, and while not grammatically correct (it should say *Slowly*), it is a catchy contrast to the way many people consider books about real estate investing to be "get rich quick" schemes. Certainly, **some books on the subject lead you to believe that everyone can get rich quick in real estate.** But if I can get them to pick up a book that says *Build Real Estate Wealth* on the cover, I'm a step closer to a sale. And if the information in my book is truthful about how the average person can invest in rental real estate and truly enjoy the journey, then *they* are step closer to their financial goals if they can connect with the information.

Stating that "everyone can get rich quick in real estate" is *partly* true though. But **the only true part is that you *can* get rich in real estate**. It's just probably not going to be quick, and not everyone can do it. In fact, nobody can do it unless they get a good education on the subject, and apply themselves diligently, unless they receive an inheritance of properties with management in place. **If you are reading this, I am probably not out of line to predict there is a strong likelihood you will find some level of success in rental real estate, and that you will be adding to your income and net worth over time.** So, let's drill deeper into this rich/wealth subject.

Most people equate being rich with being wealthy. They *are* synonyms as are the terms well-to-do, affluent, prosperous, and well off. But their meanings are not the same. I wish I could use something other than *Rich* in the subtitle, because **my real purpose is to give you the tools to accumulate *wealth*, not just money. There is a difference.**

I feel the difference between "rich" and "wealth" is like the differ-ence between "knowledge" and "wisdom." I equate knowledge with the

accumulation of facts, but wisdom is the ability to put those facts to good use. You can have lots of information at your disposal, but if you do not possess wisdom, you are more likely to make the wrong decision. Conversely, people with wisdom can make great decisions without many facts. They just know how things work together. As a parallel to this comparison, "rich" means the accumulation of money, while wealth points to knowing how to handle riches. To me, <u>wealth represents the happiness or fullness in your life that you feel because of what you have.</u> You can have lots of money while still feeling miserable because the things you have acquired with your cash do not make you happy. On the other hand, even if you have little cash or few possessions, <u>you can feel wealthy because of your relationships and the fact that your physical needs are met</u> by the cash and possessions you *do* have.

Some of my favorite song lyrics are contained in "Take It to the Limit" by the Eagles. I'm not sure which of the composers (either Randy Meisner, Don Henley, or Glenn Frey) wrote the lines, but their insightfulness impresses me every time I hear the song. Verse two addresses taking the love you could express to others and instead spending it on buying the time to make more money. The question is then posed as to whether a presumably neglected loved one would stick around if everything fell apart.

To me, **this is a warning against accumulating cash and possessions at the expense of draining dry the relationships in your life that make you feel wealthy**. The writer, while aware of the monetary rewards of his hard work, is perhaps recognizing his neglect of his loved one. While acknowledging his revelation, he is checking in with his loved one to see if he has gone too far.

I participate in a few real estate masterminds, and I am often in private conversations with others who are in some phase of the business. In both settings, as well as when conversing with friends or family, I often offer up the same advice. When discussing issues that have arisen between competitors, contractors, suppliers, friends, family, or anyone who has a story where money is part of the equation, **I am known to state something that makes people recenter their thinking back to what is really important. I tell them that, if I had a choice between losing all my money or losing all my relationships, I would**

choose to lose all my money in a heartbeat because my relationships can help me get my money back. On the other hand, if I lost all my relationships while keeping all my money, how could I enjoy my money alone? Love beats money every time.

The bottom line is that it is better to keep a relationship intact than to obsess over some perceived slight or to try to squeeze every dime out of a situation when the other party may feel taken advantage of. <u>Don't make a withdrawal from a good relationship just to make a deposit into your bank account</u>. That "paint" does not look good on you.

You might think I am trying to say that money cannot buy happiness, but I actually do not think that is universally true if you know how to handle your cash. Certainly, the lack of enough money to acquire the necessities of life can create unhappiness. Conversely, having abundant cash can create the happiness of not having the stress of scarcity. But the happiness that comes from material things is only part of the wealth equation. **Though some level of happiness can be found in having "things," the concept of money buying happiness in *relationships* has its limitations. Abundance must take its proper place in your life, or it will influence you to ruin your relationships**.

Notice I said that abundance will *influence* you to ruin relationships. I did not say the abundance will ruin your relationships; *you* will ruin your relationships if you have the wrong attitude about abundance. Money is not the root of all evil. The *love* of money (the wrong attitude about it) is the root of all evil. **If you can combine being rich in material things with the right relationship with your abundance, then you will be truly wealthy.** I can present a few ideas on this subject in this book, but I believe a right relationship with abundance is best understood through a right relationship with God, our Creator. You can explore more about that in the Bible.

Since 1987, Jeff Pizzino, APR (Accredited in Public Relations) has worked either in-house or as a PR/marketing communications consultant for a number of varied organizations. He founded his current venture, AuthenticityPR, in 2008, and often functions as a chief communications officer for his clients. Jeff is adept at securing press coverage, preserving corporate reputation, fine-tuning messaging, strengthening corporate culture, and embracing authentic communications. He has an M.B.A. in

Management from Western International University and a B.A. in Communications from Brigham Young University. His About.Me profile says he "embraces customer-centric practices, transparency and simply '**doing the right thing**' at all times."

In his early years as a freelancer, Jeff contributed an article to the Fall 1995 edition of *Financial Freedom Report Quarterly* entitled "Putting Some Old Money Myths to Rest." I saved that article because I especially liked his busting of two myths. I have added the bold type emphasis.

Jeff calls Myth #6 "Being Wealthy Is All About Material Possessions." He says, "There is more to being wealthy than 'he who dies with the most toys wins.' **There's a huge difference between accumulating money and being wealthy. Above all, never pursue money at the expense of your health, peace of mind, loving relationships, and just enjoying personal activities. Money is a means of creating wealth; wealth is a means of creating a great life. But personal joy must be cultivated along the way.**" What *he* said.

Myth #7 is called "The Acquisition of Wealth Is A Win/Lose Game." He asks, "If the rich keep getting richer, do the poor keep getting poorer? Thanks to inaccuracies in the media and omissions at our nation's universities, the truth regarding this matter is seldom heard. Here's the reality of the situation: **Your NOT becoming rich will benefit no one. But you becoming rich benefits others in an abundance of ways.** Wealthy individuals build factories which create jobs that help the economy. They invest in real estate which provides housing to renters who cannot afford to buy their own home. They also make tax contributions to the community, support churches, charities, scholarships, (as well as) educational and hospital improvements. **It's a fact that the more wealth and opportunities you create for yourself, the more wealth and opportunities you create for others.**" Well said, Jeff.

I have heard it said that most people would tell you that to turn $100 into $110 takes labor, but a billionaire would say that to turn $100,000,000 into $110,000,000 is inevitable. This points to more than a difference in mindsets. **Money begets money, and it is important to note that giving money away is part of the equation for getting money. Being wealthy involves the satisfaction of helping other people with your resources. Remember, it is not a win/**

lose game if you are playing it right. Wealthy people don't hoard money; they keep it moving by making contributions and investments.

During the Gilded Age in the United States in the late 1800's, the industry titans would say that it is shameful for the rich to die with their money. That is why you see so many Carnegie libraries. Andrew Carnegie, one of the richest men in the history of the world, sold his steel company and retired from business. He then set about in earnest distributing his fortune. In addition to funding libraries, he paid for thousands of church organs throughout the U.S. and the world. Also, during the 19th century, it became fashionable for the middle class to make financial contributions to organized charities. Many current billionaires, led by Warren Buffett and Bill and Melinda Gates, have signed a pledge to give away half of their fortunes to charity. And still, their fortunes grow.

Though you may like the idea of making large contributions to charity, you probably have the desire to leave money to your descendants. There are lots of good reasons to do that, but Warren Buffet once cautioned that **you should give your kids enough money so they can do *anything*, but not so much that they can do *nothing*. Part of feeling wealthy is feeling productive, even though you have enough money to do anything you want.**

Capital is anything you own that makes you money or means. If, through real estate investing or any other source, you accumulate capital beyond your basic needs, you have a question to ask yourself. **Are you going to be the kind who just takes enrichment and doesn't give back? The rich have a responsibility to give back to the communities from which they get their capital.** Some (but probably not enough) of the rich's resources are taken by taxes for public operations. But more is required voluntarily beyond taxes from people who have far more than they need for their own sustenance and pleasures. **Considering how this can impact the relationships in your life, doing so is an example of how you can improve from being rich to being wealthy.**

The author is unknown, and there are many versions, but this insightful writing is worth reprinting:

MONEY, what can it buy?

A bed, but not sleep.

Food to eat, but not an appetite.

Books to read, but not intelligence.

Elegance, but not beauty.

A house, but not a home.

Medicine, but not health.

Luxury, but not culture.

Pleasure, but not happiness.

A cross around your neck, but not eternal life.

A bench in church, but not paradise.

Yes, I know that some evil, stingy people appear to be blessed with great riches. Such wealth could be the passing profits of sin that God plans to snatch away. But I believe that, in the big picture, God blesses people He can trust to be "good stewards" of the capital He gives them whether they are believers or not. Just as in the Bible where God used nonbelieving people or nations to accomplish His purposes, He seems to use anyone He chooses to do good things with their capital. The evil person may not realize the role they are playing. The stingy person who gives nothing to charity may at the same time be operating a business that blesses many with good jobs. But if you really want to get God's attention, be a good steward with what He gives you, and be generous and maybe even sacrificial.

You cannot outgive God. I am not saying you should give to get, but I have noticed that the more I give away, the more comes in. Let me take that thought a step further. God was the author of any invention that ever made anyone a dime. To accomplish His purposes, He chose for whatever reason to introduce it through whomever we now recognize as the inventor. **If you are asking for wealth for yourself, you must be willing to be "used," i.e., be a "steward"** who both invests wisely for a good return and gives some of their fortune for the betterment of others.

To my friends who associate themselves with a religious belief system that preaches tithing, I want to inject the following commentary regarding my beliefs about charitable giving. Tithing, as a biblical principal, means the giving of ten percent of one's income to God. You may not choose to tithe, or you may not feel it is possible at this time. You may not even know what tithing is, but you may be curious about it. All of that is perfectly okay, because we are all on our own journeys. So, I apologize in advance to any readers who come away thinking my views are too matter of fact or heavy handed. But I can tell you this is where I landed after no small amount of studying and practice. Perhaps, if you look for yourself at what the Bible has to say about tithing and giving, you may arrive at a position similar to mine. Here are some things for you to consider on your journey:

- Tithing is to be done to your local church where you are spiritually fed, and which would respond if you were in need as a member or regular attender. Your contributions to other charities or national religious organizations are not part of your tithe.

- Your tithe is calculated on your gross income on your paycheck if you have a W-2 job, not on your net pay after taxes or other deductions.

- Your tithe is calculated on your gross income from other sources against which you do not have any expenses. Examples would be interest, dividends, lottery winnings, Social Security, trust fund distributions, monthly insurance settlements, child support and alimony.

- If you are self-employed or otherwise have expenses related to obtaining your income, your tithe is calculated on your net income after your expenses. More specifically, if you perform a service or operate a business, then tithe on what you withdraw from your business for personal use. Obviously, not all your profits are withdrawn while they are being made. Another example would be that if you buy a property for $50,000, then put $20,000 into it, and finally sell it for $100,000 less $8,000 in costs to sell it, your tithe would be on your net profit of $22,000 assuming you were able to pay out all $22,000 to yourself.

- The principal of tithing pops up throughout the Bible, but the most notable reference is in Malachi, the final book of the Old Testament. Throughout the Bible, God tells us to *trust* Him in everything, but not to *test* Him in anything...except in one instance...tithing.

- In Malachi, Chapter Three, after God points out to Malachi that the people are robbing Him in their tithes and offerings, He says in verse 10, "Bring the full tithes into the storehouse, that there may be food in my house; and thereby *put me to the test,* says the LORD of hosts, if I will not open the windows of heaven for you and pour down for you an overflowing blessing." Other translations say something like, "...and see if I will not throw open the floodgates of heaven and pour out so much blessing that you will not have room enough for it." If blessings from God could be in a bucket, they would be pressed down and running over for tithers. Test Him.

- **We shouldn't think we are being sacrificial or even generous if we tithe. Tithing is a requirement from God, so it's the least we can so. If we tithe, we are being *obedient*, and not *generous*.** After we have given our tithe to our local church, if we give even more time or money to our church or to any other charity or individual in need, then we are being generous. Beyond that, if we are so generous with our time or money that it hurts, *then* we are being sacrificial.

- God will get His work done with or without us, but those who follow His commands, and allow themselves to be used by Him as good stewards of our time and money, will receive the greater blessing. **He doesn't need our money, but *we* need the experience and the enjoyment of giving it.**

- We all came into this life with nothing, and we will leave it with nothing. Every person's increase in capital along the way is only by God's grace, whether we are a believer or not.

Secularly, these concepts are related to the Law of Reciprocity and its sister, the Law of Attraction. The Law or Principal of Reciprocity basically states that you are likely to get back what you give out in any matter from relationships to finances. The Law of Attraction encourages people to shift from a scarcity mindset to an abundance mindset. I encourage you to research both of these ideas.

While I recommend being generous with your profits, I also believe you have the right to decide where that generosity lands. **Operate your business carefully to make a profit, and then give as much care to choosing the causes you help.** This book is about making money in the rental real estate business. I want to caution you to keep your business a business, and not let your business become a charity. Specifically, **do not let your tenants force you to decide which less fortunate people you give your money to, which is what happens when you let them slide on their rent. If you let tenants take advantage of you, then you are effectively allowing them to turn themselves into your favorite charity!**

Having highlighted the contrast between being rich and being wealthy, I don't want to lose sight of the fact that you are reading this to learn about making cash in the real estate game. So far, this chapter has dealt more with your mindset regarding the *use* of money to this point, but I want to continue with some direction about the *accumulation* of cash.

It should be apparent to you that the more you have access to cash, the more power you have. The more power you have, the more cash you can accumulate. But you must exercise discipline with your money regarding your expenditures. **Wisdom and common sense must be employed when handling the expenses of your business, the profits you reinvest, your contributions to others, and the money you spend on yourself. Otherwise, you will spend all the cash that comes in, and you will not actually move ahead with the growth of your business, the extent of your investments, or the improvement of your lifestyle.** It will be like treading water where there's lots of activity to stay afloat, but you're not getting anywhere. As the money slips through your fingers, you are losing the power it could bring, so you end up back where you started.

Lottery winners and athletes, who suddenly get large amounts of cash, often go broke because they don't know how to handle money. It's too much for them to deal with all at once. Lacking foresight, they apparently believe there is a never-ending supply of cash for them, so they make little effort to keep from spending all that comes in. On the other hand, **people who incrementally build their wealth get better and better at handling larger and larger amounts of income and the expenditures related to creating that income. That's another reason for getting rich slow(ly)!**

I am sure that among your objectives for investing in rental real estate is to add security to your future, but you also want to raise your standard of living along the way. I totally agree with both of those objectives, but **you must strike a balance between depriving your personal life for the benefit of your business, and depriving your business for the benefit of your personal life.** While it is a common strategy to make sacrifices in your personal life for your business, I firmly believe you must "make it real" along the way by rewarding yourself with the fruits of your labor. Otherwise, after a while of experiencing no enjoyment, you will begin to believe there is no point to making the sacrifices, and you will lose enthusiasm for carrying on. **The key is to reward yourself enough along the way, so you notice the improvement in your condition, but not so much that you impede your progress.**

You must work out the mechanics of maintaining that balance yourself. The question usually gets down to how much of your increased net monthly cashflow resulting from your newest property getting rented, or how much of that chunk of money from selling your last flip, will go back into the business, and how much will be used to do something nice for yourself or someone else. Read on for one way to approach the issue.

Let's say you want to buy something expensive; especially something that will depreciate and not produce income...like a $30,000 extra car. Instead of just using your cash to buy the car (which would take $30,000 out of your available resources for investing), get a loan for the car. Then, buy an income-producing asset like another rental property which will throw off the cashflow to cover the payments on the car. You could buy the property for all cash to maximize the cashflow, but if you want to maximize your leverage, use all or part of the $30,000 for a downpayment on the property. Doing the latter will reduce your cashflow due to the mortgage payments, so make sure you still have enough to cover the car payments.

Five years later you will have a depreciated car worth far less than what you paid for it. *But* you will still have the equity you put into the property *plus* the equity that grew in the property. Additionally, you will enjoy the increased net monthly cashflow after the payments on the car loan are finished. Your tenants will have bought you *all* of this if it is the case that the original $30,000 came from profits from other rentals you already own! If you had blown the $30,000 by paying cash for the car, then five years later all you have is the depreciated car. Do you see the difference? **Don't be afraid of useful debt. Just buy income property that produces the cash to cover the payments.** Are you beginning to see how, once you get started, this thing just rolls on and on?

It's also important to moderate your tastes by not purchasing things at the upper end of your income level just because you can. **Always live beneath your means**. Some people think they just can't spend any less on their life than they do, so they rarely have any money left over. This can even happen to high income earners who commit to all kinds of loan payments, vacations, club memberships, and toys so that they have nothing to cover an emergency. They are treading water with their finances. **The fact is that whatever your means are at any given time, it's possible to live beneath them, and save money. It just takes deciding to live in a certain stratum, and the discipline to carry out the decision. Then, as your income increases due to wise investing, you can move to a higher stratum, but always one that is below your means.**

Another way to put it is to say that, if you are in the game because you want to *spend* a million dollars, you are less likely to *make* a million dollars. This is because you won't spend less than you make along the way. **You must enter the game knowing the path requires regular saving for emergencies, for short-term larger expenditures like special occasions, for long-term expenditures like home improvements, and investing in income-producing assets.**

It's tempting to say the way to attack this is to set goals such as a goal to own a certain number of rental units or a goal for the number of houses you flip this year. That's fine, but there may be a better way to look at it. I have heard that **it is better to raise your standards than it is to just increase your goals**. More successful people have higher standards. I believe this applies to the standards you follow for the way you conduct yourself in all phases of your life as well was the standards you impose on your properties, your relationships, the people working for you, and anything that is taken into your body or your mind. **If you raise your standards away from whatever is not good for you, success will follow.**

I know there was a lot to take in philosophically in this chapter beyond the mechanics of investing in rental real estate. It may cause you to reevaluate the way you think about your finances, and not to just take action to make an investment.

Whether you do *something* or do *nothing*, a year from now you will be different. The question is the degree to which you will be different, and in what direction you will change.

I will conclude by encouraging you to use your ability to handle your personal and business money to create cash. Use your *cash* to create *wealth*. Use your *wealth* to create a great *life*. Find *joy* in your great *life*. Share your *joy* with your *relationships*. Your *relationships* will help you create more cash, and the cycle will start again.

HOW TO PAINT A PICTURE WITH YOUR PERSONAL FINANCIAL STATEMENT

I started the last chapter about your "paint" or image with reference to how bankers will judge you based on your credit report. I want to continue in this chapter with a discussion of the other main source of data that banks will use to determine your suitability for a loan. **As part of your loan application process, banks will want you to "paint a picture" of yourself with a Personal Financial Statement.** This is an all-encompassing survey of the income, expenses, assets, and liabilities of you and any co-applicant.

Every bank has their own form, but the purpose and the categories of information are the same. This statement would cover the personal aspects of your existing financial picture, and it would be accompanied by any financial statements related to, for example, the specific property you are trying to borrow money to buy. If you already have an operating business or property, those financials would be attached, but only the net value of that business or property along with the net income (or loss) from its operation would be fed onto designated areas on the Personal Statement to be combined with your personal assets and income. **The ultimate aim of this form is to present to the bank a bottom-line view of your net income and your net worth as of the date of the statement.** They then apply their secret ratios and other qualifiers to decide on whether to give you the loan. It goes without saying that **you will want your Personal Financial Statement to look as attractive as possible with both the <u>information contained</u> as well as the <u>appearance</u> of the data entered.**

You can **consider the upcoming discussion to be a reference when the time comes for you to prepare a Personal Financial Statement**. Hopefully you can glean some tips to help you present the right information in the right way. Incompleteness will count against you as will inaccurate, unclear, or unnecessary information. Typically, these statements are filled out by hand, so **use your best <u>printing</u>**, or have someone with better printing write in the information for you.

Let's begin with **the two equations they teach you during your first week of Accounting 101.**

- First, <u>net income is equal to gross income less expenses.</u> Revenues and expenses are compiled on what is known as an Income Statement. Pretty straightforward. Most people understand this to be the way a business determines net profit, but **the banker wants to dig deep into how your business and employment resources mesh with your personal spending habits**. Presumably, cash comes to an individual or family from employment, businesses, investments, or some sort of guaranteed source (Social Security, lottery winnings, trust fund, or insurance awards, for example). The recipient(s)/applicant(s) then spend that money, and the bank wants to see how well you are doing with that. The banker will be thinking about:

- Where do you get your money from?
- How much do you get?
- How likely is your income to continue at the rate shown, and for how long?
- What regular commitments (including their nature, amount, and duration) do you have for the cash you receive?
- What is your discretionary spending?
- How much do you have left over after your obligations and your discretionary spending?
- What percentage of your income is committed to debt service and, in particular, for housing expenses?

- Secondly, net worth equals assets less liabilities. Assets, liabilities, and net capital are compiled on what is called a Balance Sheet. What you have, less what you owe, is your capital, or the amount that would be left over if you sold everything and paid all your debts. The banker wants to evaluate whether there would be enough money to pay off your loans if everything went south by looking at:

- What assets do you have?
- What are your assets worth now?
- How likely are those assets to change in value up or down, how much will that change be, and when will that change occur?
- How much cash do you have?
- Where do you keep your cash?
- What assets to you have that can quickly be turned into cash such as stocks?
- What assets do you have that would take longer to turn into cash such as your personal residence?
- What assets are you claiming that are not easy to assign a value to such as your furniture, jewelry, or art collection?
- What assets do you have pledged against existing loans like for your car?

o   What is the percentage of the loan vs. the value of the asset pledged?

o   What are the reasons for and the balances on any existing loans?

o   Which loans must be paid off in the near future?

o   Which loans can be paid off in the long term?

o   Which loans are paid off with regular payments, and which are due all at one time? When is their payoff?

o   Which loans, if any, do you plan on paying off when you get the loan for which you are applying?

o   Do you have any loans that do not need to be paid back at a specific time, such as a credit line balance or a loan on your life insurance policy?

o   Are there any obligations of a third party for which you are responsible, such as when you cosign on a child's car loan?

o   Are any of your assets tied up in a lawsuit?

o   Do you show back taxes of any kind as a liability?

o   What is the percentage of your cash and near-cash assets compared to your relatively illiquid assets?

Still, your Personal Financial Statement is only part of the picture. The banker will combine this information with your credit report to see if you are including all your obligations, and to evaluate how consistent you have been at meeting your obligations. All this, combined with your experience in the area of the loan, their general impression of you, and whatever other ingredients to their secret sauce they are looking for you to supply, will determine whether you get the loan.

Now, **I want to give you some pointers about the line items you are likely to encounter on your bank's Personal Financial Statement form.** The first section is where the personal information about the applicants is entered. This is where you and any co-applicant enter your legal name, personal address, phone numbers, email address, birth date, and Social Security Number. With your signature, the lender can now run your credit report. In this section, or in a separate general information section, you may also be asked for:

- Whether or not you are a U.S, citizen
- The name of your employer
- Your job title
- How long you have been employed there
- Your relationship to the co-applicant
- If you own your residence, or if you rent
- How long you have lived at your current residence
- The type of business you are in
- How long you have been in business
- How many dependents you have
- Whether you are a party to a lawsuit or legal filing
- Whether you have declared bankruptcy within a stated timeframe
- Through what year your income tax returns have been filed
- If any of your tax returns are being audited
- The information about any debt or obligation that you have personally guaranteed

The statement is then divided into sections to organize your personal Assets, Liabilities, Income, and Expenses. The lines will give you a spot to enter the pertinent dollar amount, but most of those amounts are transferred from a separate chart in another part of the form where you are to list the details as to how you came up with the number entered on that line.

I want to emphasize that if you own a business entity, for example an LLC that holds rental property, you will create a stand-alone statement that shows the assets, liabilities, and net worth of that entity. This statement would accompany your personal statement. Your share of that net worth would be transferred to your Personal Financial Statement and shown as an "other asset" in the long-term asset section based on your percentage of ownership. If you have multiple entities, you must make a separate statement for each entity. **Do not try to enter business assets and liabilities on a personal statement form, only your share of the net worth of the business.**

Even if you own your rental properties in your personal name as opposed to in an entity's name, I recommend you prepare a separate statement showing the Income Statement and Balance Sheet for the operation of those properties, and attach it. Then, **transfer only your net income and your net worth from those forms onto the appropriate areas of the banker's statement**. This will keep your Personal Financial Statement looking cleaner and easier to understand for the banker because only your personal picture is presented on their form without trying to jam the operation of several rental properties into the space allotted. Your rental properties are better highlighted on their own statements, and footnotes can be added to call out any special information.

Regarding an Income Statement for rental property which is attached to a Personal Financial Statement, the purpose of this statement is to demonstrate net cash flow, not net taxable income. For a tax return, only the interest portion of a loan payment is counted as an expense. Also, depreciation is a deduction, but it is not a cash-out expense. However, to demonstrate your cash flow to the banker, **disregard any deduction for depreciation, but subtract the full amount of any loan payments (interest and principal)**.

What I am about to say is key to your approach in preparing any Income Statement and Balance Sheet which is to be attached to a Personal Financial Statement. While the Balance Sheet must reflect the amounts of any assets or liabilities as of the moment the statement was prepared, the Income Statement is to reflect the future, not past history. This is called a pro forma income statement because it predicts how a business will perform given the best information you have for the period selected. The banker will have your past tax returns to back up what you are saying now, but the banker is looking to establish your net cash flow moving forward. Typically, the statement is a representation of the current calendar year, so the numbers you use for income and expenses will be a combination of known data and your projections for the remaining part of the year.

The same holds true for when you enter your income from your job. If, because you can make a reasonable calculation, you expect a different amount for a bonus this year compared to last year, then include the current year's bonus in your total and not last year's bonus. **Whatever facts are known going forward about your personal finances, that's what you use.**

On the other hand, you can't make your pro forma with the assumption that you will purchase or sell a certain number of rental units before the end of the year, because that is an unpredictable wish list. But if you have already bought or sold properties earlier in the year, then prep your pro forma reflecting the plusses or minuses to your income and expenses. **I find it helpful to present a statement that shows the current monthly gross rents per property less deductions for the monthly average of the annual expenses for each property.** Footnotes can be used to point out when any of the properties were purchased or sold that year, and how that impacted your cash flow. Of course, this is done on a per entity basis. **Then, annualize (multiply by twelve) whatever your monthly net income is as of the date of your statement**, and enter that on the appropriate line on the banker's Personal Financial Statement.

First, let's look at the Assets section on the banker's form. The lines build from your most liquid asset, which is cash, to your more illiquid assets. **The first lines will refer to what are called "current assets."** These are assets that are either cash or they can be turned into cash quickly. Examples are:

- Cash on hand and in checking accounts, savings account, or money market accounts

  - The banker is looking at two things here. First, they want to see how much cash to which you have access compared to your expenses, so they can judge your liquidity or how long you could operate if your income was interrupted. Secondly, the chart for determining your entry for this line will also ask you to list the financial institution where the account is held. The banker may be looking to require you to move deposit accounts to their bank.

- Accounts receivable from sales

  - Presumably, payments will come in within thirty days.

- Tax refunds to be received

  o If you've done your tax returns for the year, and you are owed a refund, enter it here.

- Inventory of items to be sold in the course of your business

  o The banker will consider whether you have too much unsold inventory, or not enough to keep your business going.

- Prepaid expenses that are a credit against future obligations

  o Prepayments reduce cash out in the near future.

- Marketable securities such as stocks and bonds that are sold on an exchange

  o These could be turned into cash within days if need be.

- Cash value of life insurance policies

  o If necessary, policies with a cash surrender value can be cancelled in exchange for the cash. Or the policy likely affords its owner the privilege of getting a loan against the cash value of the policy on demand. Such a loan may not need to be paid back unless the owner cancels the policy or dies. The chart on the bank's personal statement form for your life insurance policies will also require you to list the owner of the policy, the beneficiary, the face amount of the policy, the insurance company, the cash value, and any loans you have against the policy. You will want to be sure to list any term life insurance policies you have even though they do not have a cash surrender value. That is because, in addition to seeing how much of a source of cash your policies could be, the banker is looking to see if you have adequate life insurance.

- Notes receivable from individuals or other entities

  o The chart for this entry may allow you to separate the ones that are good accounts and the ones that are doubtful to be collected. Only notes that are likely to be paid off within a year should be listed as a current asset. Doubtful accounts or notes due more than a year from the date of your statement should be listed as long-term assets.

The second group of lines on your statement are for what are called "tangible long-term assets." These are assets that physically exist, but they cannot be turned into cash quickly. Some examples are:

- Motor vehicles
  - Vehicles can certainly be turned into cash, but it may not be prudent to sell them to pay off current debt. Consequently, they are considered to be long-term assets.

- Equipment and fixtures used in the course of your business
  - These are looked at in the same way as vehicles.

- Land and buildings
  - Vacant land or real estate with buildings on it may take a while to sell, so they are long-term assets. The same chart for listing your real estate assets will also ask for the amount of any mortgages against them. It allows the banker to see at a glance whether you are over-leveraged.

- Long-term mortgages you own that are secured by someone else's real estate
  - Although there is an active market among investors for mortgages, or notes as they are called, they are typically sold at a discount to their face value. Full repayment at the original amount of the loan is subject to the terms of the loan agreement, so if the payoff is more than a year away, they should be listed at their face value as a long-term asset.

- Non-marketable securities

  o Stock you own in privately held companies is not easily sold, nor is it easily valued because it is not traded on a public exchange. On your personal financial statement, such stock is segregated on the supporting chart, and you must enter your best guess as to the value. The banker may or may not give much weight to the value of privately held stock. It depends on whether your ownership in the company is central to the reason for the loan.

- Intangible assets

  o While each category of assets mentioned so far contains either physical assets or financial assets, worth can also be derived from intangible assets that cannot be seen. The problem is that it is hard to assign an accurate value to intangibles, so their value on a balance sheet is questionable in the eyes of a banker. If you place these on a balance sheet, make sure you have a good explanation for the value you used. The more common types of intangible assets are:

    ◆ Good will
    ◆ Intellectual property such as copyrights or patents

Right beside the Assets section, you will find the Liabilities section. Like the way the asset lines build from the most liquid current assets to long-term assets, the lines in the liability section start with the most urgent current or short-term liabilities and build to long-term liabilities that are not due for more than a year. Here you will find:

- Wages payable

  o I will mention them here because they certainly are a good example of a current liability, but they are not called for on a typical Personal Financial Statement form. Individuals do not typically have wages they are personally paying. Even if they are a sole proprietor, and their business has employees, the assets and liabilities of that business would be compiled separately on an accompanying statement. The net worth of that business would then be entered on their Personal Financial Statement as a long-term asset.

- Accounts and bills payable

  - For a business, these would be suppliers or subcontractors that must be paid to keep the business running. However, for the purposes of a Personal Financial Statement, your banker is asking about your obligations such as:

    - Credit cards, store charges, or other credit accounts

      - If you pay these off in full each month, then provide the total current balance of all the accounts added together, but make a notation that you pay in full each month.

    - Short-term notes due to friends, relatives, and business associates
    - Short-term notes due to banks

- Taxes payable other than income taxes

  - This is where you would enter any taxes due like property taxes or homeowners association dues.

- Unearned revenue

  - If you've already been paid for something you haven't done yet, and you'll need to pay back the money if you don't perform, it's a liability you must list.

- Income taxes payable

  - Your banker wants to know if you have paid all your federal, state, and local income taxes. If you already did your tax returns for the year, and you had taxes due, then enter the amount due here if you haven't already paid it. If you've already filed and paid, then make a side notation to that effect. You may also be asked as to through what year your tax returns have been filed, and whether any previously filed returns are being audited or challenged.

The next group of lines are for long-term liabilities. These are liabilities due more than a year from the statement date. Some examples are:

- Vehicle and other personal property loans

  - The statement would have a chart where you could list each loan including what it's for, when it's due, the amount of the monthly payment, the date you began the loan, the property's value when you bought it, its value now, the current balance, and the lender.

- Liens and assessments payable

  - An example would be if your municipality put in water or sewer lines for your property, and they haven't made you pay for your share all at one time.

- Loans against your life insurance policy.

  - As mentioned earlier, these loans typically do not need to be paid back unless the owner cancels the policy or dies, but you would still list this type of loan on your statement as it appears on the chart where you list your life insurance policies.

- Real estate mortgages

  - This is where the total amount of your mortgages is entered. You would pull it from the chart that lists all your personally owned real estate. As discussed earlier, mortgages on rental property held in an entity are shown on that entity's balance sheet, not on your Personal Financial Statement.

- Any other obligations you have that are not due to be paid within a year from the statement date.

The Personal Financial Statement form will then have a line to total all your liabilities followed by a line to arrive at your net worth. Subtract your liabilities from your assets to find your net worth. **The total of your liabilities and the amount entered for your net worth will be on the next line, and this figure must be the same as the total of all your assets.**

Next, let's cover the section for providing the facts about your income. Again, this would be your personal income, and only your share of the net income from any entities of which you are a part would be transferred from the attached statements. The types of income your banker wants to know about are the following:

- Income from your job

  - Whether you are hourly or salary, you will need to back up your entry with paystubs and/or two or three years of tax returns. They may ask for a breakdown between salary, bonuses, and commissions.

- Income from investments

  - Most commonly, this is from dividends or interest.

- Income from a business or rental properties

  - This is where you would enter your share of the net profit shown on any attached statements. Keep in mind, this number should reflect your net cash flow after mortgage payments are made, and should not include a deduction for depreciation.

- Income from other sources

  - Here you would list sources such as alimony, child support, lottery winnings, disability payments, Social Security benefits, or trust fund payments.

Finally, the banker wants to look at how you are spending your personal cash. Much of the data entered here would have to be estimated, so do your best to pull meaningful figures from your household record keeping. Although many of these are discretionary, your purpose is to paint a picture of what your lifestyle dictates. Your banker is curious about these areas of expenditures:

- Income taxes

  - If all your income taxes are paid through your paycheck withholding, you will not have an entry here. But if you make quarterly tax estimates and/or typically pay tax when you file your return, this is where to provide that information.

- Other taxes

  - The banker is looking for property taxes, or any other non-income-based taxes.

- Insurance payments

  - Total all your homeowners, life, health, disability, accident, personal umbrella, vehicle, RV, long-term care, and any other personal insurance premiums.

- Mortgage or rent payments

  - Enter your mortgage payments on all real estate held for personal use, but don't include the part that goes to a tax or insurance escrow. Those payments would be entered in the tax or insurance categories. Include rent for your personal residence plus rent you pay for extra locations like a storage unit.

- Vehicle payments

  - Total your personal on-road vehicle payments. Payments on business vehicles would appear on an attached pro forma statement for your statement.

- Other loan payments

  - Total your personal off-road vehicle, RV, swimming pool, personal loan, furniture, and any other consumer loan payments.

- Medical expenses

  - Most people have some fixed medical expenses, like for prescriptions or regular treatment, plus miscellaneous medical costs for doctor visits and the like. Just enter a reasonable amount based on your history and your known facts.

- Utilities

  - Total your gas, electricity, water, sewer, trash, heating oil, propane, cable TV, internet, and anything of this nature for your personal residence.

- Condo/homeowners association dues and assessments

  - Enter these amounts if you have them.

- Other expenses that comprise your lifestyle (lumped together as one entry)

  o Personal vehicle operation (gas, inspections, repairs, supplies)

  o Entertainment

  o Vacations

  o Groceries and food supplements

  o Clothing and footwear

  o Gifts

  o Cell phone payments

  o Fitness club memberships

  o Hobbies

I know. It sounds like it would be a lot of effort to dig up these numbers, but **once you do it for the first time, it will be easy to tweak the numbers for future statements. For your personal benefit and the benefit of your business, learn to keep track of your personal expenses. You probably see the necessity of tracking your business expenses, but doing the same with your personal expenses will pay big dividends**. The two main reasons for being able to lay your eyes on where your personal money is going are:

- It will help you make wise decisions with the cash that makes it out of your business or job and into your personal pocket. It's eye-opening to see where you are *actually* spending your money vs. where you *think* you are spending it. You might find you could spend more on one area, or that you are spending too much on another. Plain and simple, **it's the basis for making a personal budget, and a budget is necessary to keep you on track for living beneath your means. Spending less than what you make, and putting money aside for regular expenses, emergencies, long-term savings, and investment opportunities, will actually *raise* your standard of living, not take away from it.**

- It will make it easier to quickly enter accurate information on a Personal Financial Statement. **The banker will be impressed that you have not entered a list of "guesstimates."** Remember, this statement is your chance to personally shine with the bank. The details about the new property you want a mortgage for will be evaluated separately, but **if it doesn't look like you have a good handle on your *personal* expenses, it will count against you.**

As a practical matter, there probably will not be enough lines in the "estimate of annual expenses" section of the form. It will likely have specific lines for taxes, insurance premiums, and mortgage or rent payments, but otherwise you can label the lines under "other expenses" yourself. Give major categories like vehicle payments and utilities their own line, but combine smaller categories as much as necessary to make everything fit. **Keep it neat.**

In many cases, providing an updated Personal Financial Statement annually will be part of the requirements from your bank once you have the loan. This is especially true if you have a large loan with them, or if you have several loans with the same bank. They want to develop a relationship with you, and part of that is requiring you to annually submit things like this statement along with your personal and entity tax returns. The fact is that **you may gain more from the exercise of preparing the statement than your banker will get out of it in terms of seeing where adding rental real estate to your life has gotten you.**

To conclude this discussion, I hope you develop an interest in tracking the growth of your income and net worth. Forgive me if I sound nerdy, but I consider doing my tax returns to be my "playoffs," and doing my annual Personal Financial Statement in April after I have filed my tax returns to be my "Super Bowl." Each year, I can hardly wait to see what our new net worth is!

13

SELLING RENTAL PROPERTIES (FIXTURES)

Although you build the foundation of your investment property portfolio by acquiring properties, **reaping the profits from selling them is like adding fixtures to your newly constructed building**. Just before the flooring and trim are installed, the fixtures represent the finishing touches whose functions allow the building to be put to use. Fixtures, in their various forms, represent completion of the process that gives the structure meaning. In other words, although you created the physical space for it, until you install the plumbing fixtures, it's not a bathroom. Similarly, the profits from the sale of an investment property are like a stamp of completion on your project, and the beginning of usefulness. Each time you add a fixture, a structure becomes more useful. **Each time you profit from a sale, like when you install a fixture, the portfolio structure you have created becomes more useful to you in terms of providing the cash to meet your**

financial goals. Getting a chunk of cash from the sale of a property is a tangible way of seeing how useful it was to add rental real estate to your life! Profits make the real estate experience *real*.

If you've looked ahead to see how long this chapter is, you've probably noticed this chapter is significantly shorter than the others, even though the subject matter is obviously key to adding rental real estate to your life. After all, if you've added it, at some point you must subtract it. The reason for fewer pages here is simply that I have already discussed most of the facets of an investment property transaction. In Chapter Two, which is about acquiring properties, I explored subjects such as:

- Searching for property that fits your criteria
- Negotiating the deal to buy the property
- Checking out the facts relating to the property (doing due diligence)
- Financing the purchase
- Preparing for the closing

If you think about what it would be like on the opposite side of the equation in the above areas, much of what you need to know regarding selling your rental properties will become clear to you. This will be especially true if, by the time you go to sell a property, you have already been through the purchasing of multiple properties. By then, you will know how to connect with your potential buyers, how to negotiate the deal, how to present the facts about your property for buyers to evaluate, what financing options to offer, and what to expect while preparing for the closing.

Whether the pollsters and economists say real estate is in a buyers' market or a sellers' market at the time you want to sell, don't worry that it will be difficult to sell your rental property. Think of yourself in the position of a buyer...maybe the buyer *you were* when you bought the property you are about to sell. At any given time, there are investors in that position who are hoping to find a good deal on a decent property. Their definition of what is suitable to them is dictated by the stage of their investment career they are in at the time.

Just like tenants who rent because of where they are at in life, investors acquire and dispose of property as it suits their investment life.

You probably will not have to list your properties with a Realtor when you want to sell them. **If you, as I have strongly suggested, have actively involved yourself with your local real estate investment community, you will already be acquainted with bona fide buyers looking for off-market opportunities**. If you are trying to sell outright, you will probably be able to suggest resources for conventional borrowing. Otherwise, you will likely have suggestions for creative ways for your buyer to finance the deal.

If you have developed a reputation for keeping up your properties and being good at selecting your tenants, then the buyers will be even more interested. They'll be willing to pay a premium for not having to deal with deferred maintenance (because you've already done it), or for not having to throw out lousy tenants (because you have good ones). Chapter Three includes a discussion about the physical preparation of an apartment for a tenant, and Chapter Eight is about house flipping. Much of what I would have to say about preparing a rental property for sale is contained in those two chapters.

Rental real estate is not a fad. It is an integral part of any nation's housing supply, and countless places of business depend on not having to own the building out of which they operate. There is a natural supply of people with a need to rent where they live or operate their company, and the owners of rentals are coming and going routinely. **Buyers will always be trolling for deals.**

Before we leave this chapter, I want to tack on a couple of pointers for when you are selling investment property.

- Especially for a flip, which is intended to be sold as rapidly as possible after the completion of its rehab, do not *chase* the market with the sales price you offer; *be* the market. This is in reference to when there is a declining market. When you are chasing a market, it means you are lowering your price too little too late, so you are always overpriced, and your property takes too long to sell.

- Unless you are a wiz at it yourself, consult with your tax advisor about the ramifications of selling your property. There are considerations regarding the best tax year in which to have a gain or loss to report, as well as the different ways your gain or loss would be reported based on what method of creative financing was used when you sold.

- Certainly, when your buyer has prepared the contract that will be followed by everyone during the sale of your property, run it past your legal team before you sign it. Do you remember how, when you are the one buying a property, you like to present the seller with your own contract which has all the stuff you want in it, and not so much for the seller? Now it's time to beware when you are the seller.

To summarize my thoughts on selling an investment property:

- To sell quickly at a great price, take care of your property during your ownership, and manage it properly so that you keep good tenants who pay top rents.

- Discuss the timing of your sale as well as the impact of different ways of selling with your accountant before you enter a sales contract.

- Do enough research to price your property properly.

- Start with letting your investor friends know you want to sell, but otherwise market your property wherever you go to look for property.

- Use the negotiating skills you've learned as a buyer to switch to the other side of the equation.

- If you are selling your property through a broker, you have your Realtor to lean on. But if you are selling it yourself, run the contract past your attorney before you sign...even if you prepared the contract yourself.

- Reinvest your profits, but also treat yourself after the sale...at least a little.

Of course, it may be the case that at least some of the investment properties you buy may never be sold by you. Perhaps you will acquire some legacy properties that are eventually inherited by your heirs, or maybe they will be transferred into a trust you create with beneficiaries. You may even choose to gift property directly to family members, friends, or charities while you are still alive. There are lots of possibilities, but those discussions are for another time. Right now, though, I think it's time to move on to the "back office" element of my argument for adding rental real estate to your life.

14
BEST PRACTICES (FLOORING)

Much of this book has centered on instructing you on the methods and processes of operating an investment portfolio containing rental income properties. I have also expounded on the necessary mindset and philosophies needed beyond just performing the tasks required of a landlord. But as we taper away from the "how to" type of information that is specific to land lording, **I want to emphasize some ideas that could be applied in about any business where the owners are hands-on operators.** You could say this refers to your "back office" operations.

Some like to refer to "really good ways of doing business" as "best practices," so we'll go with that. **Since best practices are what you stand on when conducting your business, they are like the flooring in the imaginary building we have been constructing**. Floors are solid, sturdy, and unchanging, and they can be either attractive or unattractive. So more specifically, I'm referring to the floor *coverings* which are among the last things the builders install before they stop tracking in dirt. **Like paint on the walls in the chapter about the impact of wealth, the floor coverings are what people judge you on as you make the principals you stand on visible to others**. Yes, there has been a floor in our building all along during construction, just like we have the inner and unspoken GPS we all use to navigate this thing called life. When you lay fancy flooring for all to see, it is like when you let everyone else intersect with the best practices on which you stand.

Certainly, this is not an exhaustive discussion on how to run your life, but these are some things which came to mind that I believe to be useful in addition to the rental property-specific concepts already covered. **You routinely hear about employing principals in your life and business such as honesty, integrity, promptness, loyalty, responsibility, recognition of others, continuous learning, time management, planning, communication, innovation, team building, goal setting, and perseverance.** These are all great concepts to follow, and I recommend all of them. However, in this chapter I am going to take a more "nuts and bolts" approach on both financial and personal topics. **Contained here are specific ideas on how to do things that will help you succeed and/or avoid unnecessary trouble**, and the first is insurance.

INSURANCE

Something I have always been a proponent of is to **have adequate insurance in place for both your business and personal life. You owe it to yourself, your family, and your customers to do so.** The disruptions in life caused by not being covered or not having the right coverage can be devastating when added on top of whatever the underlying calamity was. The good news is that **not being underinsured or uninsured is completely within your control.**

Many view insurance, at least in certain areas of coverage, to be too expensive or an unnecessary expense. **My thinking is that insurance does not cost... it pays**. You may never have a significant insurance claim for which you are paid, but it is payment enough to have the peace of mind from being able to operate your business or your life knowing that an act of nature or an accident will not seriously derail you financially. **I certainly do not advocate filing numerous claims on any of your policies. In fact, I advocate having coverage from a variety of types of policies with the intention of filing as few claims as necessary**. Do this by carrying as high of a deductible as you are comfortable with for each policy, and remember the insurance companies (which share huge databases on the claims you have filed) rate you more based on the *number* of claims you have filed as opposed to the *dollar amount* of the claims.

My philosophy is to **cover my butt with insurance in every reasonable way while making the premiums a basic cost of doing life/business** which I just accept in exchange for peace of mind. I am not going to gamble on having inadequate coverage, but I will do everything I can to keep the cost down by routinely evaluating each policy for cost, coverage, and customer service.

For your rental properties, I've already covered property and commercial liability umbrella policies near the end of Chapter Two, but other types of policies to consider are:

- **Business location insurance**

  - This would be coverage for the operation of your office, even if your office is inside your personal residence...in fact, *especially* if the office you operate your business from is in where you live. **Your homeowners or renters policy is not likely to offer any coverage for your office equipment, data loss, business fraud, or liability protection for people coming to visit you for business purposes.** You should speak with your agent about filling any coverage gaps. Having an office in your home can sometimes be covered by a special endorsement on your homeowners policy, but it can also be covered as a designated location on a blanket property insurance policy with your rental properties.

- **Insurance connected with having employees (or partners)**

  - If you have W-2 employees, you will be required to get certain insurance like workers compensation, but you may also choose to offer health insurance or disability insurance. Other coverages related to employees include employment practices liability, and employee benefits liability.

o You would also want to make sure that somewhere in your general business policies you have liability coverage for your employees working around tenants in case your employee harms a tenant or their possessions. A related optional feature to consider is real estate managers errors and omissions coverage, not only for your employees who act as property managers, but also for you and any partners in your entity who manage properties.

Each year before renewal time, an underwriter will review your commercial property policy to determine what premium the carrier will charge you for the upcoming year. They take into consideration a variety of factors, not the least of which is whether they still like the property on the policy, and whether you have filed any claims. **Leading up to your renewal, it would be worth having a discussion with your commercial property insurance agent about the possibility of the agent asking the underwriter for any credits (discounts) for your good behavior**. Each year, a couple of months in advance of my annual renewal date, I send an email to my agent detailing anything we may have done at any of the properties in the past year to lessen the likelihood of a claim. I list any new roofs, upgraded electrical services, new furnaces or hot water tanks, and similar improvements. **Especially impressive are safety upgrades** like railings or new exterior steps. I also remind our agent about our routine practices like requiring tenants to carry renters insurance, our no pets and no smoking policies, inspections for working smoke and CO detectors, and the fact that we maintain a full-compliance rental occupancy license with the local code enforcement office. My agent then passes my email to the underwriter, and they discuss how much less they can charge me now that they know how hard I am trying to keep claims to a minimum.

For your personal life, it's important to be buttoned down with your coverage because an event that devastates your non-business finances and/or physical health (or that of family members for which you are

responsible or for which you *want* to be responsible) can indirectly affect your business. For example, if you must draw too much cash from your business for your personal obligations, you could bankrupt the business. Make sure you consider the following:

- **Life insurance**

  - **The earlier in your life you buy it, the better**. The older you are when you apply, the higher the premiums will be based on your age, as I'm sure you know. But there are other factors that come into play when the insurance company is deciding how much to charge you, and the older you get, the more likely those factors will apply to you. Some examples are a dangerous occupation or hobby, a health condition, or an acquired disability.

  - My suggestion is that you **take the time to sit down with a good insurance agent or two, or three**, and get a tutorial about the distinct types of life insurance. The common ones are whole life, term, and universal.

    - Whole life builds a cash value in addition to the death benefit, and it insures you until you die. This is the type of policy you can borrow against for any reason.

    - Term does not build any cash value, and it only insures you for a specific number of years until the coverage ends. However, compared to whole life and universal, its premiums are the cheapest for the same amount of coverage.

    - Universal allows the premium to be less than whole life, but it still builds a cash value because the cost of the coverage is initially lower. However, if you keep the insurance long enough, the cash value is automatically used up by the carrier to cover the higher cost of the coverage considering your age.

  - Once you learn about the various options for life insurance coverage, you can make an educated assessment of what best suits you and, most importantly, your heirs. **Your need for life insurance may be minimal when you are young, but that's the best time to buy it because the premiums are cheap, and you are presumably healthier**. The growth in cash value will be significant over your lifetime. Coverage is most needed when you are collecting people in your life such as a spouse or children because that's the period when you are least likely to have a stash of cash to lessen the financial blow to your family if you die. So, maybe a combination of whole life and term insurance would be appropriate then. In your later years, with fewer people depending on you, your need for life insurance may dwindle if you have put away some cash for your estate's expenses, so it would be okay if your term insurance expires.

- **Health insurance**

  o Here, as with property insurance, one of the biggest considerations is the amount of the deductible with which you are comfortable. Routine medical issues may be easy to absorb, but catastrophic illnesses or injuries can change your financial life for years to come. You may be lucky enough to be covered by your parents' or your spouse's policy from their employment. Otherwise, pay for the bells and whistles you can afford, but at least insure against a major calamity.

- **Disability insurance**

  o I think that disability and long-term care insurance are two of the hardest sells for an insurance agent whether his client is old or young. When we're old, it's too expensive. When we're young, the premiums are cheap, but we still think we're bullet-proof, so we don't believe it's worth buying. We can't imagine being in the position to use it. The fact is that a debilitating injury or illness can strike anyone. Health insurance will pay to get you well again, but it will not replace the income you lose out on along the way. Disability insurance may be part of your benefits package from your job, but especially if you are self-employed, **disability insurance could be, aside from health insurance, the insurance you will be the gladdest you bought when the time comes to file a claim.**

o Disability insurance pays you when you cannot trade your time for money (work). Has it occurred to you from reading this book that disability insurance might be the only type of insurance on this list (with the possible exception of life insurance) that can be replaced by owning assets that produce income, such as rental real estate?

- **Accident insurance**

  o Accident insurance pays specific amounts for specific injuries or treatments brought on by accidents, not illnesses. For example, a set amount might be paid if you visit an ER after a fall, and another amount if you sustain a broken bone. Accident insurance is commonly offered through an organization to its members at a group rate. It is inexpensive, and it is best used to give you some extra cash to use to cover your deductibles and copays from your health insurance. Because of its low cost, the benefits are not large dollars, but it probably also has a death benefit, but only if you die from an accident.

- **Long-term care insurance**

  o See my comments on disability insurance. This can be a hard sell to young people, and it's expensive for older people to open a new policy when they are so close to the time when they might use it. However, I think you have until well into middle age to get a policy at a decent price. You may never use this policy, but it will certainly benefit your heirs if you ever go into a nursing facility long-term. **There are few events that drain someone's estate like the cost of a stay in a nursing home during the final years or even months of your life.** Paying a small monthly premium for decades may pay off in the end.

- **Homeowners insurance**

  - If you own your personal residence, you know this is a must...even if you no longer carry a mortgage on it. My advice is the same as for the coverage on your investments properties. That is to **keep your premium down by carrying as large of a deductible as you feel comfortable with, and avoid filing anything except significant claims.**

  - There are many endorsements or extra features to consider with homeowners policies. Some of the more worthwhile ones are:

    - Sewer and drain backup (If you think your basement is prone to this, at least install a ball valve in your floor drain so water cannot get past it.)

    - Earthquake endorsement if you are on a fault line

    - Extra coverage for collections, jewelry, or other personal property

    - Extra coverage for outbuildings like pole barns

    - Identity theft or cyber event protection (If you can't get it with your homeowners, then buy it from another source. You'll probably need it eventually.)

    - Coverage to replace *all* the roofing or siding if what is there can no longer be matched for a small repair.

    - Office-in-the-home related coverages

- **Renters insurance**

  - If you rent your personal residence, make this a requirement for yourself just like you make it a requirement for your tenants. Make sure you have adequate coverage for your personal property, cyber events, and a home office. Then, evaluate your liability coverage limit. You don't want to have to pay out of pocket to rebuild your landlord's property if you accidentally burn it down!

- **Flood insurance**

  - Flood damage is not covered by your homeowners insurance, so if you are in a flood plain, you must buy this separately.

- **Personal liability umbrella insurance**

  - Just like how the commercial liability umbrella policy described in Chapter Two adds to your investment property insurance, this insurance adds coverage on top of whatever liability limits you carry on your underlying personal insurance like your home, auto, or RV policies. Your underlying policies may seem like they have a lot of coverage, but $1,000,000 isn't the same as it used to be. Personal umbrella policies are cheap, considering.

- **Auto insurance**

  - You must carry it by law, of course. But the question is, how long after you've paid off your car loan should you carry collision? Obviously, the cost for collision coverage is a significant part of your premium, so it's a big consideration. Personally, although I tend to keep my vehicles for a long time after any loans are paid off (if I even had a loan on it), I have never cancelled my collision coverage. The cost for even the smallest amount of damage is just too high on a vehicle you want to keep. Again, like with property insurance, **the solution is to carry a high deductible to keep your premium down, and not file petty claims.**

- **RV insurance**

  - My advice here is the same as for auto policies, especially for motor homes, larger campers, boats, motorcycles, airplanes, or any other costly toy that moves. However, when it comes to smaller off-road vehicles like four-wheelers and dirt bikes, considering the abuse these things take, you may want to only obtain the liability coverage (as required by law) if you don't have a loan against it.

ESTATE PLANNING

The making of wills, trusts, and other estate planning instruments is beyond the scope of this book, but I want to bring it up in this section of the book just to remind you of the importance of having such things. **Not everyone needs to create trusts or even more involved estate plans, but everyone should have a will.**

Some people are hung up on creating their will because they think it will bring on their death. Or they just don't believe they have enough assets to warrant the trouble. But the facts are that you're gonna die when you're gonna die, and **like it or not, your state has already made you a will in case you don't have your own**. Every state has laws that dictate what happens if you die intestate or without having made a will. Those laws spell out how your property is to be divided between your spouse and children or any other heirs, and **it may not be how you would have wanted it.**

You can author a valid will on your own, but I recommend you have help from an attorney. Compared to the ramifications of your death, the cost of preparing a will is inexpensive. There are so many issues for your eventual heirs that can be addressed and resolved by a will that you might not think of everything by yourself. **If you don't put it in your will, it's going to be decided by the government or the court system, and that will chew up time and your estate's cash.**

A good estate lawyer can also help you navigate more advanced estate planning tools that would be appropriate for the size and nature of your estate. My hope is that you create so much wealth with your real estate investing activities that you unquestionably need to have this conversation with your attorney. But at the very least, have a will.

MEDICAL DIRECTIVES

Your closest family or friends should have a good idea as to how you want to play it when it gets to the end. The problem is, when it gets to that point, you probably won't be able to tell them at that moment. The good news is that you can tell them ahead of time with a Living Will. Whereas a Last Will and Testament dictates things that happen after you die, a Living Will gives directives while you are still alive.

Living Wills and similar documents let everyone from medical staff to your loved ones know what to do if you are incapacitated and no longer able to tell them what your wishes are. Under what circumstances do they resuscitate you? How long until they "pull the plug?"

Living Wills can easily be prepared yourself. Many medical organizations or social agencies offer them as a form where you can fill in your name and check the boxes you want. Give a copy to those whom you have designated as the decision-makers.

BEING CONSIDERATE TO YOURSELF AND YOUR HEIRS

You do not want to leave a mess of an estate when you die, nor do you want to have everything in order but with nobody else knowing what needs to be done. I am all about minimizing the disruption in my life from calamities, and I feel the same way about making it easy for my heirs in the event of my death. **What follows is a list of things you can do to reduce the recovery time from the things that could happen to you (which most people go through life betting will not happen to them).** While most of these tips are useful while you are alive, they are also considerate to your heirs who must figure out your business on top of grieving your demise.

For others living in my household and me, I mostly want to prepare for the unlikely event of our house being destroyed by fire or a natural disaster like a tornado. Insurance, of course, is going to replace our house and belongings, but **I am concerned here with reducing the threat of the loss of important records that would be needed to restart our lives**. As an extension, your heirs will appreciate your efforts. You can keep the tearing out of hair to a minimum for yourself and your heirs when something bad happens by doing prudent things such as:

- **Have as many fireproof safes as you need to store all your important documents.**

  o Keep a chart of all the combinations in each safe, but don't even bother locking them. Granted, you may want to keep certain valuables like money and precious metals in a locked safe, but this isn't about keeping people out of the safe; this is about protecting documents, and making sure you and others can get into the safe quickly following a traumatic event.

  o Unless you are concerned with flooding, keep at least some of your safes in the lowest part of the building where they won't fall through the floor in the event of a fire, or get sucked out by a tornado. But keep them several inches off the floor to avoid water that can rise from a sump pump that stops working or water from a fire hose that can't drain out.

- **Organize all your important documents and put them in the fire safes.**

  o Insurance policies of all kinds
  o Estate planning documents
  o Living wills
  o Trust agreements
  o Business formation papers
  o Stock certificates, especially for non-publicly traded corporations
  o Depreciation records for business capital assets
  o Investment and banking information
  o Vehicle titles
  o A list of every online account you have with usernames and passwords
  o A list of everything you carry around in your wallet or purse with photocopies of credit cards and other ID's (front and back)
  o Passports
  o Birth certificates
  o Immunization records

- The cards they give you if you had cataract surgery or other implants
- Flash drives and any external hard drives used for computer backups
- Gift cards
- Paper evidence of tickets to events
- Paper evidence of plane tickets, travel plans, and reservations
- Employee benefits package folders
- Original Social Security card
- Important Social Security benefits correspondence and documentation
- Diplomas
- Other people's burial instructions you will need to use
- Other people's estate planning documents entrusted to you
- Powers of Attorney you have been given including Living Wills
- Marital prenuptial agreements
- Divorce papers
- Adoption papers
- Criminal records
- Child abuse clearances for working with children
- Animal pedigree information
- Receipts, user manuals, and warranties for important purchases
- Your personal journal
- Important photos and videos

Any of this stuff could cause you grief if it were to be destroyed, but it is so easy to keep it protected. **Can you imagine the trouble you would go through to replace even *one* of the items I have listed after it was destroyed?** Now that you are thinking about it, you can probably come up with additional items from your own life that should be on the list.

You might have noticed I did not include tax returns on the list. It would certainly be reasonable to keep tax returns in your fire safe. However, tax returns, especially for successful real estate investors, can take up a lot of room. I prefer to keep them in metal filing cabinets, which will offer them some degree of protection from a fire or the elements. The same for any important paper receipts for the year, especially if you've already uploaded them to the cloud. If they were to be destroyed, photocopies of old tax returns can be obtained from the IRS.

- **Every few years or so, or whenever there has been a substantial change in operations, make a video of how to operate your life and your business.**

  o Have someone else take the video so you can be shown on camera. This way, you can have two hands free to point to things and move items around.

  o **The purpose is to make it easy for your next of kin to step in immediately after your death or disability**, and for them see where everything is kept for the operation of your life and your business. If you have rental property, someone needs to know who to collect rent from...today! Bills need to be paid without interruption. Your accounting system must be kept updated. Personal obligations must be cancelled.

  o Go over the information they will need to use immediately first, but ultimately open every cabinet and drawer that contains something they will need to know about, while showing what's in there and talking about its relevance. Get detailed when necessary.

  o Download your video onto an external media like a flash drive, and give a copy to the appropriate persons with instructions to watch it immediately after your death or disability.

- **Every several years, especially if you have made significant changes to your home or possessions, make a video for use with an insurance claim.** Your insurance carrier is happy to pay you for the loss of everything in your home to a fire, but you must give them a list! The video takes away the need to try to remember everything you lost.

  o Like in the business and life operations video, have someone else operate your camera so you can more easily open drawers, cabinets, and doors while shifting things around for a better view.

- o Get the exterior and interior, room by room, in every nook and cranny. This will really pay off if you have a claim from theft, loss, or destruction.
- o Give others a copy in case yours gets destroyed in the same catastrophic event for which your claim is being filed.

BANK ACCOUNTS

To put it bluntly and briefly, **balance every one of your checkbooks (both business and personal) every month without exception**. It's just plain good bookkeeping practice. I believe some people fail to do this because they think it's too hard to do, or that it doesn't matter.

First, it's not that hard to do if you can add and subtract. You don't even need to know how to multiply and divide. Any employee at one of the desks in the bank lobby would be more than happy to demonstrate how it's done, and help you understand it.

Checks that make a carbon copy when you write them are great, but you must also enter them in your check register. **Reconciling the account balance shown on the bank's statement to the running balance in your check register depends on every transaction in the account being entered into your register**, so you must be diligent in entering automatic payments or ones you have made online.

All that happens when you are balancing your checkbook is that you are starting with the balance the bank says you have on the statement, and then you add the deposits you have made which the bank does not know about yet (because they were made after the statement cutoff date). Then, you subtract the checks or other deductions the bank does not know about (because they haven't cleared your account yet). If the result doesn't equal the latest balance in your check register, just go back and compare the transactions on the statement with the entries in your register. You will find the error and make the necessary correction.

Secondly, **it *does* matter that you keep an accurate check register and that you reconcile your checking statement to your register**. If you don't, you are setting yourself up for an unnecessary heartache when your checks start bouncing because you thought there was more money in there than there is. Also, you may miss a legitimate deduction for your business because it never made it from your check register into your accounting records.

Not being aware of the actual balance in your checking account can surprise you in the opposite direction from having bounced checks. You may find you have more money in there than you thought. I will never forget how that happened with one of my first large accounting clients. One of the first things I did for them was balance a checkbook that had long been neglected. I found over three thousand dollars they didn't realize was there!

Also, **I want to reiterate the importance of keeping separate checking and savings accounts for your rental property operations from your personal accounts, even if you own your properties in your own name and not an entity's**. Have bank accounts dedicated solely to your rentals. This is not a legal requirement, but it will help you present a much clearer picture of the success of your income properties vs. your personal finances.

Finally, as I presented in detail in Chapter Three, **it *is* the law that you keep your entity's bank accounts separate from your personal ones**. Sometimes, it could be advantageous to keep separate checking accounts for different properties, even if the properties have the same owner.

SAVINGS

Saving or putting aside money for the future must be an integral part of the financial activities of any family or business. Having savings puts you in a position to not only take advantage of opportunities, but also to avoid financial debacles. **The best way to save is to do it automatically, routinely, off the top, and without reservation.**

Saving can only come from a surplus. After all, you are not going to borrow money just to save it! **The only way to have a surplus is to not spend everything that comes in. In other words, you and/or your business must live beneath your means to have money to save.**

There are various kinds of savings, however. Some common ones are:

- **Immediate savings for routine commitments**

    - This refers to making sure you have enough money building up throughout the month to meet regular living expenses like loan payments and utilities. These funds might only need to be retained in your checking account.

- **Short-term savings for extraordinary events**

    - I am referring to lower cost things that don't come up every month, but they are your needs or wants. These could be considered living expenses for your standard of living, so you must be sure not to let them be so great of a percentage of your disposable income that you don't have anything left to save for the long-term, all the while thinking you are "saving." Some examples would be a vacation or some new furniture.

    - Like with immediate savings above, here you are simply setting money aside for something you have planned so that you inadvertently don't spend it on something else. You may want to keep this money in a separate savings account for convenience. Maybe you won't need to keep putting money into this account once your special event has passed until you come up with your next project.

- **Long-term savings for emergencies**

    - This is money set aside for the events that inevitably pop up that make us say, "Life happens." These are things we must take care of just to stay where we are at in our strata. The purpose of these savings is to mitigate the chance of cramping our commitments we have made for building our immediate and short-term savings. If we have money in our emergency fund when a need arises, we will not have to miss a loan payment or cancel our vacation plans. Examples are medical bills not covered by insurance, or replacing an appliance.

o   It could be that you put money into this savings account, which also should be a separate account for obvious reasons, on a regular basis or in chunks. But you may determine to set a cap on the maximum to let ride in the account. This would be an amount you feel comfortable with as likely being enough to get you out of any jam...and then some.

- **Long-term savings for investments**

o   Now we are getting serious! Once you have saved for your immediate needs, special projects, and emergencies, then it gets exciting and difficult. This money is not for the expenses of your life, but rather this is when you start putting money away for things like rental properties that make you money. That's exciting, but accumulating significant cash in this account takes more discipline than the type of saving described earlier. However, as they say, no pain, no gain.

o   **When you are saving for your next investment, you really must make the decision to live beneath your means. Note that saving responsibly for routine commitments and extraordinary events, and even emergencies, is really just saving *at* your means**. Though you are acting responsibly by doing those things, you are still just treading water with lots of activity, but you're not getting anywhere better.

o   This type of saving can be hard because you don't specifically know what you are saving for. Consequently, it becomes easy to slack off from making regular deposits while you are tempted to raise your standard of living instead. **The people who make it in life are the ones capable of sacrificing instant gratification in exchange for future rewards. So, you must tap into your "inner Scrooge" to get this done.**

○ Here, I recommend depositing regular amounts in regular intervals, but also dropping in chunks when you can. The idea is to be ready when something comes along. Remember, **luck is where preparation meets opportunity**. The more you've got loaded into your investment account, the more welcoming you can be when opportunity comes knocking.

- **Long-term savings for retirement**

  ○ If you don't have a regular deduction from your paycheck for something like a 401k retirement savings account, you will have to do this on your own. (By the way, always take the maximum matching amount your employer allows. It's free money!) But that is why the government created traditional and Individual Retirement Accounts (IRA's).

  ○ Saving for retirement can also be a hard sell for young people, just like disability insurance and long-term care insurance. But it goes without saying that **the earlier you start making regular contributions, the more will be deposited and the more the miracle of compounding the earnings within the IRA will amaze you.**

  ○ Although you can close out the account or even make special withdrawals in certain cases, you won't be accessing the funds in your IRA until your retirement years. So, like with saving long-term for investments, this takes sacrifice and dedication. This is because **your contributions must come right off the top before you determine what you have left to spend on your lifestyle**, and it can be hard to visualize for what you're eventually going to use the money. What may work for you is to set up an automatic withdrawal from your checking account, so you know it's going to happen without you thinking about it. There would be no periodic decision to make as to whether to contribute to your retirement account.

  ○ There are other more specialized accounts, but the main vehicles for individuals to save on their own for retirement are traditional IRA's and Roth IRA's. I am not going to go into a tutorial about retirement accounts, but I will tell you the very basic features of these two types of IRA's to make a point.

♦ There are limits, based mainly on your age and how much earned income you have for the year, on how much one can contribute to an IRA in a tax year. There is no lifetime limit.

♦ In the case of traditional IRA's, your contributions are deducted from your taxable income for the year you make a contribution. Then, any withdrawals are added to your ordinary income in the year you receive them. All withdrawals are taxed the same regardless of whether they are a return of your principal, or from capital gains, interest, or dividends that have accumulated in the account.

♦ For a Roth IRA, there is no deduction for any contributions; you contribute using after-tax dollars. However, your withdrawals are not added to your taxable income including the amount the account has grown on top of your contributions.

♦ In each type, any capital gains or dividend income accumulates in the account with no impact on your taxable income for the year. Also, aside from a few exceptions, there are penalties if you take a withdrawal before a certain age.

♦ With a traditional IRA, right around retirement age, you will be required to take what are known as RMD's or Required Minimum Withdrawals each year. There is a formula for this. They want you to start taking the money out of your IRA so they can tax you on it, or else they will penalize you for leaving it in.

♦ With a Roth IRA, there are never any RMD's for the original account holder. You can leave all your money in the account as long as you wish.

♦ Mostly, people invest in either specific stocks, bonds, or mutual funds within their IRA's. You can own as many IRA's as you want, and do different things in each IRA.

- While most brokerage houses like Fidelity will only permit traditional financial instruments in your account that can be purchased on an exchange (like shares on a stock exchange), the type of asset the government allows in your IRA is virtually unlimited in the sense that they only state you cannot hold collectibles like art, antiques, gems, coins, alcoholic beverages, and certain precious metals, life insurance, or shares in a Subchapter S corporation. However, the source or use of any asset in your IRA is restricted in terms of you or close relatives not being able to buy, sell, or use the asset.

- The point I want to make is that **I feel Roth IRA's are the way to go** even though you don't get a deduction when you make a contribution. **Current year tax savings from deductibility are outweighed by never paying tax on the withdrawals from a Roth, which will include gobs of tax-free earnings from the growth of the account. Also, not having to take RMD's from a Roth lets you keep the money in the account for making even more investments if you don't need it on the outside.**

    - Eventually, you can start making your real estate investments within your IRA, or maybe make loans as a hard money lender. Once you turn fifty-nine and a half, withdrawals can be made from your IRA (Roth or traditional) with no penalty for early withdrawal. If you have a Roth, those profits will end up being tax-free. If you have a traditional IRA, your profits, since they will be taxed when they are withdrawn, will only be considered to have been tax-deferred.

HOW IT APPEARS ON PAPER COUNTS

Sometimes, when you are trying to evaluate a deal, a design, or directions to a spot, you just cannot comprehend it as well until you see it on paper. That can be true, but the title for this section does not refer to that at all. **I want to talk about grammar, punctuation, syntax, good word choice, and proper page layout**. I think it is surprising how often the composers of what are supposed to be professional communications appear to forget how important these elements are. They may be counting too much on the content of their message to get the desired reaction. But the fact is that **the credence (not to mention the respect given to the author) given to the subject matter of a letter, advertisement, email, or publication of any kind can be significantly diminished by impropriety in any of the ingredients of good composition.** Why would you want to fall victim to that when it takes so little extra effort to do the "write" things the right way?

I hope you already understand that using proper etiquette, manors, and speech in person-to-person professional interactions is expected. You immediately notice when someone, especially someone you don't know well and are still forming opinions about, falls short in those areas during a meeting. You expected a little more convention in their behavior. Well, guess what. It matters in print as well! Like it or not, **people you are trying to influence with your written communications are making their decisions not just on the content of your message, but also on your presentation on paper or electronic media.** At the very least, improper composition of written communications will not help you, and you won't be there in person to offer your apologies and correct yourself when it's noticed.

Aside from math courses, the classes I took in primary and secondary school which have served me the most in the real world are English and typing. I still remember the teacher who taught us where commas go in sentences, and where they don't. What I am writing about in this section was mostly learned from my English instructors, but typing class had some bonus usefulness. Not only did I learn touch typing on a keyboard, but I also learned about the proper layout of a letter. I realize that a different standard has evolved for emails, but the standard for letters remains the same. **The standard for letters dictates the placement on the page of the following:**

- **The heading**

  o This can either be against the left margin or in the upper right of the page. It contains the sender's full return address, and the date is either on the first line or the last line. Your phone number, if included, would alternately be on the final line.

- **The recipient's name and full address**

  o This is started on the fourth line down from the heading (three blank lines in between), and all the way to the left margin. Use their full name with any prefix such as Mrs. or Dr. followed by the address to which your letter will be mailed.

- **The salutation**

  o This is the second line down from the last line of the recipient's address (one blank line in between). Most of the time, this line starts with "Dear" followed by the same name used above, or whatever name you use to address them in person. Put either a comma or a semicolon after their name.

- **The body**

  o This is the second line down from the Salutation. The body is your message to the recipient. Paragraphs no longer need to be indented, but there is one blank line between each paragraph if you don't indent. The blank line is optional if you indent, but it looks better even if you do.

- **The complimentary close**

  o This is the second line down from the final line in the last paragraph of the body. With letters that are typed on a word processing program, as opposed to handwritten, the close is typically started against the left margin. People tend to center the close on the page for handwritten letters instead. The close is something appropriate that seems acceptable as having come from the sender. People use words like "Sincerely," or "Yours Truly," here. Note that both words are capitalized, and the words are followed by a comma.

- **The signature line**
  - o Your signature would appear below the complimentary close. Also, especially if you need to spell out your name (because your signature is hard to read), or if you need to emphasize your name and title, type your name on the fourth line down from the close against the left margin so that your signature appears in the blank space in between. Then, type your title just below your name.

- **Enclosures and the names of additional recipients**
  - o It's optional, but at the bottom of the page you can list the items the recipient will find in the envelope with the letter. This is also where you would name anyone else who is receiving a copy of the letter. Type "CC:" against the left margin. Follow this with one space, and then enter the names.

Typing class also taught me the correct way to form an address. Everyone knows the street address goes on the next line below the recipient's name, but the next line is often formatted wrongly. The correct way is to type the city, followed by a comma, then one space followed by the name of the state or the abbreviation for the state. Then, after two spaces, enter the ZIP Code. Alternately, on the mailing envelope but not in the letter document, the ZIP Code can be on its own line below the city and state. So, the city, state, and ZIP for the Whitehouse would be Washington, DC 20500. (Yes, I know the District of Columbia is not a state.)

I believe the reasons that poorly composed communications frequently make it out the door fall into three camps. The writer:

- **Knows how to write well, but fails to proofread adequately**

  - It's tempting to think you got it right the first time. Take the time to look things over carefully. At least use the spellcheck feature of your word processing program. Read every word. Check punctuation and sentence structure. Make sure your thoughts flow together sensibly. Do not try to make too many points in one paragraph. **You must work harder to have the reader perceive the same emphasis on your printed words as compared to your emphasis if you were speaking to them in person.**

- **Does not know the fundamentals**

  - If you lack skills in composition, you can learn them or at least improve them with a little effort. Tutorials are available to refresh (or correct) what you learned in school. In the meantime, getting help from someone knowledgeable to look over your work before you send it out will pay big dividends.

- **Does not believe the fundamentals are important**

  - If you're still in this camp, please reread the two opening paragraphs of this section. People reading what you have written are noticing your errors, and it matters to them. There is much to be gained by raising the bar on how you communicate, whether it's in person or in print.

SUPPORTING CAST MEMBERS

In Chapters One and Three, I presented lists of team members you are likely to need while you operate a real estate investment business. These are people or businesses with whom you will interface *within* your business. Now, **I want to present a list of team members you will need in your private life *outside* of your**

business who will influence you in both business *and* personal endeavors. There are always supporting cast members behind any person's successes. These folks can provide the ingredients for success that you cannot provide yourself. They probably will not be apparent to those in and around your endeavors who see your successes, but they all play a significant role as supporting cast members behind the scenes. Here are some of the roles to be filled in the production of a successful life:

- **Esteem builders**

    o They make you feel good about yourself and worthy of success.

    o They respect you and are enthusiastic about you.

- **Cheerleaders**

    o They encourage you to succeed and nurture you during challenging times.

    o They help you through a crisis even if you don't know the cheerleader closely.

- **Celebrators**

    o They reward you when you have done something well.

- **Financiers**

    o They give you good financial advice.

- **Role Models**

    o You may never actually meet this person, but they give you a pattern for what you want to do, or who you want to be like.

- **Contacts**

    o You don't have to be friends or even social acquaintances, but these are people you can call on for help because they can connect you.

- **Constructive critics**

  - They play devil's advocate to stir up your creative juices.
  - You trust them to tell you the truth while not tearing you down.

- **Sponsors**

  - Beyond being a contact, they intercede on your behalf to help get jobs, promotions, positions, etc.
  - Find sponsors by helping these people out in a crunch, or being involved with projects where you rub elbows with them.

- **Public relations specialists**

  - They are business associates, bosses, friends, and others who spread good words about you because they are fans.

- **Technical supporters**

  - These are good people to help you with tasks you do not know how to do, want to do, or have time to do.

Perhaps, while reading this, some people came to mind who could fill these roles in your life. **If you already have people in any of these roles, never stop nurturing those relationships**. If there are still some holes in your cast to fill, hopefully this list will inspire you to see where to put in some effort to develop some new relationships.

I hope you see this chapter on best practices as containing useful information to apply in many aspects of your life, not just for investment property. **There are many common denominators between successful people outside of the core knowledge or skill they possess** in their chosen field. But let's get back to real estate, and wrap this up in the next chapter.

45

THE CONCLUSION (LANDSCAPING)

When you build a new home, the final area of attention is the landscaping. The installation of the lawn and plantings signals the conclusion of the construction process. It's when the building contractors leave, and you can start making your house a home. It's time to give your property the accents you prefer, and make it your own. In a similar fashion, **you have built your allegorical house throughout this book, and this conclusion is when you can take possession and do what you want with it**. At this point, you are prepared to take what you have learned about rental real estate, and apply it to your life. **My charge to you now is to possess (claim for yourself) this structure/real estate investment business which is in front of you. Believe it's for you because you can do it *your* way. Live in it, and make it your home the way it suits you best. Add it to your life without regrets because you have the tools to handle whatever comes up.**

I hope that, after you have read this book, you no longer believe that real estate investing is for other people, and not for you. My purpose was for you to be inspired to give it a try, and significantly alter your life for the better. I am counting on any readers who are stuck in a JOB (stands for Just Over Broke) to gain control over their finances and time with the information I have presented. But **I also wrote this for the readers who prefer to stay in a vocation related to their passion, and who wish to augment their income with rental real estate or house flipping so they can have some nice extra things or a more secure retirement than their job allows.**

You may not be ready to invest yet, and you fear the opportunity to get into rental properties will pass you by. First, remember that **you do not have to know everything before you get started**. Secondly, unlike technology or trend-based businesses, **one of the advantages of the rental property game is that little about it changes**, at least not quickly. Nothing happens that suddenly makes your product outdated. There can be subtle changes in the laws or in décor preferences, but you'll never have to scrap a warehouse full of outdated inventory with rentals or flips.

There is nothing magical or mystical about investing in real estate. There is no key to find for a door that will open to a room of closely held secrets that will give you an advantage. Anyone can gain access to the necessary techniques through readily available education. **Successful investors simply apply over and over the fundamental systems that can be learned by having a desire, making a commitment, and exercising discipline.**

So, you might ask, how have I prepared you to enjoy the journey of rental property investment? The first answer is by putting you in the right mindset. I have discussed a helpful mindset or attitude to maintain both before you start investing *and* after you are successful.

The next part of the answer is that I have given you the tool of knowledge. It's up to you to use your knowledge and turn it into wisdom. In other words, you now have the necessary theoretical and practical education which can empower you to act intelligently.

Education removes fear. The lack of fear creates confidence. Confidence minimizes discouragement from setbacks. Not feeling

discouraged means regrets are quickly forgotten. Sometimes you win, and sometimes you learn. So, either way, you're further ahead having learned one more thing not to fear.

Recently, I was chatting with a young girl operating a lemonade stand as I enjoyed a cool glass. I explained that my first lemonade stand was located only about three blocks away, and that I had eventually become a multi-millionaire. I gave her the following input on making that happen for her:

- Figure out what your dreams really are.
- Get educated, and make a good plan.
- Don't take advice from anyone you wouldn't want to trade places with.
- Never give up

In addition, I hope you will accept this final advice:

Watch your environment—it produces your thoughts.
Watch your thoughts—they lead to your words.
Watch your words—they lead to your actions.
Watch your actions—they set your reputation.
Watch your reputation—it influences your limits.
Know your limits—they determine your destiny.
Envision your destiny—you will avoid negative environments.

Here's the bottom line. If you are still thinking you will regret adding rental real estate to your life, consider this:
It's better to regret what you *did* do, than to regret what you *did not* do. What will the landscape of your financial house look like this time next year?

So, are you going to do this real estate thing, or not?!

16
BONUS FROM "REAL ESTATE STEVE" SZUMIGALE

The author would like to express his sincere gratitude to Steve for contributing this extremely useful slice of his knowledge to the book. His description of the following techniques for buying and selling investment property can propel you to your next level. You can read about Steve in Chapter Two, "Acquiring Properties" in Phase Five, "Financing the Deal."

Let's hear from Real Estate Steve:

> My goal here is to show you that you can become filthy stinking rich by simply choosing the right vehicle to generate wealth. Got your attention? Not all vehicles are created equal. **What I am about to show you here is information that you likely could go 10 lifetimes without encountering, so pay close attention.**

So, who am I? I am the founder of Freedom Sky Real Estate, a holdings company located in Erie, Pennsylvania. More importantly, I am a husband, father, mentor to 75 to 100 (and growing) real estate investors, and a friend. I am also a patriot to this great country, and I put God first into family, business, health, and all aspects of life to achieve greatness in life in all categories including health, wealth, and love. I have been inside over 5,000 properties, and I have been involved with our real estate holdings company in over 100 real estate deals. I also hold an active real estate license with a broker, and I've been attached to over 500 transactions, helping buyers and sellers. That puts my national ranking in the top 5% of real estate agents nationwide for most of my years since I was licensed in 2010. My focus right now is growing Freedom Sky's business into a $50,000,000 to $100,000,000 empire, and through its significance, cause impact to thousands of people like you to help you have an easier life that creates fulfillment.

In 2016, I discovered something that I know you will pick up on too: Cash Flow = Freedom. I realized that it was better to keep 100% of a property by owning it, and getting paid on it repeatedly, than it was to get a 2% to 3% broker commission for selling property since you only could get paid one time, and then you would have to do it again. When I first started, I had all the things working against me that could have all been excuses. I had no money, bad credit, bad mindset, bad addictions, lacked confidence, and I had a lot of life's baggage like one can accumulate over the years. Any one of those things could have stopped me from greatness, let alone the full gamut of them. **You can have the life of your dreams, or you can make excuses, but you can't do both!**

The point that I am making is that I am just a common person like you, and I tell you this so you can relate and realize that you could do it too. People like a good war story that shows the main character persevering into something great. No one cares about your past unless it affects them, as everyone likes happy endings. **You do not need to be perfect to inspire others**. People will be inspired by how you deal with and overcome your imperfections. Fast forward to the time I am writing this. I have personally bought and sold over $16,000,000 worth of real estate deals, and I am currently holding all high-quality assets that carry a valuation of $10,000,000 to $11,000,000, and we keep growing! Are you ready to see how it is that we built a massive real estate portfolio that made us multi-millionaires? You could be the next one. Let's do it!

Why Real Estate? You can start immediately without money, credit, or partners, with little to no risk, and make substantial amounts of money quickly both inside and outside your retirement accounts. How would your life change if you could add $20,000 a month to your current income by working part time? **The truest and the most profitable way to become a successful real estate investor is to become a "Transaction Engineer" who knows the ins and the outs of each different kind of real estate deal, and who possess the abilities to pair them with one another to maximize profit potentials, reduce costs, and minimize risks.** By understanding and implementing multiple purchase and exit strategies, it gives you the unprecedented competitive advantage that nine out of ten investors overlook when different situations with properties arise.

Let's start by looking at the 10 Different Kinds of Real Estate Deals:

1. Pretty House

   o Owner Finance
   o Subject To / Wrap Around Mortgage
   o Lease Purchase

2. Quick Turn Ugly House

   o Wholesale Buyer
   o Whole-tail

3. Work-4-Equity

4. Rehab to Retail / BRRRR

5. Short Sale Ugly House

6. Short Sale Pretty House

7. Option

   o No Money & No Credit

8. A.C.T.S. (Assignment Contract & Terms)

   o Overleveraged

9. Multi-Family

   o 2 Units / 4 Units

10. Commercial / Syndication

   o 6+ Units / 20+ Units

The skilled and seasoned investor will be able to generate the lead, make the seller call, negotiate the deal on the phone by asking a series of questions, and then to see on the spot the desired exit strategy that would provide the biggest profits.

The real estate investment business can be broken down into two different sides which are the Pretty House side, and the Ugly House side. The Pretty House side is where you can buy nice and attractive single-family and multi-family properties with no money or very little money down by using creative financing methods.

1. The Pretty House Business

The Pretty House Business is the most profitable way to increase your cash flow and grow wealth. It is a Factory that Prints Money. The KEY to this is TERMS. No Terms equals No Deal. The three main methods of acquisition are as follows:

- o Owner Finance
- o Get the Deed Subject To the Existing Mortgage
- o Lease Option

In the Pretty House Business, the real money is in receiving non-refundable option deposit/payments, monthly cash flow, debt pay down, appreciation, forfeited down payments, and equity pay-offs.

Let's break each one of them down as follows:

What is Seller Financing?

Definition: Also called owner financing, seller financing is a practice by which the seller of a property acts as a lender for the buyer of the home, and takes back a mortgage and a note.

The mortgage attaches to the property as collateral for the loan. The promissory note, or the promise to repay per certain terms, can be foreclosed upon by the lender for failure to keep the agreement.

- Can be in the form of first position mortgage, second position mortgage, or wraparound mortgage.

What is Subject To?

Definition: Buying a property subject to the existing mortgage. It means that the seller is not paying off the existing mortgage, and the buyer is taking over the payments while not personally guaranteeing the note to the bank. The unpaid balance of the existing mortgage is then calculated as part of the buyer's purchase price.

- The deed transfers, but you do not "Assume the Loan."
- The method of taking title is vitally important: The title must go into a Trust. A Warranty Deed transferred to a Trustee creates an exemption from Due on Sale requirements because "A transfer into an inter vivos trust in which the borrower is and remains a beneficiary" is exempt.

o   Reference: Garn-St. Germain Depository Institutions Act of 1982. This Act's language strikes the due on sale clause, and prohibits the bank from calling the loan due as long as the title was taken by warranty deed to trustee, and the trust's language conformed to the Act.

What is a Lease Option?

Definition: An agreement that gives a renter a choice to buy the rented property during or at the end of the rental period. It also precludes the owner from offering the property for sale to anyone else. When the term expires, the renter must either exercise the option or forfeit it.

- A longer-term lease is used, so that they have time to acquire the ability to own. Typically, two to three years, but can go longer.
- The owner retains title to capture tax benefits.
- The Tenant/Buyer (we call them residents) pays a fee, a Non-Refundable Option Deposit (NROD), today to have the right to buy the property at an agreed price later.
- The resident pays a monthly payment to occupy the property.
- Residents are responsible for all improvements and repairs to the property after the first 30-day warranty period which covers the heating/cooling system, plumbing, and electrical systems.
- The lease has Limited Rules vs. Traditional - "Pets Allowed"
- Buyers get to have the "American Dream" early - "All Credit Accepted."

What is a Non-Refundable Option Deposit (NROD)?

Definition: Money deposit(s) paid on a property for the exclusive right to buy it for an agreed length of time.

- $5,000 to $50,000 is not uncommon. The BIGGEST that we have experienced was $200,000.
- The average in our city is $12,500.
- The more EXPENSIVE the home, the BIGGER the NROD.
- The NROD is a credit toward the purchase price at closing.
- It is non-refundable.

Most of the time, Lease Options are used by investors for exit strategies. It is not usually desirable for investors to buy using Lease Options, as you do not get to acquire the deed. If you do decide to buy on a lease option, you should only pay $1.00 or no more than 3% of the purchase price for the option. That way you can turn around and, by reselling the option, get more money from the person that is going to occupy the property. Again, the main reason to not use them when buying is that you need to be in full control of the property by having the deed, so that you no longer need the seller for any reason.

Some examples of when you *would* buy on a Lease Option are when the property is overleveraged, or the seller has a unique situation that would potentially challenge the due on sale clause in the note (like a home equity line of credit or HELOC). Or perhaps a local bank with which you already have a relationship, monitors daily transfers, and your taking on one of their properties subject to could potentially ruin that relationship.

The best use of lease options is as an exit strategy on properties *you* sell to *others*, because that is when you can COMMAND BIG MONEY for the properties and collect BIG non-refundable option payments. Another great reason to use them when selling a property is that you can depreciate the asset during your ownership, because it becomes a rental property until you sell it to the option holder.

These non-refundable deposits are the "Hunks and Chunks" of big money that you can pull from a real estate business without giving up the property. They are the cash lifeblood that can be used to waterfall your company's growth into unprecedented phenomena. When you sell a property, you typically get to collect a big check one time, and then the goose is dead. However, when you collect a non-refundable option deposit, it is typically within range of the same amount as you would receive from selling the property. **In the meantime, you still get to receive the income from the spread on the rents, depreciate the property for tax benefits, pay down the mortgage and create more equity, experience potential appreciation, and also use the property for leverage to buy other assets or to liberate cash.**

The plan for you is to get paid big money to acquire properties through receiving non-refundable option deposits. Then, cash flow these properties along the way from the spreads that are there between collecting rent and paying the mortgage, collect forfeited deposits from option terminations, and then recollect another deposit or sell the property in the future for massive gains and a big chunk of money. We want you to remember this strategy as being called "Its and Bits & Hunks and Chunks!"

Now get out there and go get these deposits! $20,000 / $25,000 / $15,000 / $50,000 / $200,000!

THE SKY IS THE LIMIT!

Let's see what happens when you become a "Transaction Engineer" and use two of the ten different types of real estate deals to lock up a property.

In this example, we purchased with Subject To and exited using Lease Option. Let's take a closer look:

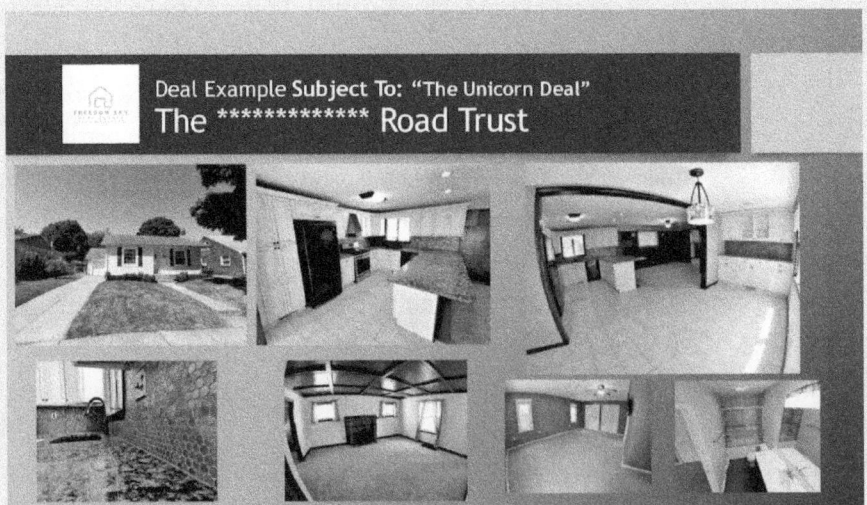

Deal Example Subject To: "The Unicorn Deal"
The *********** Road Trust

THE #'S !!!

$219,900 Lease Option Price (ARV)
$186,000 Purchase Price
          (Debt Takeover)
$0   Down
+$33,900 Profit from Potential
          Future Sale

$30,000   Non Refundable Option
          Deposit/Payment (NROD)

THE #'S !!!

$1,750 Rent Income
$1,150   PITI (Seller Loan We Took
          Subject To)
+$600   Monthly Passive Income

$189,900 Tenant Buyer BAL at 60 Mos
$163,400   Mortgage Balance at 60 Mos
$26,500 Profit from Debt Pay Down

💰 BIG HUNKS & CHUNKS 💰

+$33,900 Difference Between Sales Price & Purchase Price
+$36,000 Difference Between Rent & PITI $600 x 60 Months
+$26,500 From Debt Pay Down

$96,400 TOTAL DEAL PROFIT!!

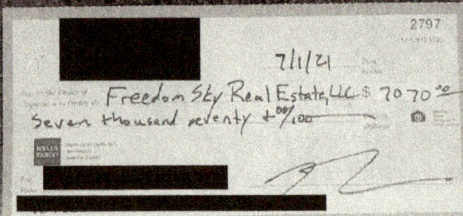

We just made $30,000 in a couple of days!

Can I spend the $30,000? Yep. Every dime. You do not have to bring it to the closing if the tenant/buyer ends up exercising their option. Statistically, only about 15 to 20% do end up buying. We are happy for them if they do, and are okay with it if they do not, as the deal gets more profitable with time and appreciation. All profit other than the rental income is taxed at long- term capital gains rates, and the option payment is NOT TAXED until the deed transfers or the tenant/buyer defaults, whichever comes first.

Wow! How many checks like this do you have to get in a month to become free of a job?

MINDSET. To whom are you listening? **If you listen to the judgements and opinions of people who are not where you want to be in life concerning the major pillars of existence of health, wealth, and love, you will remain broke, with no love. Your health will decline under the stresses of your actions. Never take financial advice from people that are not in the game, as it is too easy to feed you BS from the sidelines.** Money cures most things, and if it doesn't then there is a major problem likely to do with health or from your lengthy past of doing nothing to expand your progression of health, wealth, and love. You are either growing or dying; there is no complacency. Life is a fight, and it is 100% worth it to do it full send!

Free advice is almost always worth what it costs to acquire. Nothing. Good advice is almost never free. Cling to someone who is where you want to be going, and duplicate how they got there. Then, add your personality to the endeavor!

If you choose to learn these concepts and implement them over the course of your lifetime, you will set up you and the future generations of your family to experience a financially free and independent life. However, there are two sides to the sword, with money on the one side and mindset on the other. You must teach *both* for your legacy to not be lost or squandered in the next one to two generations. You must *become* to *attract*. Want some more?

Let's look at another example using Seller Financing:

Unicorn Deal Example: Seller Financing
"The Golden Goose"   PA 16504

THE #'S !!!

$169,900 Lease Option Price (ARV)
$151,500 Purchase Price TERMS:NO INTEREST, 15 YR AMORTIZATION, 3 YEAR BALLOON
$0   Down
+$18,400 Profit from Potential
          Future Sale

$17,500   Non Refundable Option
          Deposit/Payment (NROD)

THE #'S !!!

$1,750 Rent Income
$1,275   PITI
+$475 Monthly Passive Income

$154,900   Tenant Buyer BAL at 36 Mos
$121,200   Mortgage BAL at 36 Mos
$33,700 Profit from Debt Pay Down

💰 BIG HUNKS & CHUNKS 💰

+$18,400 Difference Between Sales Price & Purchase Price
+$17,100 Difference Between Rent & PITI $475 x 36 Months
+$33,700 From Debt Pay Down

$69,200 TOTAL DEAL PROFIT

2023 DEAL UPDATE:

- Tenant Buyer did not Buy
- Refinanced to a 30 Year Mortgage
- Appraised Value is $202,000 up from Approx $151,500
- Tenant Buyer agreed to stay another 3 to 5 more years and then buy at that time for Minimum $202,000 to $210,000
- Rent was Increased from $1,750 to $1,950 per month.
- THIS WILL RESULT IN $100,000+ TOTAL DEAL PROFIT

Now you are starting to see what becoming a "Transaction Engineer" really looks like. You can see that you are able to buy properties with no banks or credit by using creative financing strategies instead of traditional methods. The aim for you is to fully understand, underwrite, and diagnose a property by knowing the 10 Different Kinds of Real Estate Deals, and then being able to pair the deal with the proper exit strategy by linking it with the most profitable option for you at the time. This is the true "art of real estate investing."

Once you master these concepts, you will possess the ability to generate wealth upon command. It does not matter what your experience is financially, whether your credit is bad or good, if the economy goes up or down, or who is in the White House / government because you will be able to generate wealth and cash flow in any city in the United States. You should think to yourself that once you know, understand, and can implement these strategies, if someone gave you $1,000 and put you in any city in the USA, you could become a millionaire again in a few short years with the wisdom and knowledge that you possess. It is timeless.

Let's take a deeper dive into the other types of real estate deals.

2. Quick Turn Ugly House

Wholesale Buyer

Wholesaling is the process of locating properties at extremely discounted prices, and then quickly selling your contract to another end purchaser, who is typically an investor, for profit. These properties are usually distressed and in need of repairs. You will need to check your state laws regarding wholesaling, as in some states you will assign your contract to the end purchaser, but in others you will release your contract. In a few, wholesaling is not permitted. Your financial interest in the contract precludes you from needing to have a real estate license in most of the states. **Wholesaling is a great way to get started in real estate investing, and it is one of the two quickest ways to get cash now, with the other being to retain deposits and down payments by getting a non-refundable option deposit/payment.**

Wholesaling is a great short-term investment strategy, and it can become the focus of a real estate investing business. Predominantly, when you are a "Transaction Engineer," you wholesale properties that are undesirable for holding long-term. You do it to gain quick cash now, and to increase existing cash flow. Otherwise, the focus is always to hold properties while pulling the most cash out of them, while at the same time using the methods of the 10 different kinds of real estate deals. To become successful at wholesaling, you need to be able to identify and purchase properties well below MAO (Maximum Allowable Offer). **The recommended formula is 70% x ARV (After Repaired Value) – Repairs = MAO. The spread of the amount that you buy below MAO is your potential profit.**

To recap, wholesaling is a way to buy and sell real estate contracts, and a great way for you to get started in real estate investing. Lastly, on the other end of the spectrum of this category, is called whole-tailing (a combination of the words wholesale and retail) which is when you would sell to an owner occupant instead of to another investor. Typically, they will pay more than an investor, but they are a lot more challenging to find.

3. Work for Equity

Work for Equity is an exit strategy for properties that require extensive repairs which will need to be made to sell them. The cost of the repairs, when added to the purchase price, exceeds the current after repaired value (ARV) for the property. Generally, these properties have a hard time being sold via FSBO (For Sale by Owner), on the MLS, or to an Investor / all-cash buyer. There is little to no profit margin to be made by an investor who would want to buy it, and it needs too many repairs for a lender to want to offer financing. However, there are a lot of buyers who will gladly do the work with their money and labor if you give them a slight discount, and make it easy to purchase the home with a lease purchase or owner financing.

Remember, over half of Americans do not qualify for a bank loan, yet they still need housing. By gaining the 1% of knowledge (that 99% of other real estate investors and the public lack) on a strategy like this, it will enable you to be the magnet that attracts these types of properties. You will know how to pair them with their end user, all while helping the original seller and creating big profits for you. The buyers that you find by using this technique will make you a whole lot more money by:

- Fixing the property for you at their cost of materials and labor
- Paying an option deposit to be able have a term to buy the property in the future
- Paying down the existing mortgage with their rent payments
- Reducing your tax liability from short-term to long-term gains tax
- Providing monthly cash net flows
- Possibly defaulting or choosing not to exercise their right to buy the property in the future, and leaving you with a rehabbed / improved property and a forfeited option deposit

If all goes well and as planned, the buyer will exercise their option in the future, as the property would be repaired enough to qualify for a bank loan. The seller will then get their debt paid off, and you will get a BIG Check!

4. Rehab to Retail / BRRRR

Real Estate Rehabs are when investors purchase a property, complete renovations, and then sell the property for a profit. This technique is called flipping. **The recommended formula is 70% x ARV (After Repaired Value) – Repairs = MAO (Maximum Allowable Offer) for properties under $300,000, and 80% x ARV for properties over $300,000.** You will likely pay all cash for these properties. The key here is to use other people's money (OPM) such as hard money loans from individuals or companies, and seller financing.

Evaluating the property with proper repair estimates that leave you a desired profit margin is a forever changing art that fluctuates with both the housing markets and the cost of the materials. **Your success with your evaluation of the purchase is directly dependent on the speed at which you can properly estimate repairs and get a signed contract**, as there typically are other buyers interested in buying the same property. You should be able to roughly estimate the repairs and overall renovation for a property in five to fifteen minutes on your initial walk through. It does not have to be perfect, but must be within the range of the above formula for profit success.

Evaluating the property, coming up with a correct budget that complies with the above formula, finding qualified contractors, and getting the right permits are the foundations for success with the next steps of the process. The next steps are demolition, exterior renovations, interior renovations, and then completing the exit strategy. The average profit across the United States for flipping a house is between $20,000 and $30,000.

A sister strategy to Rehab to Retail is called BRRRR (Buy, Rehab, Rent, Refinance, Repeat). This method is a real estate investment approach that involves improving a distressed property, renting it out, and then doing a cash-out refinance on it to fund further rental property investments. Since most lenders require you to have 25% of equity into the property to qualify for their financing, the BRRRR method often will use all your forced appreciation (profit) from your rehab as the equity for your loan, leaving little to no cash-out from the refinance. This technique may at times require you to bring the cash difference to the closing to satisfy your existing private or hard money lender and to comply with the lending requirements of the new lender. However, this would stabilize the debt on the property over the long term, and you would then be getting the property for FREE.

As a company, we are not a big supporter or believer in the BRRRR method, as we believe that cash should not be left or buried in a piece of property. The real estate strategies that we are sharing with you produce big checks up front and do not leave it in the property. Another reason that we are not a big supporter of BRRRR is that it will require you to personally guarantee (PG) the debt on the property. If something goes wrong in the future that is not in your control i.e., war, pandemic, government change, catastrophic loss, considerable damage from a tenant, lawsuits, the lender can sue you on the note that you personally guaranteed on this property. The lender could not only come after you to reclaim the property, but also could attach the balances to your other assets that you own as well. Personally, I have seen the above ruin marriages, families, children's perceptions of parents, and the reputations of investors who became foolish with their management of debt when paired with those uncontrollable circumstances as mentioned above.

You need to build your business with BRICKS, and not on a house of cards, from the day you get started! The better way, if you are going to use this method, is to pair the Rehab to Retail Strategy to the BRRRR Method by using a Lease with Option Strategy to exit. Let's call it a BRRRR on STEROIDS or BRRLOR (Buy, Rehab, Refinance, Lease Option, Repeat). That way, you still get a huge Non-Refundable Option Deposit (NROD) from the new resident/tenant, and you can defer the repair obligations for the property to them. You can keep the same monthly cash flow spreads, as well as keeping the property. This method will require you to find a good mentor that has done a few of these successfully, since there are a lot of lending requirements and legal language that must be disclosed correctly to avoid potential future lawsuits. You will also want to talk to your private or hard money lender to make sure that they are comfortable with this method upfront before doing it, because if you do not do it correctly, you could be putting their loan in jeopardy by unknowingly clouding the title. Most attorneys do not know how to set these up correctly, and the only way to know if you are doing it right is to get someone experienced to help you. Soup to nuts, **to do these, YOU will need to cling to a Mentor and learn!**

5. Short Sale Ugly House

A Short Sale in a real estate transaction is an offer on a property at a price that is less than the amount of the mortgage. In this category, the Short Sale technique is used with properties in disrepair that are also known as "Ugly Houses". **Short Sales typically occur or become eligible when the property has a total repair cost that exceeds the current property value when added to the balance on the mortgage.** This is usually the result of a financial hardship of the owner via a decline in health, death, displacement from a job, separation from a spouse, or other financial responsibilities for the medical problems of loved ones.

The proceeds of a short sale will all go to the lender, and the lender MUST approve the Short Sale in advance. The lender then has two options. They could forgive the remaining balance, or pursue a deficiency judgement that would require the former homeowner to pay all or part of the difference. In the case of an estate or death of the borrower, there is no one to obtain a deficiency judgement against, so the lender is more likely to collaborate with you as a buyer instead of listing it with a real estate owned agent (REO agent) on the MLS system. Each state varies, and in a very few states, the lender must forgive the difference to the borrower. However, in most states the deficiency judgement will stand, thus requiring the borrower to pay the difference between what was owed on their mortgage and the amount the bank accepted from the short sale deal. This will ruin their credit as well as potentially lead to bankruptcy.

Your job as a real estate investor is to know the process, check your state's laws regarding pre-foreclosures, foreclosures, and short sales, and ask the right questions. More importantly, you should first see if you can help the seller by getting a loan modification. If you cannot accomplish that, then you should investigate a short sale.

You want to create win-win scenarios with the sellers, even if it means paying them a few thousand dollars at closing to get the job done.

When seeking a short sale, you will first want to get an authorization to release information, signed by you and the seller, on file with the lender. That document will then enable you to ask the right questions. The first question that you should be asking the lender is if there is Private Mortgage Insurance (PMI) on the property, because if there is, the insurer is ultimately responsible for paying the lender the amount of their loss on the property. Therefore, the insurer will also have to sign off with the lender to get the property approved for the short sale. An appraisal is always required.

If the property does in fact have PMI, the lender will consider the sale on a regimented price reduction process at a percentage of appraised value in "as is" condition to approve the sale. Some examples would be the Federal Housing Administration (FHA), which will approve sales in the first thirty days at 88% of the appraised value, after thirty days at 86%, and then after sixty days they will drop to 84%. Fannie Mae (FNMA) will approve 84% from day one, and is typically more flexible over time. The same goes for the Veteran's Affairs (VA) Home Loans which start at 85% of the "as is" appraised value, and go down from there over time.

You also want to pay attention to the condition of the property, as it likely will not be eligible for FHA and VA loans due to its current condition. If a major item like a roof or furnace is due for replacement, conventional financing may not like it either. To buy it, you would need to use an all-cash offer.

It takes prolonged periods of time to get through the short sale process, and the lenders do not always know what other branches are doing during the process. For example, just because you are working with the short sale department, that doesn't mean the foreclosure department hasn't already started, or will start, getting possession of the property during your short sale process via a third-party law firm. **You need to know the right questions to ask at the given point in time during the Short Sale process, and the only way to do that is to cling to a mentor who has experience with these types of transactions.** Short Sales can be extremely profitable for real estate investors.

6. Short Sale Pretty House

This is the same process as Short Sale Ugly House, however the houses generally do not need much repair, if any. They are ready to be sold to a retail buyer, and will qualify for all the types of financing. The same processes in the above section 5 apply.

7. Option

No Money & No Credit

Options employ a real estate contract that has an arrangement where the seller gives the buyer an exclusive right (but not an obligation) to purchase the property for a given price that is set for a specific length of time. The buyer pays the seller a deposit or premium for the right of the option, and then in exchange the seller must sell the property to the buyer according to the terms of the preexisting contract. The buyer has the length of time in the agreement to exercise the real estate option. Some heavily used and profitable exit strategies would include:

- Wholesale the option to another buyer for profit.
- Close on the property, and then lease option it to a new resident.
- Close, and then retail sale the property.
- Close, and rent the property.

In fast appreciating time periods and/or nonlinear real estate markets, or real estate markets that fluctuate dramatically in values (for example, Las Vagas, Jacksonville, Arizona, Florida ocean cities, etc.) with typical swings in a calendar year between 10% and 50% on average, options are huge ways to control property without ownership while you wait to see if the market swings in your favor.

In commercial real estate and in land development, an option is a great way to tie up a property with a smaller deposit, and then push your due diligence along to further see if the land is suitable for your use. Often this will include re-zoning exploration including a change of zoning classification, or a change of land use codes and/or variances, paired with cost and financing suitability, to verify that the project is worth doing and profitable. Real estate options are a terrific way to tie up a property to make a whole lot of money in real estate.

8. A.C.T.S. (Assignment Contract & Terms)

Overleveraged

Assignment Contract and Terms is an agreement using terms to purchase a property, and then assigning that same agreement to another owner-occupant for a fee. Typically, but not always, the property is overleveraged. Your contract to buy the property involves terms to buy it such as using owner financing, lease option with the right to sublease, take over debt subject to, or a straight option for cash. It then uses the strategy of finding a buyer or a tenant buyer (a buyer that leases the property and pays a non-refundable option payment to occupy and has an exclusive right to buy the property at a pre-determined price point). Next, you collect a fee and assign the agreement back to the seller, and you are out.

If the exit strategy is a true ACTS deal, then upon exit you will have no more relationship with the buyer or the seller. The advantages to sellers are several. This method may be their only way out, if the home is overleveraged, to avoid loss of their credit. And they have you doing all the legwork and the prescreening along with the marketing at no cost to them. The sellers get to retain ownership to protect their credit and avoid the due on sale clause, while enjoying an income stream to offset the monthly mortgage payment and the debt reduction if they want to get a new loan. They also have *you* just in case a new tenant needs to be installed at a future date.

Yes, these can be repeat cash cows and paydays for you. The advantages to your buyer are also several. They get to enjoy immediate occupancy, and for some that is important. They have no obligation to buy the home, and will only have a loss of their deposit if they do not end up exercising their option to purchase. They also have a longer lease term to qualify for their financing to buy it with no additional money if their loan allows it.

You get several advantages using this method. You get to have cash now by getting a fast and easy assignment or release fee. You really have no costly entanglements, and you have no closing costs. You have very little to no risk involved, and you do not use your money or your credit. The selection process for the existing market can be large and untapped with overleveraged properties, making it easy to get sellers to agree to favorable terms. This method also saves deals that you have turned down before which were quality houses that typically attract quality people. This one extra arrow in the quiver of your real estate investing business is sure to make you a ton of money while helping sellers and buyers alike.

9. Multi-Family

2 Units / 4 Units

Multi-dwelling unit or (MDU) is a classification of housing where multiple separate housing units for residential occupants are contained within one building or several buildings within one complex. The advantages to multi-family real estate investing are countless. Multi-family real estate can reduce vacancies and risk with the occupancy of the other units in the building offsetting the missing revenue occurring from the vacant units. You also can scale a real estate portfolio to a larger number of units faster with multi-family than with single-family, as you can buy more units at one time. For example, **buying a 30-unit apartment building is a lot easier and much more time-efficient than buying ten different single-family homes.**

Another massive advantage to multi-family is that you can force the appreciation of the values of properties that are five units and more by simply increasing the revenues while reducing the expenses, and then simply divide the net income by a similar property's capitalization rate to indicate a value. This property valuation method, known as the income approach, can drive profits and valuations, as well as being able to increase leverage responsibly. By contrast, the sales analysis approach uses recent comparable sales to support values, and it is limited to what has been selling on the open market.

Brand new investors can find great investment opportunities with multifamily properties, and they can even choose to live in one of their multifamily units, making it an owner-occupied property, to reduce their living costs. Multi-family real estate investing is not all upside though, as you likely are to have higher repair costs and more intense management responsibilities in exchange for less risk. You will need to decide if you are going to self-manage or hire an employee manager or a property management company. Your size and scalability are directly adjacent to properly sustained management.

It is important to note that, in most states, it is against the law for an individual who is not an employee of a company, and who has no ownership or interest in the managed property, to be a property manager for another owner without possessing a real estate license that is tied to a broker. To legally manage property for someone else, you must be an employee of that company, have an ownership interest in the property/company, or have a real estate license that has a broker attached to it.

Property management duties may include finding and screening tenants, collecting the rent payments, maintaining the properties by overseeing repairs and expenses, handling compliance and regulations, and dealing with evictions. Property management is 100% the most important part of generational real estate wealth, since without sustained cashflow now, there is no way to maintain the property, pay down debt, and secure future legacy wealth. **Getting them under contract is one thing, but properly managing them over the years to become free and clear is a separate skillset that comes with hands-on experience.**

Multi-family real estate investing is a great tool to add to your toolbelt, along with the other nine different types of real estate deals, to generate cash now, pay down debt, and scale a portfolio faster than using only a few of the methods discussed here. It is a backbone of real estate investing and growing portfolios of scale.

10. Commercial / Syndication

5+ Units / 20+ Units

Real estate syndication is a method of pooling capital from multiple investors for the common goal of acquiring real estate. Sponsors typically source a prospective deal to match the three principal areas of lending requirements of liquidity, net worth relative to asset size, and experience rating to be able to purchase property that otherwise may be out of their current financial reach. The syndicator is also known as the sponsor, and is tasked with acquiring the property, renovating it, managing it, and making sure that the equity holders get paid. They are responsible for the disposition or selling of the property. **To be the syndicator, you typically must have real estate and management experience, can locate and source noteworthy deals, and are able to raise capital to fund them from the limited partners.**

The other major players within real estate syndications are the investors. They are referred to as Limited Partners. Being a Limited Partner is a wonderful way to invest in real estate "passively" without all the work that goes into getting the assets to perform. Limited Partners supply the capital for the equity piece of the purchase, which can range from 20% to 35% of the purchase price. Investors then rely on the Sponsor to use their experience rating, net worth, and liquidity to qualify with a lender to obtain the debt piece, which is typically 65% to 80% of the purchase price. **As limited / passive members of the real estate syndication, they will be the source of capital and thus get to own a pro-rata share of the real estate based on their investment amount as compared to that of other Limited Partners.** They will get to share in the cash flow, equity, debt pay down, appreciation and depreciation, as well as in any refinance proceeds when the asset is stabilized.

Most single-asset syndication deals, as compared to investment funds that buy several properties, are restricted to accredited investors only. Individuals need to satisfy one of two criteria to be an accredited investor:

- An annual income of at least $200,000 ($300,000 for a joint filing as a couple) for the past two years, OR
- A net worth of at least $1,000,000 excluding the value of your primary residence.

Profits for a real estate syndication are largely dependent on your role, and the exit strategy. Some projects elect to split profits equally, but many real estate syndicates do not, as it would not be a fair practice based upon work and risk level. Every project is different. It's common for passive investors to receive about 70% to 80%, while the syndicator gets about 20% to 30%. Investors usually earn more because they put in more money, however the sponsor may also get paid an acquisition fee and management fees to make sure that the project remains on schedule. Partnering with other investors in a real estate syndication to purchase a property is a great way to be able to buy an asset that you wouldn't be able to afford otherwise.

As I wrap up this discussion, I want to congratulate you for reading this book! You now are aware of the existence of what 99% of the population could go 10 lifetimes without encountering. "You know not what you have done." **You now are thinking to yourself, can I do this? The answer is YES with mentoring from someone who is massively successful using these methods.** You will not find "the how" on YouTube University. Your plan is to GO and get fifty deals worth $50,000 to $100,000. Your Life Will Change! Not just one of them will make you rich, but enough of them will make you "Free," and then the cash flow and wealth accumulation will follow in abundance. You will get filthy stinking rich along the way! **Your path to success is to take unprecedented massive and determined action. I love real estate investing because it provides cash flow to sustain living, depreciation to offset your taxable income, equity from paying down debt, appreciation into the future which builds**

free wealth, and is a great hedge against inflation. Plus, you can borrow tax free funds by leveraging your assets to create more cash as your portfolio permits.

Your next steps to execute are that you need to find a mentor with a mentoring program that encompasses the 10 different types of real estate deals so you can learn the business the correct way, and to avoid the costly pitfalls of:

- Having no experience
- Paperwork requirements
- Lack of people connections
- Not knowing what to do, or what to say
- How to sell
- Where to find the deals
- How to protect your assets
- How to reduce your tax consequence
- How to estimate ARV and MAO
- All creative and regular financing methods
- Understanding markets

The list is pretty much endless as to what you can learn from a good mentor. The money that you will pay to learn will be far less than what it costs in lost deals, court hearings if someone sues you, or damage to the people who you could potentially hurt from not knowing how to set up deals up appropriately by using the correct paperwork.

A mentor will shave decades off your learning curve, and quite frankly is necessary to achieve results in the business. Looking back, I can remember several occasions when someone asked me, "Steve, what should I do with the $30,000, $50,000, or even $100,000 that I have saved up? I want to get into real estate." My answer was always to pay a mentor and learn, because that little bit of money will bloom and grow into 10X, 20X, 50X or even a 100X when you have the right information at your fingertips.

Mentors are rare to find, and a great mentor for you will need to be actively working in the business, yet still have time to teach you. I do actively take new students on only if I think we are absolutely a match, and if they really want it and will take unprecedented massive, determined action. PM me on social media or send me an email to **steve@freedomsky.com,** and we can schedule a strategy call. Your future success will be 100% dependent on your ability to not only obtain the correct information, but to be able to properly put it into action. This, like Joel Miller says, is the difference between knowledge and wisdom.

Now go and get those BIG CHECKS!

And the author adds, as Steve would say, "BOOM!"

DID YOU ENJOY THIS BOOK?

Please consider leaving your fellow readers a review of this book to tell them how *Build Real Estate Wealth* impacted you.

JoelMillerBooks.com

INDEX

ABOUT THE AUTHOR

I first became curious about the prospects of investing in rental properties when someone built sixteen townhouses on my newspaper route in junior high. After obtaining a BA in accounting, I opened an accounting practice while also pursuing my other passion which was to pioneer the professional mobile disc jockey business in our area. Not long after that I began to add income properties to my (already busy) life. I soon sold the accounting practice as my involvement in real estate continued to grow, but my DJ business existed nicely with my rental properties for thirty-five years and 5051 appearances.

Along the way I began flipping houses (before "flip" was a real estate term), and I've done well over one hundred flips. I retired from the DJ business in 2011, and since then I have grown my rental investment portfolio. Eventually, in 2018 I became a hard money lender to many other investors, and I discovered a real desire to boost newer investors in their journeys with whatever wisdom from my own experiences seemed appropriate.

While contributing many years as a leader of the professional organization for landlords in northwestern Pennsylvania, I became the lead instructor of our Landlord 101 class which is a sixteen-hour seminar on becoming the best landlord you can be. Landlords find the class beneficial whether they're still looking for their first rental or if they already have several dozen units. Additionally, I created classes on house flipping and hard money lending.

I have been an occasional contributor over the years to professional magazines in both the real estate and the mobile disc jockey worlds, and after a bunch of podcast appearances, peers began encouraging me to write a book. Out of a perfect storm of investing experience, business knowledge, podcast appearances, professional writing, and a desire to teach, *Build Real Estate Wealth: Enjoy the Journey of Rental Property Investment* has been born. I hope you like it as much as I have liked pouring out what's in my head onto these pages!

You can find Joel Miller on Facebook and LinkedIn. A YouTube instructional video series is planned. A listing of upcoming appearances and publications is available at:

JoelMillerBooks.com

www.ingramcontent.com/pod-product-compliance
Lightning Source LLC
Chambersburg PA
CBHW030449210326
41597CB00013B/596